# THE SECURITY RISK HANDBOOK

*The Security Risk Handbook* assists businesses that need to be able to carry out effective security risk assessments, security surveys, and security audits. It provides guidelines and standardised detailed processes and procedures for carrying out all three stages of the security journey: assess, survey, and audit.

Packed with tools and templates, the book is extremely practical. At the end of each explanatory chapter, a unique case study can be examined by the reader in the areas of risk assessment, security survey, and security audit. This book also highlights the commercial and reputational benefits of rigorous risk management procedures. It can be applied to corporate security, retail security, critical national infrastructure security, maritime security, aviation security, counter-terrorism, and executive and close protection.

This text is relevant to security professionals across all key sectors: corporate security, retail security, critical national infrastructure security, maritime security, aviation security, counter-terrorism, and executive and close protection. It will also be useful to health and safety managers, operations managers, facilities managers, and logistics professionals whose remit is to ensure security across an organisation or function.

**Charles Swanson** is a professional security and risk management specialist and lecturer. He is a Chartered Security Professional, Fellow of the Security Institute, and currently the Senior Tutor on the MSc programme in Security and Risk Management with Linx International and the University of West London. He has lectured in risk management, counterterrorism, and information security (cyber) to a global audience. His first book published by Routledge was titled *Professional Security Management: A Strategic Guide.*

'I think this is a fantastic idea. Speaking to security professionals on such a regular basis, there is clearly an appetite for support and education in these areas. Therefore, I believe there would be significant demand for a handbook of this type'.

**Mattew Bull**, Editor, *International Security Journal*

'I have known Charles Swanson for many years in a professional capacity and consider him to be a recognised and leading security professional who is both expert in security consulting, as well as in the field of professional security training courses and education.

In my professional opinion, and having seen Charles's proposal, I believe that a book of this nature will fill a gap in available publications of the kind. Indeed, I would certainly purchase a copy of the book'.

**Mike Bluestone**, Chartered Security Professional,
Director, Corps Security

'For today's security departments, professionals and consultants, the need for a consistent and homogenised approach to the practical elements of security is imperative. In my view, the creation of a publication of this nature has a real opportunity in this sector, and considering how influential Mr. Swanson is, and that he is an industry thought leader, I can think of no better person to author this resource'.

**Sarah Hayward-Turton**

# THE SECURITY RISK HANDBOOK

## Assess, Survey, Audit

*Charles Swanson*

Routledge
Taylor & Francis Group
LONDON AND NEW YORK

Cover image: © Getty Images

First published 2023
by Routledge
4 Park Square, Milton Park, Abingdon, Oxon OX14 4RN

and by Routledge
605 Third Avenue, New York, NY 10158

*Routledge is an imprint of the Taylor & Francis Group, an informa business*



*British Library Cataloguing-in-Publication Data*
A catalogue record for this book is available from the British Library

ISBN: 9781032030340 (hbk)
ISBN: 9781032030357 (pbk)
ISBN: 9781003186335 (ebk)

DOI: 10.4324/9781003186335

Typeset in Joanna
by codeMantra

Access the Support Material: www.routledge.com/9781032030357

I dedicate this book to the memory of a very close friend who kept me company and probably helped me to retain my sanity through the dark days of the Covid pandemic. When I was researching and writing this book, very often alone at home, because my wife Elly was at work, Barney was always there, but on 6 August 2021, the vet told us that Barney had an aggressive fungal infection that was inoperable. Elly and I made the decision to relieve Barn of his pain, and the following day we said goodbye to him.

Some weeks later my three-year-old granddaughter Beatrix said that Barney was now in heaven taking a rest.

I hope so.

Good night and God bless mate.

# CONTENTS

# OPENING STATEMENT

I sincerely believe that the security industry in the UK, as an example, is populated with professionals of the highest calibre, and I am sure that could be said for other geographical areas such as the USA, Europe, Australia, the Far East, etc. However, once again, using the UK as a focus, the greatest challenge for the sector, in my opinion, is a lack of governance and leadership. Unlike other professions such as law or medicine, which are both regulated by a single institute[1] the security profession is not. In order for a citizen of the United Kingdom to be able to practise medicine, he or she will be required by law to hold minimum qualifications.

To practise as a Doctor, the applicant will require a bachelor's degree in medicine (MBBS) or surgery (BMBS) that has been recognised by the General Medical Council (GMC). That is only the beginning.

After graduation with a medical degree, he or she will need to complete several years' of postgraduate study, where they will specialise in a specific area of medicine.

They will also need to pass a Disclosure and Barring Service (DBS) check to certify that they are safe to work with members of the public.

To commence Doctor training at medical school, all applicants will need to have a minimum of 3 A grade A Levels, including Physics and Biology. They will also need at least 5 GCSEs in grades 7–9/A-A*, including English and Mathematics.

There is an equally robust process before anybody in the United Kingdom can practise as a Lawyer, which becomes even more rigorous if the choice is to study to become a Barrister.

In the UK today, and I suspect this is common in most nation states, anybody can refer to themselves as a Security Consultant, without any form of qualifications. With the exception of the Register of Security Professionals,[2] I believe there is no rigorous process for gaining professional recognition.

There is no uniformity of process or recognised discipline of academic qualifications, and because of that flaw, a person can leave the military or police on Friday, and by Monday they can refer to themselves as Security Consultants.

How can that make any sense whatsoever?

Royal Charter issued to the Worshipful Company of Security Professionals in this is a point worthy of debate because once again in my opinion it is the catalyst for all of the arguments and debates you will find in this book.

The security industry needs to be a regulated profession, as described by GOV.UK[3] as:

'Regulated profession' is a term which is defined in the Professional Qualifications Bill. It means a profession which is regulated by law in the UK or a part of the UK. 'Profession' includes an occupation or trade, or any subdivision and specialism within a profession. The Bill sets out that a profession is regulated by law where there is a legal requirement to have certain qualifications or experience (or meet an alternative condition or requirement) in order to undertake certain professional activities or use a protected title.

As a profession, we need a single point of focus, and critically we need to identify a structure where security professionals can be recognised for the skills and qualifications they have today, not the historical shackles that we are still too often bound by.

Rant over!

## Notes

1 For solicitors it is the Law Society, and for Medical Doctors it is the General Medical council.

2 https://www.charteredsecurityprofessional.org/ Accessed on 20 March 2022.

3 https://www.gov.uk/government/publications/professions-regulated-by-law-in-the-uk-and-their-regulators/uk-regulated-professions-and-their-regulators Accessed on 18 March 2022.

# BOOK AIMS

This handbook has been written to assist security and other professionals in carrying out the Security Risk Assessment, the Security Survey, and the Security Audit, in that order; what I refer to as the Risk Journey.

To my mind, the most important section of this process is the Security Risk Assessment, because without it, carrying out an effective Security Survey or Security Audit is illogical.

To put it bluntly, the aim of the Security Risk Assessment is to try to understand what the likelihood is of an attack against an asset, and what the impact would be if such an attack were to be successful. After that there is a responsibility to offer the best possible risk management advice to the client; advice that is logical, effective, deliverable, and proportionate to the risks and costs to the business.

This is not an academic publication.

Except for the fact that I will be encouraging you to think like a criminal (more of that later), the contents of the book will not be underpinned by criminological theory or debate about crime causation. This is a practitioner's handbook which will I hope, assist you in understanding risk, but more importantly help you to appreciate and recognise the most effective means of carrying out a Security Risk Assessment, a Security Survey, and a Security Audit. The Risk Journey.

Throughout the book, I will be referring to the professional carrying out the three procedures as the Security Auditor. More of that later.

The Security Auditor carries out a critical process, one that is vital to the delivery of the Security Survey and the Security Audit.

Assess-Survey-Audit.

The Risk Journey.

When I was considering this book, I asked a number of trusted colleagues why the handbook was needed, and there were some extremely interesting and honest replies.

> *There is, in my opinion, a significant knowledge gap in the market at both practitioner and client levels, which I believe the proposed book will go a long way in redressing.*
>
> Head of corporate risk

> *The subject of the next book proposal by Charles is one of significant importance to the security profession as there is currently a distinct lack of understanding and common interpretation of security risk assessments, security surveys, and security audits across commerce, industry, and government bodies.*
>
> Corporate head of crisis management

> *I note that the book will be primarily aimed at security professionals who may have a remit to carry out security reviews, which will include the Security Risk Assessment, the Security Survey, and the Security Audit. In my professional opinion, and having seen Charles's proposal, I believe that a book of this nature will fill a gap in available publications of the kind. Indeed, I would certainly purchase a copy of the book.*
>
> Director of security consultation

> *I have now had an opportunity to review Charles' proposal for the new book and I concur with his statement regarding the Aims and USP of this book. I believe this proposed book will be a unique and highly effective guide for the wider security and risk market.*
>
> F1 racing head of global security

## Definitions

As I see it, this is the crux of the problem, because the security industry uses a variety of definitions, with no credible means of uniformity or alignment. So here are my definitions of those processes that I believe constitute the risk journey.

The Security Risk Assessment

*The Security Risk Assessment is an appreciation of the measure of risk related to the asset being protected.*

The Security Survey

*The Security Survey is a physical examination of all security systems in situ.*

The Security Audit

*The Security Audit is the measurement of conformity to all agreed security standards.*[1]

Today, more than ever, organisations are vulnerable to the threat of physical and cyber means of attack from sophisticated and aggressive criminals and terrorist groups. To prevent or mitigate such risks to their physical and digital systems, and as the basis for any organisational security review, businesses need to be able to carry out effective Security Risk Assessments, Security Surveys, and Security Audits.

Presently there are no harmonious or recognised international standards for carrying out either a Security Risk Assessment, a Security Survey, or a Security Audit, and that leaves the security industry and businesses unnecessarily exposed to risk.

For too long, organisations particularly in the United States and the UK have walked blindly into adverse security and risk situations, in the hope that those chosen to carry out a Security Review, or Security Audit, perhaps even a Security Risk Assessment; whatever title is in vogue at that moment in time, are competent. Unfortunately, today there is still a chasm between those who understand what I refer to as the Risk Journey and those who do not. My argument is that without security and business justification, companies are investing huge sums of money on systems and procedures that are very often not fit for purpose, and consequently they are often pointless and ineffective, if not dangerous, because they may generate a false sense of security.

The procedures and protocols for supporting companies and protecting their assets must be part of a coordinated and more importantly, a standardised effort, hence the title *The Security Risk Handbook: Assess, Survey, Audit.* However, of critical importance, and this will be constantly referred to in the book, is an understanding of security from a criminal perspective. It is futile designing, installing, and commissioning any form of security system purely from the purview of the Security Manager, because far too often ego and vanity take over and it is easy to be swayed by what the system can achieve, as opposed to identifying systems limitations, which the criminal will monopolise at the first opportunity. That is why, before and whilst the Security Risk Assessment, the Security Survey, and the Security Audit are carried out, it is imperative that the security professional is constantly thinking like a criminal.

## *Aims*

To explain the criticality of understanding and implementing a risk management system that begins with a Security Risk Assessment, and then moves on to the Security Survey before finally carrying out the Security Audit.

To provide *standardised* detailed processes and procedures for carrying out all three stages of the journey; *Assess, Survey, and Audit.*

## Note

1 This may refer to international standards such as ISO 27001, or internal standards perhaps set during the Security Survey.

# LIST OF FIGURES

# LIST OF TABLES

# INTERNATIONAL SECURITY STANDARDS AND REGULATIONS

The following International Security Standards and Regulations cover a range of sectors that will be to the advantage of the Security Auditor to have a good working knowledge of, and they will consist of ISO's,[1] British Standards (BS), international regulations, and initiatives.

## *International Organisation Standards (ISO)*

| | |
|---|---|
| ISO 9001 | Quality Management Systems |
| ISO 14000 | Environmental management |
| ISO 18000/1 | Information Technology |
| ISO 18788 | Management Systems for Private Security Operations |
| ISO 22301 | Business Continuity Management |
| ISO 22320 | Security Resilience, Emergency Management, Guidelines for Incident Management |
| ISO 27001 | Information Security Systems Management |
| ISO 27032 | Information Technology, Security Techniques, Guidelines for Cyber Security |
| ISO 28000 | Supply Chain Security |
| ISO 28007 | Guidelines for private maritime security companies (PMSC) that provide privately contracted armed security personnel (PCASP) on board ships. |
| ISO 31000 | Risk Management |

## *British Standards*

| | |
|---|---|
| BS 11200 | Crisis Management |

## *International Sip and Port Facility Security (ISPS) Code*

The ISPS Code was enacted as a direct impact of 9/11, and it concentrates on the security of a selected band of ships, and all port facilities servicing those vessels. A number of initiatives were also introduced as a result of the introduction of the Code.

| | |
|---|---|
| CSI | The Container Shipping Initiative was introduced to ensure the safe passage of maritime containers to and from the USA. |
| TAPA | Transported Asset Protection Association is aimed at ensuring a safe supply chain passage of cargo. |
| C-TPAT | Customs-Trade Partnership Against Terrorism aims to make US borders safer and more secure. |
| AEO | Authorized Economic Operator is a European Union initiative which intrinsically aims to mirror C-TPAT in Europe. |
| Safe Ports | The Security & Accountability for Every Port Act is another US initiative designed to safeguard US ports. |

## *Websites*

The following websites are open source and are helpful to the Security Auditor.

| | |
|---|---|
| CPNI | The Centre for the Protection of National Infrastructure<br>www.cpni.gov.uk |
| Home Office | The Home Office<br>https://www.gov.uk/government/organisations/home-office |
| SIA | The Security Industry Authority<br>https://www.gov.uk/government/organisations/security-industry-authority |
| ICO | Information Commissioners Office<br>https://ico.org.uk/ |
| NCSC | National Cyber Security Centre<br>https://www.ncsc.gov.uk/ |
| GCHQ | General Communications Headquarters<br>https://www.gchq.gov.uk/ |
| BSI | British Standards Institute<br>https://shop.bsigroup.com/ |
| BRC | British Retail Consortium<br>https://brc.org.uk/ |
| Security Institute | The Security Institute<br>https://security-institute.org/ |
| ASIS International | American Society for Industrial Security<br>https://www.asisonline.org/ |
| CAA | Civil Aviation Authority<br>https://www.caa.co.uk/home/ |

| | |
|---|---|
| USCBP | US Customs and Border Protection<br>https://www.cbp.gov/ |
| IMO | International Maritime Organisation<br>https://www.imo.org/en/ |
| Interpol | International Police Organisation<br>https://www.interpol.int/ |
| Europol | European Police Organization<br>https://www.europol.europa.eu/ |

## Note

1 The **International Organization for Standardization.** https://www.iso.org/home.html Accessed on 21 March 2022.

# GLOSSARY

**AACS** Automatic Access Control System
**AI's** Assignment Instructions
**AIR** Active Infrared
**ANPR** Automatic Number Plate Recognition
**AQ** Al Qaeda
**ARC** Alarm Response Centre
**Assets** Something of importance that requires protection
**BRC** British Retail Consortium
**BMS** Building Management System
**BNC** Bayonet Neill Concelman
**BTP** British Transport Police
**CAA** Civil Aviation Authority
**Cat 5** Category 5 CCTV cable
**CBDO** Chief Business Development Officer
**CBRN** Chemical, biological, radiological, and nuclear.
**CCTV** Closed Circuit Television
**CEO** Chief Executive Officer. Head of the Board of Directors.
**CFO** Chief Finance Officer. Responsible for financial decisions.
**Chartered Status** A form of accreditation.
**CIO** Chief Information Officer
**CISO** Chief Information Security Officer

**CMP** Crisis Management Plan
**CPTED** Crime Prevention Through Environmental Design
**Company Secretary** The organisations legal advisor. He or she may be a qualified lawyer
**CONTEST** UK Counter Terrorism strategy
**CP** Close Protection
**CPA** Crime Pattern Analysis
**CPNI** Centre for the Protection of National Infrastructure
**CPO** Close Protection Officer
**CRAVED**[1] Retail acronym for a theft process
**CSO.** Chief Security Officer
**CSO** Company Security Officer (Maritime)
**CSR** Corporate Social Responsibility. A self-regulating business model that helps a company be socially accountable to itself, its stakeholders, and the public
**CTU** Counter Terrorism Unit
**CTSA** Counter Terrorist Security Advisor
**CQA** Close Quarter Assassination
**Cyber** The use of computers
**Cybercrime** The use of computers to commit a crime
**DiD** Defence in Depth
**DNA** Deoxyribonucleic acid: a nucleic acid that is the main constituent of the chromosomes of all organisms (except some viruses)
**DOB** Daily Occurrence Book
**DPA** Data Protection Act
**DRP** Disaster Recovery Plan
**Dual Tech** Dual technology
**DVD** Digital Video Disk
**EAS** Electronic Article Surveillance
**FM** Facilities Management
**FOI** Freedom of Information Act
**Gap analysis** The difference between where an organisation or process is currently, and where is needs to be
**GDPR** General Data Protection Regulations
**GMT** Greenwich Meantime
**H&S** Health and Safety
**HDMI** High-Definition Multimedia Interface

**HGV** Heavy Goods Vehicle
**HID** High Intensity Discharge
**HPS** High Pressure Sodium
**HR** Human Resources
**HTR** Hostile Target Reconnaissance
**HVM** Hostile Vehicle Mitigation
**ICO** Information Commissioners Office
**ICT** Information Communications Technology
**IDS** Intruder Detection System
**IED** Improvised Explosive Device
**Impact** The result of an occurrence or the result of an attack
**IMO** International Maritime Organisation
**Infrastructure** The basic facilities, services, and installations needed for the functioning of an organisation
**INGO** International Non-Governmental Organisation
**ISO** International Organization for Standards
**IQ** Islamic Qaeda
**IRA** Irish Republican Army
**ISPS** Code International Ship and Port Facility Security Code
**K&R** Kidnap and ransom
**KPI** Key Point Indicator
**LAN** Local Area Nertwork
**LCD** Liquid Crystal Display
**LED** Light Emitting Diode
**Likelihood** The probability that something will happen
**LPS** Low-Pressure Sodium
**MD** Managing Director.
**Mitigation** Measures taken to reduce an impact
**MI5** British Security Services
**MMF** Multi Mode Fibre
**MOI** Ministry of the Interior
**MSc** Master of Science. A recognised academic qualification
**National grid** UK power supply system
**NCA** National Crime Agency
**NGO** Non-Government Organisation.
**NHS** National Health Service. The UK national health organisation
**NTS** UK gas supply system

**NVR** Network Video Recording
**OCG** Organised Crime Group
**OR** Operational Requirement.
**OT** Operational technology
**PA** button Personal Attack button
**PESTLE** Political, Economic, Socio geographic, technological, Legal and environmental
**PAL** Publicly Accessible Location
**PAS** Publicly Accessible Specifications
**PBIED** Personnel Borne Improvised Explosive Device
**PCRS** Proximity Card Raeder System
**PFSO** Port Facility Security Officer
**PFSP** Port Facility Security Plan
**Phishing** A scam of sending e-mails from a fake Web site to illegally obtain password information
**PIDS** Perimeter Intruder Detection Systems
**PIN** Personal Identification Number
**PIR** Passive Infrared
**PIRA** Provisional Irish Republican Army
**PoS** Point of Sale
**PSS** Public Space Surveillance
**Principle** The VIP being afforded close protection
**PTZ** Pan, tilt and zoom
**QRT** Quick Reaction Team
**Qualitative** Relating to the quality of substance
**Quantitative** Relating to the quantity of a substance
**QMS** Quality Management System
**R&D** Research and Development
**Residual Risk** Risk in place after risk treatment
**Reed Contacts** Part of an IDS used to protect doors and windows
**RFID** Radio Frequency Identification
**Risk** The probability of a negative occurrence
**Risk Acceptance** The level of risk that is acceptable
**Risk analysis** The initial process of assessing the likelihood and impact of an adverse event
**Risk evaluation** Quantifying the potential impact of a risk
**Risk identification** Identifying the relevant level of risk

**Risk Journey** Assess, survey, audit
**Risk Treatment** Actions taken to control the risk
**RTG** Rubber Tyred Gantry
**SCP** Situational Crime Prevention
**SCS** Supply Chain Security
**Security Auditor** The Security Professional responsible for carrying out the Security Risk Assessment, the Security Survey and the Security Audit
**Shrinkage** The term used to cover the difference between recorded and actual stock
**SIA** Security Industry Authority
**SLA** Service Level Agreement
**SME** Subject Matter Expert
**SMF** Single Mode Fibre
**SMT** Senior Management Team
**SOLAS** Safety of Lives at Sea
**SOP** Standard Operating Procedures
**SSA** Ship Security Assessment
**SSSA** Store Security Self-Assessment
**SSO** Ship Security Officer
**SSP** Ship Security Plan
**SWOT** Strengths, weaknesses, opportunities, and threats
**Synopsis** A brief outline or general view, as of a subject or written work; an abstract or a summary
**Teams** A virtual means of communicating
**TFT** Thin Filmed Transistor
**TEU** Ten Equivalent Unit (a maritime steel container)
**The Security Audit** A measurement of conformity to all agreed security standards
**The SRA** Security Risk Assessment
**The Security Survey** The Security Survey is a physical examination of all security systems in situ
**Terrorism** The use of violence and/or fear to achieve an ideological or political goal
**Threat** A statement of intent to do harm
**Threat Assessment** The means of identifying levels of threat
**TK** Tiger Kidnap
**TL** Team Leader

**UK** United Kingdom
**UPS** Uninterruptable Power Supply
**USA** United States of America
**UVBT** Under Vehicle Booby Trap
**VAW** Vehicle as a weapon of attack
**VBDS** Video Based Detection System
**VBIED** Vehicle Borne Improvised Explosive Device
**VCR** Video Cassette Recorder
**VGA** Video Graphics Array
**VIP** Very Important Person
**VLCC** Very Large Crude Carrier
**VMD** Video Motion Detection
**VSS** Video Surveillance Systems
**Vulnerability** A weakness in the system
**WAN** Wide Area Network
**Zoom** A virtual means of communicating

## Note

1 Concealable, Removable, Accessible, Valuable, Enjoyable and Disposable.

# ACKNOWLEDGEMENTS

As with my first book *Professional Security Management: A strategic guide,* I have received so much advice, guidance, and inspiration from a group of security professionals and friends with the highest possible standards of professional integrity. I would like to thank the following people:

Sarah Hayward-Turton, Mike Bluestone, Doug Cook, Doctor Mike Mc Donagh, Rick Mounfield, Andrew Nicholls, Brendan McGarrity, Bruce Braes, Dave Galt, David Gill, Professor Martin Gill, Demelza Staples, Martin Bird, Mathew Bull.

Thank you all.

There are also a number of very close friends, who once again have been at the end of a telephone line, or even a Zoom or Teams call whenever I needed them.

Thank you, Geordie Beck, for always having confidence in me, and Doctor Stefano Dela Salla, my friend in Venice who has consistently had such trust in my professional abilities. John and Joan, our friends in Liverpool, as always, have given me encouragement from day one. My mate Ian (Scouse) Kelly. Thank you all.

Unbeknown to them, once again, my beautiful and loving granddaughters, Darcy and Beatrix who believe their Ga Ga (me!) can do just about anything, including a high kick (in joke).

But as ever, a very special thanks goes to my wife and absolute soul mate Elly, who has borne the brunt of me at times living in my study, with mood swings that she didn't deserve. Without you Ell, I couldn't have survived the time researching and writing this book. Thank you.

# FOREWORD

The Security sector cannot be described as a profession under any of the defining characteristics you may find in your research, but it is full of professional people. People of integrity and altruism. Professionals who value the journey of learning and never sit back in the belief that they know it all. I know this because for the past five years (2017–2022) I have had the privilege of working with some of the most incredibly giving and selfless professionals that are keeping people, places & assets safe and secure; they are Government Security Professionals, Corporate Security leaders and consultants in disciplines ranging from cyber security and engineering through the full range of business continuity and organisational resilience to the men and women who place themselves in danger every time they go to work at the frontline.

In this book, Charlie starts by authenticating my opinion above. He highlights what Doctors and Lawyers must maintain in order to practise their trade. In our sector, all we can do is encourage our people to be the best version of themselves. Many will pursue continuing professional development with assiduous dedication. Others will not.

For those who value learning and development, there needs to be a simple suite of contemporary knowledge that challenges and improves upon the trends that are accepted. In the case of this book, Charlie brings together three key elements of assessing security and presents them in a succinct and most logical 'Risk Journey' that frankly makes me question why we have not been working this way in the past. It is the most obvious example of common sense that shines a floodlight on the obfuscation we so often endure but worse, inflict on our clients.

The mark of a great teacher is their ability to present a complex problem in a manner that makes sense and leaves no room for confusion. What Charlie has given the reader is a well-organised and structured guide that sets a cadence through each chapter, that I personally find comforting. As an operational guide, the information is instinctively well placed and easy to find. The risk assessment followed by the security survey, topped off with an audit to ensure the recommendations mitigate the initial risks. The specialisations are documented in the same order in each chapter in all three sections which will make this book the 'goto' in any professional's library.

This book encourages the reader to research, the answers to the security problems are not found here. This book gives the reader the tools to find their own solutions and present the evidence in a logical way without ambiguity. What more does a modern security professional, or their client want?

The Risk Journey is a perfect analogy.

Rick Mounfield MSc CSyP FSyI
Chief Executive of The Security Institute 2017–2022

# INTRODUCTION

## What this book is all about

> *Listen, but take nobody's word, and accept nothing on face value. Trust only one source, and that is evidence-based research.*
>
> (Swanson, 2021)

Answer this question *What is the difference between a Security Risk Assessment, a Security Survey and a Security Audit?*, because that is what this book is all about!

Within the security sector, there is too often a lack of cohesion and understanding in relation to best practices surrounding the security review.[1] This inconsistency lies behind terminology, with phrases such as Security Risk Assessment, Security Survey, and Security Audit being quoted without any thought given to what I refer to in this book as *The Risk Journey.*

Ask yourself another question. How many people do you know who are qualified or formally trained to carry out either a Security Risk Assessment, a Security Survey or a Security Audit? I suspect the answer is limited, and that makes no sense, because in one form or another the Security Risk

DOI: 10.4324/9781003186335-1

Assessment, the Security Survey, and arguably to a lesser extent the Security Audit are carried out frequently, but really without clarity and rationale.

I have taught security risk assessing, security surveying, and security auditing for over twenty years, and I have carried out assessments, surveys, and audits worldwide for a cross section of clients, with a single common denominator: Confusion.

Confusion that has manifested itself in terms of disjointed and at times misleading scopes of work.

But why?

I believe this is the result of poor communications and understanding of what the client wants and needs, but how can a Security Consultant or professional Security Manager understand what the client needs if the client is actually unsure of his or her requirements.

**Security consultant to client, *What do you want from the review?* Client, *I don't know, you tell me, you are the security expert.***

Touche!

Very often, at the behest of the insurance broker, the compliance function of the business will initiate a programme of Security Risk Assessments, Security Surveys, and Security Audits, but the problem of course is that the compliance team is focused on ensuring that the programme meets the requirements of the insurer and that perhaps three or four security assessments are carried out, or five security surveys, or maybe five ISO 27001 security IT audits. Who knows? The concern is that neither the insurer nor the compliance function generally has any idea what the assessment, survey, or audit consists of, and it ends up being what is too often referred to as, and I hate to say this, a 'tick box' exercise.

This means that the insurance broker is happy...

Compliance and probably the Chief Security Officer (CSO) are proud of their achievements...

And of course, the Board can assure shareholders that the organisation is secure...

But realistically, exactly what has been achieved?

Conformity to a compliance programme that nobody really understands.

*We are back to square one where nobody has paid any attention to the risk journey, and that makes no sense.*

In order to address the problem, this book will be divided into four sections:

- The Security Risk Assessment.
- The Security Survey.
- The Security Audit.
- The Conclusion.

The risk assessment, survey and audit will be relatively generic in terms of their initial introduction, but once you move to the specialist sectors such as corporate security, retail security, maritime security and so on you will realise that there are in fact a number of differences in approach and implementation. In my opinion and experience it is extremely difficult to approach the assessment, survey, or audit with absolute generic equality, so flexibility and individuality are critical. Think outside of the box; think like a criminal.

## Chapter 1. Risk and the Security Risk Assessment

The first part of this section will explain what the Risk Journey is, and why it is important for you to understand the concept, before you explore the Security Risk Assessment. In this part of the section, you will be introduced to risk, before examining risk component parts, or elements which are critical in terms of understanding the process of risk, and through the use of an effective template, how risk is measured during a Security Risk Assessment. The section will also cover the intricacies of risk perception, risk communication, and the risk appetite, before going onto examine various risk mitigation methods.

Part 2 of the section will offer advice and guidance about how you can use the theories and concepts of the Security Risk Assessment in the following diverse areas:

Corporate security
Publicly accessible locations (PAL)
Retail security
Critical national infrastructure security
Maritime security
Aviation security
Hostile environment security
Close protection
Counter-terrorism[2]

As with the Security Survey and the Security Audit, I have attempted to maintain uniformity throughout the book, but because of the range of diversity you may notice a number of places in the three disciplines that seem at odds with the mainstream approach. For example, the Security Risk Assessment, Security Survey or Security Audit carried out at a corporate location, which is relatively constant, will of course be different to those processes carried out at a retail outlet, or within a hostile environment.

## Chapter 2. The Security Survey

Part 1 of Section 2 will focus on the generics of the Security Survey and will in the first instance argue that the Security Survey is the second stage in the Risk Journey and logically should be carried after a credible Security Risk Assessment has been completed. A Security Survey is a physical examination of all security systems in situ often referred to as the 'boots on the ground' approach, where uncomfortable questions often need to be asked, and documentation is perused that is particularly sensitive. It is at this stage where very often the diplomatic skills of the Security Auditor are severely tested.

The Security Survey will be divided into six steps.

1. Reasons for the survey.
2. Preliminary research.
3. Preparation.
4. Implementation of the survey (boots on the ground).
5. Post survey de brief.
6. The survey report.

Part 2 of this chapter will mirror Part 2 of Chapter 1, describing how the Security Survey may be applied to a number of diverse environments, with an acknowledgement that there will be deviations from the standard approach.

## Chapter 3. The Security Audit

Part 1 of Chapter 3 will introduce you, to the third and final element of the Risk Journey, the Security Audit. Here I emphasise the argument that this is the only logical approach to any form of organisational security review, and that there is an absolute symbiotic relationship between the three elements.

The Security Audit is a means of measuring whether the standards identified during the Security Survey are being maintained and conformed to. Once again, Part 2 of this chapter will see you being guided through a number of Security Audits carried out after Security Surveys in a diverse range of environments.

## Conclusion

The book will conclude with arguments about the credibility of the Risk Journey, and the need for uniformity and single governance overviewing the security industry. I also, once again make the argument for the title of the Security Auditor, who must be a recognised security professional and ambassador for the industry.

## Pause for thought, reflection, and research

Throughout the book, there will be sections where you will be asked for your thoughts on what may be a new area for you, referred to as *pause for thought*. There will also be times for *reflection*, this will be when you have studied an area that perhaps may be particularly significant, and you will be asked to take a little time to reflect on what you have learned. Finally, there will subjects that you will be asked to *research* in order for you to be comfortable with current trends and definitions.

# The security review (for lack of a better term)

*Pause for thought*

What is a security review, and why is there the need to have one carried out?

The Security Review is the beginning of the Risk Journey, because generally, by virtue of the fact that an organisation, ostensibly through the offices of the Executive Board of Directors, has decided that its strategic security approach may not be providing sufficient cover to meet the threat from crime and terrorism, and it now requires some form of review. But what does that mean?

This is the first of many hurdles and ambiguities that will be met when attempting to decide exactly what is required, and what form the Security Review will take.

The process may begin when the Company Secretary receives a communication from the insurance broker insisting that a security review is carried out before the next years premiums are decided. Equally, it may be intelligence from either the police or the country security services informing the Chief Security Officer that the threat of a cyber or terrorist attack is extremely high, and the organisation is *advised* to have a security review of its assets carried out by a competent person (s).[3] Perhaps a new branch is due to begin operations, during which it will be symbiotically connected to the remainder of the organisation, and a security review is necessary to ensure that the new location is not a security Achilles heel, a vulnerability.

Whatever the reason may be, the CEO is likely to be under pressure, and is probably convinced that there may be weaknesses in the organisation's security structure; and in order to fulfil his or her shareholders expectations, funds will be released to have a security review of the entire organisation carried out. This is the beginning of the Risk Journey, but who is involved?

## Identification: What's in a title?

> *Pause for thought*
>
> In your opinion, is the title of the person carrying out the Security Risk Assessment etc., important, and if so, what would be your choice?

This is probably one of the most difficult sections of the book, because the above is a mysterious character, with a plethora of titles and qualifications that are generally hard to synchronise.

Although this may be outside the scope of the book, I believe it is worthy of examination and debate.

In my previous book *Security Management: A strategic guide*, I tackled the thorny issue of identifying the Security Auditor, and I maintain the argument in this book.

Reading some of the feedback received, this may seem to be irrelevant, but in my opinion the first task is to identify a title that is appropriate to this professional.

I am of the opinion that the title most likely to be recognised throughout the security sector, and probably other business sectors is that of the Security Auditor.

Auditors are recognised in most sectors as the professional who can be relied upon to accurately measure competency and compliance levels, and that should be applied to the person who carries out the Security Risk Assessment, the Security Survey and of course the Security Audit.

There will be arguments not only about the title of the Security Auditor, but also about his or her qualifications and experience, and in my opinion, this particular auditor should hold a vocational qualification in a security-related topic, an academic qualification,[4] and should have at least five years' experience in the field. Ideally, he or she should possess Chartered Status and be licenced, with status and licence being evaluated periodically.

So for ease of reference and identification, for the remainder of the book, irrelevant to the security process being carried out,[5] I shall refer to the security professional involved as the Security Auditor.

How's that for a controversial statement!

## Notes

1 The overarching process that investigates how an organization may be protected from risk. This will be covered later in the book.

2 Covered in the Security Risk Assessment as a section, and then mentioned as a threat throughout the remainder of the book.
3 Whatever that means.
4 Bachelors or Master's degree.
5 The Security Risk Assessment, the Security Survey, or the Security Audit.

# 1

# RISK AND THE SECURITY RISK ASSESSMENT

> *Pause for thought*
>
> Your starter for ten. In your own words, describe what is meant by the term, 'risk'.

A professional colleague of mine……

*"Looks like a really interesting project, but it could be contentious as there are many views about the security risk assessment…."*

My reply…….

*"That's the problem. There are too many forms of security risk assessing, which then has a knock-on effect when the survey and audit are carried out. I want to encourage discussion and debate, but I'm aiming at standardisation".*

DOI: 10.4324/9781003186335-2

## The Risk Journey

Figure 1 is a graphical representation of the Risk Journey: Assess, Survey, and Audit.

My argument is that to carry out an overall security review, there must be a coordinated approach, revolving around the Security Risk Assessment, the Security Survey, and the Security Audit, in that order. The logic behind my approach is that it is pointless carrying out a Security Survey if the risk to the organisation or person is unknown. Equally, the Security Audit has no value if standards have not been set and adhered to during the Security Survey, or in support of British or international standards.

So, this book will have an overarching process that focusses on the Risk Journey message, and that will permeate throughout. Assess, Survey, and Audit.

Before discussing the process of risk assessment, it is critical to understand risk itself, and those component parts or elements of risk that must be taken into consideration if an effective and balanced risk assessment is to be carried out.

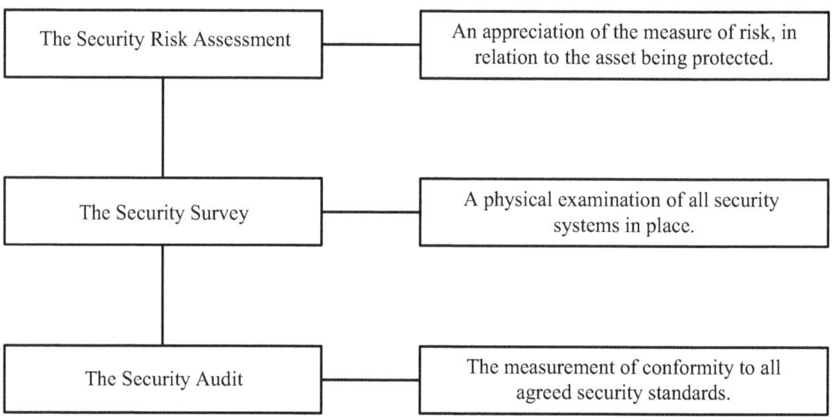


*Figure 1* The Risk Journey.

## Risk

Risk is not new. There has always been a contingent edge to life. What has changed is the nature and definition of risk (Franklin, 1998).

Drennan et al. (2007) further argue that risks are all around us. In the air we breathe, the food we eat, and the knowledge we rely upon to build our societies. But how do we define risk?

Risk is often quoted as being the likelihood of a negative occurrence, and that is a legitimate argument, but in my opinion, it epitomises the sometimes-simplistic approach to a concept that has been in existence since time began.

> ### *Reflection*
>
> Take a little time to think about how you see risk and think about how it affects you in your everyday life.

Adam (1995) in his acclaimed publication, simply named *Risk* argues that *the decisions that are made in the face of uncertainty involve weighing the potential rewards of an act against its potential adverse consequences.* That to me is the seminal argument surrounding the concept of pure risk, rewards, and adverse consequences.

One definition begins with risk as the probability that a particular *adverse event* occurs during a stated period of time, or results from a particular challenge. As a probability in the sense of statistical theory, risk obeys all the formal laws of combining probabilities. Explicitly or implicitly, it must always relate to the 'risk of (a specific event or set of events)' and where appropriate must refer to exposure to a hazard specified in terms of its amount or intensity, time of starting, or duration. There is a further argument that all risks are conditional, often related to perception, although often the conditions are implied by context rather than explicitly stated.

An *adverse event* is an occurrence that produces harm and with risk defined as above; a *hazard* is seen as the situation that in particular circumstances could lead to harm, where *harm* is the loss to a human being (or to a human population) consequent on *damage*, and damage is the loss of inherent quality suffered by an entity (physical or biological).

Of course, that is the view from a particular body of expertise, but not everybody views risk in such a focused and scientific manner. That is referred to as risk perception.

*Reflection*

Ask yourself this question "Are you risk-averse or are you prepared to take risks that other people may not?". It's all about perception.

## Risk perception

There have been extensive studies in understanding how individuals perceive risk (Engemann, 2018), and as human beings, we see risk individually, and generally from a different perspective, with variables such as age, experience, social standing, and even levels of education.

A good example of the above is how young children strike the balance between safety and excitement. The behaviour of children, driven by curiosity and a need for excitement, yet curbed by their sense of danger, suggests that these junior risk experts are performing a balancing act. In some cases, it is a physical balancing act; learning to walk or ride a bicycle cannot be done without an accident. In mastering such skills, they are not seeking a zero-risk life; they are balancing the expected rewards of their actions against the perceived costs of failure (Adam, 1995).

Pidgeon et al. (1992) defined risk perception as 'people's beliefs, attitudes, judgements, and feelings, as well as the wider social or cultural values and dispositions that people adopt, towards hazards and their benefits', arguing that risk perception is not simply an individual process but has to be understood against the societal and cultural background.

Never believe that you have the only opinion when it comes to understanding risk. Always listen to others.

From a corporate perspective, functions within an organisation may agree about the importance of risk management but will inevitably approach risk from a different angle. Take the Senior Management Team at British Utilities (BU).

### Case Study 1: Project Imperial Hubris

*Hubris means deadly pride. Thinking you can do things better than anyone else.*

Rick Riordan

### The company: British Utilities (BU)

BU is a fictitious London-based gas/oil exploration and development multinational company, with offices and operations spanning all seven continents: employing approximately 75,000 people.

In 2020, the organisation recorded a turnover of $275.4bn, with profits after tax amounting to just over $4bn.

However, since a drilling accident in the Gulf of Aden in 2015, when nineteen employees were killed, with an oil spillage consisting of 4.6 million barrels, and with litigation and clean-up charges of over $45 bn, BU has struggled to regain market share and is currently aggressively attempting to recall past glories.

As with the majority of other corporate entities, BU has a divided Executive Board when the subject of risk perception and risk management are concerned, and internal debate is far from unusual.

### The key protagonists

- **Sir Ian Kelly OBE Chief Executive Officer (CEO)**
  Sir Ian took over the reins of the business a little after the drilling accident; a time when the brand and reputation of BU were at an all-time low. His remit from the board was to build a new brand which reflected a significantly developed environmental approach to energy provision, whilst ensuring the company was delivering an increased profit, year on year to its shareholders,
  He is currently under a great deal of pressure.
- **Karen Gibson MBA Chief Finance Officer (CFO)**
  Karen also joined the business after the Gulf of Aden crisis, with instructions from the board and company shareholders to always ensure that the accounts 'balanced', particularly after the disastrous financial outcomes related to litigation and clean-up costs.
  Ms Gibson sits on the Executive Board.
- **Russ Rowe MBA Chief Business Development Officer (CBDO)**
  Russ Rowe (we will see more of Russ later in the book), has a reputation in the company, and within the industry, for

stopping at nothing to 'make a sale', 'do a deal' and grow the business. His hero is Peter Drucker, who once said *'Economic results are earned by leadership, not by mere competence. Profits are the reward for making a unique, or at least a distinct, contribution in a meaningful area; and what is meaningful is decided market and customer'* (Drucker, 1955). Russ has this quote in a frame on his wall, and as far as he is concerned, profit is everything and risks are there to be taken.

Mr Rowe sits on the Executive Board.

- **John Beck QGM MSc Chief Security Officer**
  John is a former police Superintendent, and after a glowing first career has powerfully influenced BU to focus on security and the safety of assets. He possesses an MSc (Distinction) in Security Risk Management, and fully understands the business needs of the company. Although surprisingly, given his former career, he is slightly risk averse.

  Mr Beck sits on the Executive Board.

The four Board members are experts in their own rights, and each one looks at risk from a different perspective.

*Debate*

Examine the above case study and offer arguments that will support all sides of the debate. Try not to be biased either way.

## Risk component parts

As mentioned earlier, there is often confusion when attempting to arrive at a decisive and clinical definition and understanding, with explanations of risk often being offered in the terms of threats or vulnerabilities. Very often, such elements are identified as running alongside risk, when in actual fact, they are critical parts of the overarching concept of risk. Risk is a theory; its component parts constitute the practical application of the concept. Let me be a little clearer.

The component parts or elements of risk are:

- Assets
- Threats
- Vulnerabilities
- Likelihood
- Impact
- Acceptance
- Treatment

## *Assets*

> *Pause for thought*
>
> What is an asset? And what do you believe the three most important assets are in your work environment?

In general terms, assets tend to take on a tangible value when represented from a financial perspective. Accounting coach.com[1] when defining an asset, argues that assets are '*things that are resources owned by a company and which have future economic value that can be measured, and can be expressed in monetary terms. Examples include cash, investments, accounts receivable, inventory, supplies, land, buildings, equipment, and vehicles.*'

However, the same website goes on to say that '*...some valuable items that cannot be measured and expressed in dollars include the company's outstanding reputation, its customer base etc.*'

This is the epicentre of the discussion. From the above perspective, assets tend to have a monetary value. However, such a measurement or scale is not always useful when describing assets belonging to perhaps a corporation, or a public body, where it is generally accepted that an asset is something of value that is important to the organisation and indeed may be critical in terms of crisis management or business continuity; and perhaps more importantly, brand and reputation. Financial assets are of course important, but other assets should also be given consideration.

### *BU*

Prior to the documented drilling accident in the Gulf of Aden in 2015, BU budgeted a significant percentage of its profits to ensure that the environment in which it was operating was safe, and that a robust Corporate Social Responsibility (CSR) policy was in place. The company was lauded and admired for its environmental approach to business. However, since the drilling accident, the words BU are too often associated with an organisation that puts profit before safety.

However, this differentiation between financial and non-financial institutions is not as straight forwards as it seems, and in many ways, it replicates the complexities of risk perception, in that whilst the HR department may place human beings at the very top end of their asset protection priorities, shareholders are likely to favour business protection and share value.

The IT function will be insistent that the security of information and data assets must be its number one priority, whilst public relations will insist that nothing is as important as brand and reputation.

The point being is that of course all assets are important, and in terms of risk and the risk assessment they have to be identified at the earliest opportunity if the risk assessment and the ensuing risk management process are to be effective. From the earliest stage of the risk assessment, every organisation has to have a total understanding of what must be protected, and there have to be policies and best practices in place to prioritise such a defensive strategy, whether it is people, brand, or information.

Asset protection is the beginning of the risk management process, and this should be followed by identifying and preparing for a range of threats.

## Threats

The Collins Concise Dictionary defines threat as:

1. A declaration of the intention to inflict harm, pain, or misery.
2. An indication of imminent harm, danger, or pain.
3. A person or thing that is regarded as dangerous or likely to inflict pain or misery.
4. A statement of intent (Swanson, 2020).

### *Reflection*

Think of a couple of examples of threats in your life and environment that may fall into one or more of the Collins categories.

Of critical importance is understanding the two main threats to any organisation, and they originate from man-made and natural sources.

To a certain extent, the likelihood of man-made threats can be forecast, usually through the assessment of corroborated intelligence from a variety of sources. Conversely, natural threats, identified by genre are more difficult to predict. Terrorism is probably the greatest known man-made threat today, whether it is physical with a loss of lives and the destruction of property, or digital in the form of a cyber-attack. Natural threats can come in the form of flooding, tsunamis, or perhaps volcanic disruption. As I write this book (2021) the major threat we are facing is from a global pandemic (Covid 19), which perhaps could have been forecast by means of effective modelling, although very often that is easier said than done.

## *Man-made: 9/11*

We live in an extremely complex, global society which faces sophisticated threats on a scale never experienced. On 11 September 2001, the United States of America, the greatest military power in history was attacked by an extremely competent and aggressive terrorist organisation with one plan, and that was to wreak as much havoc as possible against innocent members of the public. When two Boing 737's were flown into the North and South Towers of the World Trade Center in New York, the result was the loss of just under 3,000 souls. This was terrorism on a scale that was totally unforeseen.

### *Reflection*

In your opinion, could this have been forecast? Y/N?

### *Man-made: When the bubble burst*

The financial crisis of 2008, also known as the global financial crisis (GFC), was a severe worldwide event. Excessive risk-taking by banks, combined with the bursting of the United States housing bubble caused the values of securities tied to U.S. real estate to plummet, damaging financial institutions globally, culminating with the bankruptcy of Lehman Brothers on September 15, 2008, and the onslaught of an international banking crisis. The series of events sparked a global financial crisis, which, at the time, was the most severe global recession since the Great Depression between 1929 and 1933. It was also followed by the European debt crisis, which began with a deficit in Greece in late 2009, and the 2008–2011 Icelandic financial crisis, which involved the failure of all three of the major banks in Iceland and, relative to the size of its economy, was the largest economic collapse suffered by any country in economic history. It was among the five worst financial crises the world had experienced and led to a loss of more than $2 trillion from the global economy.[2]

> ***Reflection***
>
> In your opinion, could this have been forecast? Y/N?

### *Natural: Covid 19 and exercise cygnus*

Exercise Cygnus was a 2016 UK government simulation of a flu outbreak, carried out to war-game the UK's pandemic readiness. It involved 950 officials from central and local government, NHS organisations, prisons, and local emergency response planners. A report on the exercise was compiled the following year and distributed among selected participants.

The simulation took place over three days in October 2016 and asked participants to imagine they were fighting a fictitious 'worst-case-scenario' flu pandemic affecting up to 50% of the population and causing up to 400,000 excess deaths.

### *What did it involve?*

The scenario imagined that a new virus had emerged in Thailand in June, later identified as a strain of H2N2. Within a month the World Health Organization had declared a public emergency, triggering the UK's response plans as the world mobilised to tackle an outbreak of 'swan flu'.

For the three days of the exercise, officials were told to imagine they were managing the seventh week of the pandemic, facing a peak in demand for hospital and social care. The purpose of such simulations is generally not only to test how emergency plans would hold up under strain but also to acclimatise ministers and officials to the sorts of decisions they would be forced to make.

Mock Cobra[3] meetings were held where ministers and officials were presented with situation reports from the ground, while reporters from a fictitious news organisation called WNN published news articles, and government social media campaigns were released on the social media platform "Twister".

### *What were the findings?*

The Cygnus report was frank about the state of the UK's readiness. 'The UK's preparedness and response, in terms of its plans, policies, and capability, is currently not sufficient to cope with the extreme demands of a severe pandemic that will have a nationwide impact across all sectors', it found.

One problem was that while each government body participating in the exercise had its own bespoke plans, enabling a flexible and decentralised response, nobody in the centre had oversight over everyone else.

In the absence of any "overview of pandemic response plans and procedures", participants found it much harder to shift resources between one another so as react to unexpected rises and falls in demand for services such as social care beds.

In the language of the report, '*The lack of joint tactical level plans was evidenced when the scenario demand for services outstripped the capacity of local responders, in the areas of excess deaths, social care, and the NHS*'.

Some organisations' plans were severely out of date and sometimes referred to coordinating their response with bodies that no longer existed.

Others were relying on an institutional memory of fighting the 2009 swine flu pandemic that was slowly fading (Pegg, 2020).[4]

Whether UK government departments were exercising in the event of a form of bird flu, or perhaps a biological attack by an aggressive state actor, the crisis management approach should have been broadly similar. However, as can be seen from recent Covid 19 events, planning was poor, with totally ineffective crisis communications systems in place. We will cover the threat assessment and risk communications later in this chapter.

### *Covid 19 origins*

To the best of our current knowledge, the Covid 19 pandemic started with the transmission of the virus from an initial animal host, likely a bat, to an intermediate host, possibly a pangolin,[5] before infecting humans.

'If you go to the origin of this kind of coronavirus, then I think common sense is that bats are the original reservoir', says Martin Beer, a virologist at the Federal Research Institute for Animal Health in Greifswald, Germany.

Could this have been forecast? Y/N

## ***Threat and the threat assessment***

> ### *Research*
>
> Take a little time to research how, in your opinion, an organisation should carry out a threat assessment.

According to Smith and Brooks, writing in Security Science, 2013, a *threat assessment* is the evaluation and assessment of the intentions of people who could pose a threat to an organisation, how they might cause harm, and their ability and motivation to carry out the task.

Philpott (2013), writing in Security Consulting (Fourth Edition), argues that a threat assessment is an evaluation of events that can adversely affect operations and/or specific assets. Historical information is a primary source for threat assessments, including past criminal and terrorist events, and a comprehensive threat assessment considers actual, inherent, and potential threats.

1. Actual Threats
   a. The crime history against an asset or at a facility where the asset is located. Actual threats are a quantitative element of a threat assessment.
   b. Relevant crimes on the premises (three to five years prior to the date of the incident).
   c. Relevant crimes in the immediate vicinity of the facility (three to five years prior to the date of the incident).
2. Inherent Threats
   Threats that exist by virtue of the inherent nature or characteristics of the facility or nature of the operation. For example, certain types of facilities or assets may be a crime magnet or prone to loss, damage, or destruction (e.g., assaults among patrons in nightclubs, infant abductions from hospital nurseries, etc.).
3. Potential Threats
   Threats which exist by virtue of vulnerabilities around the asset or weaknesses in the security programme which produce opportunities for crime to occur.

So, if we agree that a *threat assessment* is:

- The evaluation and assessment of the intentions of people who could pose a threat to an organisation.
- How perpetrators might cause harm.
- The attacker's ability and motivation to carry out the task.
- An evaluation of events that can adversely affect operations and/or specific assets.

Then the next step is to understand whether the threat is actual, inherent, or potential, and the most effective means of achieving this is by use of a fictitious case study.

## *Exercise safe approach*

### *Synopsis*

You are the Global Chief Security Officer (CSO) at the headquarters of a multinational telecommunications company (TeleUK) based in Birmingpool, which is the second largest, and one of the fastest economically developed cities in the UK.

The headquarters has recently relocated to a new ten-storey multi-occupied building in the centre of the city, and you are still in the process of testing and commissioning physical and digital security systems that are predominantly ICT based.

Despite the advice offered by you and the Chief Information Security Officer (CISCO) to the Executive Board about current security systems not being fully operational presently, The Chief Executive Officer (CEO), supported by the Chief Finance Officer (CFO) and the Business Development Director (BDD) has decided that because of the recent hard-won contract to provide cloud ICT-based support for a Middle Eastern state (Duarabia), all systems must be online within the next 48 hours.

Having identified the assets to be protected, your task is to carry out a threat assessment, taking into consideration the following factors:

1. The threat of a cyber-attack against commercial targets operating within the telecommunications sector in the UK has increased by over 40% during the last twelve months. The Center for the Protection of National Infrastructure (CPNI) and the National Cyber Security Centre (NCSC) have confirmed that such planned and attempted incursions are likely to continue for the foreseeable future.
2. Duarabia has a number of enemies within the middle eastern area, all of whom would benefit from understanding the commercial capabilities of that state.
3. Any penetration of the TeleUK ICT system which led to the loss of client data would be catastrophic for the service provider and of course the client.
4. The physical frailties of the building security systems are stark, and it is known in the local ICT sector that the security of all TeleUK ICT networks is far from satisfactory.
5. TeleUK network technicians have advised you that over the last 72 hours, a number of attempted incursions have taken place. Fortunately, none of the attacks were successful, but in their opinion, it is only a matter of time before a successful breach takes place.

### *Pause for thought*

Based on four strands of the information above, write down your thoughts about the actual, inherent, and potential threats to the TeleUK ICT networks.

- **Actual threats**

  *The crime history against an asset.*
  - There have been a number of attempted breaches of the company's ICT networks.
  - The threat of a cyber-attack against commercial targets operating within the telecommunications sector in the UK has increased by over 40% over the last twelve months.
- **Inherent threats**

  *Threats that exist by virtue of the inherent nature or characteristics of the facility or nature of the operation.*
  - Because of the recent critical contract to provide cloud ICT-based support for Duarabia, all systems must be online within the next 48 hours.
- **Potential threats**

  *Threats which exist by virtue of vulnerabilities around the asset or weaknesses in the security programme which produce opportunities for crime to occur.*
  - The physical frailties of the building security systems are stark, and it is known in the local ICT sector that the security of all TeleUK ICT networks is far from satisfactory.

Based on the above information, it appears that the TeleUK network is at serious risk from a number of threat vectors, but how can that be effectively communicated in a simple manner that is easy to understand?

## *The threat matrix*

Table 1, the Threat Matrix© illustrates several options that will assist the Security Auditor in having an understanding of the threat, the exposed asset (s), the potential impact, and any mitigation or treatment strategies that may arise.

*Table 1* The Threat Matrix© (Copyright Swanson, 2020)

| *Threat by type* | *Threat* | *Exposed asset (s)* | *Potential impact (s)* | *Treatment* |
|---|---|---|---|---|
| Actual | Attempted kidnap. | CEO | Impact on brand and reputation | Review all executive protection protocols. |
| Actual | Attempted network breach. | Company ICT network | Loss of data security. | Enhanced ICT protection |
| Inherent | Likely breach of all cloud services. | Company ICT network | Loss of major contract | ICT risk awareness |
| Potential | DDOS attack. | Company network | IT down time | Enhanced IT protection |

DDoS, Distributed Denial of Service.

## *Key takeaway*

*As with the definition of risk, the threat assessment is likely to be subjective, and the assessor therefore must keep an open mind, based on the judgement of evidence-based research.*

## *The Crime Pattern Analysis (CPA)*

Whilst no threat can be ignored, it is probably logical to argue that crime is the most common threat to all organisations and the criticality of A Crime Pattern Analysis (CPA) cannot be overstated.

The College of Policing in the UK says that analysis identifies patterns and inconsistencies in information. It enables the analyst to draw inferences from them so that operational decisions can be made on actions to take. This might include:

- enforcement activity
- additional information gathering
- a crime and disorder reduction strategy.

It supports strategic decision-making and the tactical deployment of resources to prevent, reduce and detect crime and disorder. It also identifies effective practice and lessons learnt through a review of tactical and strategic activity.

Analysis provides an insight into what is happening and why. It clarifies and details:

- what has happened
- why this is important
- context around the bigger picture
- what could happen next.

An important part of the analyst's role is to move beyond simply describing what has happened and to add value by providing a richer interpretation of intelligence.[6]

Crime is of course analysed in exactly the same manner, but it will require a different form of access dependent on the country involved.

Probably the easiest website to access for crime analysis in the UK is www.police.uk. Simply by inserting a post code the researcher will have access to crime and investigations in that area. Go to www.police.uk now and insert E14 5DY.[7]

Whatever the threat, and irrelevant of its source, the threat will always look for a path of least resistance or a means of *exposing the asset*, generally referred to as a vulnerability or a weakness in the system, referred to as a vulnerability.

### *Research*

Go to www.police.uk and analyse the crime situation where you live or work.

## *Vulnerabilities*

### *Pause for thought*

Some obvious vulnerabilities to any system or location will include access control, poor policies, and procedures, and so on. However, for this pause for thought give some consideration, and identify vulnerabilities to your organisation that may not be so obvious.

Dictionary.com defines vulnerability as 'openness to attack or hurt, either physically or in other ways; susceptibility'. An example being, '*We need to develop bold policies that will reduce the vulnerability of the organisations ICT network*'[8]

So far, we have examined the importance of asset identification, and the relevant threat scenarios that if successful may diversely impact that asset. We also looked at the importance of a threat assessment, in relation to calculating actual, inherent, and potential threats and the mitigation strategies required to protect the asset.

When discussing vulnerabilities, it is important to understand that particular entities can, and usually are, assets and vulnerabilities at the same time. For example, as we will discuss later, people can be a company's greatest asset, if selected effectively and managed in a way that brings the best out of them. However, a member of staff poorly selected, or mismanaged, could easily become a major vulnerability, increasing the risk to the organisation.

A well-designed, installed, and maintained automatic access control system can be a major asset as it will ensure that only authorised personnel are able to enter a building or access an ICT network. However, if that system is not fit for purpose, and does not have an Operational Requirement (OR), it is a vulnerability because it allows unauthorised access, and exposure to risk. An Operational Requirement is a means of assessing whether a system or systems are operating to the standards required to mitigate risk. CPNI has an excellent approach to the OR. Go to www.CPNI.gov.uk ad search for Operational Requirement.

It is probably fair to say that the greatest vulnerability to be found in any environment is the human being, whether that is an on-duty Security Officer who may be bored, or an ICT technician who is taking short cuts, and ignoring security protocols. I would recommend any Security Auditor to place this vulnerability at the top of their list!

However, what we need to do now is examine, *from the criminal perspective,* any vulnerabilities that may assist in exposing the asset to attack.

A major vulnerability that can be very quickly observed by the criminal is 'over engineering', that is to say, overcomplicating systems without thinking about the consequences, particularly from an end-user perspective. If the Security Officer, for example, does not totally understand the systems in place to secure an area, it is possible that such systems may be ignored.

An excellent example of this is the presence of patrol logging systems that are in abundance globally, recently described by an international provider of such systems by saying that:

> The guard patrol system provides you with the data and reports needed **to ensure your staff are visiting specific locations as part of their duties.** You simply fix checkpoints in areas that require attending, this can be inside and outdoors. Staff then carry a data collector on their round which they present to each checkpoint to record their presence. At the end of the round, the data including the time, date and checkpoints visited can be downloaded into the reporting software.[9]

Figure 2 illustrates a small data centre protected by a perimeter wall. The Security Officer is expected to patrol the inside of the wall every two hours, and during each patrol, he/she must connect the patrol guard reader with points 1–5, evidencing the fact that the Security Officer has visited every point during his/her petrol.

*Pause for thought*

Taking into consideration the guard patrol system, can you see any security issues in Figure 2?

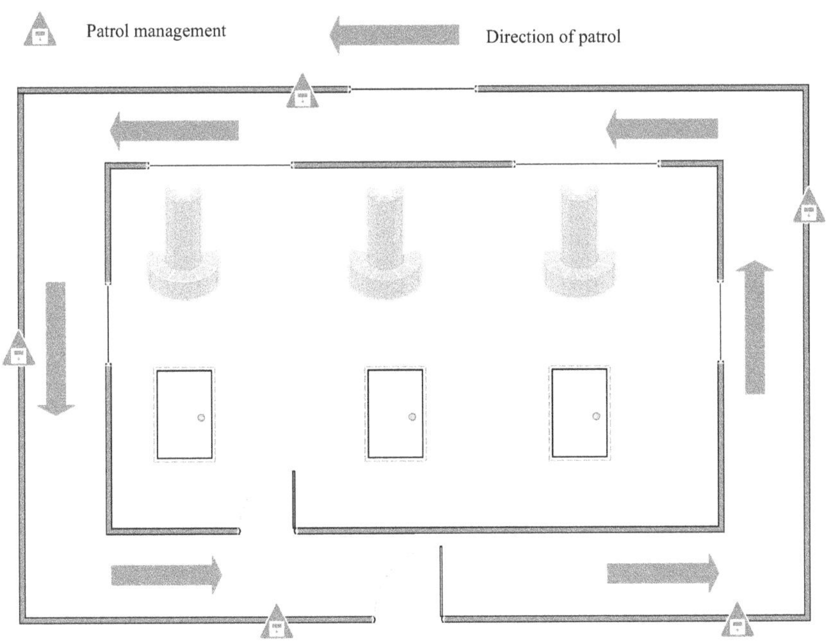


Figure 2 Guard patrol.

Remember that **the guard patrol system provides you with the data and reports needed to ensure your staff are visiting specific locations as part of their duties.** And of course, assuming that technically the guard patrol system is functioning correctly, every time the Security Officer swipes or contacts the patrol management point there will be evidence of that visit.

Excellent.

The client or the auditor should feel confident that all patrol connecting point protocols have been carried out effectively and professionally, and that the patrol has been a success.

Excellent. But has it?

Yes, every patrol point has been contacted, and perhaps from the perspective of the manager or client, for auditing purposes that is sufficient but does it mean that the perimeter fence is secure?

Let us once again refer to how this is seen by the criminal.

The first consideration must be the expectations of the Security Officer whilst on patrol. He or she understands that in the first instance, their performance, in terms of the guard patrol requirements is critical, as the client

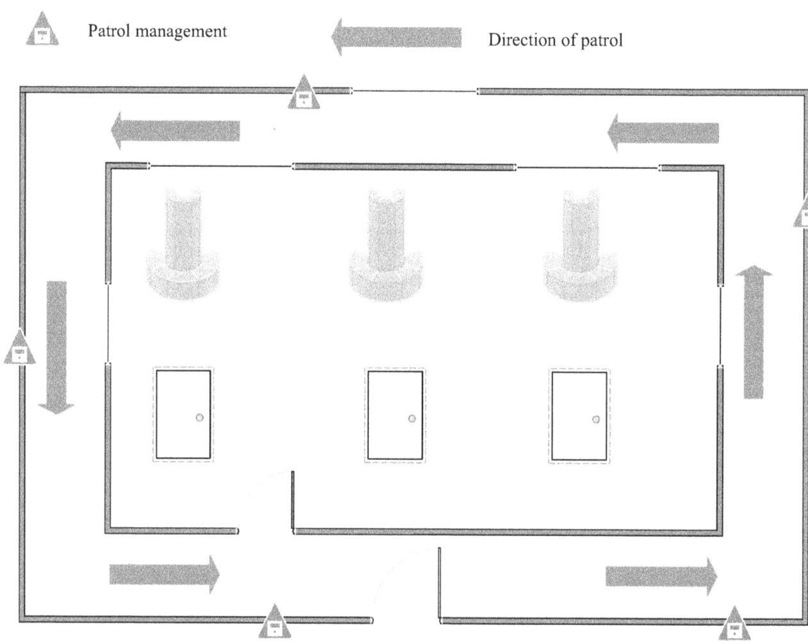


Figure 3 Guard patrol 2.

will ultimately be measuring their performance by interrogating the patrol records. So, they understand that they must move unfalteringly from point one to point two, from point two to point three, and so on; so that is their first consideration, but what about any activity or issues between points?

This puts the Security Officer in an invidious position, as time may not be on his or her side, and they have to make contact with all points during their patrol; the criminal knows that only too well!

Let us begin to think like a criminal again.

It is extremely likely that the potential burglar will have carried out some form of reconnaissance and will know that once the Security Officer has struck point 4, which is located on the northern side of the east wall, he or she will have to move around a corner, where they will have point 5 firmly in their sights. The criminal is also aware that the internal Intruder Detection System (IDS) is temporarily inert because the Security Officer's movement would activate it, added to this, an insider colleague of the criminal has left the window on the eastern wall insecure. That's it then. Once the Security Officer has struck point 4, and is steaming towards point 5, the burglar is likely to enter the corridor via the east window and will immediately have access to the data centre. Job done.

### *Pause for thought*

Who is at fault in this scenario? Is it the fault of the client who is insistent that the first priority for the Security Officer is to adhere to the guard patrol schedule, or does the blame lie with the Security Officer for ignoring all activity in between points? What do you think?

### *Key takeaway*

*Human actions or reactions can be the greatest vulnerability to any organisation, and far too often, vulnerabilities will not be admitted, but they will still exist!*

Another significant area of vulnerability, which is intrinsically linked to over-engineering is arrogance-induced indifference. That is to say, we believe the systems in place are invincible, and therefore the perpetrator of any offence will attack another location (displacement), or adopt the mind set of 'It will never happen to me'.

So, whilst limited security protection methods, or poor policies, plans, and procedures may be seen as vulnerabilities, to my mind, the greatest vulnerability in any system is the presence and arrogant domination of a human being.

The next step is to identify how likely it is that an attack will take place, and that is far from easy.

### *Likelihood (sometimes referred to as the probability)*

> *Pause for thought*
>
> How would you measure the likelihood of an attack against an asset, for example, the attempted breach of an ICT system? What would you take into consideration?

It is relatively easy to identify an asset within the organisation, and through effective and corroborated intelligence, and critical statistical analysis, a threat assessment can be designed and documented. It is also quite straight forward to carry out a vulnerability assessment to identify those weaknesses that impact the organisation. Assets, threats, and vulnerabilities are largely tangible and are therefore relatively easy to identify. Measuring the likelihood of an attack is not quite as straight forward because by attempting to measure likelihood, we are in fact trying to forecast future events! Hmm...

So, what do we need to do?

Very often when I am teaching risk or security surveying, I will ask my students how to measure likelihood, and nine times out of ten the answer coming back to me will be to examine past incidents; and that is normally where the contribution ends. Of course, a statistical analysis of historical data has to be part of the overall approach for the measurement of likelihood, but it is certainly not the entire answer.

If an assessor were reliant on past incidents, believing that a number of attacks during a said period, at a common location, it could be extrapolated to argue that there would-be future attacks at that location. However, if no attacks have ever been recorded at a particular area, over a said period of time, does that mean there will be none in the future? Of course not.

Let us look at what is actually meant by the term "likelihood'.

Quite simply, as defined by the Cambridge Dictionary, likelihood is the chance that something will happen.

So, returning to the factors and variables involved in assessing the likelihood or the chances of a criminal event occurring, it is correct to take into consideration historical statistical information, but that is only a single element that requires examination and extrapolation. There are several other factors and variables that must be examined and added to the process before we can come to any credible conclusion about likelihood, and we are back to the component parts or elements of risk.

- **Assets**: In terms of assets and their relationship with likelihood, the Security Auditor has to look at the issue from two perspectives, those of the risk owner and the potential perpetrator. The risk owner must have a clear understanding of the importance or perhaps the criticality of the asset to the organisation. As for the attacker, if successful, what will he or she do with the asset? So how important is the asset to the risk owner, and how attractive is it to the criminal?
- **Threats**: The Security Auditor must calculate where the threat is coming from, what it consists of, and whether it is realistic. For instance, if the threat is evidenced to be credible, in a form that is realistically dangerous, then it may be argued that the threat to the asset is high.
- **Vulnerability**: It is highly unlikely that the criminal will carry out an attack unless a credible weakness is identified. However, remembering how important it is to think like a criminal, it must be borne in mind that the criminal may be aware of vulnerabilities in the system that the auditor is blind to.
- **Impact**: This is likely to be the deciding factor as to whether or not the criminal or terrorist caries out the attack; what will the impact be if they are successful? The perceived impact may be an overriding factor, even after control measures have been taken into account. The likely impact may be so critical that the criminal will take a chance, because of the levels of success.

After likelihood, the next stage to consider is the impact of an attack on the asset.

## Impact

Impact is the result of a positive event or a successful attack and is often substituted by the term consequence.

As an example, the general consequences or impact of enforcing a 'lock-down', during a pandemic, when certain restrictions are imposed on a population, is to reduce the levels of infection. The result of a positive event.

Alternatively, the same lockdown, whilst reducing the impact of the infections is extremely positive, it was proven during the Covid 19 pandemic that the same restrictions had a negative impact on children's education and the mental health of a significant percentage of the UK population.

The impact however is unlikely to be static, only being measured on one occasion; often the impact has consequential aspects to it.

For instance, the impact of the terrorist attacks against the Twin Towers in New York on 11 September 2001 was initially measured in terms of the death toll on the day, with approximately 3,000 people being killed. However, consequentially, the impact of the attack was also measured by other variables, such as the invasion of Afghanistan, the introduction of the International Ship and Port Facility Security Code (2004), or the change in the US psyche and approach to terrorism.

When Lehrman Brothers ran into trouble in the United States during 2008/2009, the impact was a global recession at a level not seen since 1929.

Therefore, when a risk assessment is carried out, the impact or consequences of a particular threat, when measured by the likelihood of such a threat determines how the risk will be treated; or perhaps not! This is referred to as risk acceptance or the risk appetite.

## Risk acceptance

Whilst risk is generally believed to be '*...the likelihood of a negative occurrence...*' very often a decision is made by the risk owner, normally the Executive Board to accept the level of risk that has been assessed, and this can be for a variety of reasons. However, from a business perspective, the security function or security department is likely to be viewed as being risk averse;

the team that doesn't understand business-critical decisions, only attest to the belief that risk must be avoided at all costs. Why is that?

This cultural bias may originate from the fact that historically the Security Manager has adapted to the security sector as a second career, or role, after serving twenty or thirty years as either a police officer or a member of the armed services, where generally risks are not gladly accepted.

Banks must be protected from 'villains' and opposing forces must not be given quarter.

It doesn't help of course when the former police sergeant or army Warrant Officer, now a 'corporate' Security Manager during his or her annual appraisal is advised by their line manager, maybe the CSO, that the prime role of any Security Manager is to protect the assets of the organisation (no matter what!) at all costs.

Suddenly they are tasked to carry out a Security Risk Assessment of their location, a bank, and from the assessment, every crime known to man is examined, with the result that (in the eyes of the assessor, notwithstanding cost) all risks highlighted in the assessment report MUST be treated, and risk has to be eliminated if the organisations assets are to be protected. This is when it becomes personal, and that is a critical mistake.

To be engaged in a Security Risk Assessment is to all intents and purposes similar to being centrally involved in a serious criminal investigation, in which the collection of credible evidence is critical to the outcome of the case. During the assessment, the Security Manager or perhaps Operations Manager will be required to gather evidence of the highest calibre, that when presented to the Executive Board will lend credence to his or her opinion about the risks to that organisation. The Security Risk Assessment consists of evidence relating to the likelihood of a risk and the impact that risk will have on the victim (organisation), and during research and compilation, it is not unusual for the assessor to become extremely attached to his or her research and the consequent findings. This may be to the point where he or she believes (subconsciously) that they are the owner of the risk, and subsequently (in their minds) it is their responsibility to decide how such a risk should be treated.

Of course, it is not their responsibility, that decision lies with the owner of the risk, who has commissioned the Security Risk Assessment.

The assessor will present their findings, and the risk owner will decide:

a. Is the Security Risk Assessment credible? Does it make sense?
b. Does the risk require treatment, if so, what attention should be given to the recommendations in the Security Risk Assessment report?
c. Should the risk be accepted?

> *Pause for thought*
>
> Why would the CEO accept the risk?

There are a number or reasons why the risk may be accepted, generally referred to as the risk appetite.

1. The organisation may constitute some form of financial institution which needs to 'take' risks to grow the business.
2. The cost of accepting and implementing the risk treatment recommended in the Security Risk Assessment may exceed the potential financial losses involved in accepting the risk. This will be evidenced once a Cost Benefit Analysis (CBA) has been performed, and a business case submitted.
3. The risk owner may not trust the recommendations made in the Security Risk Assessment report, and he or she may decide to maintain the status quo.

Should the risk owner decide not to accept the risk, he or she will have to decide which treatment measures are to be adopted in order that the risk does not negatively impact the organisation.

### *Key takeaway*

*The decision to accept risk is made by the risk owner (normally the CEO or designate), not the Security Risk Assessor.*

## Risk treatment

Having covered the potentially thorny and probable political issues relating to risk perception and acceptance, we now need to move on and examine a number of ways in which a risk may be treated. However, before we tackle treatment methods, we need to clear up potential confusion relating to two aspects of risk treatment. To prevent or mitigate?

> *Pause for thought*
>
> What is the difference between prevention and mitigation?

**Prevention:** *The act of preventing something, or things that people do in order to prevent something.*[10]Prevention is relatively straight forward, in that we decide upon a strategy or strategies that will, to the best of our abilities stop any criminal activities, referred to as a crime prevention strategy.

**Mitigation:** *A reduction in the harmful effects of something.*[11] It is of course impossible to prevent all criminal or terrorist activities, but in order to lessen the impact of an attack, we introduce mitigation procedures and protocols. It may not be possible to prevent a cybercriminal attacking our network, but if sufficient mitigation protocols are in place, the attack is likely to have less of an impact.

Back to risk treatment!

Having discussed risk acceptance, it is generally agreed that there are four means of treating a risk, which are to:

- Avoid
- Reduce
- Spread
- Transfer

## Risk avoidance

Complete risk elimination is impossible, but it is conceivable to eradicate individual and specific risks by avoidance. Using the example of BU which has an ambition to drill for oil and gas in an area of high terrorist activity, a clear means of eliminating the risk of a terrorist attack is to cancel extraction operations. If exploration work is not carried out, then of course there is no danger of the threat from terrorism against the company in that location. The problem of course is that whilst the threat from terrorist activity in a particular area has been eliminated, the risk of reduced income has been introduced, and that may not be economically or politically acceptable to the Board; nor is it likely that it will be financially tolerated by the company's shareholders.

### *Risk reduction*

Risk reduction is usually achieved when some form of risk treatment is introduced, either physical or digital. This may include target hardening, which refers to extra layers of physical security being introduced, or when protecting digital systems, it may be more effective firewalls and ant-virus software, or more efficient security protocols.

### *Risk spreading*

Probably the most radical means of treating risk is to spread it. In the 1550s, after having its fleet constantly attacked by pirates (Normally English!), who were able to identify those vessels with the most attractive cargos (gold, spices, and so on), the Spanish government commissioned Pedro Menéndez de Avilés to deliver a system that would protect Spanish assets. de Avilés introduced the world's first convoy system, which would ensure that if it were attacked by pirates, a number of vessels would be able to make good their escape. Spreading the risk.

This can be applied in a number of ways today, with the transportation of high-cost goods being transported in a fleet of vehicles, on a diverse route system, as opposed to carrying the entire asset in one mode of transport. Basic common sense.

### *Risk transference*

Risk transference refers to a third party being responsible for the risk management of an entity, and this usually means the intervention of an insurance provider. For example, before an aircraft can take off, or a vessel begins its journey at sea, it must be insured. Should the plane be hijacked, or the ship be attacked by pirates (for example), the insurer will bear a great deal of the brunt of any financial implications.

### *Residual risk*

It is important to understand that, unlike a hazard, conceptually risk cannot be eliminated, but it can be treated. However, there has to be a realisation that even though the identified risk has been treated, it has not been eliminated, and this is known as residual risk. Residual risk refers to the level of risk still in existence after treatment.

### *Example – BU*

BU have recently invested a great deal of funding on physical security measures designed to protect its Head Office in London. Systems installed include a new digital Closed-Circuit Television (CCTV) system, automatic access control with a no-pass back facility, and an upgraded IDS. The Security Manager and her team are extremely proud of the project and have reassured the Executive Board that staff and property are now safer as a result of the upgrade.

Of course, the first question posed by the CEO/CFO is:

*'Does that mean risk has now been reduced to zero?'*

Of course, the answer is no, because whilst the Security Manager and her team are proud of their achievements, they are aware that there are still criminal elements who pay scant regard to such 'shiny systems', and there is still therefore a risk of being attacked by unimpressed offenders.

### *Key takeaway*

*It is generally accepted that risk cannot be eliminated, but individual risks can be treated.*

## The Security Risk Assessment process

The Security Risk Assessment process offers the Security Auditor the opportunity to examine a number of factors, such as assets, threats vulnerabilities, and so on, which when calculated will arrive at a risk factor.

To understand the Security Risk Assessment process in a tabular format, Figure 4 is designed to take you through the requirements of the assessment, beginning with asset identification, and finishing with risk treatment.

This is now where we move from what may have been seen as an academic approach to risk, to the practical methodologies of measuring and treating risk in a number of sectors. The risk assessment is by no means a straightforward process, and whereas when auditing there are clear guidelines relating to conformance, the Security Auditor, without

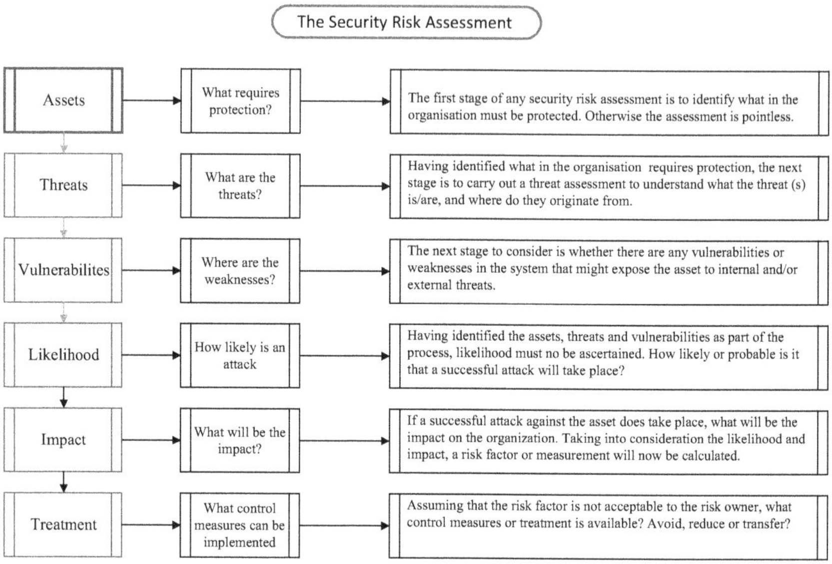


*Figure 4* The six-step Security Risk Assessment process.

such guidelines or standards is expected to gather and collate evidence relating to risk, before presenting it to the risk owner. However, let us not be under any illusion that the risk assessment, security or otherwise, is 100% reliable. The risk assessment is just that; it is an assessment, an assumption, or even a calculated and perhaps scientific guess; but it is not 100% accurate.

Remember, the objective of the Security Auditor is to collect and collate evidence relating to risk, before presenting his or her findings to the risk owner. Decisions relating to how that risk is treated lay with the owner of the risk, not the risk assessor. This is the time for the assessor to remove him or herself from the decision-making process because unless further investigations are required, that is their job done...at least for now!

It is also important to understand where the risk analysis fits in here. According to Newsome (2014), the risk analysis helps to identify and understand the risks ahead of the risk assessment, which in turn is a practical step towards choosing which negative risk should be controlled (mitigated or treated), and which positive risk should be pursued and how to communicate risk management.

Fischer (2013) when discussing risk analysis make a number of good arguments relevant to this book when he says that the first step in risk analysis is identifying the threats and vulnerabilities. Many threats to business are important to security, but some are more obvious than others. That is applicable when you look at the individual and diverse environments in part two of this chapter.

Let us refresh our memories before we move on.

**The six-step Security Risk Assessment process**

1. **Identify the organisation's *assets*.**
   This has to be the first step in the Security Risk Assessment process because if we do not understand what requires protection, the remaining steps of the assessment will be pointless. Before an attack, the first step the aggressor takes is to identify those entities and functions that are key to us and the organisation, namely the assets.
2. **What are the *threats* to the organisation?**
   Step two is the identification of the threats pertinent to the organisation by way of a credible threat assessment. Who and what do we anticipate defending ourselves and the organisation against?
3. **What *vulnerabilities* or weaknesses have been identified?**
   The criminal or terrorist will forensically examine all of our security systems in an effort to identify a weakness, or exposure, through which he or she may be able to carry out their attack (s). We must be on the front foot by identifying such vulnerabilities before an attack.
4. **What is the *likelihood* of an attack?**
   This is by far the most difficult task in the Security Risk Assessment, and it is a phase when we must be in a position to foster the thoughts of any Subject Matter Expert relevant to the threat.
5. **What would be the *impact*?**
   Once we have knowledge of the assets, threats, vulnerabilities, and likelihood of an attack, we will be in a position to calculate any possible impact. Once again it is critical to consult experts.
6. **What *mitigation* strategies or treatment may be recommended.**
   With all of the evidence now in our possession and an understanding of the likelihood and impact of an attack, we will be in a position to recommend the correct mitigation strategies or risk treatment.

### *Key takeaway*

*The Security Risk Assessment is the first step in the Risk Journey.*

## *Security or safety?*

There has always been contention between security and safety, and this is reflected in debates surrounding risk assessment. It is generally agreed that a Security Risk Assessment is designed to protect people and organisations from premeditated risk when there is a perpatrator who wishes to consciously cause damage. However, from a Health & Safety (H&S) perspective, when the risk is normally accidental, the central aims of the risk assessment are:

- An identification of what can cause injury or harm (to the asset).
- What is the likelihood of harm?
- Whether hazards (not risks) can be eliminated.
- What actions or protective measures can be introduced to control the risks?

Let us analyse the above criteria from a H&S viewpoint, and also from the lens of the Security Auditor in Table 2.

So, my argument, which I suspect may be contentious, is that whilst the H&S Risk Assessment tends to focus on accidental injuries such as slips and trips, etc., the Security Risk Assessment concentrates on the malicious, premeditated attack. However, my further declaration is that

*Table 2* The risk comparison analysis

| *Aims* | *Health & Safety* | *Security* |
|---|---|---|
| What can cause injury or harm | Slips and trips | A cyber-attack |
| What is the likelihood of harm? | Low | Moderate to high |
| Whether hazards (not risks) can be eliminated | Yes. Effectively managed housekeeping | Difficult, as the criminal is on the front foot |
| What actions or protective measures can be introduced to control the risks | The introduction of protocols and procedures | ICT procedures; fire walls; anti-virus software, etc. |

the methodology employed for both risk assessments is broadly the same, as is the aim, which is to protect the asset from any form of exposure that may cause harm. A broken leg (slips and trips) or a loss of data (the cyber-attack).

ISO 31000 describes the risk assessment as:

- Risk identification
- Risk analysis
- Risk evaluation.

## *Types of risk assessment*

There are three recognised types of risk assessment.

- **Qualitative**:

All three types of assessment examine the likelihood and impact of a threat, with the Qualitative format tending to deliver a text-based, opinion-oriented measurement. This form of assessment is based on a qualitative research approach which we will see in the examples to follow.

- **Quantitative**:

The quantitative assessment will examine the likelihood and impact of a threat, but this type of assessment will use a mathematical approach, before delivering a measurement based on a weighted score.

- **Semi-quantitative**:

The semi-quantitative assessment is a hybrid, which will utilise a combination of the qualitative and quantitative approaches, delivering a maths-based score, coupled with a text-related explanation of the score. For the purposes of this section, and indeed this book we will use a semi-quantitative Security Risk Assessment procedure.

So, the most effective means of understanding the above definition and approach is to look at a practical case study, from which we will be able to carry out a risk assessment.

We will use BU.

### *BU*

As you may recall, BU is a fictitious London-based gas/oil exploration and development multinational company, with offices and operations spanning all seven continents: employing approximately 75,000 people.

Initial exploration surveys have been carried out in a hostile environment in the Middle East (The Kingdom of Saudubai), within a region that has extremely high levels of terrorist activity, intrinsically aimed at western nations and organisations. Collation of the first data sets indicates an area of exploration where *it is likely that high yields of oil* could be extracted, with an extremely profitable return on investment, which is exactly what the Executive Board is receptive to.

However, in a stable and safe environment that is of course acceptable, and indeed welcomed by the board, but Chief Security Officer John Beck argues that *the area of exploration in question is anything but stable, with increasing rates of terrorist activity.* As far as he is concerned the risk of a terrorist attack, with the possibility of fatalities and the destruction of company assets is beyond his, and therefore the company's risk appetite. In order to evidence his arguments, Mr Beck will need to carry out a Security Risk Assessment (described later in the book), to clarify the risks involved, before requesting an action plan from the Executive Board of Directors.

Every known and accepted form of risk assessment will be reliant on the knowledge of likelihood or probability multiplied by impact or consequence. However, using BU as an example, and in order to carry out a successful Security Risk Assessment we must be able to identify the following:

> *Pause for thought*
>
> Is Mr Beck correct, and what process do you think the Security Risk Assessment should follow?

### *Assets*

In terms of BU, the assets are divided into several areas:

- People
- Data and information

- ICT/OT
- Equipment and infrastructure
- Oil
- Brand and reputation.

### *Threats*

The main threat appears to come from high levels of terrorist activity in the area where BU are intending to drill; however, there is always the possibility, or maybe probability of a cyber-attack.

### *Vulnerabilities*

Vulnerabilities are as follows:

- Poor intelligence.
- Reliance on local resources for defence of all sites.
- Ineffective power supply.
- A weak or inconsistent IT national framework.

### *Likelihood*

The likelihood of an attack depends on several factors:

- How BU defences are perceived by potential perpetrators.
- The importance of all BU assets to the attackers.
- The potential for calling a halt to all future exploration.
- The publicity arising from the attack.

### *Impact*

The impact could be:

- Loss of life.
- Loss of data.
- Damage or destruction of infrastructure.
- Loss of oil revenues.
- Damage to brand and reputation.

Another means of measuring or preparing for the above is to carry out ether a SWOT or PESTLE analysis (or both). The SWOT analysis is designed for an organisation to take a detailed look at itself, whilst a PESTLE analysis allows the company to carry out an appraisal of potential external factors that may impact operations.

## *SWOT*

SWOT (Strengths, Weakness, Opportunities, and Threats) is an analysis that can be carried out to examine a project, department, organisation, or entire sector, no matter the size.

It is especially useful at the beginning of a project. But it also gives organisations a good framework for reviewing where they stand as progress is made, and for trying new ideas and solutions.[12]

> ### *Reflection*
>
> Think how SWOT can be used to measure BU.

### *BU: SWOT*

- **Strengths**

BU is a world-renowned oil and gas exploration organisation, with unrivalled experience in the industry, ranging from initial assessments to product delivery.

- **Weaknesses**

The organisation is still reeling from the aftereffects of the accident in Yemen, and a combination of litigation fear and new members of staff and management means that presently BU is not as confident as it might be. There is also, of course, the internal struggle between security and business development.

- **Opportunities**

This is a significant opportunity for BU, not only to grow the business and command market share but also to re-establish itself as a world leader in the field of oil and gas exploration.

- **Threats**

The vultures are circling, and competitors will be closely examining every move made by the company in the hope that strategic mistakes will be made that can be capitalised on.

## *PESTLE*

PESTLE analysis is a strategic framework used to evaluate the external environment of a business by breaking down the opportunities and risks into **P**olitical, **E**conomic, **S**ocial, **T**echnological, **L**egal, and **E**nvironmental, factors. PESTLE analysis can be an effective framework to use in corporate strategy planning and for identifying the pros and cons of a business strategy.[13]

### *Self-challenge*

Think how PESTLE can be used to measure BU.

## *BU: PESTLE*

- **Political**
  In terms of BU, there are two areas of politics that are applicable here, internal, and external. As already mentioned, there is an ongoing dispute within BU involving the security function and the business development team, with neither party being prepared to yield to the logic of the other. Externally, Saudubai is essentially a war-torn state that has not experienced any form of political stability for two decades. It is currently, in theory, a monarchy, with the House of Saud having ruled over a reluctant and downtrodden population for nearly three hundred years. However, an insurgent republican movement called The Peoples Liberation Movement (PLM) is threatening an insurrection against a monarchy that is extremely unpopular. All government departments have been infiltrated by the PLM, and it is virtually impossible to be awarded any form of work contract without the permission of a local PLM grandee.

- **Economic**
  In theory, the Saudubai economy should be self-sufficient as there is an excess of natural resources, in particular oil, meaning that oil exports should afford the nation state a very healthy economy. However, like in a number of mineral-rich countries, corruption is rife, and living conditions for the indigenous population are exceptionally poor. Gross Domestic Product (GDP) has not grown for more than ten years and is significantly below average levels for the region. Consequently, western customers, prepared to deal in US dollar are made welcome with open arms.

- **Socio geographic**
  The Kingdom of Saudubai (KoS) is a deeply religious state, with a 94% Muslim population. There is a National Health Service (NHS) of sorts, although in reality, if medical assistance is required, the flashing of US Dollars will always help the patient to 'jump' the queue. There has been a population growth of approximately 2%–4% year on year, with 22% of citizens being over 75 years of age.

  Spending on defence and security has increased significantly since the mid-1990s and was about US$67bn in 2019. Saudubai ranks among the top ten nations in the world in government spending for its military, representing about 11% of GDP in 2019. Its modern, high-technology arsenal makes Saudubai among the world's most well-armed nations, with its military equipment being supplied primarily by the United States, France, and Britain. According to Jones Fighting Armies in 2018–2019 KoS became the world's third largest arms importer, receiving six times more major arms than in 2015–2017. Major imports included 100 combat aircraft from the UK, 75 combat helicopters from the United States, 4 tanker aircraft from Spain and over 200 armoured fighting vehicles from France. Saudubai has a long list of outstanding orders for arms, including 27 more combat aircraft from the UK, 154 combat aircraft from the United States, and a large number of armoured vehicles from Italy.

  The Saudubai National Defence and Security Forces (SNDSF), through the Defense Ministry, is highly influential in terms of all national decisions, including trade.

- **Technological**
  Over the summer of 2018, with little notice, Saudubai issued a royal decree mandating the establishment of the Authority for Data and

Artificial Intelligence. The royal decree also ordered the creation of the Center for Artificial Intelligence. KoS officials were given 120 days (until the end of December) to make the necessary preparations.

The KoS national communications company, SaudCom has several extensive contracts with the likes of BT (UK), Deutsche Telekom (Germany), and France Com (France) to provide a backbone of landline and cellular communication hubs, alongside a significant investment in cloud and smart technology.

- **Legal**

  There is often uncertainty regarding the difference between political and legal factors in the context of PESTLE analysis. Legal factors pertain to any legal forces that define what a business can or cannot do. Political factors involve the relationship between business and the government. Political and legal factors can intersect when governmental bodies introduce legislature and policies that affect how businesses operate.

  Legal factors include the following:

  - Industry Regulation
  - Licenses & Permits.
  - Labour Laws
  - Intellectual Property

- **Environmental**

  BU exploration impacts directly on the environment, because drilling and explosive investigations may cause minor earth tremors which will affect the local population. To this end, the company must ensure that all actions are taken to ensure that the local and national environment is safe. In particular, BU has invested significantly in Corporate Sustainability Responsibility and Corporate Social Responsibility programmes, ensuring that carbon footprint reduction efforts are made, and transitions into renewable material and energy sources are developed to protect the environment and the indigenous population.

  We have covered BU's potential political issues, and as far as legal liabilities are concerned there are equally important and problematic areas of concern.

  Whilst KoS is an established nation state, with a mature judicial system, as with politics and the economy, bribery and corruption are rife. BU must ensure that all legal areas are covered, and that there is an embedded local legal representation within the judiciary.

### *Key takeaway*

*The SWOT and PESTLE analysis are excellent measurement tools for assessing an organisation from within, and also from an external perspective.*

## Security Risk Assessment-BU

*The Security Risk Assessment is a process that identities threats from hostile actors who have the intention of causing harm by criminal acts.*

In this section, we will examine a number of Security Risk Assessments designed to protect BU assets from a range of threats. We will use semi-quantitative metricise, which will offer a scored weight and a textual explanation for each decision. There are no hard and fast rules when designing a risk assessment template, the style and design are dependent on the organisation and what it requires the template to communicate and achieve. Security Risk Assessment, Security Survey, and Security Audit Templates are provided in the book, and they will be available in PDF form from the Routledge e-learning platform at www.routledge.com/9781032030357.

## BU

### Scenario 1: Travelling to and in a potentially hostile environment

**Scenario: The CEO and CFO intend to travel to The Kingdom of Saudubai (KoS), to begin contract negotiations with the Ministry of the Interior (MOI)**

- Asset (s): CEO and CFO
- Threat: Kidnap and Ransom (K&R)
- Vulnerability: Travelling in an unknown, potentially hostile environment.
- Likelihood: According to local police intelligence, the likelihood is *high*.
- Impact: *High* in terms of brand and reputation. Loss of knowledge (Table 3).

*Table* 3 Travel in a potentially hostile environment *before* risk treatment. Quantitative weighted scoring, and qualitative textual decision

| **Impact** | *1 (Very low)* | *2 (Low)* | **3 (High)** | *4 (Very high)* | *5 (Catastrophic)* |
|---|---|---|---|---|---|
| **Likelihood** | | | | | |
| 1 (Very low) | | | | | |
| 2 (Low) | | | | | |
| 3 (Medium) | | | | | |
| **4 (High)** | | | **12/25** | | |
| 5 (Very high) | | | | | |

## *Synopsis*

Briefly, it can be seen that following advice from local police intelligence sources, the likelihood of the CEO and CFO being kidnapped and held for ransom is high (4), and after taking into consideration such an occurrence the Executive Board of BU has declared that the impact could also be high (3). With a score of 12/25 (3 × 4) The Board has decided that the risk is beyond any risk appetite and has asked for risk treatment options.

## *The Security Risk Assessment gap analysis*

Based on the evidence we are able to obtain, and having carried out the Security Risk Assessment, we are at the point where we understand the levels of risk that the organisation faces, and by speaking to the risk owner, we will be able to quantify exactly how the organisation is likely to act.

Using the above synopsis from Table 3, we know that the impact of the CEO and CFO being kidnapped is high (12/25), and that is unacceptable to the Executive Board, who have stipulated that the current risk is unacceptable, and some form of risk assessment must be applied (Below 12/25).

We know where the organisation currently is in terms of risk, and we also know what the expectations of the risk owners are.

This is the Security Risk Assessment gap analysis (see Figure 5).

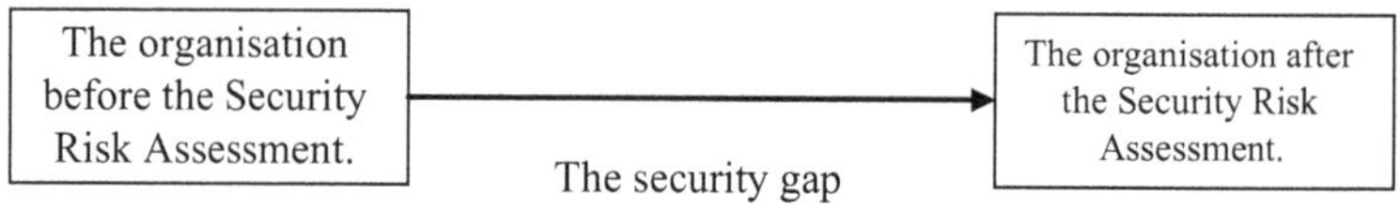


*Figure* 5 The security gap analysis.

## *Risk treatment options*

1. Accept: No.
2. Transfer: Currently unacceptable to the company insurance brokers without treatment.
3. Avoid: This would impact the business development plan for operations considerably.
4. Reduce: Yes.
    a. Deliver a detailed hostile environment training course to all involved (CEO and CFO)
    b. Select a secure means of travel.
    c. Identify a 'safe' means of accommodation.
    d. Arrange for executive protection.
    e. Enlist local protection/liaison forces.
    f. Ensure that all communications and means of transport are secure and fit for purpose.
    g. Ensure that the CEO and the CFO travel and are accommodated separately (Table 4).

*Table* 4 Travel in a potentially hostile environment *after* risk treatment. Quantitative weighted scoring, and qualitative textual decision

| | **Impact** | 1 (*Very low*) | 2 (*Low*) | 3 (*High*) | **4 (*Very high*)** | 5 (*Catastrophic*) |
|---|---|---|---|---|---|---|
| **Likelihood** | | | | | | |
| 1 (Very low) | | | | | | |
| **2 (Low)** | | | | | **8/25** | |
| 3 (Medium) | | | | | | |
| 4 (High) | | | | | | |
| 5 (Very high) | | | | | | |

### *Post-treatment*

Because treatment measures have been taken, the likelihood of K&R will be reduced to *low*, although the impact will remain *very high* if the attack is successful. The measurement is now 8/25, and that reduction is accepted by the Board.

## *Scenario 2: Placement of a Vehicle Born Improvised Explosive Device (VBIED) after exploration has begun*

**Scenario: An attack by means of a mobile VBIED against the processing area of the plant to cause as much carnage as possible**

- Asset: Personnel, property, and infrastructure
- Threat: VBIED
- Vulnerability: Poor access management and corrupt local employees.
- Likelihood: According to local police intelligence, likelihood is *high*.
- Impact: *Catastrophic* in terms of casualties and damage (Table 5).

### *Synopsis*

Briefly, it can be seen that following advice from local police intelligence sources, the likelihood of a VBIED being delivered is high, and after taking into consideration such an occurrence the Executive Board of BU has declared that the impact could be catastrophic. With a score of 20/25

*Table 5* Placement of a VBIED *before* treatment has begun. Quantitative weighted scoring, and qualitative textual decision

| | **Impact** | 1 (*Very low*) | 2 (*Low*) | 3 (*High*) | 4 (*Very high*) | **5 (*Catastrophic*)** |
|---|---|---|---|---|---|---|
| **Likelihood** | | | | | | |
| 1 (Very low) | | | | | | |
| 2 (Low) | | | | | | |
| 3 (Medium) | | | | | | |
| **4 (High)** | | | | | | **20/25** |
| 5 (Very high) | | | | | | |

the Board has decided that the risk is beyond any risk appetite and has asked for risk treatment options.

### *Risk treatment options*

1. Accept: No.
2. Transfer: Currently unacceptable to the company insurance brokers without treatment.
3. Avoid: This would impact the business development plan for operations considerably.
4. Reduce: Yes.
    a. Produce and disseminate robust Standing Operational Procedures (SOP) and instructions for dealing with all forms of terrorist activity.
    b. Carry out a security assessment of the perimeter (s).
    c. Ensure that Defence in Depth has been achieved.
    d. Ensure that all aspects of access control have been examined, and any vulnerabilities have been addressed.
    e. Ensure that all physical security (including manned guarding) has been examined and is fit for purpose.
    f. Test all forms of communication being used at the plant.
    g. Carry out drills and exercises to take account of all possibilities.
5. Spread: Unlikely to be feasible as the process is carried out at one location (Table 6).

*Table* 6 Placement of a VBIED *after* treatment. Quantitative weighted scoring, and qualitative textual decision

| | **Impact** | 1 (Very low) | 2 (Low) | 3 (High) | 4 (Very high) | **5 (Catastrophic)** |
|---|---|---|---|---|---|---|
| **Likelihood** | | | | | | |
| 1 (Very low) | | | | | | |
| **2 (Low)** | | | | | | **10/25** |
| 3 (Medium) | | | | | | |
| 4 (High) | | | | | | |
| 5 (Very high) | | | | | | |

### *Post-treatment*

Once again, if all of the treatment recommendations are accepted and successfully implemented, the likelihood that a successful VBIED attack will take place is low. However, once again, if the attack is successful the impact will be catastrophic.

## *Scenario 3: Breach of the company ICT/OT network*

**Scenario: Breach of the company ICT/OT network to compromise and fatally damage all IT communications**

- Asset: ICT/OT network
- Threat: Cyber attack
- Vulnerability: Reliance on external support (SaudCom).
- Likelihood: According to global IT intelligence services, the likelihood is *high*.
- Impact: *Very high* (Table 7).

### *Synopsis*

Global IT intelligence sources have confirmed that the likelihood of a cyber-attack against BU is high, and after taking into consideration such a possibility, the Executive Board of BU has declared that the impact could be very high. With a score of 16/25, the Board has decided that the risk is beyond any risk appetite and has asked for risk treatment options.

*Table 7* Breach of the company ICT/OT network in order to compromise and fatally damage all ICT communications, and Operational Technology *before* treatment. Quantitative weighted scoring, and qualitative textual decision

| **Impact** | 1 (Very low) | 2 (Low) | 3 (High) | **4 (Very high)** | 5 (Catastrophic) |
|---|---|---|---|---|---|
| **Likelihood** | | | | | |
| 1 (Very low) | | | | | |
| 2 (Low) | | | | | |
| 3 (Medium) | | | | | |
| **4 (High)** | | | | **16/25** | |
| 5 (Very high) | | | | | |

## *Risk treatment options*

1. Accept: No.
2. Transfer: Currently unacceptable to the company insurance brokers without treatment.
3. Avoid: This would impact the business development plan for operations considerably.
4. Reduce: Yes.
    a. Ensure that all IT systems are protected by policies, plans, and procedures in accordance with ISO 27001[14]
    b. Liaise with HR to ensure that all IT staff and management (local and the UK) are security vetted.
    c. Carry out a covert penetration test of the network
    d. Ensure that all physical security measures conform to the recent security survey, and that all OT systems cannot be compromised.
5. Spread: Ensure that back up occurs regularly, and that where possible, ICT/OT tasks are carried out by a range of networks (Table 8).

### *Post-treatment*

Once again, if all of the treatment recommendations are accepted and successfully implemented, the likelihood that a successful cyber-attack will take place is low. However, once again, if the attack is successful the impact will be very high.

*Table 8* Breach of the company ICT/OT network in order to compromise and fatally damage all IT communications, and Operational Technology systems *after* treatment. Quantitative weighted scoring, and qualitative textual decision

| | **Impact** | 1 (Very low) | 2 (Low) | 3 (High) | **4 (Very high)** | 5 (Catastrophic) |
|---|---|---|---|---|---|---|
| **Likelihood** | | | | | | |
| 1 (Very low) | | | | | | |
| **2 (Low)** | | | | | **8/25** | |
| 3 (Medium) | | | | | | |
| 4 (High) | | | | | | |
| 5 (Very high) | | | | | | |

### *Reflection*

During this section, we examined the Security Risk Assessment.

Take some time to reflect on what you have learned from the section, and then write one or two sentences about how you would carry out a Security Risk Assessment at your place of work, or at home.

## Risk communication

### *Research*

A great deal has been written about risk communication. Take a little time to research what you believe to be the most acceptable definition of the concept.

During, and once a Security Risk Assessment has been carried out, effective and transparent Risk Communication is critical, and it is all about having the ability to manage two-way communication in order to ensure that all parties involved are aware of the risk (s) that may pertain to them and their organisations. Central to this is the relationship between the expert and the layperson[15] (Swanson, 2020).

Another definition of risk communication was published by the National Research Council (NRC)[16] in 1989 in which it was argued that *risk communication is an* ***interactive*** *process of exchange of information and opinion among individuals, groups, and institutions.*

*Interactive* is the key word. The NRC argues that risk communication is an interactive dialogue between those who are facing risk and those who have some capacity for controlling or reducing that risk. For example, according to this definition, when a factory is built, the organisation that constructed it has a responsibility for interacting with area residents to help them understand any potential risks that may be caused by the factory and its emissions into the air and water. If an organisation simply announces to area residents that its new factory is *safe*, the organisation has not met the interactive expectation established by the NRC.

Instead, the organisation should share the information residents need in order to determine the risks and economic benefits of the new factory. Through this interaction, residents can better determine whether they (1) perceive a risk or (2) are willing to tolerate (accept) the risks because the potential benefits outweigh them (Ulmer et al., 2011).

So, it is all about honesty and transparency.

### *Key takeaways*

*Effective, honest, and transparent risk communication can make the difference between a well understood risk, and a potential crisis/disaster.*

As mentioned earlier in this section, risk communication is very often impeded, or at best misunderstood because of perceived arrogance displayed by so-called experts. Very often a 'them and us' situation occurs because subject matter experts have little or no confidence in people less qualified than themselves, and this is then extenuated by lay persons because they have no faith in the faceless authorities who refuse to communicate clearly with them.

As I write this book, the UK is in the eye of a Covid 19 pandemic that will likely develop into an endemic situation that we must live with for the foreseeable future. On 26 February 2021, the UK Covid 19 death toll reached a figure of 127,000 departed souls, and the constant criticism laid at the feet of the UK government has been its inability to clearly communicate the risk of Covid 19 during the twelve months (so far) of the pandemic.

Government ministers (Experts) claim the advice and guidance given to the public (Lay persons) has been clear since the pandemic began, but numerous media outlets have quoted stories of UK citizens complaining that all government messages have been confusing.

Sound familiar?

An example of such confusion can be argued in terms of the debacle surrounding the wearing of face coverings. On 14 June 2020, a senior government minister stated on a well-known political programme that face coverings would not be required under any circumstances, as they did not reduce the possibility of infectious spread. The following day, the Prime Minister announced on the BBC that with effect that day, face coverings will be worn on all modes of transport, and in shops.

I am relatively sure that the government Director of Communications, or whatever his or her title may have been, was confident that circumstances had changed between the 14th and 15th of June, and that the latter announcement was in keeping with the recognised communication strategy of the day. I have no intention of becoming politically involved here but did anybody in that gargantuan communications department give any thought to how the two conflicting messages would be received by 'the man and woman on the street; I doubt it.

My mantra as far as security risk communications is concerned is honesty, honesty, honesty.

I absolutely understand that every organisation is to a certain extent driven by internal politics, but during several decades of practicing security risk management (I will get it right eventually!), I can honestly say that to the best of my ability I have always looked my customers and colleagues in the eye and said it as it is (Table 9).

### *Key takeaway*

*Honesty and integrity! Simple as that.*

## ***Back to BU-Saudubai and risk communications***

### *Synopsis*

Global Counter-Terrorism intelligence sources have affirmed that the likelihood of a terrorist attack against the BU drilling location in Saudubai is *high*, and the impact would be *catastrophic*.

*Table 9* The threat of terrorist activity in Saudubai *before* treatment

| | **Impact** | 1 (*Very low*) | 2 (*Low*) | 3 (*High*) | 4 (*Very high*) | **5 (Catastrophic)** |
|---|---|---|---|---|---|---|
| **Likelihood** | | | | | | |
| 1 (Very low) | | | | | | |
| 2 (Low) | | | | | | |
| 3 (Medium) | | | | | | |
| **4 (High)** | | | | | | **20/25** |
| 5 (Very high) | | | | | | |

The result of the Security Risk Assessment is concerning. This is extremely sensitive information, and it is at this stage that the CSO, John Beck has to produce a communications plan in order that the appropriate members of the Senior Management Team (SMT) are informed in the correct manner and at precisely the right time.

Figure 6 is an organisational chart of the relevant members of the BU Executive Board.

> *Self-challenge*
>
> In terms of the results of the Security Risk Assessment, who, in your opinion should be informed of the results, by what means, and in what order. In terms of the Executive Board, Mr. Beck reports directly to the CEO, but he is aware of the political sensitivity of the information in his possession.

The BU scenario is perhaps an unusual representation of this risk communications issue, and we will revisit it towards the end of this section, however for now we will continue with the process in hand using the communication of a risk assessment, but in perhaps a less politically volatile environment, using a fictitious case study.

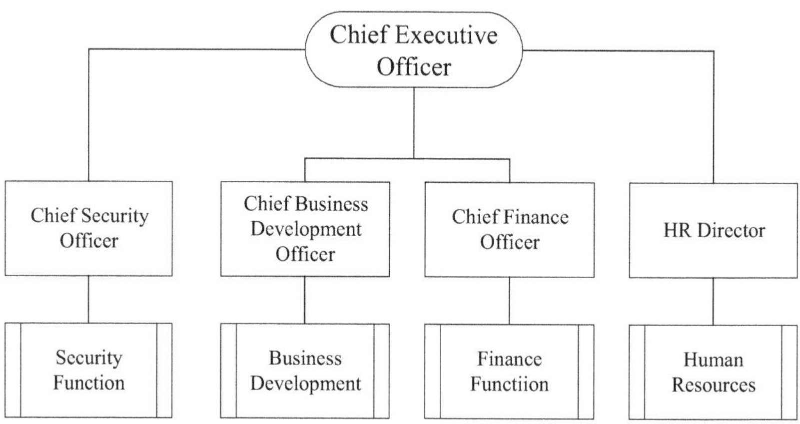


*Figure 6* BU executive board.

## *Project-Nemesis*

In order to develop the theme, we will examine the delivery of a risk assessment report to an established and trusted client, offering two options and we will build into the scenario a number of variables, such as crime rates, that could present us with a challenge, or challenges. Options A and B will illustrate different outcomes from the Security Risk Assessment, potentially requiring different responses.

## *Client: Ve-Systems Data Centre*

We were commissioned to carry out a risk assessment, focusing on potential burglaries being carried out against a data centre located in a business park in the South of England. The data centre is protected by a 3-metre welded mesh fence through 360 degrees. There is no manned guarding support, with the reception area being occupied 0800–1700hrs Monday to Friday by a lone receptionist.

Crime rates, including burglary, are below the national average, and the business park employs a 24/7 security team, and physical security systems such as Video Surveillance Systems (VSS), access control, intruder detection, etc. are extremely high.

Security systems within the data centre are also of a high standard, with 24/7 security cover.

As the result of our research, Table 10 indicates that the likelihood of a successful burglary is low (2/5) but the impact of such a successful attack would score very high (4/5) offering an overall risk-weighted score of 8/25.

*Table 10* The threat of terrorist activity in Saudubai *after* treatment

| | **Impact** | 1 (Very low) | 2 (Low) | 3 (High) | **4 (Very high)** | 5 (Catastrophic) |
|---|---|---|---|---|---|---|
| **Likelihood** | | | | | | |
| 1 (Very low) | | | | | | |
| **2 (Low)** | | | | | **8/25** | |
| 3 (Medium) | | | | | | |
| 4 (High) | | | | | | |
| 5 (Very high) | | | | | | |

## *Advice to client (abridged)*

### *Option A: Maintain the status quo*

As the result of a Security Risk Assessment carried out at the Ve-Systems Data Centre, Pegasus Business Park, Aldershot, Hants on 01 February 2021, it is recommended that no enhanced physical security measures are added to the existing configurations, as the likelihood of a successful attack in the form of a burglary is low. However, should an attack be carried out against the Data Centre network, which is successful, the impact is likely to be very high, and it is recommended that IT contingency plans are in place to mitigate such an attack.

If the above advice is accepted, it will be an indication that the levels of risk identified fall within the levels of acceptable risk determined by the risk owner, the CEO.

### *Option B: Enhanced response*

Crime rates, including burglary, are above the national average, with the business park offering physical security cover Monday to Friday, daylight hours only. Physical security systems in place (VSS, access control, intruder detection, etc.) are unlikely to deter, detect, or delay an attack.

Security systems within the data centre have not been upgraded for three years and may not be fit for purpose.

As the result of our research, Table 11 indicates that the likelihood of a successful burglary is *high* (4/5) and the impact of such a successful attack would score *very high* (4/5) offering an overall risk-weighted score of 16/25.

*Table 11* The risk of a successful burglary *before* mitigation

| | **Impact** | 1 (Very low) | 2 (Low) | 3 (High) | **4 (Very high)** | 5 (Catastrophic) |
|---|---|---|---|---|---|---|
| **Likelihood** | | | | | | |
| 1 (Very low) | | | | | | |
| 2 (Low) | | | | | | |
| 3 (Medium) | | | | | | |
| **4 (High)** | | | | | **16/25** | |
| 5 (Very high) | | | | | | |

### *Advice to client*

As the result of a Security Risk Assessment carried out at the Ve-Systems Data Centre, Pegasus Business Park, Aldershot, Hants on 01 February 2021, it is recommended that enhanced physical security measures are added to the existing configurations, as the likelihood of a successful attack in the form of a burglary is high. Should an attack against the Data Centre network be successful, the impact is likely to be very high, and it is recommended that ICT contingency plans are in place to mitigate such an attack.

#### *Enhanced physical security measures*

It is recommended that the following enhanced physical security measures are considered as a matter of urgency:

1. A Microphonic Perimeter Intruder Detection System (PIDS), signalling to a remote Alarm Receiving Centre (ARC), which will provide a Security Officer Quick Reaction Team (QRT) to investigate any potential intrusion.
2. An external and internal Video Surveillance System (VSS) that is fit for purpose and conforms to all Information Commissioners Office (ICO) regulations, and national legislation.
3. Light Emitting Diode (LED) security lighting to support the perimeter fence.
4. A perimeter and internal Volumetric Intruder Detection System (VIDS) that also signals to the ARC.
5. An Automatic Access Control System (AACS) which encompasses a dual configuration of a Proximity Card Reader System (PCRS) supported by a Personal Identification Number (PIN) code.

All technical specifications will be detailed within an addendum Operational Report attached to this document.

Once the above specifications are implemented, the likelihood of a successful attack will be low, but if the attack takes place and is successful it will still have a very high impact. Table 12 indicates that if the security advice offered is accepted and implemented, the likelihood of an attack will be low, however, should an attack against the Data Centre network be successful, the impact is likely to be very high, and it is recommended that

*Table 12* The risk of a successful burglary *after* mitigation

| | **Impact** | 1 (*Very low*) | 2 (*Low*) | 3 (*High*) | **4 (*Very high*)** | 5 (*Catastrophic*) |
|---|---|---|---|---|---|---|
| **Likelihood** | | | | | | |
| 1 (Very low) | | | | | | |
| **2 (Low)** | | | | | **8/25** | |
| 3 (Medium) | | | | | | |
| 4 (High) | | | | | | |
| 5 (Very high) | | | | | | |

ICT contingency plans are in place to mitigate such an attack. The revised risk can be seen in Table 12.

The above risk assessment method is quite generic, so for the next section of the book, we will examine a number of sectors with unique security and risk profiles. Beginning with corporate security.

### *Key takeaways*

*No Security Risk Assessment is a 'one size fits all' solution, rather, the Security Auditor is reliant on evidence researched during his/her initial investigations. Equally, control measures must be introduced that are suitable and proportionate for that particular survey.*

## Security Risk Assessment of unique sectors

In this part of the book, we will investigate how the Security Risk Assessment process can be addressed within specialist areas, beginning with corporate security.

## Corporate security

### *Pause for thought*

What is meant by the term 'corporate security'?

It was with trepidation that I chose to begin this section by examining risk and how it can be managed in a corporate environment; trepidation because unlike, for example, retail security, which is well understood, or maritime security, which is relatively easily defined, corporate security is often an unknown and difficult concept to explain.

Whilst researching for this book I consulted a number of search engines in anticipation of finding a definition of the term corporate security, but with limited success. I refined the search and used the phrase corporate security management, again without much luck. However, Cabric (2015) says that *corporate security management provides practical advice on efficiently and effectively protecting an organisation's processes, tangible and intangible assets, and people*, before going on to argue that *corporate security management explores the diverse structures of security organisations in different industries. It shows the crucial corporate security competencies needed and demonstrates how they blend with the competencies of the entire organisation.*

I am sure the above arguments are entirely correct and accurate, but I am really no closer to understanding how the security industry defines the term corporate security. Enter Professor Martin Gill, who in his excellent publication *The Handbook of Security* (2014) allows Lippert and Walby to argue that the notion of corporate security evokes the image of an in-house security office located in the basement of a private corporation headquarters or in an old shack on the premises tasked to protect the asset, to coordinate or monitor access and egress in facilities, and to ensure the physical safety of executives and other employees from internal and external threats.

We are at last getting somewhere.

Dalton (2003) took this a stage further when he examined what he referred to as the transformation in corporate security, which he divides into four phases. He calls the first phase the 'green shack' era. If someone were to ask for security in the organisation, a worker might respond by saying 'Go round back to the little green shack', referring to the lowly position they occupied in the organisation, and the lack of corporate security resources.

Dalton calls the next phase the 'physical security' era when many corporate security units were named 'loss prevention' branches. The focus was on the protection of tangible assets at points of entry and egress. What we today refer to as access control management.

In Dalton's next 'corporate security' phase, units were referred to as such, and took on many more tasks than mere physical security. This is when, at last, business mangers came to view corporate security as part of their overall business plan (thank goodness), and as a best business practice.

Dalton calls the final phase (and here we go) the 'total asset protection 'era, where protection of tangible and intangible assets and a more global outlook came to characterise corporate security.

Hurrah!

So, for the purpose of this book, I am going to define corporate security as:

*'The protection of corporate assets, tangible and intangible, symbiotically related to the success or failure of the corporation'.*

Before we move on to consider what the Corporate Security Assessment looks like, it will help if we are to study an example of a corporation.

### *BU*

You may recall that BU is a fictitious London based gas and oil exploration and development multinational company, with offices and operations spanning all seven continents: employing approximately 75,000 people.

In 2020, the organisation recorded a turnover of 275.4 billion U.S. dollars, with profits after tax amounting to just over 4 billion US dollars.

However, since a drilling accident in the Gulf of Aden in 2015, when nineteen employees were killed, with an oil spillage consisting of 4.6 million barrels, and with litigation and clean-up charges of over 45 billion US dollars, BU has struggled to regain market share, and the company is aggressively attempting to recall past glories.

## The Corporate Security Risk Assessment – 50 Canada Way, Pegasus Wharf, London. E14 5DY

Reference Number: SecRa/CW/01/22.

> *Reflection*
>
> Just to refresh our minds, what is meant by the term Security Risk Assessment?

*The Security Risk Assessment is a process that identities threats from hostile actors who have the intention of causing harm by criminal acts.*

Corporate security is '*The protection of corporate assets, tangible and intangible, symbiotically related to the success or failure of the corporation.*'

The Head Office of BU is located at 50 Canada Way, Pegasus Wharf, London. The building is 35 stories tall has access from an adjacent road, and from an underground shopping mall. 50 Canada Way has open access on a 24/7 basis and is protected by Security Officers contracted from Pegasus Security. At any one time, there will be up to 5,000 occupants of the building.

An integral part of any Security Risk Assessment is understanding the levels of crime in the area where the assessment is to take place and to achieve that a Crime Pattern Analysis (CPA) should be carried out.

## *Crime Pattern Analysis (CPA) – E14 5DY*

The postcode E145DY indicates an area of London that is devoted to financial and corporate business. Although cybercrime and terrorism are not covered in this form of CPA, it is safe to say that they will be classified as two of the most serious threats to the business community.[17] In terms of general crime, the greatest fear for this community will be related to robbery and burglary, which are in fact relatively minimal. The greatest levels of crime originate from anti-social behaviour, violence and sexual offences, and theft (in its many forms).

Take a little time to familiarise yourself with www.police.uk

So, as with other sectors covered in this book, corporate security is unique in that its risk components differ from other sectors. We will now take a look at the risk components at BU, before carrying out a number of risk assessments that are distinctive to this sector, and we will use the same running order that was applied earlier in the book.

## *Risk component parts*

- Assets
- Threats
- Vulnerabilities
- Likelihood
- Impact
- Acceptance
- Treatment

### Assets

*Something of importance that requires protection… corporate assets, tangible, and intangible…*

> *Pause for thought*
>
> In terms of priority, what do you believe the three most critical corporate security assets are?

First, you may recall that Dalton argued that the final phase (and here we go) *is the 'total asset protection 'era, where the protection of tangible and intangible assets and a more global outlook came to characterise corporate security.*

The predominant assets to be found at 50 Canada Way are:

### People

Whether they are members of staff and management, visitors, contractors or members of the emergency services, the protection of people has to be the first consideration taken by the Security Auditor.

### Building and infrastructure

The structure of the building and its supporting infrastructure must be protected, otherwise, an attack could lead to loss of life and massive physical damage.

### Information and data

For a number of reasons, information and data are significant assets to BU at 50 Canada Way, and they must be protected.

### Brand and reputation

One of the company's greatest assets is its brand and reputation as people feel safe when entering the building and have a sense of protection. Brand and reputation must be protected.

## *Threats*

*A statement of intent.*

> ### *Reflection*
>
> What do you think are the most relevant threats to BU at Pegasus Wharf?

It is easy when thinking about threat scenarios in a Security Risk Assessment to allow the mind to go on a spending spree that includes all forms of threats from low-level theft to terrorism, and everything in between. However, whilst it is not within the purview of the Security Auditor to prioritise asset protection, that responsibility lies with the risk owner, it is important to understand that the risk assessor is responsible for researching threats to his or her client's assets, and like every other aspect of risk, he or she must communicate those threats clearly and transparently.

Back to 50 Canada Way.

You may recall that when we first examined the threat, we decided that there are two types: natural and man-made. Whilst there is the possibility of natural incidents threatening 50 Canada Way, that also applies to every other type of environment in that vicinity. So, for the purpose of this study, we will concentrate on manmade dangers that threaten the location at Pegasus Wharf, and there are a number of threats that will concern the Senior Management Team at BU.

In no particular order of priority, here are some of the threats to the building:

### ***Social disorder***

As can be seen in the CPA, anti-social behaviour accounts for approximately 50% of all crimes committed within the post code and must be considered during the Security Risk Assessment. In August 2011, riots took place in London, resulting in attacks against 2,815 homes and businesses, with 205 people injured, at a cost of over 200 million UK pounds. Retail outlets were attacked, as were corporate institutions such as banks and high-rise business locations.

## *General crime*

According to the Crime Pattern Analysis for Pegasus Wharf, notwithstanding anti-social behaviour, the greatest crime threats that will realistically impact the location are:

- Violence and sexual offences
- Theft
- Burglary
- Robbery
- Criminal damage and arson

All of the above should be taken into consideration when the Security Risk Assessment is carried out, and realistic control measures to treat the crimes should be recommended.

Mitigation strategies such as:

- CCTV
- Lighting
- Access control
- IDS
- Manned Guarding
- Policies, plans and procedures.

## *The insider threat*

The above criminal offences are generally, although not specifically, carried out by external criminals, but of course, the insider threat can emanate, and be committed by anybody 'inside' the organisation. From the receptionist at the front entrance to the Chief Executive Officer (CEO) in his suite on the executive floor.

Insider threats emanate from users with legitimate access to company assets who use such a privilege, whether maliciously or unintentionally, to cause harm to the business. Insider threats aren't necessarily current employees, they can also be former employees, contractors, or partners who have access to an organisation's systems or data.[18]

Detection and mitigation of the insider threat is an intricate skill, and if there is suspicion of such a threat, specialist support should be sought.

### *The cyber threat*

> *I am convinced that there are only two types of company: those that have been hacked, and those that will be. And even they are converging into one category: companies that have been hacked and will be hacked again.*
>
> Robert S Mueller III, Director of the FBI (Evans, 2019)

The threat of a cyber-attack against any corporate body must be taken seriously during the Security Risk Assessment, as this is an area of crime that is probably growing at a greater pace than any other threat vector. BU is reliant on Information Communication Technology (ICT) and would therefore be an ideal target for cyber criminals. As with the insider threat, specialist support should be sought when tackling cybercrime.

### *Terrorism*

The threat of a terrorist attack against a corporate organisation cannot be ignored, but there is an absolute reliance on corroborated intelligence and support from credible sources such as police Counter Terrorist Security Advisors (CTSA), MI5, the National Crime Agency (NCA) and so on. It is extremely difficult to assess the likelihood of a terrorist attack, but it must be recognised as a serious threat, and mitigation strategies such as those carried out to deter general criminals should be considered. Terrorism is normally accepted as low likelihood, high consequence.

### *Kidnap and Ransom (K&R)*

Kidnap and ransom is a politically delicate area, but it must be covered during the assessment. There are a number of reasons why the CEO of BU may be targeted by kidnappers, with a ransom outcome being the most likely. However, it maybe that the kidnappers require particular information about the company, or perhaps the criminal is making a statement about his or her skills in this area.

Experience tells me that some corporate senior managers do not appreciate the fact that they may be targets for kidnappers, however, as with all other threats covered in this section kidnap and ransom cannot be ignored. Once again, specialist support is critical.

### Assassination

Although the likelihood of an assassination attempt against the CEO is very low, as with all other threats it cannot, and must not be ruled out. Remembering that BU is contemplating gas exploration operations in a high-risk area, there is the possibility, however unlikely that one of the terrorist groups operating in that area may wish to make a statement by killing a senior member of BU. This may be a warning against exploration, or it may be to attack the share value of the company.

### Vulnerabilities

Just to refresh our minds, what is meant by the term Security Risk Assessment?

> *Reflection*
>
> Think of five vulnerabilities that may be found at BU Pegasus Wharf.

Every organisation has its share of vulnerabilities, its weaknesses, and that is how the aggressor exposes and attacks the asset. The criminal, as we have discussed, looks at his or her target from a completely different angle to the designer who specified the access control system or had installed the CCTV network. The criminal is actively seeking a vulnerability, whether it is the fact that the access control system has not been configured to include a 'no pass back' facility, or perhaps the fact that the camera covering the goods inward rear entrance is blocked by 'temporary' storage, that has actually been there (temporarily) for twelve months. Unfortunately, it is easy for the designer or the Security Manager to miss such apparently obvious vulnerabilities as they may be so immersed in other aspects of their work.

The criminal is a fresh pair of eyes, as the Security Auditor must be when carrying out the Security Risk Assessment. It is also important to understand the environmental differences between light and hours of darkness, as it is almost two different worlds. Once again, the criminal understands that the external CCTV system may not be supported by sufficient lighting to make it effective, or that at 5 am, the Security Officers are tired and have a habit of retiring to the CCTV suite for the final couple of hours of their shift.

Some notable vulnerabilities at 50 Canada Way are:

- People and apathy.
- Access control.
- Intruder Detection Systems.
- Poor lighting.
- CCTV.
- Policies, plans, and procedures.
- Communications.
- ICT systems.

I could go on, but for a security professional carrying out an effective Security Risk Assessment, thinking like a criminal will help him or her to identify the above and more. The next stage of the Security Risk Assessment is to think about the likelihood of criminal activity, and what impact it may have on the organisation.

## *Likelihood and impact*

### *Likelihood*

> *Reflection*
>
> Can you remember the most effective means of estimating likelihood?

As discussed, this is arguably the most difficult area when a risk assessment is being carried out, because in reality, we are attempting to forecast future events. Keep the saying below in mind.

*Jack of all trades, master of none.*

Previously we identified several threats that are pertinent when thinking about 50 Canada Way, but what we have to do next is to identify some agreed level of likelihood in relation to each offence, and this is where professional collaboration is needed, as the Security Auditor cannot be a subject matter expert in all fields of security.

*He or she must seek out the professional opinion of experts in various subject matters.*

For example, unless trained and qualified, it is unlikely that the Security Auditor will be a cyber subject matter expert, but for the purpose of this section, he or she has been tasked with estimating the likelihood of a cyber-attack against the ICT network at 50 Canada Way.

### *Reflection*

If we agree that the Security Auditor is not a cyber subject matter expert, how is he or she expected to arrive at a level of likelihood in relation to a cyber-attack against 50 Canada Way?

A basic premise of Security Risk Assessing and Security Surveying is to understand one's own skill sets and to always be armed with a data base of contacts with skills other than yours. In this particular scenario, we have a situation where the threat is against an asset that the Security Auditor has little knowledge of, but he has a data base containing contacts, and in it of course are the ICT network specialists who operate from 50 Canada Way. This is an opportunity for the assessor to deliver the intelligence he or she has to the systems engineers, and ask them, in their opinion, what the likelihood is of the BU network at 50 Canada Way being attacked?

Very probably they will consider the intelligence now in their possession, before delivering an evidence-based opinion of such a likelihood, and whilst that is not guaranteed to be absolute, it is considerably closer to reality than if the conclusion had been arrived at by the Security Auditor alone.

## *Impact*

Once again, as with the likelihood conundrum, it is doubtful that the Security Auditor will be able to make a considered, and accurate evaluation of the impact of an attack against the ICT network at 50 Canada

*Table* 13 The risk of an attack against the ICT network *before* mitigation

| ***Impact*** | 1 (*Very low*) | 2 (Low) | 3 (High) | **4 (Very high)** | 5 (Catastrophic) |
|---|---|---|---|---|---|
| **Likelihood** | | | | | |
| 1 (Very low) | | | | | |
| 2 (Low) | | | | | |
| 3 (Medium) | | | | | |
| **4 (High)** | | | | **16/25** | |
| 5 (Very high) | | | | | |

Way, but he or she knows an SME who will be able to. Armed with the knowledge of a range of attack possibilities, network engineers should be able to make correct and accurate calculations about the impact of an attack.

In Table 13, based on intelligence and evidence presented, it has been decided that the likelihood of an attack against the ICT network is *High* with the impact being *Very high*. The next stage is to present the findings to the risk owner for consideration, and hopefully, a decision will be made about the appropriate risk treatment required.

## *Risk treatment*

To refresh our memories, and leaving aside risk acceptance, there are four recognised means of treating risk, and they are:

- Avoid
- Reduce
- Transfer
- Spread

So once again referring to 50 Canada Way, one of the most concerning threats derives from cyber-crime, and the risk owner, after consulting the Security Auditor, and reading his or her report, has to make a decision on how his or her assets are to be protected.

### *Avoid*

The only practical way of avoiding an attack against organisational assets it to remove those targets. If we were speculating an attack against, for instance, gas exploration operations in a hostile environment, and the decision was made to avoid such a risk, then the risk owner would need to consider termination of operations, and the removal of all assets from the location where the threat is emanating. That is relatively straight forward, and ultimately achievable.

The situation at 50 Canada Way is slightly more complicated because there are an array of operations being carried out by BU personnel that are symbiotically related, making it incredibly difficult to avoid the risk.

> ### *Reflection*
>
> How would you avoid a cyber-attack against the ICT network at 50 Canada Way?

The threat against the gas exploration operations is physical i.e., a terrorist attack to kill and destroy property and infrastructure, whereas the threat to the ICT network in the UK is digital, and therefore, the removal or physical transference of ICT hardware would have little or no effect. In my opinion, and this is bound to be contentious, if an aggressor is determined to carry out a cyber-attack, short of him or her being apprehended by law enforcement, or completely closing down all ICT operations, there are no means to avoid the attack. The risk owner must then consider how the threat is going to be mitigated, and thus reduced.

### *Reduce*

We have already covered risk reduction in the scenario surrounding Table 12, and once the appropriate mitigation strategies have been implemented[19] at 50 Canada Way, it is likely that the risk will be reduced.

See Table 14 which shows that the likelihood *after* mitigation strategies have been introduced, has been reduced from high to low, but if an attack is successful the impact will still be very high.

*Table 14* The risk *after* mitigation strategies

| | **Impact** | *1 (Very low)* | *2 (Low)* | *3 (High)* | **4 (Very high)** | *5 (Catastrophic)* |
|---|---|---|---|---|---|---|
| **Likelihood** | | | | | | |
| 1 (Very low) | | | | | | |
| **2 (Low)** | | | | | **8/25** | |
| 3 (Medium) | | | | | | |
| 4 (High) | | | | | | |
| 5 (Very high) | | | | | | |

## *Transfer*

Transference of the risk is the third means of treating it, for example to an insurance provider, who will cover the financial cost of any accidents or malicious attacks. Even an organisation as large as BU does not have the financial resources to protect its people and infrastructure from a wide range of risks, so the company will pay an insurance broker to cover the cost of an incident.

However, vicarious liability legislation does not release the risk owner from ensuring that the risk is being effectively managed.

## *Spread*

The most effective means of spreading the risk in this situation is by ensuring that the data is constantly backed up, and where possible stored at several sites.

## ***Summary***

*The threat of an attack against the ICT network at 50 Canada Way was deemed to be High, with an impact that was estimated to be Very High (16/25). The risk owner (CEO) after consultation with the Security Auditor and relevant stakeholders decided that the most effect means of mitigation was to reduce the risk. After risk treatment was complete it was decided by all parties that the risk of a cyber-attack had been reduced to low likelihood (8/25) but remains a high impact should an attack be successful.*

So, as argued earlier in the book, establishing exactly what is meant by the term corporate security is difficult, not so when examining mass events held at publicly accessible locations (PAL).

## Publicly accessible locations (PAL)

*With some exceptions (e.g., on transport security and for certain sports grounds),* ***there is yet no legislative requirement*** *to consider or implement security measures at publicly accessible locations.*[20]

How can that possibly be logical?

One of the many security issues when considering mass events is the fact that people are there to enjoy themselves, and there is a tendency for them to let their guard down.

Manchester Arena. May 2017

At 10.31pm on Monday 22 May 2017, suicide bomber Salman Abedi detonated an Improvised Explosive Device (IED) in the foyer of the crowded Manchester Arena.

The devastation caused by the device – which contained nails, screws, and bolts – was horrific.

23 people of all ages were killed and 1,017 injured – many of them teenagers and children.

Just hours earlier thousands had turned up to the Arena to watch American pop sensation Ariana Grande.

Doors opened for the sell-out concert at 6 pm with many of the 21,000 fans given tickets for the show as birthday and Christmas presents.

But just as Ariana finished her encore the device was detonated in the venue's foyer, near Victoria train station.[21]

There were of course accusations that the authorities had failed to secure the arena, and that the emergency services were slow to respond, none of which, as far as I am aware were supported by sound evidence. It is easy and indeed cheap to deliver accusations without merit, but that is not what this section is about.

After the attack, the question that should have been asked is this:

*"What form of risk assessment, if any was carried out prior to the attack, and if the risk assessment had been carried out, who was it carried out by, what were the findings, and how were they communicated?"*

Twenty-two lives were lost, and one hundred and twenty people were injured, some critically.

## Case study – The Manchester Arena bombings

*On 22 May 2017, towards the end of a pop concert being delivered by Ariana Grande at the Manchester Arena, an Islamist suicide bomber, Salman Ramadan Abedi (SA), detonated an Improvised Explosive Device (IED), killing himself, and 23 people who were leaving the arena. 1,017 people were injured.*

### *The inquiry*

Sir John Saunders, having acted as the Coroner responsible for conducting the Inquests arising from the deaths in the Manchester Arena terror attack on 22 May 2017, was appointed to chair the Manchester Arena Inquiry by the Home Secretary in October 2019.[22]

The report was published in June 2021 with some startling findings, but it is not within the scope or spirit of this book to offer opinion about the inquiry. However, some of the lessons that must be learned can be highlighted for discussion, with the aim of ensuring that an attack like this is never allowed to happen again.

- **Perimeter size**
  Sir John is of the opinion that had the perimeter been pushed out, or extended, there is the possibility that this may have deterred Abedi.
  - *Whilst it is impossible to agree or disagree with the Chairman's views, an extension of the controlled perimeter would have meant that the bomber would have needed to travel a greater distance, but perhaps more importantly, in terms of Crime Prevention Through Environmental Design (CPTED), he would have been exposed to greater scrutiny by security staff, the police and the general public.*
- **The risk assessment**
  In the report, the inquiry Chairman argues that at the time of the attack, those responsible for the security of the venue had in place a generally written risk assessment covering its activities. Sir John says that *it was inadequate, in that it failed to adopt a rigorous approach to the assessment of the risk of a*

*terrorist attack and did not identify what steps should be taken to reduce that risk.*

In any event, it did not form part of the event management company's planning or procedures at the time of the Ariana Grande concert.

- *The risk assessment is the foundation of all security strategies, and if the inquiry report is accurate, not to have carried out a specific counter-terrorism assessment for the concert was a major flaw.*

- **CTSA advice**
  In terms of CTSA advice, Sir John was quite specific in his views of the process, arguing that the *voluntary nature* of the CTSA system and the lack of any specific duty to identify and mitigate the risk of terrorism means that the system is inadequate to provide a proper level of protection to the public. He further argued that the CTSA did not consider and advise on what security was required to protect against an attack by a person-borne IED in the City Room, particularly during egress or ingress.

  The CTSA culture at the time meant that organisation management teams were not invited to participate in the CTSA process. In my opinion, security at the Arena would have benefitted from management involvement in that process.

  - *There is absolutely no question about CTSA's involvement in event security, and I advise all event security managers to work closely with the counter-terrorism experts. However, I would further advise such management teams to ensure that all aspects of counter-terrorism advice are considered, and that may mean seeking council from a physical security subject matter expert as part of the risk assessment process.*

- **Police support**
  As the result of examining police logs, and statements taken after the event, the inquiry Chairman is convinced that the British Transport Police (BTP), is to a certain extent responsible for a lack of mitigation in relation to the effects of the attack. Sir John argues that:

- When planning the deployment of officers to police events at the Arena, BTP failed to give adequate consideration to the threat of terrorism.
- No written risk assessment was conducted by BTP for the Ariana Grande concert or events generally. BTP should have prepared a written risk assessment which expressly considered the threat from terrorism for every event attended by a substantial number of people.
- The CTSA culture at the time meant that organisations management were not invited to participate in the CTSA process. Security at the Arena would have benefitted from management involvement in that process.
    - *Once again, in my opinion, all security managers should engage in dialogue with local police forces, but as with CTSA's support, the security function must be prepared to commission specialists in risk assessment and physical security.*
- **SIA Training and general security awareness**
  During the inquiry, it became apparent that there were a number of training issues, that in the opinion of the Chairman should have been addressed by the event management teams before the event. Sir Joh highlighted the following training vulnerabilities and flaws:
- The management team should have ensured that its CCTV operators were in possession of SIA CCTV Public Space Surveillance (PSS) licenses.
- The management team did not provide adequate CCTV-specific counter-terrorism training for its senior staff, despite requests from both people who should have received it. This was a significant failure.
- The management team should have made counter-terrorism refresher training compulsory for stewards.
- Had the management team taken robust steps to ensure that all of its staff had completed their training diligently, and provided a practical opportunity to demonstrate their knowledge and build their confidence, it is possible that the two Security

Officers would have acted more decisively to escalate a member of the public's concerns regarding SA.

- There were also concerns about the levels of patrol and search training which the Chairman argued were inadequate.
  - *Whether it is event security, corporate security or the security of any other sector of the industry there is no excuse for inadequate training. As mentioned, it is not within either the scope or the spirit of this book to criticise organisations for the stance taken in terms of how they carry out their security strategies.*
  - *However, there is sufficient evidence to make a compelling argument, that whilst in the short term the investment can appear financially significant, in terms of long-term planning, effective security training and awareness can, and has often in the past, saved lives.*

If I may say so, the inquiry report is exceptionally well researched and written, and once again, in my opinion, it will be to the benefit of all security professionals to download and read it at:

https://manchesterarenainquiry.org.uk/chairman

## Martyn's law

One of the 23 people killed as a result of the suicide attack against concert goers at the Manchester arena was a young man by the name of Martyn Hett. After the atrocity, a group now known as Survivors Against Terror, led by Martyn's mother Figen Murray and Nick Aldworth, a retired Chief Superintendent in the Metropolitan Police bravely took it upon themselves to bring pressure to bear on the UK government to ensure that such an attack never happens again. They have produced a document titled *Martyn's Law: Proposed new legislation to provide better protection from terrorism for the British Public.*

This paper proposes the introduction of new legislation to provide better protection from terrorism for the British Public. It is produced in honour of the life of Martyn Hett and the 35 other people murdered, and hundreds injured, by extremists in the UK in 2017. Its aim is to help reduce the number of families who have to go through what their families have by making the UK better protected from terrorism and more prepared to deal with its consequence, while maintaining a free and open society. Martyn's Law should therefore be a key part of delivering the UK's wider Counter Terrorism Strategy 2018 (CONTEST).

Once again, I recommend it as essential reading for any security professional interested in ensuring that the UK public remains safe.

It can be found at:

https://democracy.manchester.gov.uk/documents/s13150/Appendix%20 1%20-%20Martyns_Law_Final_Report.pdf

## Protect duty

On 26 February 2021, the UK government set out it plans for the safety of the UK population from terrorist attacks.

Protect Duty is part of the Government's commitment to improving protective security and preparedness in public places.

In a Home Office paper, the UK government said that on 26 February 2021 it had set out its proposals on a new Protect Duty; a legal requirement for public places to ensure preparedness for and protection from terrorist attacks.

The Protect Duty delivers on a manifesto commitment to improve the safety and security of public venues and spaces, drawing on lessons learned from previous terrorist incidents.

The proposals have been championed by victims' groups, including the Martyn's Law campaign, which was established by Figen Murray, who tragically lost her son, Martyn, in the Manchester Arena attack in 2017.

Figen Murray, the mother of Martyn Hett, one of the 22 victims of the Manchester Arena attack said:

> *Today is a major stride towards making our country safer from terror attacks. I want to thank the government for taking this step. To make Martyn's Law a reality is of huge relief, and I look forward to making a lasting difference with all of those who have supported it.*

The full version of the announcement can be found at:

https://www.gov.uk/government/news/government-sets-out-plans-to-protect-public-places-from-terrorist-attacks

Back to event security.

*Pause for thought*

What is meant by the term 'event security'?

## The publicly accessible locations (PAL) Security Risk Assessment–Liverport Arena, Liverport Docklands, LE1 2BB

Reference number: SecRa/LA/02/22

The Liverport Arena stands in Liverport Docklands and has the capacity to allow 12,000 standing guests to attend a mass event such as a pop concert.

There are five main entry points, and five emergency exits, all of which, during a concert will be manned by contract Security Officers.

There is a capacity for 2,000 private vehicles in the underground car park, with additional spaces available in other local parking areas surrounding the arena.

An integral part of any Security Risk Assessment is understanding the levels of crime in the area where the assessment is to take place and to have an understanding that a Crime Pattern Analysis (CPA) should be carried out.

## Crime Pattern Analysis (CPA) – LE1 2BB

The postcode LE1 2BB indicates an area of Liverport that is devoted to hospitality and entertainment. Although cybercrime and terrorism are not covered in this form of CPA, it is safe to say that they will be classified as two of the most serious threats to any community. In terms of general crime, the greatest fear for this community will be related to robbery and burglary, which are in fact relatively minimal.

The highest levels of crime originate from anti-social behaviour, violence and sexual offences, and theft (in its many forms).

Take a little time to familiarise yourself with www.police.uk

So, as previously mentioned in corporate security, event security is unique in that its risk component parts tend to differ, to a certain extent, from other sectors. We will now take a look at the risk components to be found at the Liverport Arena, before carrying out a number of risk assessments that are distinctive to this sector, and we will use the same running order that was applied earlier in the book.

### Risk component parts

- Assets.
- Threats.
- Vulnerabilities.
- Likelihood.
- Impact.
- Acceptance.
- Treatment.

### Assets

The most prominent assets to be found at the Liverport Arena, in no particular order of priority are:

#### *People*

Whether they are members of staff and management, visitors, performers, or members of the emergency services, the protection of people has to be the first consideration taken by the Security Auditor.

#### *Building and infrastructure*

The structure of the arena and its supporting infrastructure must be protected, otherwise, an attack could lead to loss of life and massive physical damage. The infrastructure at a mass events location is diverse and complicated, and a great deal of planning is required to protect this extremely important asset.

#### *Information and data*

There will be a great deal of sales data and prediction that is important for planning future events, and that is a critical asset that must be protected.

#### *Brand and reputation*

One of the arena's greatest assets is its brand and reputation as people feel safe when entering the location and have a sense of protection. Brand and reputation must be protected.

## Threats

*A statement of intent.*

> ### *Reflection*
>
> What do you think are the most relevant threats to the Liverpoort Arena?

The threats to any mass event are many and varied, and in no particular order, we will now examine the threats as we see them impacting the Liverpoort Arena.

### *General crime*

From the Crime Pattern Analysis (CPA), it can be seen that the three most vociferous crimes in the area are violence and sexual offences, anti-social behaviour, and public order, with the first two, certainly having the potential to impact the arena during, let us say, a pop concert. Of course, there are other offences that may be of concern to the security team, examples being drugs, theft, and vehicle crimes.

### *Cyber crime*

Whilst sensitive data found in a corporate or critical infrastructure environment won't be held at an entertainment location such as the Liverpoort Arena, there will be data relating to forthcoming events, sales, staff, and security. Such information and data will attract a criminal who requires intelligence before an attack, and therefore the threat of cybercrime must be taken seriously by the Security Auditor during the Security Risk Assessment.

### *Arson and criminal damage*

In an area where offences of anti-social and public order are significant, the threat of arson and criminal damage must always be taken into consideration during the Security Risk Assessment.

### *Alcohol induced violence*

Unfortunately, alcohol is far too often the cause of violence, particularly when the sale is uncontrolled, and most mass event locations are often close to public houses and bars, and of course, the sale of alcohol is allowed if the premises is licensed. The Security Auditor must ensure that security practices are in place to control intoxicated personnel before, during, and after an event.

### *Terrorism*

The marauding attacks at the Bataclan in November 2015, and the suicide bomber who detonated an explosive device at the Manchester Arena in May 2017 are testament to the fact that terrorists see such mass events as legitimate targets. The threat of a terrorist attack against the Liverpool Arena is very real and must be considered during the Security Risk Assessment.

### *Vulnerabilities*

As already mentioned earlier in the book, every organisation has its share of vulnerabilities, its weaknesses, and that is how the aggressor exposes and attacks the asset. Once again it is critical to understand that the offender does not look at vulnerabilities and weaknesses from the same lens as the Security Manger. A vulnerability from the Security Manager's perspective, is far too often a weakness, and whilst an unserviceable CCTV camera covering the rear fire exit is a nuisance, and funds must be sought to have it repaired, to the criminal that camera is a means of entering the building unseen.

The Security Auditor must adopt the same approach as the criminal, that is to say, he or she must look at potential vulnerabilities as aids to the offender.

Some notable vulnerabilities that may be found at the arena are:

- People.
- Access control.
- Intruder Detection Systems.
- CCTV.
- Policies, plans, and procedures.
- Communications.
- ICT systems.

I could go on, but to a security professional carrying out an effective Security Risk Assessment, thinking like a criminal will help him or her to identify the above and more. The next stage of the Security Risk Assessment is to think about the likelihood of criminal activity, and what impact it may have on the organisation.

## ***Likelihood and impact***

### *Likelihood*

> ### *Reflection*
>
> Can you remember the most effective means of estimating likelihood?

As mentioned on a number of occasions, estimating (and that is what it is, an estimation) the likelihood of an attack is the most difficult consideration taken during a Security Risk Assessment, but it is a critical element of the process.

Again, as previously argued, the basic premise of Security Risk Assessing and Security Surveying is to understand one's own skill sets and to always be armed with a data base of contacts with skills other than yours.

The most worrying threat to any mass event, is a terrorist attack, and just as the Security Auditor involved in risk assessing 50 Canada Way had the common sense to take advice from a cyber subject matter expert, for the Liverpool Arena, advice from counter-terrorist and physical/ICT security experts will need to be sought.

#### IMPACT

Whilst calculating the impact of a terrorist attack is perhaps more straight forward than assessing its likelihood, it is still a specialist area, and unless the Security Auditor is qualified and experienced in the field, once again

*Table* 15 The risk of a terrorist attack against the Liverport Arena *before* mitigation

| **Impact** | 1 (*Very low*) | 2 (*Low*) | 3 (*High*) | 4 (*Very high*) | **5 (*Catastrophic*)** |
|---|---|---|---|---|---|
| **Likelihood** | | | | | |
| 1 (Very low) | | | | | |
| 2 (Low) | | | | | |
| **3 (Medium)** | | | | | **15/25** |
| 4 (High) | | | | | |
| 5 (Very high) | | | | | |

advice should be sought from counter-terrorism and physical security subject matter experts.

In Table 15, based on intelligence and evidence presented, it has been decided that the likelihood of a terrorist attack against the Liverport Arena is *Medium* with the impact being *Catastrophic*. The next stage is to present the findings to the risk owner for consideration, and hopefully, a decision will be made about the appropriate risk treatment required.

## *Risk treatment*

To refresh our memories, leaving aside risk acceptance, there are four recognised means of treating risk, and they are:

- Avoid
- Reduce
- Transfer
- Spread

Having received the Security Risk Assessment, the Board of Directors at the Liverport Arena now have to decide what risk treatment is appropriate for their situation. Current risk levels are not acceptable. Do they opt to....

### AVOID

Feasibly, the only means open to avoid the assessed terrorist attack is to cancel the event, and that maybe necessary if it is believed that no other means are available to counter the threat. However, evidence of likelihood will need to be compelling because the financial repercussions of cancellation would need to be considered and debated.

### REDUCE

To reduce the threat of a terrorist attack against the Liverport Arena, the Board of Directors would have to sanction a number of physical security upgrades to the existing security systems in place, and such amendments would need to satisfy any police concerns. Consideration must also be given to the comfort and acceptance of those attending

*Table 16* The risk of a terrorist attack against the Liverport Arena *after* mitigation

| | **Impact** | 1 (*Very low*) | 2 (*Low*) | 3 (*High*) | 4 (*Very high*) | **5 (*Catastrophic*)** |
|---|---|---|---|---|---|---|
| **Likelihood** | | | | | | |
| 1 (Very low) | | | | | | |
| **2 (Low)** | | | | | | **10/25** |
| 3 (Medium) | | | | | | |
| 4 (High) | | | | | | |
| 5 (Very high) | | | | | | |

an event. For example, it is quite straight forward to recommend an enhanced search programme, but the reasons and rational will need to be explained to all attendees.

#### SPREAD

If an event is promoted, it will take place in the arena, making it impossible to choose to spread the risk as an option. However, it is aways wise to have an alternative venue if possible.

#### TRANSFER

The event at the arena will have to be covered by adequate insurance agreements, so to a certain extent, the risk is being transferred.

Table 16 illustrates a reduction in the risk level after methods have been implemented to reduce the risk. The likelihood is now low (2), due to the security upgrades, but if a terrorist attack took place and was successful, the impact would still be catastrophic (5). This reduces the risk level from 15/25 to 10/25.

### *Summary*

*The threat of a terrorist attack against the Liverport Arena was deemed to be Medium, with an impact that was estimated to be Catastrophic (10/25). The risk owner after consultation with the Security Auditor and relevant stakeholders decided that the most effective and relevant stakeholders decided that the most effective means of mitigation was to reduce the risk. After risk treatment was complete it was decided by all parties that the risk of a terrorist attack had been reduced to a low likelihood (10/25) which means it still has a catastrophic impact should an attack be successful.*

Having so far examined corporate security and publicly accessible location mass events, we now move onto look at how the Security Risk Assessment may go some way to protecting the retail environment.

## Retail security

Researching the global cost of retail crime proved to be extremely difficult, with most estimates relating to the year 2008. However, according to the British Retail Consortium (BRC) 2020 Retail Crime Survey,[23] the total cost to British Retailers was £2.1 bn,[24] and during the same period, 424 violent or abusive incidents occurred each day. According to Forbs, the cost of retail crime in the United States during the same period was $46.8 bn.[25]

For the purpose of this section, we will use the shopping centre that is located beneath 50 Canada Way.

## Retail Security: Canada Way Shopping Centre

Reference number: SecRa/CWSC/03/22

Canada Way Shopping Centre is accessed from the ground floor of 50 Canada Way, with stairs, lifts, and escalators being available. It is a single-story retail area, with 125 shops, bars, and restaurants accessible to the public. The shops include jewellery, clothing, fashion accessory, department stores, electronics, beauty and health, stationery, and pet care.

Opening hours are:

Monday to Friday 9am–8pm

Saturday 10am–7pm

Sunday 12pm–6pm

There is access to the shopping centre from an underground car park, and there is direct access to London Underground (Tube).

Security is provided by Pegasus Security, with Security Officer support being available on a 24/7 basis, with the following duties being carried out.

- Security Control Room management.
    - Alarm and CCTV management
- Static security at strategic locations around 50 Canada Way and throughout the shopping centre.
- Security Officer patrols, with and without canine support.
- Security Incident Quick Reaction Force (SIQRF).
- Police liaison.
- First response.

*Table 17* Tangible and intangible retail assets, in no particular priority

| *Tangible assets* | *Intangible assets* |
|---|---|
| People | Brand and reputation |
| Property | Sales forecasts |
| Infrastructure | Perceptions of security |
| Data and information | Intellectual property |
| Sales and turnover | Values and culture |

As with corporate security and mass event security, we will now examine retail security risk components in an alternative tabular format, before looking at a number of Security Risk Assessment examples (Table 17).

### *Assets*[26]

*Pause for thought*

What do you believe the three most important retail security assets are?

*Table 18* Critical assets at Canada Way Shopping Center

| *Assets* | *Examples at Canada Way Shopping Center* |
|---|---|
| People | Staff and management; members of the public; security staff and contractors. |
| Property and produce | The shop itself and the produce held within. |
| Infrastructure | Electricity and gas supplies; fresh water; air conditioning; IT framework. |
| Data and information | Data and information held on all servers and any cloud access. |
| Sales and turnover | As with any business, increased sales and turnover are tremendous assets. |
| Brand and reputation | After people, potentially the greatest asset to any organisation. |
| Sales forecasts | If accurate and communicated effectively, positive sales forecasts are critical to business development and growth. |

So, as with other sectors, the first part of any risk assessment, security or otherwise is to identify the assets which require protection, but it is not within the remit of the risk assessor to prioritise such protection, that onerous task lies with the risk owner.

In terms of the Canada Way Shopping Center, Table 18 gives an indication of the most critical assets that must be protected.

As mentioned earlier in the book, the identification of assets to be protected is a critical first step, closely followed by an understanding of where the threat comes from.

## *Threats*

The Crime Pattern Analysis (CPA) at Figure 7 informs us that the most potent threats to that post code are anti-social behaviour, followed by violence and sexual offences, with theft, shoplifting, and burglary also being hilighted. However, statistics from the BRC inform us that retail crime in the UK from 2019 to 2020 cost the sector £2.1bn, and there were 424 violent or abusive incidents each day. To that end, it is logical to examine the following threats.

### *Violent and abusive behaviour*

Staff are not going to subject themselves to the possibility of violence and abusive behaviour, and if the store management team that employees them has taken little or no precautions to protect them, they will let their feet do the talking; and will leave. Equally, shoppers are not going to entertain or accept any threats of violent or abusive behaviour and will obviously only shop in a secure and safe retail outlet elsewhere.

The Security Risk Assessment (SRA) must take into consideration all physical precautions introduced to ensure the safety and security of staff and shoppers. Equally, the Health & Safety at Work Act (1974) sets out the general responsibilities that employers have towards employees and members of the public. Often referred to as a duty of care. As with other specialist sectors, the Security Auditor is not required to be Health & Safety qualified (although that would be a significant advantage) but he or she should be acquainted with relevant legislation and regulations and have access to a qualified Health & Safety advisor.

### Theft

Within retail, theft is often mistakenly referred to as 'shrinkage', which is actually defined as:

*'The loss of a retailer's inventory from shoplifting, employee theft, supplier error/fraud, cashier errors, and other causes. The two biggest causes, by far, of "retailer shrinkage" are **shoplifters and employee theft**.'*[27]

So, whilst it is technically incorrect to refer to certain aspects of shrinkage as loss through stealing, shoplifting and staff theft account for a significant percentage of the discrepancies.

### Burglary

Although during non-trading hours, all outlets will be secured, and there will be a significant Security Officer presence, the standard of IDS fitted will vary, from basic door and window contacts to extremely sensitive and sophisticated perimeter and volumetric internal alarms signalling to the Security Control Room or an off-site Alarm Receiving Centre (ARC). The smaller bespoke shops, with limited sales capacity, will likely be protected by basic systems, whilst jewellery and high-ticket value clothes stores will have a sophisticated, monitored IDS. The Security Auditor must take all options into consideration.

#### Arson and criminal damage

There are numerous reasons which explain why a shop has been set alight, or had graffiti sprayed on its windows and doors, or had the windows and doors attacked. It may be a revenge attack carried out by a former employee who has been fired, wrongly, in his or her eyes. It may also be as simple as a vandal attack by thoughtless criminals with no logical explanation. Whatever the reason it must be included in the Security Risk Assessment.

#### Cyber

This is a relatively new threat vector for retailers, but e-crime is on the increase and has been exacerbated by the Covid 19 pandemic. Blog.netop.com[28] offers four cybersecurity trends that they argue retailers need to know, which are:

### *Phishing scams*

Email phishing occurs when attackers send legitimate-looking emails to customers posing as a retailer. People open the email, click on a link, and soon enough, malware is installed, and information is poached from the retailer and their customers.

### ***Machine learning***

Using an intricate system of bots that are guided by algorithms, attackers can gather data like passwords and credit card information. Retailers who are the victim of such attacks can lose money, and even have to shut down completely to resolve botnet attacks.

### ***Data breaches caused by unauthorised access***

Data breaches involve the leak or loss of data and remain a common cybersecurity trend even in 2020. Cybercriminals use data breaches to access cloud networks to view, copy, and transmit data for malicious purposes. For retailers, it's not just the stolen data, but the brand reputation that creates major problems.

### *Supply chain*

Retailers rely on a vast supply chain network to keep business and inventory moving, but with the increased use of cloud computing, digital communication, and reliance on vendors, the supply chain has become a common attack surface.

In order for the threat to realise, and therefore be successful, the aggressor needs exposure to the asset, and that is generally gained through some form of weakness or vulnerability.

### ***Vulnerabilities***

One of the greatest security vulnerabilities for any retail outlet is the fact that sales are sacrosanct, and profit is difficult; every penny must be accounted for, probably more so than in any other business environment. There is a tendency for security spending to be at times over scrutinised and perhaps reduced, but of course, this is not applicable to all brands. Certain brands will be given a low priority, until of course, an incident occurs, and the business loses money, or a member of staff is injured.

Another major weakness is the fact that members of staff are very often placed in a position of trust, and at times, for any number of reasons that faith is betrayed. Perhaps it is exceedingly easy for staff to disable the CCTV system for a crime to be committed unseen, or perhaps switch off the loop alarm so that an expensive piece of equipment can be removed without being detected.

There is often a reliance in retail on Electronic Article Surveillance systems (EAS).

The EAS system is activated when a Radio Frequency Identification (RFID) tag, attached to a product passes between the EAS readers.

This will instigate some form of alarm, normally sound and vision, and the Standard Operating Procedures (SOP) will dictate that a response is required, either by an on-duty Security Officer, or a member of staff. However, this is where and when problems too often occur, for the following reasons.

- Technology
  As advanced as the EAS technology is today, there is still a tendency for the system to false activate, and there are several means of circumnavigating the EAS,[29] meaning that very often staff have little confidence in the system, uttering such explanations as '*It's OK mate, it's always going off, no worries. On you go*'.
- Response
  As mentioned above, false alarms very often elicit an apathetic response to the activation, and therefore the reaction is limited. Equally, there is the conundrum of how a Security Officer or member of staff is *expected* to respond. What should be the outcome if the person activating the EAS runs out of the shop, and into the high street or car park? Is the Security Officer or member of staff expected to give chase, with the possibility of being attacked? I would advise that this is not the correct action to be taken.

  What should be the response to an EAS activation if there are ten people entering the store, and ten shoppers leaving at the same time? Which of the twenty should be challenged? This scenario should be examined during the assessment, and the Security

Auditor should be looking for evidence that all members of staff and contract Security Officers are protected from placing themselves in danger by pursuing a fleeing criminal. Once the assets, threats, and vulnerabilities have been identified in relation to the retail outlet, the Security Auditor must endeavour to measure the likelihood of an attack and its impact.

## *Likelihood and impact*

### *Likelihood*

If you recall, retail crime in the UK from 2019 to 2020 cost the sector £2.1bn, and there were 424 violent or abusive incidents each day, and added to this is the extreme vulnerabilities of the sector. I believe the likelihood of a retail outlet being attacked is high.

As mentioned earlier, it does of course depend on the shop or store in terms of the product being sold, and the levels of security deployed to deter crime. But the fact that most of the goods stolen are moved on very easily, and criminal investigations into retail crime are quite low as far as police priorities are concerned, would, in my opinion, encourage rather than deter retail crime.

In terms of the shopping centre below 50 Canada Way, the likelihood would depend on the individual shop or store being targeted, but there is also 24/7 on-site security which must be taken into consideration.

Don't forget displacement, which sees the attacker take on the small, less protected shop, as opposed to the larger store, which has deployed CCTV, security lighting, and a well-designed, implemented, and monitored IDS.

### *Impact*

As with likelihood, the impact felt by the retailer is dependent on the ability of the outlet to absorb an attack. For a small bespoke shop, with minimum turnover, the impact of an attack or a series of attacks could be disastrous. Whilst a well-branded outlet, with considerable footfall and a high turnover may be able to absorb the impact of let us say a burglary easier than the smaller adjacent shop. Of course, that is in terms of financial loss, but another impact which must be taken into consideration is the safety and morale of staff, who may feel abandoned if security is seen as a low priority in their place of work.

### Risk treatment

As with the scenario relating to corporate security, we still include the following means:

- Avoid
- Reduce
- Spread
- Transfer

However, I believe that before we look at the four means of treatment, we need to examine the retail risk appetite, which I would argue is quite high. The risk appetite of a retail outlet may be perceived as high because everyday sales are critical and retail operates within a unique business model, where risks are almost, albeit covertly, acceptable in order to make a Dollar!

Experience advises me that during a retail Security Risk Assessment, the assessor must be aware that security expenditure often presents itself as a low priority when compared to day-to-day footfall and sales. I can think of no other sector where the security function is looked upon as being an out-and-out cost centre, and for that reason, the Security Auditor must be slightly more vigilant to the fact that security expenditure is often difficult to justify.

#### Risk avoidance

Risk avoidance for any business community is difficult, because as explained earlier, very often in order to avoid risk, the operation has to be curtailed. Remember the exploration example? To a certain extent, risk avoidance is more difficult for retailers, because the only realistic option is either the postponement of business development in terms of new builds or the closure of current locations; neither of which is financially acceptable

#### Risk reduction

As with other sectors, for retailer's, risk reduction is the only logical option, and this has to be argued during the Security Risk Assessment. Table 20 displays the likelihood and impact of an overnight burglary at a store below 50 Canada Way, with the threat emanating from organised criminals who are intent on successfully stealing consignments of high-end expensive clothing, worth approximately £200,000. The likelihood is high because of the value of the goods which can easily be moved on, and the impact would be very high because of the financial loss and the damage to the brand and reputation.

### *Spread the risk*

Particularly in high ticket outlets, it would be wise to ensure that expensive stock, where possible, is held at a number of locations, or perhaps have the minimum stock in the shop, with the remainder held at a warehouse or distribution centre. Spreading the risk is difficult in this situation, but it should be considered.

In order to reduce the risk from 16/25 to an acceptable level, it has been decided to upgrade the current CCTV system which is monitored at an Alarm Receiving Centre (ARC), to increase the capacity of the IDS, which is also monitored, and ensure that the store is visited every hour during closing times by the shopping centre security team. It is likely that this will reduce the risk. See Table 20.

The overall risk factor has been reduced by 50%, with the likelihood of an attack now being rated as Low. However, should the attack be successful the impact will still be very high.

*Table 19* The risk of an overnight burglary, *before* risk treatment

| **Impact** | *1 (Very low)* | *2 (Low)* | *3 (High)* | ***4 (Very high)*** | *5 (Catastrophic)* |
|---|---|---|---|---|---|
| **Likelihood** | | | | | |
| 1 (Very low) | | | | | |
| 2 (Low) | | | | | |
| 3 (Medium) | | | | | |
| **4 (High)** | | | | **16/25** | |
| 5 (Very high) | | | | | |

*Table 20* The risk of an overnight burglary, *after* risk treatment

| **Impact** | *1 (Very low)* | *2 (Low)* | *3 (High)* | ***4 (Very high)*** | *5 (Catastrophic)* |
|---|---|---|---|---|---|
| **Likelihood** | | | | | |
| 1 (Very low) | | | | | |
| **2 (Low)** | | | | **8/25** | |
| 3 (Medium) | | | | | |
| 4 (High) | | | | | |
| 5 (Very high) | | | | | |

### *Transfer*

The normal procedure for risk transference is through the reliance of insurers brokers, and of course, all retailers must have the appropriate insurance cover to ensure that premises are safe, and that they are (to a certain extent) protected against crime. Also, very often retailers choose to utilise a self-assessment process whereby the store manager is responsible for carrying out a Security Risk Assessment based on a model produced by the security function, but in my opinion, this task lies with either the security function lead or a trusted and qualified security consultant.

### *Summary*

*The threat of a burglary against a high value retail outlet was deemed to be High, with an impact that was estimated to be Very High (16/25). The risk owner after consultation with the Security Auditor and relevant stakeholders decided that the most effective means of mitigation was to reduce the risk. After risk treatment was complete it was decided by all parties that the risk of burglary had been reduced to a low likelihood (8/25) but means it still has a very high impact should an attack be successful.*

### *Key takeaway*

*Perhaps more than any other sector, the retail industry is reliant on people, and that must be the primary asset.*

Moving on from retail security, we will now examine the requirements to assess and protect critical national infrastructure.

## Critical national infrastructure security

> *Pause for thought*
>
> Take a little time to think about these two questions:
>
> 1. What is meant by the term Critical National Infrastructure?
> 2. How is it affected by interdependency?

Before we begin to examine this section, it is important to note that in the UK CPNI is responsible for all critical national infrastructure security.

In his excellent book *Critical Infrastructure: Understanding its component parts, vulnerabilities, operating risks, and interdependencies*, Macaulay (2009) defining critical infrastructure says that they are the organisations delivering goods and services in an economy that are fundamental to the functioning of society and the economy.

In the UK, the Centre for the Protection of National Infrastructure (CPNI) argues that National Infrastructure means those facilities, systems, sites, information, people, networks, and processes, necessary for a country to function and upon which daily life depends. It also includes some functions, sites, and organisations which are not critical to the maintenance of essential services, but which need protection due to the potential danger to the public.[30]

In a recent UK Government paper titled *Public Summary of Sector Security and Resilience Plans* (Cabinet Office, 2017),[31] critical infrastructure services are noted as:

- Chemicals
- Civil Nuclear
- *Communications*
- Defence
- Emergency Services
- Energy
- Finance

- Food
- Government
- Health
- Space
- Transport
- Water

### *National infrastructure interdependency*

> **Just a thought**
>
> In your own words, what is meant by the term interdependency?

When discussing interdependency, Macauley says that it may best be understood in the context of dependency: to be partially or entirely reliant upon another for the same goods or services. Interdependency is a bi-direction, two-way version of dependency with degrees of intensity: both are partially or entirely reliant on each other. This of course applies to critical infrastructure.

For example:

A: A *communications centre* is reliant on *water and power*. Without such, it will fail.
 A1: *Power supply* is reliant on *water* and *communications*. Without such, it will fail.
 A2: *Water supply* is reliant on *power* and *communications*. Without such, it will fail.
B: *Transport* is reliant on *power in the form of fuel supply*. Without which it will fail.
 B1: *Fuel supply* is reliant upon *transport*. Without which it will fail.

So, a security professional carrying out a Security Risk Assessment at a communications centre will of course consider and examine the assets, threats, and vulnerabilities of the location, but he or she must also be cognisant of the fact that the risk assessment may have an interdependency effect on other critical infrastructures in the chain.

In terms of severity, I am not comparing the importance of a nuclear power station to a corner shop, but remember that CPNI described critical infrastructures *as facilities, systems, sites, information, people, networks, and processes, necessary for a country to function and upon which daily life depends*. It is therefore reasonable to assume that such Security Risk Assessments will be overseen by government offices, but that is not to say that the assessment will not be outsourced, and that is why there has to be continuity of standards.

## Critical national infrastructure security – 50 Canada Way, Pegasus Wharf, London. E14 5DY

Reference number: SecRa/CWDC/04/22

Fictionally, for reasons of national security, a restricted data centre has been constructed on the 35th floor of 50 Canada Way, with its data halls containing sensitive information that if accessed by hostile state actors may carry a threat to the UK. I must emphasise that under normal circumstances, CPNI will be responsible for all aspects of critical national infrastructure security, but very occasionally expert witness evidence may be required for balance or validation. It is also worth pointing out that CPNI recognise Chartered Security Professionals and will very often offer them information and intelligence that is not open source.

### *Reflection*

Take as long as you feel necessary, as this is particularly important. Please list the following in relation to the 50 Canada Way data centre.

**Assets**: List three critical assets (in order of criticality) that you believe relate to the data centre.

**Threats:** List three threats to the data centre. What are they, and where do they originate from?

**Vulnerabilities:** List three vulnerabilities that may expose the data centre assets to attack.

**Likelihood:** In your own words, what is the likelihood of a successful attack against any of the listed assets.

**Impact:** What may be the impact of such a successful attack?

**Treatment:** How should we treat the risk?

*Table* 21 Several tangible and intangible retail assets, in no particular priority

| *Tangible assets* | *Intangible assets* |
|---|---|
| People | Brand and reputation |
| Property | Sales forecasts |
| Infrastructure | Perceptions of security |
| Data and information | Intellectual property |
| Sales and turnover | Values and culture |

## Assets

So, as with other sectors, the first part of any risk assessment, security or otherwise is to identify the assets which require protection, but it is not within the remit of the risk assessor to prioritise such protection, that onerous task lies with the risk owner.

In terms of the 50 Canada Way Data Center, Table 22 gives a tabular indication of the most critical assets that must be protected.

## Threats

This is a data centre that constitutes a significant section of the UK's critical national infrastructure; therefore, we must assume a worst-case scenario, and that it is the inevitability that a hostile actor knows that it stores restricted data. It should then be assumed (dependent upon corroborated

*Table* 22 Critical assets at 50 Canada Way Data Center

| *Assets* | *Examples at Canada Way Shopping Center* |
|---|---|
| People | Staff and management; members of the public; security staff and contractors. |
| Infrastructure | Electricity and gas supplies; fresh water; air conditioning; IT framework. |
| Data and information | Data and information held on all servers and any cloud access. |
| Sales and turnover | As with any business, increased sales and turnover are tremendous assets. |
| Brand and reputation | After people, potentially the greatest asset to any organisation. |
| ICT hardware | By virtue of the fact that the top floor of 50 Canada way is a data centre, there is advanced and extremely sensitive ICT hardware that must be protected. |

intelligence) that the attackers' target would be data and information, but the question that must be asked is, 'Is it the intention of the attacker to steal or destroy the data, physically or digitally'. Once again, it is likely (we have problems if I am wrong here) that the data is protected to the highest level, and that it is constantly backed up to several platforms, and therefore destruction at source (the data centre) is a pointless exercise. It is therefore my estimation that the attacker (through cyber means) will attempt to acquire the data.

My three threats are:

- A cyber-attack to illegally acquire data and information.
- A physical attack to destroy the data centre.
- A media attack to inform the public of the operations being carried out at the data centre.

### *Vulnerabilities*

The mere fact that there are a number of sophisticated systems in place, administrated by a diverse workforce, means that there will inevitably be weaknesses to be found at the data centre. Remember that the criminal will be searching for vulnerabilities that will expose the asset to attack, such as:

#### *Physical access control*

The attacker will be looking for some form of access control weakness that will afford him or her entrance to the floor, and ultimately the data halls in which the hardware is to be found.

#### *Digital access control*

The cyber hacker will be looking for a means of electronically accessing information and data stored on the network.

#### *Insecure backup*

It is possible that when the data is backed up it may initially be transferred on insecure means, and it is the transference of the data that is the vulnerability.

## *Likelihood and impact*

### *Likelihood*

As with other aspects of security previously covered in this section, the likelihood of an attack against a critical infrastructure node is incredibly difficult to forecast, but it is such a crucial aspect of the Security Risk Assessment that it cannot be ignored. That of course doesn't make it any easier.

Remember what is meant by the term 'likelihood'.

*The probability of occurrence*

Likelihood, not dissimilar to risk perception is subjective, and every professional involved in risk management will look at likelihood from an alternative perspective.

Remember that the assets, threats, vulnerabilities, and impact must also be taken into consideration when examining likelihood.

In terms of the data centre, which has assets that are critical to the protection of the UK, threats emanating from advanced aggressive state actors, and potential vulnerabilities because of the diversity of variables, I believe the likelihood of some form of attack is very high.

### *Impact*

Dependant of course on the data and information stored on the network, it is difficult to measure the impact, but let us take a worst-case scenario, and that is a situation where defence information is stolen, then the impact is likely to be very high, and potentially catastrophic.

### *Risk treatment*

As with the scenario relating to other Security Risk Assessments, we still include the following means:

- Avoid
- Reduce
- Spread
- Transfer

However, I believe that before we look at the four means of treatment, we need to think about the critical infrastructure risk appetite, which I would argue is very high. If a corporate institution is successfully attacked, let us suggest that it is the victim of a very sophisticated cyber strike, it is likely the worst-case scenario is that the business will fold, and shareholders may lose fortunes, in terms of financial investment.

If a retail outlet is attacked, it may be that the store or distribution centre is robbed or burgled, but unless it is an armed attack, the worst-case scenario is that the retailer will lose a certain amount of stock, and possibly cash, but that's about it.

However, if the data centre on the top floor of 50 Canada Way is breached, and information is stolen, it may impact the nation, which could mean loss of life or lives. Therefore, the risk acceptance or appetite at a critical infrastructure is extremely high because lives and the security of the nation are at risk. So let us examine risk treatment.

### *Risk avoidance*

As previously mentioned, for a number of reasons risk avoidance is in many ways the most difficult choice for the risk owner to make, because, in reality, this means that the operation has to be terminated. In terms of critical infrastructure that is close to impossible, because the country needs power, water, food, and in this example, secure storage and transmission of sensitive data and information. Therefore, the option of risk avoidance has little credibility.

### *Risk reduction*

Currently, it is estimated by network subject matter experts that the likelihood of an attack against the data centre is very high, with an impact that is also very high, giving a risk measurement of 20/25 (4×5). This measurement must be reduced.

In order to reduce the risk from 20/25 to an acceptable level, it has been decided to ensure that all physical and electronic access is upgraded, data transference will be end-to-end encrypted, and all data will be backed up four times during a twenty-four-hour period.

### *Spreading the risk*

The protection of critical infrastructure is an excellent example of how to spread the risk, an example being the national grid. Should a power station be taken offline, for whatever reason, there is resilience built in to ensure that

*Table* 23 The risk *before* any mitigation is taken into consideration

| | **Impact** | 1 (*Very low*) | 2 (*Low*) | 3 (*High*) | **4 (*Very high*)** | 5 (*Catastrophic*) |
|---|---|---|---|---|---|---|
| **Likelihood** | | | | | | |
| 1 (Very low) | | | | | | |
| 2 (Low) | | | | | | |
| 3 (Medium) | | | | | | |
| 4 (High) | | | | | | |
| **5 (Very high)** | | | | | **20/25** | |

*Table* 24 The risk *after* any mitigation is taken into consideration

| | **Impact** | 1 (*Very low*) | 2 (*Low*) | 3 (*High*) | **4 (*Very high*)** | 5 (*Catastrophic*) |
|---|---|---|---|---|---|---|
| **Likelihood** | | | | | | |
| 1 (Very low) | | | | | | |
| 2 (Low) | | | | | | |
| 3 (Medium) | | | | | | |
| **4 (High)** | | | | | **16/25** | |
| 5 (Very high) | | | | | | |

another source picks up the load and is able to supply power. The same applies to data capture, with storage being distributed across a number of data centres.

It is likely that the measures described above will reduce the risk to a high likelihood, with an impact that would still be very high, offering a risk measurement of 16/25 (4 × 4). See Table 24.

### *Risk transference*

As opposed to the reliance on insurance brokerage, transference in relation to the data centre will be reliant on end-to-end encrypted data being constantly backed up, and if the data centre receives a physical attack, the secondary and tertiary data centres will bear the responsibility of storing data from 50 Canada Way.

### ***Summary***

*The threat of data theft from a government Data Centre was deemed to be High, with an impact that was estimated to be Very High (20/25). The risk owner after consultation with the Security Risk Assessor and relevant stakeholders decided that the most effective means of mitigation was to reduce the risk. After risk treatment was complete it was decided by all parties that the risk of data theft had been reduced to a high likelihood (16/25) but means it still has a very high impact should an attack be successful. Unlike the previous Security Risk Assessment, the likelihood of a successful attack against a government Data Centre, after treatment is still believed to be high, meaning that this is a dynamic situation that will need to be constantly monitored.*

### *Key takeaway*

*A term to remember in relation to the protection of critical national infrastructure is interdependency.*

We will now move on to maritime security.

## Maritime security

Reference number: SecRa/MS/05/22

The abominable and horrendous attacks against the Twin Towers in New York on 11 September 2001 didn't only affect aviation security, rather it impacted the global maritime sector in a manner never foreseen.

As the result of the attacks by Al Qaeda, which claimed more than 3,000 innocent souls, a risk assessment carried out by the International Maritime Organisation (IMO) declared that the next major target would be either a ship or a port.

On 22 December 2002, at an IMO meeting in London to discuss Safety of Lives at Sea (SOLAS), the International Ship and Port Facility Security Code (ISPS) was enacted, and that was to change the face of maritime security as we knew it.[32] Prior to the introduction of the ISPS Code, there had been no laws or regulations that stipulated how a vessel, or a port must be security protected. So, for this section we will concentrate on two areas of the maritime sector, ships, and port facilities.[33] As with other sectors examined so far, we will research maritime assets, threats, vulnerabilities, likelihood, and impact, before recommending risk treatment.

### *Assets*

> *Pause for thought*
>
> In your opinion, what is the most important asset on board a ship or within a port facility?

Maritime assets are not dissimilar to assets found in other sectors, in terms of how they are identified and prioritised, but of course, the environment is quite unique. Let's take a look at the assets to be protected at sea and on land.

### *People*

Whether it is the Officers and crew of a 20,000 TEU[34] container vessel sailing through hostile waters, or perhaps the driver of a Rubber Tyred Gantry (RTG) at Felixstowe Container Terminal, people are at the heart of the maritime industry. As such, all efforts must be made to ensure their safety.

### *Property and infrastructure*

The container vessel and its cargo, or the port facility holding 20,000 40-foot containers, both have property and infrastructure that must be protected.

### *Data and information.*

The lifeblood of all maritime operations and movements must be protected.

## Case study: Antwerp container terminal

Between June 2011 and May 2013, all container traffic within the Port of Antwerp was monitored by cyber criminals acting on behalf of a South American drugs cartel. The attackers were able to install keylogging software in the port ICT network which allowed them to covertly control all container movement, meaning they were able to unload drugs from the remotely controlled containers, allowing the cartel to move drugs in and out of Antwerp.

By the time the Dutch and Belgian police had infiltrated and apprehended the criminals, it was thought that drugs with a street value of about 170 million US Dollars had been moved through the port. Of course, the illegal movement of drugs was of great concern, but imagine if it had been arms and explosives that were being transited through the port for purposes of terrorism.

### *Brand and reputation*

Once again, as with other sectors discussed so far, the brand and reputation of a shipping line, or a particular port are critical for their credibility as a safe investment, and also to ensure that those employed by the company feel safe and secure at all times. The positive development of the Port of Antwerp took a great deal of time, investment, and commitment, and its reputation as being one of the most technically established ports in the world was not achieved overnight. However, such a great brand could have been destroyed quite literally with the stroke of a key, had it not been for an exceptionally committed ICT workforce, and some very professional police investigations.

### *Threats*

This is where it becomes complicated.

The ISPS Code argues that there are a set of clearly defined threats to ships and port facilities, examples being:

- Damage to, or destruction of, the sip or a port facility, e.g., by explosive devices, arson, sabotage, or vandalism.
- Hijacking or seizure of the ship or persons aboard.
- Smuggling weapons or equipment, including weapons of mass destruction.
- Use of the ship itself as a weapon or a means to cause damage or destruction.
- Blockage of a port entrance, locks, approaches etc.
- A nuclear, biological, or chemical attack.

In my opinion that is far too broad, and we need to look at specific threats which will severely impact the maritime environment if carried out successfully.

#### *Piracy*

Murphy (2010) explains that piracy, very simply, is unlawful depredation at sea involving the use or threat of violence, but not necessarily involving robbery. It has been around for centuries, and this is how it was commonly understood for a very long time, certainly since the end of the seventeenth century. The threat is cyclical, with the level of threat depending on the national and international situation at the time.

For instance, during the period 2010–2014, there were 358 piracy attacks by Somali pirates, with this number dropping to 8 attacks between 2015 and 2019. However, statistics show that the threat of Somali piracy during 2020 began to grow again.

When carrying out either a Ship Security Assessment (SSA) or a Port Facility Security Assessment (PFSA) it is always wise to take into consideration the threat of piracy, particularly in unstable waters.

### *Terrorism*

> ***Research***
>
> Take a little time to research the terrorist attacks against the USS Cole and the MV Limburg.

When compared to land or aviation terrorism, the threat of an attack by terrorists against a maritime target is less likely. However, as the attacks against the *USS Cole* and the *MV Limburg* illustrate, if the opportunity arrives and the terrorist believes the attack will be successful, he or she will no doubt strike. Therefore, ruling out a maritime terrorist attack would be foolish.

Attacking a ship at sea is always going to be exceedingly difficult because the logistics are so complicated, and of course, ISPS certificated vessels are likely to be more security aware, and potentially prepared for an attack.

However, attacking a ship when she is tied alongside a port facility, or attacking the facility itself is of course less complicated, and to a certain extent, the terrorist is offered the same options that he or she would receive if they were attacking a corporate structure. One of the best means of defence offered to the port facility management team or the ship's master is to ensure that their property and people are protected by the ISPS Code, which although not infallible, it does offer a great deal of advice and guidance in terms of countering the terrorist threat. I would therefore urge all maritime security risk assessors to first of all confirm that the ship holds a Ship Security Plan (SSP), and that the facility is protected by being in possession of a Port Facility Security Plan (PFSP).

#### CYBER

During recent times, the threat from cyber criminals, and to a lesser extent cyber terrorists has grown exponentially and is now seen as the greatest threat to society; and that of course includes the maritime industry.

From a Security Risk Assessment perspective, the examination of cyber risk is complicated, mainly because very little detail is, for obvious reasons, made public. However, that should not deter the security risk assessor from investigating this threat, because as explained, cyber is probably one of, if not the gravest threat to the maritime industry.

### *General crime*

Of course, because a vessel is sailing on the high seas, or is tied alongside a port facility doesn't mean that it (and the port facility) is immune from general crime, and when the maritime Security Risk Assessment is being carried out, be it an SSA or a PFSA, the following crimes must be taken into consideration.

- Theft
- Arson
- Criminal damage
- Robbery
- Burglary
- Assault

## *Vulnerabilities*

In many respects, maritime assets are as vulnerable as any other target selected to be attacked, the difference of course is that in this respect we are covering sea-going vessels and facilities that serve them.

The ISPS Code, when covering vulnerability in terms of the Ship Security Assessment (SSA) and the Port Facility Security Assessment (PFSA) states:

The security assessment should include:

Identification of weaknesses (vulnerabilities), including human factors, in the infrastructure, policies, and procedures.

This advice seems to me to be rather light, and I believe that the maritime security assessor should be examining the ship or the port facility for the following vulnerabilities:

### *Access control*

How easy is it to illegally enter the port facility, and once inside is it possible to climb the ship's gangway before accessing all areas of the vessel? If the port facility and/or the ship is ISPS Code compliant, access control will be dependent on what level of security the ship or facility is at.[35]

### *Integrated security systems*

The term integrated security is often misunderstood and because of this may be difficult to assess. The security risk assessor should examine all systems in place, such as CCTV, access control, intruder detection, and lighting, to ensure that they complement and support each other. Attention should be given to the three Ds and one R:

- Deter
- Detect
- Delay
- Respond

A credible integrated security system should be able to demonstrate achievement of the three Ds, with an effective guard force that can respond to any alarm activation.

### *Policies, plans, and procedures*

The reality of life is that such documentation may not exist, and even if it does it may not be fit for purpose, or the client may decide not to share it with the assessor. Documentation to be examined if possible, during the Security Risk Assessment is as follows:

### *Assignment Instructions (AIs)/Standard Operating Procedures (SOPs)*

If the ship (unlikely) or the port facility (possibly) is protected by a contract manned guarding service, there will be a set of AIs in place, which will be owned by the guarding company and driven by the client. AIs are a set of documents that set the duties and responsibilities of the guard force, and they should be reviewed regularly by the client and the guarding company to ensure at they are current and fit for purpose. AIs are a legal requirement for all contract guarding support in the UK and should be examined during the Security Risk Assessment. If the ship and or port facility is protected by an in-house security team, their roles and responsibilities should be contained in some form of SOPs, although that is not mandatory.

### *Emergency response manual*

Such procedures may be contained within the AIs/SOPs, or they may be a standalone document. In whichever form they exist, they are drawn to provide advice and guidance for staff, management, and the security team about how to react to a number of emergency situations, both man-made and natural, such as:

- Fire
- Flood
- Storms
- Power outage
- Terrorism
- Cybercrime/terrorism
- Kidnap and ransom

### *Crisis Management (CMP) and Disaster Recovery Plans (DRP)*

It is unfortunately too often argued that crisis management and disaster recovery do not fit within the purview of the security function, but I beg to differ. Very often, the main threats to an organisation are manmade security threats such as general crime, cybercrime, terrorism, and so on; and it makes absolute common sense that such threats are taken into consideration when a Security Risk Assessment is being carried out, with maritime being no exception.

The Security Risk Assessment approach should include crisis management and disaster recovery, and the approach of communicating with Subject Matter Experts, requesting to view the plans pertains to maritime just as much as it does to any other sector. Weak or ineffective CM and DR plans will equate to a massive vulnerability in relation to either a ship or a port facility.

## *Likelihood and impact*

For this section, unlike other areas covered in the chapter so far, we will look at two targets: a ship and a port facility, using fictitious case studies to examine the likelihood and impact of an attack.

### *Likelihood*

### Scenario.

### *Ships-MV Red Lion*

The MV *Red Lion* is a UK flagged Very Large Crude Carrier (VLCC), with a dead weight of 200,000 gross tons, carrying just under two million barrels of crude oil, and is due to transit the Straits of Hurmuz. She is carrying her load from Al Jubay in the Kingdom of Saudi Arabia to Salalah in Oman

The straits of Hormuz run north to south, with Iran commanding the northern flank, and Oman in the south.

Relations between the UK and Iran are tense, with Iran threatening to defend her shores and economy by attacking any vessels that she believes to be a threat. The Iranian navy is the largest and most powerful in the region and has a history of attacking and hi-jacking merchant vessels.

There is a small international force in the region consisting of warships from the United States, Germany, Italy, and France, based at Fujairah in the United Arab Emirates (UAE).

So, what is the likelihood of the *Red Lion* being sunk or hi-jacked?

### *Impact*

As mentioned, the *Red Lion* is carrying just under two million barrels of crude oil, the destination being Salalah in Oman.

> ### *Just a thought*
>
> Should Iran capture or sink the Red Lion, what will be the impact of that attack?

There are likely to be several impacts should the *Red Lion* be attacked and sunk or hijacked.

### *Sunk*

There is the possibility of a loss of life, the discharging of two million barrels of crude oil into the Straits of Hormuz, and the distinct likelihood of a major diplomatic incident, with the probability of some form of retaliation, which could escalate into a regional war.

### *Hijacked*

This would have less of an impact, but it would still generate a major diplomatic incident, with the likelihood of 'tit for tat' retaliation, probably in the form of an Iranian merchant vessel being taken over, until the *Red Lion* and her crew were freed.

Table 25 shows the likelihood and impact of the *Red Lion*, prior to any risk treatment, reflecting the fact that because of the assets and threats brought into the equation, the likelihood is *High* (4), and the impact is *Very High* (4) giving a risk measurement of 16/25.

### *Risk treatment*

As with other scenarios covered so far, we still include the following means:

- Avoid
- Reduce
- Spread
- Transfer

#### *Risk avoidance*

Realistically there is only one way that the *Red Lion* is able to totally avoid the risk of attack by Iranian naval forces, and that is not to transit the Straits

*Table* 25 Likelihood and impact *before* any risk treatment

| **Impact** | 1 (*Very low*) | 2 (*Low*) | 3 (*High*) | **4 (Very high)** | 5 (*Catastrophic*) |
|---|---|---|---|---|---|
| **Likelihood** | | | | | |
| 1 (Very low) | | | | | |
| 2 (Low) | | | | | |
| 3 (Medium) | | | | | |
| **4 (High)** | | | | **16/25** | |
| 5 (Very high) | | | | | |

of Hurmuz, from Saudi Arabia to Oman. Of course, if that were the decision taken there would be massive legal and economic implications, not to mention damage to the brand and reputation of the shipping line. Equally, it would reflect subservience to the Iranians.

### *Risk reduction*

To reduce the risk from 16/25 to an acceptable level, the shipping line has decided to continue with the transit, but the vessel will be protected in the following manner:

- Arrangements will be made with the international naval force for the journey to take place only at a time when friendly warships are available for protection duties, and that may mean that the *Red Lion* will travel in an international convoy of other merchant vessels sailing in the same direction.
- All ship's crew will be conversant about manning the vessel at security levels 2 or 3.
- There will be an armed response team recruited as a contingency against a small force hi-jack.

### *Spread the risk*

Of course, the most effective means of spreading the risk here would be to learn the lessons from the Spaniards in the 1550s. Distribute the load throughout a number of vessels and sail in convoy style, preferably with a naval escort.

The above measures should reduce the risk factor, from 16/25 to 10/25. See Table 26.

### *Risk transference*

In this particular example, risk transference is easily explained as it is compulsory for all UK[36] flagged vessels to adhere to the Marine Act 1906.[37] Lloyds of London is the most commonly used marine insurance broker, and in the example used here, the MV *Red Lion*, transiting the Gulf of Hurmuz will be insured, as will her crew and cargo, with the insurers carrying the risk.

*Table 26* Likelihood and impact *after* any risk treatment

| **Impact** | 1 (*Very low*) | 2 (Low) | 3 (High) | **4 (Very high)** | 5 (*Catastrophic*) |
|---|---|---|---|---|---|
| **Likelihood** | | | | | |
| 1 (Very low) | | | | | |
| **2 (Low)** | | | | **8/25** | |
| 3 (Medium) | | | | | |
| 4 (High) | | | | | |
| 5 (Very high) | | | | | |

## *Summary*

*The threat the Red Lion being attacked/sunk or hijacked was deemed to be High, with an impact that was estimated to be Very High (16/25). The shipping line after consultation with the Security Auditor and relevant stakeholders decided that the most effective means of mitigation was to reduce the risk. After risk treatment was complete it was decided by all parties that the risk had been reduced to a Low likelihood (8/25) but means it still has a Very High impact should an attack be successful.*

## *Likelihood*

### *Scenario*

#### PORT FACILITY – LIVERPORT CONTAINER TERMINAL

The Liverport Container terminal is located on the Northwest coast of England and is serviced by a first-class rail service, and direct road communications from the M62. The terminal operates on a 24/7 basis, and currently handles 1.5 million containers per year, with a workforce of approximately 5,000 full- and part-time staff and management.

Containers arrive from, and depart to all four corners of the world, with a significant number carrying very high-value products, such as computer chips and high-value ICT hardware.

The terminal is technology dependant, with all container movement being ICT automated. Crime levels at the terminal are low, but crime intelligence received from the local police is vague. So, what is the likelihood of the container terminal being attacked?

### Impact

The container terminal faces several threats, with varying impacts.

#### Cyber

As mentioned, the container terminal is technology dependant, with container movement being dictated by the terminal IT network, which of course is extremely vulnerable to attack. The cyber-attack against the Port of Antwerp in 2011–2012[38] is a good example of how relatively easy it is to attack a port IT system, and if the same happened to the Liverport Container terminal, the impact would be extremely serious.

#### Container theft (of and from)

Either in transit by road, or static within the terminal, the theft of individual fully loaded containers cannot be dismissed. Equally, illegal breach of a container has to be considered as there are so many in situ, and even with a professional guard force, and supporting technology such as CCTV and Radio Frequency Identification (RFID), theft of and from a container is a possibility.

#### Arson and criminal damage

For a number of reasons, there is the possibility of containers being attacked or set on fire by either disgruntled employees or vandals, and that form of threat could be very expensive.

### Terrorism

Whilst the likelihood of a terrorist attack against the terminal is medium, the consequences will undoubtedly be extremely high.

Table 27 shows the likelihood and impact of a terrorist attack in relation to the Liverport Container terminal, prior to any risk treatment. This reflects the fact that because of the assets and threats brought into the equation, the likelihood is medium (3), but the worst-case impact could be catastrophic (terrorism) giving a risk measurement of 15/25.

*Table 27* Likelihood and impact of a terrorist attack *before* mitigation

| | **Impact** | 1 (*Very low*) | 2 (*Low*) | 3 (*High*) | 4 (*Very high*) | **5 (*Catastrophic*)** |
|---|---|---|---|---|---|---|
| Likelihood | | | | | | |
| 1 (Very low) | | | | | | |
| 2 (Low) | | | | | | |
| **3 (Medium)** | | | | | | **15/25** |
| 4 (High) | | | | | | |
| 5 (Very high) | | | | | | |

## *Risk treatment*

As with other scenarios covered so far, we still include the following means:

- Avoid
- Reduce
- Spread
- Transfer

### *Risk avoidance*

In order to avoid risks in their entirety the terminal would be forced to discontinue all container operations, and that of course is financially and politically impossible, probably leading to the closure of the facility.

### *Risk reduction*

Risk reduction is of course feasible if the container terminal management team is prepared to invest in a series of upgrades to the current security systems in situ. If a programme of installing an integrated security system, that is to say, all systems working in synchronisation, is introduced, with the effect of target hardening the facility, it is probable that the likelihood of a successful attack would be reduced. Equally, it would be prudent for the Port Facility Security Officer (PFSO) to introduce a system of Defence in Depth, as that would add to the risk reduction.

*Table 28* Likelihood and impact of a terrorist attack *after* mitigation

| **Impact** | 1 (Very low) | 2 (Low) | 3 (High) | 4 (Very high) | **5 (Catastrophic)** |
|---|---|---|---|---|---|
| **Likelihood** | | | | | |
| 1 (Very low) | | | | | |
| **2 (Low)** | | | | | **10/25** |
| 3 (Medium) | | | | | |
| 4 (High) | | | | | |
| 5 (Very high) | | | | | |

### *Spread the risk*

If the contents of the containers are known, it would be possible to spread the risk by distributing the most attractive and higher-cost items through as many containers as possible.

The above measures should reduce the risk factor, from 16/25 to 10/25. See Table 28.

### *Risk transference*

Once again, if appropriate levels of insurance are acquired, that will transfer the risk.

### **Summary**

*The threat of a terrorist attack against the container terminal was deemed to be Medium, with an impact that was estimated to be Catastrophic (15/25). The container terminal owners after consultation with the Security Risk Assessor and relevant stakeholders decided that the most effective means of mitigation was to reduce the risk. After risk treatment was complete it was decided by all parties that the risk of terrorist attack had been reduced to a low likelihood (10/25) but means it still has a catastrophic impact should an attack be successful.*

### *Key takeaway*

*Whilst a ship is at its most vulnerable when tied alongside a berth, and a Port Facility is also vulnerable when connected to a vessel, don't rule out the threats of crime and terrorism at any other time.*

## Aviation security

> *Pause for thought*
>
> In your opinion, what were the critical mistakes made by the US government prior to and during the attacks on 9/11?

Naturally, the events of 9/11 take precedence when describing aviation security, because there was no greater example of a necessity to rethink security and risk management. On 11 September 2001, al Qaeda carried out an attack at the heart of the greatest military power probably ever known to man, an attack that apparently was so unexpected, so incredulous, that military historians and anthropologists will be debating and writing about it for years to come. In terms of security and risk management, it was so preposterous that nobody in their right mind would have rated it on a likelihood scale anywhere less than impossible; but it happened. Forecasting an attack against the Twin Towers in New York, using two commercial airliners, would have seemed madness on 10 September 2001, but the worst-case scenario happened.

When al Qaeda struck, not only were 3,000 souls lost, but the risk appetite and risk adversity of the American people escalated to a point never seen before; this could not be allowed to ever happen again, and the US government swore to eradicate the terrorist group that was responsible.

As a result of 9/11, the US government 9/11 Commission Authority carried out a number of detailed investigations into what was required to secure the US aviation sector, and this was replicated in a number of countries worldwide.

According to Price and Forrest (2009), the 9/11 Commission outlined five specific weaknesses in the US aviation system that I argue could easily be replicated on a global scale. They were:

1. Pre-screening processes that focus on detecting potential aircraft bombers rather than potential aircraft hijackers.
2. Relaxed checkpoint screening and permissive rules regarding small knives.

3. A lack of flight security measures such as Air Marshalls and reinforced cockpit doors.
4. An industry-wide strategy of complying with hijackers in a nonconfrontational manner.
5. A lack of protocols and capabilities for executing a coordinated response to multiple hijackings and suicide hijackers.

The 9/11 Commission recommended the following minimum measures to combat such weaknesses:

1. Enhanced passenger pre-screening.
2. Improved measures to detect explosives on passengers.
3. The examination of human factors issues at screening checkpoints.
4. To expedite deployment of inline baggage screening systems.
5. The intensification of efforts to screen and track cargo.
6. The deployment of hardened cargo containers.
7. The institution of risk-based prioritisation as the basis for a transportation security policy (which incredibly did not exist) and the creation of a strategic plan for aviation security).

It would be easy to look at the above recommendations and ask why such measures were not in place already, but as a species we tend not to listen to warnings, too often acting after the event.

We will now examine the component parts of risk and carry out a Security Risk Assessment. First, we will look at the assets, threats, and vulnerabilities involved in any aviation security situation, and then in the likelihood/impact section, as with the maritime study, we will divide it between two particular areas: aircraft and airports.

## Assets

> ### *Pause for thought*
>
> In your opinion, what are the most critical assets in an aviation environment?

In a very similar vein to maritime security, the aviation sector is quite unique, but the process of asset prioritisation and protection is similar to any other environment or sector so far covered in the book.

### *People*

Whether passengers on a long-haul flight, air crew, people transiting an airport or the team protecting that airport, the security of personnel must be a priority in an aviation scenario. An Improvised Explosive Device (IED) placed in the hold of a Boing 777 could cause the loss of lives in the hundreds. Equally, an IED placed in a suitcase in the centre of a departures lounge will also result in mass casualties and deaths. Of course, the terrorist is acutely aware of the criticality of passengers and employees and will strive to explore any weakness in the system that may offer him or her an opportunity to attack the asset.

### *Infrastructure*

Every airport, and all aircraft being serviced rely on being able to access facilities and logistics which allow daily operations to continue seamlessly. This of course includes all utilities such as electrical power, gas, and water facilities, without which the airport and all aircraft in use will not be able to operate. The Security Auditor should ensure that airport infrastructure is backed up, particularly the electricity supply. It is logical to suppose that every airport has some form of power backup, whether it is in the form of a direct current Uninterruptible Power Supply (UPS) for the ICT network, or an alternating current generator supplying power for the airport.

### *ICT*

One of the most critical assets to the aviation industry is Information Communications Technology (ICT), without which it is probably safe to assume the airport would be closed, with no flight movement. When we talk about ICT systems in airports today, we're not just talking about a minor system, responsible for part of an airport's operations; we are referring to the entire operation.

The majority of business processes at airports around the world – from check-in to baggage handling and from video surveillance to access control – are dependent on ICT systems and ICT infrastructure. Whether we're talking, for example, about cabling, access switches, core switches, and servers, this ICT infrastructure literally never sleeps.

For the larger airports, redundancy measures are often in place to make this 'always on' approach happen. This involves critical infrastructure such as servers being hosted in two alternative geographical equipment rooms to avoid a single point of failure.[39]

Two of the greatest defensive assets that an airport can have are Defence in Depth and integrated security systems.

### *Airport Defence in Depth*

Defence in Depth at an airport is remarkably similar to Defence in Depth at a distribution centre, or a business park, with the exception being there is more than one critical target to protect. In terms of this section, we will apply Airport Defence in Depth to protect and offer security support to a departures area, and aircraft standing on the tarmac.

We will now examine the following elements of Defence in Depth.

#### *External to the airport*

This is where reliance on law enforcement and other agencies for the security and safety of the environment outside the airport is paramount. Once again, the use of a Crime Pattern Analysis will help the Security Risk Assessor understand the criminal risk to the airport.

#### *Perimeter security and access control*

Physically, this is the first layer of the Airport Defence in Depth concept, and there is the dependency on a robust perimeter fence, supported by elements of the integrated security systems, such as CCTV, Perimeter Intruder Detections Systems (PIDS), high-security lighting systems and manned guarding. Access control to this part of the airport is normally via a public car park, from where passengers can walk or take a provided airport bus to the main airport buildings. Such car park access control is normally in the form of an automatic barrier, which is supported by CCTV, and a communications link to the Security Control Room.

### *Airport building and access control*

Access to any main airport building is very often seen as the Achilles Heel, and a potential single point of failure of airport security, because of the sheer volume of members of the public accessing this area. Using Birmingham International airport in the UK as an example, during 2019, more than 3 million people accessed the main airport building, averaging over 8,000 visitors per day.

Because of the high footfall, logistically and operationally, it would be extremely difficult to process every person entering the main building. Therefore once again there is a reliance on integrated security systems, in particular, CCTV and manned guarding to provide security support.

### *Movement through security*

From when a member of the public enters the airport property, to when he or she takes their seat on the aircraft, this is the first occasion when they will be subject to some form of control. Before passengers are allowed to enter the departure gates, they are subjected to a series of security checks, which generally include:

- An initial passport and boarding card inspection at the very first barrier.
- Perhaps a second similar security check twenty metres further on.
- They will then have to remove outer jackets, belt, and maybe shoes, and have any electronic equipment open for inspection before they and their luggage are subject to x-ray scanning.
- Having passed through the free-standing x-ray scanner, they may be subject to an inspection by a Security Officer using a handheld metal detector.
- Their luggage may be swabbed in an effort to ascertain if it contains any explosives.
- Finally, the police or security team may deploy drug or explosives detection dogs.

### *Departure's gates*

Once inside the departure gate area, passengers are forbidden to leave, unless they seek assistance from security, and provide adequate evidence as to why they no longer wish to continue with their journey. Passengers will no longer have access to their main luggage, which will be in the process of being loaded onto the aircraft. They will of course be in possession of hand luggage, but that will have been scanned, and perhaps searched.

### *Access to the tarmac*

From the departure gates to the aircraft maybe by bus, or on foot, but it will be controlled. As will directions to individual seats.

The journey from home or work to the aircraft is one that is controlled and managed from a security point of view. From the external environment to the aircraft seat. See Figure 7.

As mentioned on several occasions in this section, Airport Defence in Depth is often reliant on integrated security systems, so let us see what we mean by that term.

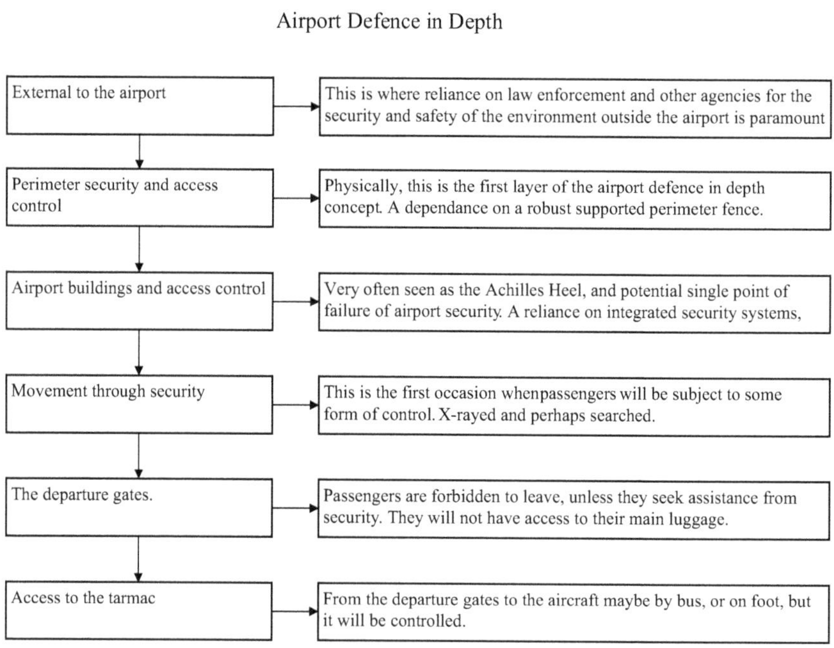


Figure 7 From home or work to the airport.

## *Aviation integrated security systems*

> *Pause for thought*
>
> What is meant by the term 'Integrated security'?

The term integrated security systems has been in use for some time, but very often there is confusion about what it actually means. Norman (2007) argues that most integrated security systems installed are designed to protect against unknown vulnerabilities, against unknown threats. They often use techniques and products that work well to the advantage of the vendor, but not always so well to the advantage of the client, and they are often more expensive than is necessary. Norman goes on to say that integrated security systems may comprise numerous subsystems, installed together into one complete, highly coordinated, high-functioning system. Typical sub-systems include, alarms, access controls, CCTV, two-way voice communication, parking control, and of course the human element, manned guarding.

Probably the most effective way of explaining integrated security systems is by way of a fictitious scenario.

## Scenario

### *Operation Swift and Sure*

After carrying out significant reconnaissance against an East Midlands cargo airport, an Organised Crime Group (OCG) has decided to attempt a burglary, in the hope of penetrating a bonded warehouse within the airport. The bonded area currently holds approximately one million packets of cigarettes, with a street value of about 15 million pounds. The plan is for the burglary team (three members) to breach the bonded warehouse, and carry five containers of cigarettes to the northern perimeter fence, before throwing them over the fence to their waiting team members, who will load them in a vehicle, and make good their escape.

Although they are not aware of the specifications of the integrated security system currently protecting the warehouse, they do know that between 0100 and 0300hrs, there is no Security Officer protection, and the inner building main gate to the south has been left insecure by a corrupt Security Officer.

...and so, it begins...

### *Phase 1: The perimeter*

The burglars have decided to climb the 2.3-metre welded mesh perimeter fence on the western side and to achieve their aims, they have brought with them a three-metre collapsible aluminium ladder. Two of the five LED pole-mounted security lights have been inoperable for the last ten days, and the criminals have assumed (correctly) that the three CCTV cameras installed to protect the fence will be useless. However, as the ladder is placed against the fence, unbeknown to the criminals, it activates a fence-installed taut wire silent intruder alarm that will signal to an Alarm Receiving Centre (ARC) two miles away, and two Security Officers will be despatched to investigate. The police will be informed, as it is a bonded warehouse.

### *Phase 2: Dead ground*

All three burglars successfully descend from the perimeter fence, still in possession of the collapsible ladder. However, the criminals are unaware that as the first member of the gang hits the floor, his presence will activate an underground pressure-driven intruder detection system, which will inform the ARC that ground penetration has been achieved. At the same time, two CCTV cameras, supported by inside fence lighting will automatically pan, tilt and zoom before capturing evidential standard footage of the burglars making their way to the insecure inner door. A police call sign has now been despatched, and it will take approximately three minutes to reach the warehouse. The criminals are blissfully unaware that they have been detected, and that they are being monitored from within the ARC, and that their descriptions and movements have been passed to the police.

### *Phase 3: Entering the warehouse. CCTV trip wire*

When the burglars are five metres from the warehouse, their images will be captured by a covert video surveillance system using thermal imaging technology, that will snare them in a surveillance 'trip wire', which means that they will be filmed, and the images will immediately be transmitted to the ARC, and if required the police control room.

### *Phase 4: Moving the stolen goods*

Believing they are free from apprehension, the criminals begin to move the, now stolen goods, to the northern perimeter fence, with the expectation that they will be able to move them over the perimeter fence line, but as soon as the first burglar descends the ladder to the outside of the location, he is apprehended and arrested by two police officers. As the other two make good their escape through the warehouse, they too are caught in the act of escape and are also arrested.

In this example, we saw CCTV/video surveillance, intruder detection, lighting (not so effective), ARC response, and law enforcement working in harmony. Integrated security is in place to protect airport assets.

## *Threats*

> **Just a thought**
>
> In your opinion, what are the main threats to the aviation sector?

There are numerous acts of criminal and terrorist behaviour that threaten the aviation sector, whether it is an attack against an airport, an aeroplane, or both; and in this section, we will examine the most prevalent and dangerous threats that the Security Risk Assessor should be aware of and consider in his or her assessment.

### *Terrorism*

Still the greatest threat to the aviation industry is from terrorist activity, whether that is a marauding gunman (men) inside an airport departure area, the placing of an improvised explosive devices (IEDs) at the same location, or the hijacking and destruction of an aircraft. To my mind, the greatest threat is the terrorists' decision to carry out an attack against a departure area, let us say, an airport of the size and complexity of Heathrow

International Airport, where there may be several thousand very vulnerable passengers waiting to board their flights. Mass casualties and fatalities would almost be a certainty.

My next concern would be that the terrorists somehow were able to smuggle arms and ammunition onto an aircraft before it is hijacked and used as a weapon, as was the case during the attacks in New York on 9/11.

## *Cyber*

It could be argued that the cyber threat to the aviation industry is no more severe than such an attack against say, a bank, or a power station. The difference of course is that a cyber attack against the aviation industry could mean planes dropping out of control to the ground.

In an article written for the Cyber Security Observatory, Jose Monteagudo, who is the CEO of Smartrev Cybersec argues that the aviation industry relies on a critically complex infrastructure integrated into multiple systems that need to be individually and holistically protected.

A thorough cyber assessment is needed involving aircraft and equipment manufacturers, air traffic control, airports, airlines, and all the other elements of the aviation infrastructure as information systems.

This should include penetration testing or red teaming where cyber experts try to gain access to the systems as well as vulnerability testing to look for flaws in security.

The key question is what makes a system vulnerable?

Two components are needed, a vulnerability and a pathway to attack that system or exploit that vulnerability. The suggestion that we do not need to patch a specific vulnerability unless there is a pathway is challenged by the possibility of not having identified an existing attack pathway.

Another especially important element to consider is the insider threat. Reports show that insider threat is on the rise, requiring employees to be educated in their role in mitigating such threats and adhering to cybersecurity policies and best practices. Processes and playbooks should be periodically reassessed and rigorously tested to ensure continuous improvement. In addition, access controls should be put in place to only allow the people who absolutely need clearance to certain areas and paths to the airport or the aircraft.[40]

Many systems in civilian aviation are potentially hackable: reservation systems, flight traffic management systems, access control management systems, departure control systems, passport control systems, cloud-based airline data storage, hazardous materials transportation management, cargo handling and shipping.

And that's before we get to computers on aircraft – flight control systems, GPS-based navigation systems, fuel gauges, fuel consumption systems, maintenance computers, and so on. The potential points of cyber vulnerability in aviation are many and growing.[41]

Cyber security and the cyber threat to the aviation sector are extremely complex issues for Security Risk Assessment, and unless the Security Risk Assessor is trained and educated in this field, it is recommended, as with all other technical risk assessments, that the assessor seeks advice form an aviation Subject Matter Expert (SME).

### *Chemical, Biological, Radiological, and Nuclear (CBRN)*

In terms of CBRN, the Centre for the Protection of National Infrastructures (CPNI) defines the threat as: The malicious use of Chemical, Biological, Radiological and Nuclear materials, or weapons with the intention to cause significant harm or disruption. The hazard posed by these materials varies:

- Chemical: Poisoning or injury caused by chemical substances, including traditional (military) chemical warfare agents and harmful industrial or household chemicals.
- Biological: Illnesses caused by the deliberate release of dangerous bacteria or viruses or by biological toxins (e.g., ricin, found in castor oil beans).
- Radiological: Illness caused by exposure to harmful radioactive materials.
- Nuclear: Life-threatening health effects caused by exposure to harmful radiation, thermal or blast effects arising from a nuclear detonation.

Within the wider definition and context of CBRN, the term 'White Powder(s)' is also often used in a mail context to describe the potential presence of a noxious substance (or hoax material) in a letter or parcel.[42]

The above description is generic, and of course, applies to airports, and that means that the Security Auditor must ensure that the airport being assessed is in possession of appropriate policies, plans, and procedures to either prevent or mitigate such risks.

Having examined aviation assets and threats, we will now look at any vulnerabilities that may be discovered in that environment.

## Vulnerabilities

> *Pause for thought*
>
> In your considered opinion what are the greatest vulnerabilities to be found within the aviation sector?

### *Humans*

As with all other environments covered so far, it is probably fair to say that the greatest vulnerability to be found within the aviation sector is the human being, and as stated earlier in the book, I would recommend any Security Auditor to place this vulnerability at the top of their list!

Probably the greatest human vulnerability at any airport is within the departures area, where members of the public have free access, and if needed egress, as the main doors are not access controlled. As mentioned earlier, an airport the size of Birmingham International Airport, which is certainly not the largest airport, can have up to 8,000 passengers entering and leaving the main departures door every day, that is a footfall of 350 passengers and other visitors every hour. It is likely that several thousand people could be in the insecure departures lounge at any one time, meaning that some form of terrorist attack, be it a marauding gunman, or placed IEDs could wreak havoc in terms of injuries and fatalities. This is where the application of Crime Prevention Through Environmental Design (CPTED) and Situational Crime Prevention (SCP) would be a major advantage and should be considered by the Security Risk Assessor, and as you will see later in the book, the Security Surveyor.

### Perimeter protection and access control

By virtue of the fact that airport perimeters are extremely large and difficult to maintain, it is reasonable to argue that there will be vulnerabilities, whether because of poor maintenance allowing for breaches, or nonfunctioning security equipment such as CCTV, lighting, and so on. It is strongly recommended that the Security Risk Assessor ensures that he or she, at the earliest opportunity traverses the length of the perimeter; don't be deterred by the size or length of the fence. As night follows day, the first time the assessor fails to circumnavigate the perimeter, there will a breach

Equally important is for an airport to have an effective search policy and procedure in place.

## *Car parking*

As mentioned earlier in this section, very often the most common form of access to an airport is via the car park, and all commercial airports are reliant on car parking for security and commercial reasons. From a security perspective, a well-managed car park means that all private means of transport are located in a controlled area, and through the use of effective CCTV and professional security patrolling, the area is likely to be as secure as possible. Commercially, of course, car parking is a massive income generator for the owners of the airport.

However, with perceived poor security and commercial development comes the vulnerability of allowing hundreds, if not thousands of vehicles to co-locate in a reasonably dense area. The vehicles are of course open to abuse in the form of theft of, or theft from them, and in terms of a terrorist attack, they leave the airport vulnerable to some form of Vehicle Born IED, although the car park is normally some distance away from the main terminal.

## *ICT reliance*

Whilst ICT is a significant asset to every aviation environment, there is today a reliance on ICT-based electronic systems, and of course, that means once again we have an asset, that unless managed efficiently can very soon become a major vulnerability. The Security Risk Assessor when examining airport ICT systems must of course include ICT-based electronic security systems, ensuring that there are fail-safe plans in the event the CCTV system fails, or the automatic access control systems deny entry, or the perimeter lights become inoperative.

### *Policies, plans, and procedures*

Security policies, plans, and procedures will no doubt be available in hard copy, and will also be held on a hard drive. The security risk assessor must ensure that the correct policies exist, and that they are secure. In the wrong hands, security documentation will give a major advantage to criminals or terrorists.

### *Aircraft security: 9/11 and then Germanwings*

#### *9/11*

One of the most violent terrorist attacks ever carried out took place on 11 September 2001, when two terrorist groups representing Osama bin Laden's Al Qaeda crashed two commercial aircraft into the North and South Towers of the World Trade Centre in New York. The aircraft were Boeing 767s and the terrorists were able to take over control of the airplanes by freely accessing the cockpit, and physically wrestling the aircraft from the flight crew.

As a result of this particular action by the Al Qaeda terrorists, all commercial aircraft were mandated to have installed cockpit doors that could not be breached from the outside, offering the flight crew an extra level of security.

#### *Germanwings*

The added layer of security introduced as the result of 9/11 was to sadly backfire some years later.

On 24 March 2015 at 0900hrs GMT, Germanwings flight 4U 9525 took off from Barcelona Airport in Spain heading for Duesseldorf, Germany, with 150 people on board. At 0930hrs, once the aircraft had reached its cruising altitude of 38,000 feet, the captain exited the cockpit, presumably to visit the bathroom, leaving the co-pilot in control, and the cockpit door was automatically secured. According to traffic control, at 0934hrs, knocking from the outside of the cockpit could be heard, but the now secure door was never opened. At 0941hrs, after a dramatic descent, the plane crashed into a mountain, killing all on board.

A later inquest suggested that the co-pilot may have been suffering from some form of depression, and it was probably a conscious decision made by him to fly the aircraft into the mountain, but that of course could not be proven.

One fact that was certain, however, was that once the cockpit door was secure from the inside, it could not be breached.

So, from a safety perspective, takeoff and landing are the most dangerous phases for any flight, but in terms of security, an aircraft, particularly a commercial airliner is at its most vulnerable once cruising at optimal altitude. Once again, the security risk assessor must take all possibilities and worst-case scenarios into consideration.

## *Likelihood and impact*

As with the maritime security section, in order to examine the likelihood and impact in relation to aviation security, we will use a fictitious case study, in which a terrorist organisation has decided to attempt the hijacking of a commercial aircraft at an international airport.

### *Likelihood*

Post Covid 19 restrictions, it is likely that the workload of security teams in all environments is going to grow exponentially, none more so, however, than those teams operating in the aviation sector, because airports are going to move from a ten percent capacity during the pandemic to 100% capacity very quickly.

Criminals and terrorists are aware of this.

## *Security Risk Assessment: Birmingpool (BPL) International Airport*

Reference number: SecRa/BPL/06/22

Birmingpool (BPL) International Airport is located in the Northwest England, and under normal circumstances, has a daily footfall of between 7,000 and 10,000 passengers every day. The airport is also an international hub, with large commercial airliners flying to all corners of the globe.

The British government has recently given support to the state of Israel during a confrontation with Palestinians in the West Bank. Islamic Qaeda (IQ), in the light of the act, has decided to teach the UK and the rest of the Western world a lesson by carrying out a marauding gun attack against an airport, in the hope of being able to hijack an aircraft to have a number of demands met.

IQ have carried out significant research and they are aware of a number of issues:

- Surprise attack: Intelligence.
- IQ have been made aware of the fact that such an attack will catch Birmingpool International Airport authorities completely by surprise because British security services do not believe that the terrorist organisation has either the determination or capacity to carry out a marauding attack.
- Police presence.
- The terrorists have decided to initiate the attack at 0600hrs, when the police and security teams are carrying out shift changes, with increased vulnerabilities. Also, passenger levels will be high as people begin to arrive for early departures.
- Security infrastructure.
- Although the airport security function deploys Defence in Depth, supported by a sophisticated integrated security system, IQ has inside intelligence and support, and ten minutes before the attack begins, CCTV, automatic access control and security lighting will be de-activated. All ground floor exits will be opened, offering the terrorists 360-degree access.
- Flight times and locations.
- IQ, once again through excellent inside intelligence, knows where all major airline gates are located, and which aircraft is on the tarmac awaiting take-off clearance.
- The need for suicide attacks.
- Although IQ has drafted plans for, and rehearsed an all-out marauding attack, deploying 16 gunmen, contingency plans are in place, should a personal borne IED attack (suicide bomber) be the only option. If necessary, two of the IQ fighter will attack the security forces, deploying PBIEDs.

## *Impact*

The primary aim of the attack is initially to wreak as much carnage as possible within the airport. The secondary aim is to enter and take over a

*Table 29* Likelihood and impact of a marauding terrorist attack *before* mitigation

| **Impact** | 1 (*Very low*) | 2 (*Low*) | 3 (*High*) | 4 (*Very high*) | **5 (*Catastrophic*)** |
|---|---|---|---|---|---|
| **Likelihood** | | | | | |
| 1 (Very low) | | | | | |
| 2 (Low) | | | | | |
| 3 (Medium) | | | | | |
| **4 (High)** | | | | | **20/25** |
| 5 (Very high) | | | | | |

full commercial aircraft, holding passengers and crew hostage until their demands to have all Israeli forces moved out of the West Bank have been met.

Based on corroborated intelligence from the UK security services, Table 29 shows the likelihood and impact of a marauding terrorist attack at Birmingpool International Airport, prior to any risk treatment. This reflects the fact that because of the assets, threats, and vulnerabilities involved in the equation, the likelihood is high (4), and the worst-case impact could be catastrophic (5) giving a risk measurement of 20/25.

## Risk treatment

As with other scenarios covered so far, we still include the following means:

- Avoid
- Reduce
- Spread
- Transfer

### Risk avoidance

In order to avoid risks in their entirety the airport would be forced to discontinue all flight operations, and that of course is financially and politically impossible because it would probably lead to the permanent closure of the airport, and submission to the terrorist organisation.

### *Risk reduction*

Risk reduction is of course feasible, particularly if the airport management team were to focus with greater detail, all vetting and screening procedures to reduce the likelihood of insider operations. There also needs to be a recruitment drive to employ security staff in greater numbers, and more of a commitment from airport police. Finally, all integrated security systems need to be examined and perhaps upgraded to lessen the chance of them being corrupted.

### *Spread the risk*

Spreading the risk is difficult because the terrorist organisation has specifically targeted Birmingpool International Airport.

### *Risk transference*

Once again, if appropriate levels of insurance are acquired, that will transfer the risk.

The above risk treatment measures should reduce the risk factor, from 20/25 to 10/25. See Table 30.

### **Summary**

*The threat of a terrorist attack against Birmingpool International Airport was deemed to be High, with an impact that was estimated to be Catastrophic (15/25). The airport Senior Management Team after consultation with the Security Auditor and relevant stakeholders decided that the most effective means of mitigation was to reduce the risk. After risk treatment was*

*Table 30* Likelihood and impact of a marauding terrorist attack *after* mitigation

| | **Impact** | 1 (Very low) | 2 (Low) | 3 (High) | 4 (Very high) | **5 (Catastrophic)** |
|---|---|---|---|---|---|---|
| **Likelihood** | | | | | | |
| 1 (Very low) | | | | | | |
| **2 (Low)** | | | | | | **10/25** |
| 3 (Medium) | | | | | | |
| 4 (High) | | | | | | |
| 5 (Very high) | | | | | | |

*complete it was decided by all parties that the risk of terrorist attack had been reduced to a low likelihood (10/25) but means it still has a catastrophic impact should an attack be successful.*

## *Key takeaway*

*As with maritime security, the protection of an airport includes defence of the terminal, and all aircraft using the airport. Defence in Depth and the use of integrated security are particularly effective when an airport requires protection.*

Increasingly, business professionals and Non-Governmental Organisations (NGOs) are being forced, for a variety of reasons, to travel to and indeed operate in hostile environments, whether on land, sea, or in the air.

The environment that is probably the most applicable for this book is the travelling and working space, very often today populated by business professionals who are either working, or from a business perspective, visiting areas where personal security is a challenge. So let us look at how such an environment can be risk managed.

## Hostile environment security

> *Pause for thought*
>
> Think of a situation where you, or perhaps a colleague may find yourselves, in which your personal security is questioned.

### *Assets*

#### *People*

In terms of travelling to and from, or working in a hostile environment, the asset requiring the greatest levels of security protection is the man or woman involved. Very often, he or she is likely to be critical to the business or its operations. For example, in an earlier scenario, we saw the CEO and CFO of BU who intended to travel to Saudubai to begin contract negotiations with the KoS Ministry of the Interior (MOI). Besides the fact that as human beings, their lives are sacred, they also carry critical seniority in an international organisation, and should anything untoward happen to them it could be catastrophic for BU.

#### *Information*

It is probably fair to say that the majority of large international business organisations will have Travel Crisis Management and Business Continuity Plans that can be activated at short notice, should a member of staff find himself or herself in a dangerous situation. Equally, forward-thinking companies will have information and data protection plans in the event of their servers or networks being attacked, and that of course is fine; but what about the manager travelling in a potentially hostile country, in possession of a laptop with information that should have been downloaded onto a separate drive before they left the UK or the United States. Everybody is in a hurry, and of course, it is complicated trying to access sales figures or R&D material remotely, so why not leave it on the laptop hard drive where it can be accessed at a moment's notice, but consider the following scenario.

### *Brand and reputation*

Prior to his journey to Saudubai, Russ Rowe was given an intelligence briefing about the threats that he may encounter in that turbulent part of the world. BU, in line with best business practice, will probably rely on such intelligence being provided by a third-party intelligence gathering company, as the gas and oil exploration company has neither the skills nor the interest in carrying out intelligence analysis, and in the UK certainly, such third-party companies are extremely adept at delivering evidence-based, high-level intelligence, which will reduce the risk to overseas travellers.

What if the intelligence briefings delivered to Russ, or perhaps more catastrophic, to the CEO and CFO were inaccurate, and had not been analysed correctly. There is every possibility that the CEO and CFO could be kidnapped for ransom, which undoubtedly BU would pay, meaning the two senior managers would be safe, but what about the reputation and damage done to an international organisation that failed to show due diligence to two of its senior managers, having to pay kidnapers to have them returned. Brand and reputation perhaps damaged beyond redemption.

## *Threats*

### *Terrorism*

Probably the greatest threat to be taken into consideration in a hostile environment is the threat of a terrorist attack because by and large, terrorist organisations aim to create publicity for their cause, and to achieve that, they prefer to kill as many people as possible. During the Security Risk Assessment, the assessor should give thought to the following terrorist methods of operation.

### *The placed Improvised Explosive Device (IED)*

The placed IED has been the most used of all terrorist weapons, primarily because it is easy to construct, very portable, and simple to hide. The container can be anything from a small briefcase to a large suitcase, depending on the levels of havoc the terrorist wants to create. During the Security Risk Assessment, the assessor must take into consideration the ease at which the IED can be deployed at the location being assessed, with the most effective means of mitigation being sound communications, detailed training, and transparent policies, plans, and procedures.

### *The Vehicle-Borne IED (VBIED)*

The VBIED generally comes in two forms.

- The Under Vehicle Booby Trap (UVBT)
- In many ways, this is a specialist weapons system because it is difficult to construct and must be attached to the target vehicle. Once attached, the device will be initiated either by means of an internal timing mechanism or by remote control, usually using a cell phone signal. The UVBT was successfully used by the Provisional Irish Republican Army (PIRA), and more recently by terrorist groups in Iraq and Afghanistan; it is designed to kill or maim occupants of the car.
- The Vehicle-Borne IED (VBIED).
- In this instance, the vehicle will carry some form of IED, whether that is in containers carried in the boot of the vehicle, or if a larger vehicle is used, such as a van or Heavy Goods Vehicle (HGV), it may be packed solid with explosives and some form of initiator (timer or remote). This form of attack option has been used globally, and over the last thirty years or so has been the most successful weapons system in the terrorist's armoury.

### *Personnel Borne IED (PBIED)*

Otherwise known as the suicide bomber, this is by far the most difficult terrorist means of attack to prevent or mitigate. The terrorist operating as a suicide bomber has a number of advantages when planning an attack. In the first instance, he or she will decide where and when they intend to carry out the attack; they are always on the front foot. The terrorist will choose the type and size of the device, and they have the option of aborting the attack should they wish or need to do so.

Once again, the Security Auditor must liaise with law enforcement agencies, and if possible, with security services to obtain the most effective and accurate intelligence. Prevention and mitigation will be achieved through detailed training programmes and exercises, sound communications, and transparent policies, plans, and procedures.

### Key takeaway

*In general terms, the probability of a terrorist attack is low, but it also has a very high impact if it is carried out. That is to say that the impact may be devastating. The Security Risk Assessor must take the threat of a terrorist attack into consideration during every assessment. The approach of "Its unlikely to happen to me" is unacceptable.*

### Kidnap and Ransom (K&R)

Kidnap and Ransom, or K&R a favoured means of attack in a hostile environment, is normally well planned and is generally initiated after Hostile Target Reconnaissance (HTR) has been carried out. Outsiders moving around this type of environment normally do themselves no favours, in as much as they are pretty easy to spot in a crowd, and unfortunately, far too often they either haven't received or have failed to listen to protective advice designed to ensure their safety.

The kidnappers will abduct their victim for a number of reasons, such as revenge, to prove a point and gain publicity, or to demand payment for the life of their target. Another type of K&R is the Tiger Kidnap.

### Tiger Kidnap

Tiger kidnapping is a specific act that pairs kidnapping with a second illegal activity. The kidnapping is conducted to coerce an individual or group into perpetrating a crime. An item or person is held hostage, and the kidnappers demand action instead of payment. Tiger kidnapping forces an innocent third party to complete high-risk, illegal work. The kidnappings are rarely reported since the very nature of the set-up means that the victims are also guilty of committing a crime.

The term 'tiger kidnapping' comes from the way a tiger stalks its prey before it strikes. Criminals use the same tactic. They learn about their victims' weaknesses before they exploit them, eventually targeting the item or person that they believe will elicit a desired reaction.[43]

### Cyber

The cyber threat in a hostile environment can come in two forms:

- The individual
- As mentioned, when we discussed Russ Rowe earlier in the book, the businessperson travelling abroad very often has a number of issues on

his or her mind from the moment they begin their journey until they have boarded the train or aircraft making its way home; and militia and organised criminal groups in hostile areas are very aware of this.

- The organisation.
- Once the organisation has begun operations in a hostile environment, it should be obvious that hostile actors, individual or organisational, are likely to initiate plans to carry out a cyber attack against the company's ICT network. For example, in terms of BU, once drilling operations have begun, there will be a plethora of sensitive data and information available, should the hackers be successful in their efforts to breach the ICT network.

## Vulnerabilities

### People

Every organisation operating in an environment that has been categorised as hostile is vulnerable to attack, and probably the greatest vulnerability is us! Remember Russ Rowe?

### *Russ Rowe (DBD) of BU fame*

Russ, our intrepid Business Development Director at BU is desperate to finalise a sale in The Kingdom of Saudubai (KoS) and has completely rescheduled his diary in order to be able to fly to the Kingdom at a moment's notice; and realising that he needs as much current information as possible to impress his hosts, has decided to download all sales figures and R&D information onto his company laptop (in contravention of company instructions).

Russ is one of many thousands of British and US businesspeople plying their trade in potentially hostile environments, whilst carrying extremely sensitive information on an insecure (except for a password!) laptop, and of course, from the time he boards his train, he is being monitored.

Let us see how this plays out.

Monday 0800hrs.

Russ boards his train from Oxford to Paddington Station, London, where he catches the Heathrow Express to Terminal 2 at Heathrow International Airport, taking the 13-hour (Business Class) flight to Joda, which is the capital of Saudubai. As soon as he has settled down on board and is about to drain his third glass of champagne, he decides to do some homework, and out comes the laptop. The extremely attractive young lady next to him has engaged him in conversation, and surprise, surprise she is also employed in the field of gas and oil exploration. Shock, horror!

Vanity has now kicked in (aided and abetted by three glasses of champagne, two glasses of wine, and a very interested and attractive young female business executive – at least that's her story and she is sticking to it!), and Russ is delicately (not) explaining to her the unique approach to exploration employed by BU, which of course means showing her some very sophisticated (and sensitive) graphics on his – yes you have it – laptop. Almost like a bolt out of the blue, Elly now breaks the glad news to Russ that she will be staying at the Ramada Hotel in Joda, and you guessed it, so is Russ. What an amazing surprise.

Tuesday 1200hrs.

After a 13-hour flight, Elly and Russ share a taxi to the Ramada Hotel, where they decide to freshen up, and after catching up with e-mails (as always) agree to meet at the hotel bar for a drink and a bite to eat.

During the afternoon, two things happen that when combined are going to shorten Russ's career with BU quite significantly.

First, Elly now knows what room Russ is staying in, and she immediately informs a colleague, who has a master key to all hotel rooms.

Second, and this is unforgivable, in an effort to ensure that he meets Elly on time when he has finished working on his e-mails, he leaves his laptop on the dressing table, as in his words, he is only fifty metres away, and he will be back in a couple of hours. What could possibly happen in that short space of time?

Well, here is what happens.

Elly's friend Mohammad, seeing Russ leave his room, now knows that he has a couple of hours before the Brit returns. You may now think that Mohammad is going to enter Russ's room and steal the computer; no that would be stupid. Mohammad is extremely proficient in accessing secure electronic equipment, and within minutes of entering the hotel room, he has the laptop open and has copied Russ's sales figures and the R&D information. All of these will be sold to the highest bidder, with Mohammad and Elly dividing the profits two ways.

After dinner, Russ will never see Elly again, and he will not know until it is far too late, that all of his companies' sensitive sales and R&D information is in the hands of a Chinese company, which will seal the deal.

Cheers Russ.

### *Access control and physical security measures*

Once operational, using BU as an example, organisations are of course vulnerable to physical attack, and measures such as Defence in Depth and integrated security are critical because without such supporting systems the operation is vulnerable to a criminal or terrorist attack.

### *ICT*

Today, ICT systems are very often the backbone of an organisation, enabling a variety of systems to be used concurrently, with maximum benefit to all end users. However, if the network is hacked, it becomes a major vulnerability, as it then allows unauthorised access to all ICT-reliant systems, such as CCTV, access control, lighting, and so on. In a hostile environment, it is very likely that adversaries, such as state actors will be constantly attempting to hack the BU ICT network.

### *Preparation*

Remember *failing to plan is planning to fail*. In a potential hostile situation, planning is critical, as is planning communication, which must ensure that all stakeholders are aware of the strategic, tactical, and operational plans before deployment. Deployment cannot take place until all preparation aspects have been authorised and 'signed off' by the Executive Board.

### *Training and awareness*

A function of preparedness is training and awareness, and this should begin as soon as there is confirmation that the contract is likely to go live, with BU personnel preparing to deploy in a hostile environment. Training and awareness programmes should aim to deliver education relating to the safety of members of staff and all company structures and infrastructures. Should sufficient levels of training and awareness not be delivered, the lives of all personnel being deployed are vulnerable, as are all aspects of the operation.

## ***Security Risk Assessment: BU drilling operations in the Kingdom of Saudubai (KoS)***

Reference number: SecRa/KoS/07/22

## *Likelihood and impact*

As with all other sections covered so far, in order to examine the likelihood and impact in relation to hostile environment security, we will use a fictitious case study, in which a terrorist organisation has decided to attack the BU drilling operations in The Kingdom of Saudubai (KoS). As intelligence has suggested, the type of terrorist operation common to this political and geographical area is the VBIED, and marauding terrorist attack using light weapons systems.

BU has recently been awarded a contract to begin exploratory drilling operations in Joda, the Kingdom of Saudubai.

After initial research carried out it is believed that significant levels of crude oil exist, making it commercially viable for BU and KoS to begin a joint venture related to the extraction of an extremely attractive mineral.

Drilling operations are due to begin in eight weeks' time, and planning for extraction is as follows.

1. Six boring platforms have been installed and are currently undergoing safety checks.
2. A compound has been constructed which houses approximately 100 engineers, processing technicians, ICT engineers, and security management.
3. A separate construction has been built 100 metres from the main compound to house 250 local staff, including drivers, labourers, security guards, etc.
4. All resources will be delivered on a weekly basis from a central supplier in Joda, including food and fresh water.
5. KoS armed forces and police have been tasked to ensure external compound safety.

Islamist Qaeda (IQ), which is the predominant insurgent terrorist organisation in the region has sworn to carry out revenge attacks against what they see as a politically motivated contract given to a western state that is particularly close to the hated United States of America.

### *Impact*

The primary aim of a terrorist attack against the BU drilling operations is initially to wreak as much carnage as possible at the site, with the secondary objective being to close down all drilling operations.

*Table 31* Likelihood and impact of a VBIED and marauding terrorist attack *before* mitigation

| | Impact | 1 (Very low) | 2 (Low) | 3 (High) | 4 (Very high) | **5 (Catastrophic)** |
|---|---|---|---|---|---|---|
| **Likelihood** | | | | | | |
| 1 (Very low) | | | | | | |
| 2 (Low) | | | | | | |
| 3 (Medium) | | | | | | |
| **4 (High)** | | | | | | **20/25** |
| 5 (Very high) | | | | | | |

Based on corroborated intelligence from the UK and KoS security services, Table 31 shows the likelihood and impact of a VBIED and marauding terrorist attack, prior to any risk treatment. This reflects the fact that because of the assets, threats, and vulnerabilities involved in the equation, the likelihood is high (4), and the worst-case impact could be catastrophic (5) giving a risk measurement of 20/25.

## *Risk treatment*

As with other scenarios covered so far, we still include the following means:

### *Risk avoidance*

This is something of a recurring theme, but once again, risk avoidance means the cancellation of all drilling operations. The Senior Management Team would be reluctant to follow such advice, as not only would it be financially disagreeable, in terms of brand and reputation it would also be politically embarrassing.

### *Risk reduction*

The risk could be reduced by taking the following steps.

- Ensure that all physical (including manned guarding) and electronic security systems are fit for purpose.
- Revisit all operational contingency plans, making sure that they are effectively communicated to all members of staff.

- Reduce traffic movement.
- Liaise with KoS police and security forces to ensure that cover is provided at all times.
- Revisit all Corporate Social Responsibility (CSR) measures to ensure that BU captures the hearts and minds of the local community.

### *Spread the risk*

The only way that risk could be spread, is to construct a number of similar platforms to ensure that drilling operations will continue, even if one of the sites is attacked.

### *Risk transference*

Once again, if appropriate levels of insurance are acquired, that will transfer the risk.

The above risk treatment measures should reduce the risk factor, from 20/25 to 10/25. See Table 32.

*Table 32* Likelihood and impact of a VBIED and marauding terrorist attack *after* mitigation

| **Impact** | 1 (Very low) | 2 (Low) | 3 (High) | 4 (Very high) | **5 (Catastrophic)** |
|---|---|---|---|---|---|
| **Likelihood** | | | | | |
| 1 (Very low) | | | | | |
| **2 (Low)** | | | | | **10/25** |
| 3 (Medium) | | | | | |
| 4 (High) | | | | | |
| 5 (Very high) | | | | | |

## Summary

*The threat of a terrorist attack against BU drilling operations in Saudbei was deemed to be High, with an impact that was estimated to be Catastrophic (20/25). The BU Senior Management Team after consultation with the Security Risk Assessor and relevant stakeholders decided that the most effective means of mitigation was to reduce the risk. After risk treatment was complete it was decided by all parties that the risk of a terrorist attack had been reduced to a low likelihood (10/25) but means it still has a catastrophic impact should an attack be successful.*

## Close protection

Reference number: SecRa/CP/08/22.

I very rarely use the term expert, but it certainly applies to a close friend and professional colleague that I have known for several years, Mr Ian Kelly, former head of Close Protection Training with the international conglomerate G4S. When asked to define close protection, Ian argued very clearly that it is: *The application of protection for another person requiring it, regardless of the many names it may attract but needing the professional services of a Close Protection Officer(s), is ultimately just that; Close Protection.*

*Whilst the 'how' 'can' and 'will' differ greatly there will be some consistent factors that will dominate provision if it is to be correctly applied; the threat assessment leading to an understanding of credible risk towards the principal; the principals, or principal's organisation/family, risk acceptance (the 'why') which together should in turn shape the principle's risk appetite especially in terms of what he/she/they want their activities/lives to look like.*

*The challenge for the modern-day Close Protection Officer is to navigate through this process; assess and communicate risk effectively but reassuringly, if propionate Close Protection is to be successfully applied. This process should also influence one important factor, which will always be present, sufficient funding to achieve 'the how'.*

Thanks Ian.

This is perhaps all about semantics. Intrinsically there is no difference, both forms of protection teams serve to ensure, to the best of their ability, the security and safeguarding of a Very Important Person (VIP), referred to in the sector as the principal. The perception of this form of protection very often paints the picture of three or four well-tanned athletic bodyguards wearing close-fitting suites, aviator sunglasses, and Rolex watches, but in reality, that is exactly what close protection is not!

From this point on I shall refer to the sector as close protection or as it is better known, CP.

This form of protection is or should be reliant on the services of 'the grey man'. The Close Protection Officer (CPO) who has the ability to blend into the background, being reliant on intelligence, excellent communications with the principal and his team, and of course the physical fitness required should the need arise. It is generally accepted that if the Close Protection Team has to fight their way out of a situation, whilst protecting the principal, they have lost before they started because they should not have found themselves in that position in the first place!

Perhaps more than any other sector, close protection is all about risk management; and understanding that if the CP team does not apply itself to the protocols and rigors of risk management, their principal is likely to be either killed or held to ransom. For that reason, I am going to describe the Security Risk Assessment, as applied to CP, in pretty much the same vein as I have with other sectors.

## *Assets*

### The principal

The primary asset in any Close Protection situation is of course the principal, as he or she is the reason for the existence of the CP team, and it is likely that their very existence is borne out of an effective threat assessment, during which it was decided that the threat to the pop star, the footballer or the corporate CEO was so great that some form of protection was needed.

**Types of principal.** It makes sense at this stage to divide the types of principal into two categories, high and low profile.

- High profile.
  For this category it is fair to say that pop stars, film actors and well-paid sports stars are the primary principals. Because of their lifestyles, and of course related to the significant exposure to the media that the likes of David Beckham or Robby Williams generate, it is probably appropriate for them to be seen to be protected by high-profile CP teams.
  In this situation, the principal, a well-known actress, who is constantly followed by the paparazzi needs an equally high-profile CP team to afford her constant and credible protection. The body language of the team metaphorically signals a very aggressive posture, warning any perpetrators or personal trespassers that such a threat will be met, if necessary, with a forceful response.
- Low profile.
  Low profile close protection does not infer that the cover is of a lower level when compared to high profile CP, rather it is an indication of the preferred profile of the principal. At the opposite end of the spectrum, when compared to pop stars and footballers, is the Chief Executive Officer (CEO) or Managing Director (MD), who may require CP cover, but prefers not to have the most aggressive, even offensive

types of bodyguards protecting them. Instead of seeking to employ the services of a team that are distinguished by their 'greyness', or better put, their ability to blend into the principal's background to be almost clones of him or her.

As opposed to the glamour-seeking high profile principal, the CEO will more attentively listen to his or her Close Protection Officer (CPO) and team, because they need to move from a to b without being detected, and upon arrival at their destination, move into the building unseen.

### *The principal's family*

During the close protection Security Risk Assessment, the assessor must take into consideration the family of the principal, even if they are not included in the CP Service Level Agreement (SLA). Despite the SLA, it is likely that the principal will very obviously be concerned for the welfare of perhaps his/her partner and their children.

### *The CP Team*

The CP Team is an asset, and it is extremely important that it is protected.

### *Vehicles, communications, and weapons*

It is highly likely that the principal will be transported in some form of a luxury vehicle, which will contain a sophisticated communications system. Of course, if protection takes place in a hostile environment, weapons and ammunition will be involved in the asset calculation, because in the wrong hands they become a threat.

## Threats

Whether close protection is being provided for either a high-profile or a low-profile client, there are a range of threats that the Security Auditor/CPO must take into consideration.

### *Close Quarter Assassination (CQA)*

This is the ultimate threat scenario, and it must be considered a worst-case situation in any Close Protection Security Risk Assessment. It is likely that politicians, and perhaps senior management are the likely target for the CQA, but it cannot be ruled out when a high-profile personality is in the media focus.

### *John Lennon*

On the evening of 8 December 1980, English musician John Lennon, formerly of the Beatles, was shot and fatally wounded in the archway of The Dakota, his residence in New York City. His killer was Mark David Chapman, an American Beatles fan who travelled from Hawaii. Chapman said he was angered by Lennon's lifestyle and public statements, especially his much-publicised remark about the Beatles being 'more popular than Jesus' and the lyrics of his later songs 'God' and 'Imagine'. Chapman also said he was inspired by the fictional character Holden Caulfield from J. D. Salinger's novel *The Catcher in the Rye*.[44]

As far as I am aware, Lennon did not deploy a CP team, and it would be foolish to speculate whether such a service would have protected him, but it proves the point that high-profile media personalities are threatened and should consider their safety. That said, very often CP is seen as a means of denying personal freedom, and it is of course the choice of the VIP.

### *Assault*

Whether it is Justin Timberlake, or David Beckham the threat of physical assault cannot be ignored. Very often it is merely an attempt to get a point across, or for the assailant to be seen by the world's media as being capable of making such an expression, and in itself is not a serious physical concern. Although politically it could be disastrous.

### *Emmanuel Macron*

On Tuesday 08 June 2021 French President Emmanuel Macron was slapped in the face by a man during a visit to a small town in southeastern France, an incident that prompted a wide show of support for French politicians from all sides.

The French president was greeting the public waiting for him behind barriers in the town of Tain-l'Hermitage after he visited a high school that is training students to work in hotels and restaurants.

A video shows a man slapping Macron in the face and his bodyguards pushing the man away as the French leader is quickly rushed from the scene.

*A bodyguard, who was standing right behind Macron, raised a hand in defence of the president* **but was a fraction of a second too late to stop the slap (there is no such thing as a fraction of a second too late!)** *The bodyguard then put his arm around the president to protect him.*

What if the assailant had been carrying an offensive weapon? A fraction too late would have been fatal.

### *Kidnap and Ransom (K&R)*

Another major threat is K&R, which is the most feared amongst the close protection community because the outcome is unknown. This particular offence or threat is unlikely to be deployed against a high-profile principal such as a pop star or footballer, but it is certainly applicable when giving consideration to the safety of the CEO or MD. The criminal or terrorist group will carry out the act in order to gain some form of competitive advantage. It may be that the victim has access to sensitive data or information, and the abductors will use all means necessary to extract whatever information they need. Also, there is the possibility of a Tiger Kidnap, although the likelihood of a Tiger Kidnap is dependent on the target.

### *Tiger Kidnap (TK)*

Tiger kidnap is a term used to describe the abduction of one or more individuals in which the abduction forms part of a robbery. A person of importance to the victim, typically a family member or loved one, is held hostage and used as collateral until the victim has complied with the requests of the offender. The victim that forms the part of the robbery will be instructed to attend their place of employment, typically a bank or financial institution, and withdraw a quantity of cash. This is accomplished by using a picture of the victim's loved one(s) under gunpoint, or through the desperate persuasion of the victim to get the assistance of their colleagues, which may be necessary to complete the act. When the money has been secured, the victim is then told of a location in which to meet the criminals to hand over the cash. TK has proven to be extremely successful for criminals over the past couple of decades.[45]

## *Theft*

### *The high-profile principal*

By virtue of the fact that the principal is likely to be a known VIP, there is a strong likelihood that he or she will be in possession of goods that are important and attractive to a thief. There are numerous stories about pop stars and Premier League footballers having either their stolen or homes burgled, with attractive assets worth significant amounts of money being stolen.

### *French football*

Seven men and a woman went on trial over a string of thefts carried out against celebrities in Paris, France.

The defendants, aged between 27 and 31, are accused of targeting high-profile figures including footballer Thiago Silva in 2018 and 2019.

An estimated €4.2m (£3.6m; $5m) in jewellery and other valuable items were taken from homes in the French capital.

Stolen items were later discovered at a flat, alongside a list of potential targets and their addresses.

Footballer Eric Maxim Choupo-Moting of Paris St-Germain was playing in a Uefa Champions League match against Liverpool in late November 2018, when he was robbed of valuables worth around €600,000 ($720,000, £510,000).

Less than a month later Thiago Silva – who was PSG captain at the time before moving to Chelsea – returned from a French league game to find that jewellery and watches were missing. His losses were put at €1.2m ($1.4m, £1m).

CCTV footage showed two suspects *scaling a drainpipe and entering his home through a window*, before carrying the stolen goods away in bags.

Other victims of the gang include French rapper Booba, TV host Patrick Sébastien, chef Jean-Pierre Vigato and a wealthy Saudi national.

Police believe the *suspects climbed buildings and entered through windows* in the victims' homes.

After an investigation involving phone taps, seven men were arrested in August 2019.

According to the AFP news agency, members of the group later admitted to some of the accusations, or claimed they were lookouts during the thefts. Two of the gang that targeted wealthy stars are said to have gone by the nicknames The Cat and Bidou.

The eighth suspect, the tenant of a flat in Aubervilliers to the north of Paris where the stolen goods were found, has denied charges including receiving stolen goods and membership in a criminal organisation, AFP reports.

There have been other high-profile thefts in the city in recent years, with at least three other Paris St-Germain players being burgled this year. Ángel Di María's family was targeted earlier this year, again while he was playing for his club.

In 2016, American celebrity Kim Kardashian was robbed at gunpoint at her luxury Paris residence.[46]

The very obvious question to be asked here, is whether the locations where the burglaries took place were ever security risk assessed, and if so, by who? I would argue certainly not by a competent security risk assessor.

### *The low-profile principal*

Theft from the low-profile principal will inevitably be different from the same offence committed against the pop star or high-profile footballer because the protected assets will be dissimilar. The CEO or MD is likely to be in possession of information and data that is attractive to the thief who will probably sell it to the highest bidder. So, this is a form of espionage, as opposed to burglary. That is not to say that the homes of the low-profile principal should not be security risk assessed, of course they should, as should their offices and places of work.

### *The insider threat*

Whether it is the high-profile pop star, or the CEO of a corporation, information will exist, that if found in the wrong hands could be problematic to the principal. Perhaps it is sensitive data about the pop stars' movements that must not be released to the press, or the confidential sales figures needed by the CEO for her next meeting with the shareholders. Any member of the CP team with access to such information must be regarded as a threat, with appropriate screening and vetting taking place before their employment. The Security Risk Assessor must be cognizant of the fact that the insider threat exists, and such a threat must be taken into consideration during all phases of the assessment.

### *Public communications*

Relatively speaking, this is one of the greatest threats to the principal, because misinformed public communications can be socially and commercially damaging, even fatal. The media are likely to amplify, and perhaps distort information about the principal that will sell headlines or media time, and whilst this is not a direct physical threat, very often the trust built between the principal and his or her CPO, who has his or her ear to the ground, can prevent or mitigate this threat. Very often the CP Team Leader or CPO can act on behalf of the principal and can stave off questions that perhaps could have been too sensitive for the principal to comment on. It's all about trust and effective communication.

## ***Vulnerabilities***

### *Poor intelligence*

As mentioned earlier in this section, close protection is based on the risk assessment, and a major component of any risk assessment is intelligence. On a daily basis, the Close Protection Team must have access to crime intelligence at every level, whether that is related to low-level crime in an area where the principal may be staying for a day or two, or terrorism intelligence in an area that the CEO is about to visit.

Intelligence can originate from a number of sources, such as local rumours picked up by the team, crime intelligence and analysis provided by local law enforcement agencies, or high-level terrorism intelligence provided by national security services.

The Security Auditor must take intelligence into consideration at every stage of the assessment.

### *Communications (public relations)*

Good communications between the principal and his or her team are critical, as are internal communications between team members, and as such, must be exercised and tested periodically, as the principal must be content that the sensitive information shared with his team is secure. Allowing information such as road movement data, hotel details, and so on to be accessed by unauthorised personnel, including of course the media could be disastrous, and some form of communications encryption should be contained with all communications systems. The military 'need to know' method is generally seen as effective, with only those team members who need access to certain material being included in the brief.

### *Weak team leadership*

Having commanded a number of close protection teams in the dim and distant past, I know from first-hand experience how difficult it can be to manage not only the safety of the principal, but the day-to-day supervision of a highly trained team of Close Protection Officers, who demand strong leadership.

The CP Team Leader is constantly carrying out dynamic risk assessments which can include anything from imminent road moves in a potentially hostile environment to ensuring that all aspects of the principal's life are being catered for, and possibly who is going to take the place of his second in command who has just resigned to spend more time with his wife and family.

The Security Risk Assessor when carrying out the assessment should interview the Team Leader in order to understand exactly what the role entails, and how it may be amended, if necessary to resolve any leadership and communications issues.

Areas such as internal promotion, training and development, and recruitment policies should be examined.

### *Poor or inadequate equipment*

Every piece of equipment used by the Close Protection Team must be fit for purpose and should be checked for operational effectiveness on a daily basis. A vehicle failing to start, with no backup is unprofessional at best but is potentially fatal if the principal is required to move at a moment's notice. Equally, communications equipment not tested regularly is almost bound to fail when required most.

The CP Team Leader should delegate the responsibility of equipment preparedness to a competent team member, who must ensure that all equipment is checked and tested daily, and this should be recorded in the equipment log.

### *Operational movement*

As already mentioned, intelligence is key to the safety of the principal, and it must be used to ensure that operational movement is safe, with situations such as not setting patterns i.e., rotating routes, moving in and out of a location, and choosing the safest route to take, but that is often easier said than done if the principal has his or her own ideas.

## *The Prince of Wales*

The Guardian newspaper reported that on 09 December 2010, a car containing Prince Charles and his wife, Camilla, was attacked as a wave of protest swept through central London in the wake of a Commons vote to force through a trebling of university tuition fees for students in England.

Protesters cracked windows and threw paint on the Rolls-Royce after it became separated from its police escort and was surrounded by demonstrators who had spilled into the West End after an initially peaceful demonstration outside parliament rapidly deteriorated and spread.

One, Ben Kelsey, said:

> There were 400 to 500 protesters there. It was fairly obvious who was in the car. It was very well lit up. Charles and Camilla looked quite relaxed at first but when they saw how many people there were they began to get worried. A few seconds later the area was packed with police. It was complete chaos.

Another witness described how a police protection officer, dressed in a tuxedo, travelling in convoy with the royal couple opened the doors of his car to beat his way through the crowds.

The royal couple had looked visibly shaken when they arrived at the London Palladium for the Royal Variety performance, but Camilla later joked about the incident, saying: 'First time for everything' as she left the theatre.

Unofficially, it was admitted that the Prince and his wife had been advised against driving through that route, but he failed to accept the advice and guidance of his CPO.[47]

## *Apathy*

Probably the greatest vulnerability impacting any Close Protection team is apathy, 'It's not going to happen to us, no worries', because that is when the principal will be attacked when his team's guard is down. Apathy can creep into a team for many reasons. It may be that the team is bored because it spends the majority of its time sitting around in cars waiting for the principal to move, or it may be because the team has never encountered action. However, the main reason for apathy is poor leadership, with the Team Leader being unable to motivate his team. Once that has been identified, triage is required to stop the motivational haemorrhaging. Again, this must be considered during the Security Risk Assessment.

## *Likelihood and impact*

### *Likelihood*

Close protection is a service delivered to reduce the likelihood of an attack against the principal through visual and intelligence deterrence. When required, the CP team will adopt an aggressive posture to make it very clear that they will protect their principal under all circumstances.

Equally, any aggressor intending on carrying out an attack against the principal will research his or her defence postures, with the CP team endeavouring to ensure that all intelligence gleaned by the potential perpetrator will lead them to believe that an attack will be defended, and that it is a futile strategy. That of course does not mean that an attempted CQA or K&R situation will not arise, and if it does, the CP team needs to appreciate operationally and tactically what the impact may be.

### *Impact*

The impact of the attack very much depends on the nature of the threat, and as mentioned earlier, the most critical adverse consequence of an attack against a principal would be death.

Table 33 shows the likelihood and impact in of an attack against a principal moving from his or her vehicle to a location, perhaps the office or accommodation, when the principal is at their most vulnerable. The gunman sees this as the ideal moment to carry out their attack because the mind of the principal will either be concentrating on entering his/her house, or what they need to do once in their vehicle, with the thought of an attack being the last thing on their mind. If the attacker sees the principal as a target worthy of attention, then the likelihood is high (4/5) and if the attack is successful the impact will be catastrophic (5/5), giving an overall risk measurement of 20/25.

*Table* 33 Likelihood and impact of an attack *before* mitigation

| | **Impact** | 1 (Very low) | 2 (Low) | 3 (High) | 4 (Very high) | **5 (Catastrophic)** |
|---|---|---|---|---|---|---|
| **Likelihood** | | | | | | |
| 1 (Very low) | | | | | | |
| 2 (Low) | | | | | | |
| 3 (Medium) | | | | | | |
| **4 (High)** | | | | | | **20/25** |
| 5 (Very high) | | | | | | |

## *Risk treatment*

As with other scenarios covered so far, we still include the following means:

- Avoid
- Reduce
- Spread
- Transfer

### *Risk avoidance*

The principal could of course decide to err on the side of safety by permanently installing him or herself with their place of residence, and it is likely that they would probably (no guarantee of course) be safe. However, that option is of course totally impracticable for a plethora of reasons. Not least is the fact that he or she will be acquiescing to the threats of the criminal, with no certainty of safety.

### *Risk reduction*

Although the scenario chosen is the attack against the principal as he or she enters/leaves a premises, the range of threats is varied and by tightening up all CP procedures, it is likely that the risk will be reduced,

### *Spread the risk*

Spreading the risk is difficult because there is only one principal. That said Charles De Gaulle whilst presiding over France chose to move in a convoy of identical Citroen saloons, constantly alternating his choice of vehicle in order to confuse a potential attacker.

### *Risk transference*

Once again, if appropriate levels of insurance are acquired, that will transfer the risk.

The above measures should reduce the risk factor, from 20/25 to 15/25. See Table 34.

### *Key takeaway*

Close protection is only as good as the communication and trust between a principal and his CP team.

Intrinsically related to close protection, one of the greatest threats to a principal is the threat of a terrorist attack, so let us now look at how we may prepare for such an event.

*Table 34* Likelihood and impact of an attack *after* mitigation

| **Impact** | *1 (Very low)* | *2 (Low)* | *3 (High)* | *4 (Very high)* | ***5 (Catastrophic)*** |
|---|---|---|---|---|---|
| **Likelihood** | | | | | |
| 1 (Very low) | | | | | |
| 2 (Low) | | | | | |
| **3 (Medium)** | | | | | **15/25** |
| 4 (High) | | | | | |
| 5 (Very high) | | | | | |

## Counter-terrorism

Reference number: SecRa/CT/10/22

Gerry Adams, when commanding the Provisional Irish Republican Army (PIRA) once threatened the Prime Minister of Great Britain and Northern Ireland, Margaret Thatcher by saying:

*'You (the government of Great Britain) have to be lucky all of the time, we (PIRA) only have to be lucky once'.*

I suspect that this is the philosophical stance taken by all terrorist groups, the fact that they may often fail in their objectives, but eventually their patience will bear fruit. That is what we in the free world must be aware of, and it must be considered at every level of counter-terrorist operations.

There is absolutely no doubt that the most difficult, and singularly critical Security Risk Assessment to carry out involves the threat of a terrorist attack.

It appears that as the result of the atrocity which killed 23 innocent people at the Manchester Arena on 22 May 2017, a piece of legislation to be referred to as Martyn's Law will be enacted.

The group Survivors Against Terror[48] describe Martyn's Law as a piece of legislation that creates a coherent and proportionate approach to protective security. They argue that it should apply to any place or space to which the public has access. For small venues, this may simply require an addition to their already mandated fire plan, for bigger more complex venues it will require a more holistic approach.

It consists of 5 requirements, arguing that spaces and places to which the public have access must:

- Engage with freely available counterterrorism advice and training
- *Conduct vulnerability assessments of their operating places and spaces.*
- *Mitigate the risks created by the vulnerabilities.*
- Put in place a counter-terrorism plan.
- Plan for the threat of terrorism.

*Martyn's Law seeks to ensure that public bodies are prepared for terrorism and are able to deal with its aftermath.*

It proposes that training and awareness are made available, and adopted, so that people can protect themselves and the communities in which they live. It will fill gaps in existing legislation while also working hand in glove with related areas of law such as planning.

From a personal perspective, I totally endorse the enactment of Martyn's Law, going as far as to argue that it should have been introduced some time ago; but of course, hindsight is a marvellous virtue, and it is a skill that we all possess.

There are two areas that are relevant to this book and the section currently being covered, and they are:

- Conduct vulnerability assessments of their operating places and spaces.
- Mitigate the risks created by the vulnerabilities.

Of course, the Security Risk Assessment covers not only vulnerabilities and mitigation strategies, but it also takes into full consideration all of the component parts of risk in order to produce a well-rounded approach to that phenomenon.

So, from my perspective, all of the above public bodies should consider not only vulnerability assessments and mitigation strategies, but they should also, and must, invest in full Counter Terrorism Security Risk Assessments.

So let us begin to look at the Counter Terrorism Security Risk Assessment and its component parts.

## Assets

The core asset that the terrorist wants to attack, and ultimately destroy is us, human beings. There are arguments that the terrorist will always attempt to generate as much media coverage as possible, and that the oxygen of publicity is the greatest weapon in their armoury. The terrorist may attack critical infrastructures, or perhaps the economy of the country they have identified as a legitimate enemy, but their long-term aim is to kill as many innocent people as possible.

## Threats

Terrorist threats are many and varied, and all options should be considered when carrying out the Security Risk Assessment. Examples of such threats are:

### *The Improvised Explosive device (IED)*

The IED comes in many forms and has been incredibly effective for the terrorist over a vast period of time. So let us examine some of the most effective IED platforms in the terrorist's armoury.

### *The placed IED*

When the Security Risk Assessment is carried out the assessor should take into consideration all locations and operations that will allow the terrorist to deploy a placed IED in a bag, a rucksack, a briefcase, or whatever container is suited to their operations. Looking at it from a terrorist perspective (thinking like a criminal), where can I place my explosive device that will have the most effect.

For example, if you are carrying out a Security Risk Assessment of a corporate building in a busy city centre, then perhaps the best location to place the IED, is hidden in a crowded reception area at 0830hrs on Monday morning. The device can then be initiated either by a preset timer within the container, or remotely by the terrorist using, for example, a cell phone.

### *The Vehicle-Borne IED (VBIED)*

The vehicle-borne IED has been the most successful weapon used by terrorist organisations worldwide. Whether it is a relatively small explosive device magnetically attached to the underside of a car, with the intention of killing the occupant, or 500 kg of high explosives packed into a van or Heavy Goods Vehicle parked alongside a building, the VBIED is a terrorist weapon of choice. During the Counter Terrorist Security Risk Assessment, the assessor must take into consideration all areas where such a threat may be successfully delivered. Underground car parks and parking close to buildings must be taken into account, and Hostile Vehicle Mitigation measures such as bollards, rising kerbs, and stout perimeter protection should be considered.[49]

For both the placed IED and the VBIED, consideration should also be given to the possibility of a secondary device, or 'come on'. This is where a suspect device or vehicle is identified, and occupants of a building are evacuated to an assembly area. The terrorist who placed the suspect device or parked the possible VBIED is likely to be aware of the evacuation procedures for the building in danger, and he or she may place another device in that area to kill and maim as many of the fleeing members of staff as possible. Under such circumstances, the Security Risk Assessor must give some thought to all evacuation procedures, including the possibility of an invacuation, when members of staff, or those in danger will remain inside the building, protected within a reinforced room.

### *Vehicle as a weapon of attack (VAW)*

This is perhaps one of the most difficult methods of attack to make contingency plans for because the majority of such incidents where vehicles have been used as a weapon of attack have occurred on public roads, where of course the responsibility for safety lies with local security agencies. The method of operation for such an attack is for the terrorist to gain access, normally to a Heavy Goods Vehicle (HGV), and after selecting a crowded area, he or she will drive the vehicle into the mass of people occupying that location, normally a road or bridge.

### *Nice, France*

On 14 July 2016 a large cargo vehicle, driven by Mohamad Lahouaiej-Bouhel, was deliberately crashed into crowds celebrating Bastille Day. This was an intentional attack by an Islamic State-inspired terrorist, who killed 86 innocent bystanders, and wounded a further 458 people. The terrorist was shot dead by French Police.

Although, as explained, the majority of vehicles as a weapon of attack incidents take place on public roads, the Security Risk Assessor must take the threat into consideration when carrying out an assessment, because the terrorist is generally on the front foot, and there is no guarantee that such an attack will not take place in a large car park, or with a business park.

### *Marauding Terrorist Attack (MTA)*

In the excellent document *Marauding terrorist Attacks: Making Your Organisation Ready*[50] the UK Government defines an MTA by saying that terrorists enter a busy area aiming to kill or injure as many people as possible. The attackers then begin marauding, travelling on foot or in a vehicle, to find and kill or injure more people. Attackers are drawn by movement and deterred by seemingly unoccupied locations as well as by anything that may take time and effort to overcome, such as a locked door. The terrorists may take hostages, resulting in a longer siege.

Attacks may conclude with the arrest, death, or escape of the terrorists. Terrorists typically use a quiet location where they expect not to be disturbed to make final preparations, ready weapons, and wait for the appropriate moment to make their final approach to the target and launch the attack. Attacks often begin in areas that are not controlled by any single organisation (sometimes called 'grey space'). Most deaths occur during the initial attack and before police are able to respond. Whilst it is correct to say that most deaths occur during the early stages, that is not always so.

### *Mumbai, India*

In November 2008, the group known as Lashkar-e-Taiba carried out twelve marauding terrorist attacks across locations in Mumbai, India. The attacks, by ten members of the terrorist organisation spanned four days, between 26 November and 29 November, when at least 300 people were killed, with approximately 300 wounded. The attacks finished when, during a gun battle with Indian special forces, all of the group, with the exception of one terrorist, were killed.

Once again, response to this form of attack will be the responsibility of law enforcement and security forces, but the Security Risk Assessor must take the threat into consideration when carrying out the assessment.

### *The suicide attacker*

By far the most difficult terrorist scenario to plan for, the suicide attacker is the epitome of the terrorist being on the front foot, deciding to carry out the attack as and when they are ready. A quite obvious downside when planning to mitigate the suicide threat is that this terrorist knows that he or she is going to die as the result of their attack, so what we do is of little consequence to them. With the exception of 9/11, when 18 terrorists realised that they would probably die as the result of them crashing commercial airlines against landside targets, contemporary suicide attackers tend to detonate some form of IED strapped to their bodies and die as a consequence.

### *7/7*

On 07 July 2005, four young Muslim males attacked the London transport system, detonating explosives carried in rucksacks on their backs. In a coordinated attack, three of the suicide bombers detonated their explosive devices at 0850hrs, on three separate underground carriages, killing 39 commuters. At about 0950hrs, the fourth terrorist exploded the device contained in his backpack on a London bus, killing 13 passengers. In total 56 people (including the terrorists) were killed and approximately 700 were injured.

Once again, responsibility for dealing with such a threat falls under the jurisdiction of law enforcement agencies and the security services, but during the Counter Terrorist Security Risk Assessment, such an attack must be taken into consideration.

### *Kidnap/hostage taking, and ransom*

Kidnap/hostage taking, and ransom is not a common form of terrorist threat, but it still exists, with the likes of Abu Sayyaf being past masters in the art. Martin (2006) in his excellent book *Understanding Terrorism* argues that the threat of this form of a terrorist attack is used for a purpose. He argues that kidnappings are conducted for different reasons; they are done sometimes to extort ransoms and at other times for purely propaganda purposes. He concedes that in the latter scenarios, the hostages are sometimes executed. Martin also argues that kidnapping/hostage-taking is sometimes used to force concessions. This is because hostage takers may influence a government's decisions by promising rewards for compliance…The release of a hostage unharmed when a ransom is paid underwrites a promise in the future. Martin says that the sequential release of selected hostages makes promises credible.

So, whilst this particular threat may not be the most common, the Security Risk Assessor must always bear its possibility in mind.

### *Cyber*

As mentioned on a number of occasions, the threat of cybercrime is well documented, and in relation to most public and private business sectors, it is one of, if not the most concerning threat. That is not necessarily the case when cyber terrorism is debated, with compelling evidence for and against its existence being offered from very credible sources.

Singer and Friedman (2014) in a section of their book titled *How Afraid Should We be of Cyberterrorism?* argue that thirty-one thousand three hundred is roughly the number of magazine and journal articles written so far that discuss the phenomenon of cyberterrorism. They say that zero is the number of people who had been physically hurt or killed by cyberterrorism at the time their book went to the press. They go on to argue that they are not saying terrorist groups are uninterested in using cyber technology to carry out acts of violence. For example, in 2001 al-Qaeda computers seized in Afghanistan showed models of a dam and engineering software that simulated catastrophic failure of controls.

I am sure Singer and Friedman have every faith in their credible arguments about cyberterrorism and loss of life, but terrorism isn't confined to murderous acts, it also relates to how frightened, terrorised people are by acts of terrorism. In my opinion, if the discussed threat exists to attack, let us say a water supply or a national power grid, and that generates fear, it is cyberterrorism. The Security Auditor should take the threat of cyberterrorism very seriously and include it in all aspects of the Security Risk Assessment.

## Likelihood

As previously explained, calculating the likelihood of any crime is difficult, and terrorism is no exception because there are so many variables. The Security Auditor must take into consideration advice and guidance offered by the likes of the National Counter Terrorism Security Office in the UK or Homeland Security in the United States. As with all other Security Risk Assessments, all worst-case scenarios must be considered. Who saw 9/11 coming?

## Impact

The impact of a terrorist attack very much depends on the nature of the threat.

Table 35 shows the likelihood and impact of a terrorist attack, in the form of a placed IED, against a corporate location (50 Canada Way). Based on advice from terrorism specialists, the likelihood is medium (3/5), but the impact will be catastrophic (5/5), giving an overall risk measurement of 15/25.

*Table* 35 Likelihood and impact of a terrorist attack *before* mitigation

| | **Impact** | 1 *(Very low)* | 2 *(Low)* | 3 *(High)* | 4 *(Very high)* | **5 (Catastrophic)** |
|---|---|---|---|---|---|---|
| **Likelihood** | | | | | | |
| 1 (Very low) | | | | | | |
| 2 (Low) | | | | | | |
| **3 (Medium)** | | | | | | **15/25** |
| 4 (High) | | | | | | |
| 5 (Very high) | | | | | | |

### Risk treatment

As with other scenarios covered so far, we still include the following means:

- Avoid
- Reduce
- Spread
- Transfer

### Risk avoidance

The avoidance of a terrorist attack against a corporate or most other locations is extremely difficult because as with other sectors this would mean the closure of the building and the cessation of all operations. Besides the massive financial cost of such a strategy, it would give a political advantage to the terrorist, who would likely believe that he or she has been successful without carrying out an attack.

### Risk reduction

Risk reduction is the most appropriate strategy as it can be achieved with the introduction of a number of risk control measures such as upgrading all physical and electronic security measures, more effective access control, increased security training and awareness, and so on.

### Spread the risk

The risk can be spread by sharing the assets in the building with other locations within the group.

### Risk transference

This would entail an increase in insurance cover, but most insurance brokers are reluctant to become too involved in Counter Terrorism.

The above measures should reduce the risk factor, from 15/25 to 10/25. See Table 36.

*Table 36* Likelihood and impact of a terrorist attack *after* mitigation

| **Impact** | 1 (*Very low*) | 2 (*Low*) | 3 (*High*) | 4 (*Very high*) | **5 (*Catastrophic*)** |
|---|---|---|---|---|---|
| **Likelihood** | | | | | |
| 1 (Very low) | | | | | |
| **2 (Low)** | | | | | **10/25** |
| 3 (Medium) | | | | | |
| 4 (High) | | | | | |
| 5 (Very high) | | | | | |

## *Key takeaway*

*The threat of a terrorist attack is often seen as low likelihood, but high impact. In my experience, it is wise never to rule out any form of attack, and always think worst case scenario.*

Once an effective Security Risk Assessment has been carried out, the next leg of the Risk Journey is the Security Survey.

That is the end of Chapter one, in which we focused on the Security Risk Assessment and how it may be applied to a number of diverse environments or unique sectors, We will now look at the Security Survey.

## Bibliography

Adam. J., (1995) *Risk* London, Routledge.

Cabric. M., (2015) *Corporate Security Management: Challenges, Risks, and Strategies* Washington Butterworth-Heinemann.

Dalton. D., (2003) *Rethinking Corporate Security in the Post 9/11 Era* New York, Butterworth Heinemann.

Drennan. L. T., Mc Connell. A., Stark. A., (2007) *Risk and Crisis Management in the Public Sector* Oxon, Routledge.

Drucker. P., (1955) *Managing for Results* London, Routledge.

Engemann. K. J., (2018) *The Routledge Companion to Risk, Crisis and Security in Business* London, Routledge.

Evans. A., (2019) *Managing Cyber Risk* Oxon, Routledge.

Fischer. J. R., (2013) *Introduction to Security* Amsterdam, Elsevier.

Franklin. J., (1998) *The Politics of Risk Society* Cambridge, Polity Press.

Gill. M., (2014) *The Handbook of Security* London, Palgrave Macmillan.

International Organization for Standardization https://www.iso.org/home.html Accessed on 21 March 2022.

International Ship and Port facility Security Code (2004) London, International Maritim Organisation.

Macaulay. T., (2009) *Critical Infrastructure: Understanding Its Component Parts, Vulnerabilities, Operating Risks, and Interdependencies.* London, CRC Press.

Pegg Writing in the Guardian https://www.theguardian.com/world/2020/may/07/what-was-exercise-cygnus-and-what-did-it-find Accessed on 22 March 2020.

Pidgeon. N. F., Hood, C., Jones, D., Turner, B., Gibson, R. (1992) Risk Perception. In Risk: Analysis, Perception and Management. Report to the Royal Society Group. London, The Royal Society. In Swanson (2020).

Swanson. C., (2020) *Professional Security Management: A Strategic Guide* Oxon, Routledge.

Ulmer. R. Sellnow. T. Seeger. M. W., (2011) *Effective Crisis Communications: Moving from Crisis to Opportunity* London, Sage Publications.

## Notes

1 www.accountingcoach.com

2 https://en.wikipedia.org/wiki/Financial_crisis_of_2007%E2%80%932008 Accessed on 05 December 2020.

3 COBR or COBRA is shorthand for the Civil Contingencies Committee that is convened to handle matters of national emergency or major disruption. Its purpose is to coordinate different departments and agencies in response to such emergencies. COBR is the acronym for Cabinet Office Briefing Rooms, a series of rooms located in the Cabinet Office in 70 Whitehall. https://www.instituteforgovernment.org.uk/explainers/cobr-cobra.

4 https://www.theguardian.com/world/2020/may/07/what-was-exercise-cygnus-and-what-did-it-find.

5 Pangolin-The WWF defines a pangolin as the only mammals wholly covered in scales and they use those scales to protect themselves from predators

in the wild. If under threat, a pangolin will immediately curl into a tight ball and will use their sharp-scaled tails to defend themselves. https://www.worldwildlife.org/stories/what-is-a-pangolin Accessed on 28 October 2021.

6 https://www.app.college.police.uk/app-content/intelligence-management/analysis/#the-role-of-analysis Accessed on 19 February 2021.

7 Outside of the UK it is recommended that local law enforcement websites are searched for criminal statistics.

8 https://www.dictionary.com/browse/vulnerability Accessed on 31 December 2020.

9 https://deister.co.uk/solutions/guard-tour-systems?keyword=%2Bpatrol%20%2Bmanagement%20%2Bsystem&device=c&network=g&gclid=EAIaIQobChMIvuecsK_47QIVCZntCh1wVAlFEAAYASAAEgKHDvD_BwE Accessed on 31 December 2020.

10 https://www.macmillandictionary.com/dictionary/british/prevention Accessed on 10 January 2021.

11 https://www.macmillandictionary.com/dictionary/british/mitigation Accessed on 10 January 2021.

12 https://www.nesta.org.uk/toolkit/swot-analysis/?gclid=CjwKCAiA05qABhBdEiwAOtGmbqB0RCUDTvqvXOUVZrlqJUiLUBZFCYT7mYgDKfnCUsvOHEEsBGl_7hoC1LoQAvD_BwE Accessed on 19 January 2021.

13 https://corporatefinanceinstitute.com/resources/knowledge/strategy/pestel-analysis/ Accessed on 19 January 2021.

14 Information Security Management Systems (ISMS).

15 The Security Auditor/SME and the Board.

16 The National Research Council (NRC) is the operating arm of the United States National Academies of Sciences, Engineering, and Medicine and is overseen by a governing board that consists councilors from each of the three Academies. https://www.nationalacademies.org/home accessed 26 January 2021.

17 For cyber crime refer to https://www.ncsc.gov.uk/, and for terrorism information go to https://www.gov.uk/terrorism-national-emergency.

18 https://securityintelligence.com/posts/what-are-insider-threats-and-how-can-you-mitigate-them/ Accessed on 24 March 2021.

19 Fire walls, more effective virus protection, increased password protocols etc.

20 Protect Duty Consultation: Making the public safer at publicly accessible locations. https://assets.publishing.service.gov.uk/government/

uploads/system/uploads/attachment_data/file/964808/Protect_Duty_Consultation_Document5.pdf Accessed on 25 May 2021.

21 https://www.manchestereveningnews.co.uk/news/greater-manchester-news/manchester-bombing-what-happened-arena-13090977 Accessed on 25 May 2021.

22 https://manchesterarenainquiry.org.uk/chairman/ Accessed on 31 October 2021.

23 https://brc.org.uk/media/674208/crime-survey-2020.pdf.

24 1.1 billion Pounds relating to crime, and 1.0 billion Pounds spent of crime prevention methods.

25 https://www.forbes.com/sites/tjmccue/2019/01/31/inventory-shrink-cost-the-us-retail-industry-46-8-billion/?sh=15ec83236b70.

26 The asset information found in tables 18 and 19 are an alternative to the system of listing assets in a text form.

27 https://www.davemanuel.com/investor-dictionary/retail-shrinkage/ Accessed on 28 March 2021.

28 https://blog.netop.com/cyber-security-trends Accessed on 28 March 2021.

29 For obvious reasons, ways of evading the EAS will not be shared in this publication.

30 https://www.cpni.gov.uk/critical-national-infrastructure-0 Accessed on 07 April 2021.

31 https://assets.publishing.service.gov.uk/government/uploads/system/uploads/attachment_data/file/678927/Public_Summary_of_Sector_Security_and_Resilience_Plans_2017__FINAL_pdf___002_.pdf Accessed on 07 April 2021.

32 For detailed information about the ISPS Code, go to https://www.imo.org/en/OurWork/Security/Pages/SOLAS-XI-2%20ISPS%20Code.aspx.

33 A port facility is a facility e.g., a container terminal serving vessels that are ISPS Code certificated.

34 A TEU or Twenty-foot Equivalent Unit is an exact unit of measurement used to determine cargo capacity for container ships and terminals.

This measurement is derived from the dimensions of a 20 ft standardized shipping container. Because standard containers can be 20 or 40 ft in length the capacity of a container ship can depend on the ratio of the two sizes. https://www.freightright.com/kb/teu Accessed on 06 December 2021.

35 There are three levels of security, security levels 1, 2, and 3. Security Level 1 is when the facility or ship is at its lowest level of security, with minimum levels of access control. Security level 2 instructs the ship and port facility

to ensure that additional protective measures are in place, including an increase in access control. At security level 3, access control generally means that only the ships crew, or those employed at the port facility will be allowed to enter.

36 Other maritime nation states will have similar legislation.

37 https://www.legislation.gov.uk/ukpga/Edw7/6/41/contents.

38 See https://www.bbc.co.uk/news/world-europe-24539417 Accessed on 26 April 2021.

39 https://www.royalhaskoningdhv.com/en-gb/blog/transport/do-you-really-know-the-status-of-your-airports-it-systems-q/10361 Accessed on 06 May 2021.

40 https://cyberstartupobservatory.com/aviation-cybersecurity-major-challenges/ Accessed on 13 May 2021.

41 https://www.weforum.org/agenda/2016/07/four-threats-to-aviation-security-and-four-responses/ Accessed on 14 May 2021.

42 https://www.cpni.gov.uk/chemical-biological-radiological-and-nuclear-cbrn-threats Accessed on 15 May 2021.

43 https://www.crimemuseum.org/crime-library/kidnappings/tiger-kidnapping/ Accessed on 15 June 2021.

44 https://en.wikipedia.org/wiki/Murder_of_John_Lennon Accessed on 22 June 2021.

45 https://core.ac.uk/download/pdf/30732899.pdf Accessed on 22 June 2021.

46 https://www.bbc.co.uk/news/world-europe-57579574 Accessed on 23 June 2021.

47 https://www.theguardian.com/education/2010/dec/09/charles-camilla-car-attacked-fees-protest Accessed on 23 June 2021.

48 https://democracy.manchester.gov.uk/documents/s13150/Appendix%20 1%20-%20Martyns_Law_Final_Report.pdf accessed on 11 September 2021.

49 Go to https://www.gov.uk/government/publications/crowded-places-guidance/hostile-vehicle-mitigation-hvm for advice and guidance from HM Government.

50 https://assets.publishing.service.gov.uk/government/uploads/system/uploads/attachment_data/file/908586/MTA_Guidance_Making_Your_Organisation_Ready__OFFICIAL__OPEN_SOURCE_FINAL_V2.3.pdf Accessed on 11 September 2021.

# 2

# THE SECURITY SURVEY

> *Just a thought*
>
> In your own words what is a Security Survey?

The previous chapter covered risk and the risk assessment, focussing on the Security Risk Assessment, and it was reasonably straight forward to define a number of terms relative to risk, thanks to numerous search engines.

It's not so easy when trying to define the Security Survey, because of the often-perceived symbiotic relationship between the survey and the assessment. As argued constantly throughout the book, there is certainly an important relationship, but it isn't symbiotic. No, in my opinion, it isn't plausible to begin a Security Survey without having carried out the Security Risk Assessment, but a risk assessment can be standalone without having to move on to the Security Survey. In fact, that is very common.

DOI: 10.4324/9781003186335-3

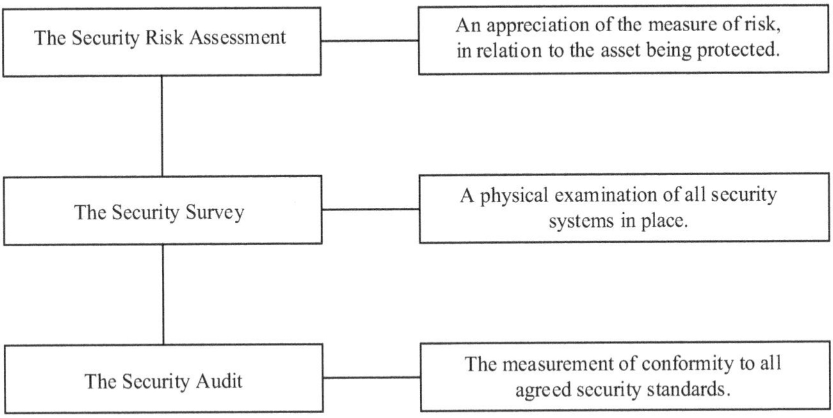


*Figure 8* The Risk Journey.

I have taught Security Surveying for several decades, and mostly my students, on day one when asked the question '*What in your opinion is the difference between a Security Risk Assessment, a Security Survey, and a Security Audit*', will either glaze over, or mutter something totally incomprehensible, but mainly, they don't know. That is key.

Remember how the Security Risk Assessment was defined earlier:

*The Security Risk Assessment is a process that identities threats from hostile actors who have the intention of causing harm by criminal acts.*

That is straight forward, but what is a Security Survey?

## Defence in Depth (DiD)

Before we examine the meaning of a physical Security Survey, critical to the process is a concept often referred to as Defence in Depth.

Interestingly, if you search for Defence in Depth, you will be met with a series of search solutions focussing on the protection of ICT systems, which of course is fine, but what we are now going to look at is how the concept helps us to protect the physical attributes of a target location.

Defence in Depth begins at the outside of the perimeter fence, and is incrementally introduced as the attacker attempts to advance towards the target, which for example is a nuclear processing plant. The idea is that his or her movements will be impeded by the integrated security system, which will either discourage their attempts or will assist in him or her being apprehended.

### *The Security Survey*

In their book *Risk Analysis and the Security Survey* (2012), Broder and Tucker quote Momboisse (1977) who defined the Security Survey as:

> *...a critical, on-site examination....to ascertain the present security status, identify deficiencies or excesses, determine the protection needed, and make recommendations to improve the overall security of the operation.*

I would simplify that by arguing that a Security Survey is the opportunity to examine all existing security systems to ensure that they are fit for purpose.

*Do they do what they were designed to do?*

So, having digested the contents and findings of an appropriate Security Risk Assessment, the next stage is to examine all security systems at the location/site in question, but this must be achieved in a logical and orderly manner, with the first task being the establishment of effective communications with the client. Critical to any Security Survey is understanding the customer's requirements, and the need to understand the scope of the survey.

## The customer

## Understanding customer needs

This is where a considerable percentage of security professionals struggle, an area of the survey that is critical, understanding the customer and the customer's needs. There are several considerations that must be examined, and research has to be undertaken before you even speak to your customer.

Some of the considerations will be:

### *Have you begun discussions with the customer/customer representative?*

From the moment you begin a dialogue with either the customer or his/her representative, keep a log of all conversations for reflection and audit purposes.

### *What is the role or position of whoever it is you have begun discussions with?*

This is critical, because far too often a junior manager or supervisor may begin the process, but he or she may not have operational or commercial authority for contractual negotiations. Ensure that you are speaking to the 'decision maker'.

### *Does the customer understand the concept of the Security Survey?*

This can be particularly sensitive, because the customer may have his or her perceptions about the definition of a Security Survey, and it can often take high levels of diplomatic skill to explain what is actually required.

#### *Key takeaway*

*Diplomacy is the key to a successful Security Survey.*

### *Does the customer have a scope of work?*

Once again this is critical, because the point of contact may not have the authority to draw up a scope of work, or the client may not understand the term. Remember, it is unlikely (not impossible of course) that the customer will be a security professional, so once again diplomacy is key.

### *Have costs been considered/discussed?*

It is likely that there will be some form of security budget, but you will need to wait until you believe it is the right time to discuss costs. This is a real test of operational diplomacy. Don't be seen as a used car salesman (No disrespect to vehicle salespersons of course).

### *Are there any operational or commercial sensitivities that may be confidential?*

The Security Survey by its very nature will be commercially and operationally sensitive, and you will need to investigate any increase in such sensitivities. It may be that the survey is being commissioned after a member of staff has been compromised or dismissed, so once again, diplomacy is the order of the day.

### *Has a Security Risk Assessment been carried out, and if so, has the customer seen the results?*

Ideally, a risk assessment will have been carried out in relation to the organisation and location, and the customer will have seen the results. This is a great opportunity for you to explain the relationship between the Security Risk Assessment and the Security Survey.

### *Have all laws and sector regulations been taken into account?*

All global locations will be legislated for and will be required to conform to national and international law. Sectors such as maritime, aviation, national infrastructure, and terrorism will have unique legislation and regulations that the Security Auditor must, at the earliest opportunity take into consideration and adhere to.

I cannot overstate the criticality of good customer communications, because this is an area where so many security professionals fail, or perhaps fall at the first hurdle. The implementation of a Security Survey can be seen as the ultimate test of confidence and indeed confidentiality because the Security Auditor is likely to witness operations and speak to on-site personnel, which brings with it of course, a need to prove confidentiality. The customer may insist that some form of Non-Disclosure Agreement (NDA) is signed, which will be legally binding, and really is the ultimate means of establishing confidentiality. Always read the small print of any legal document, and that of course includes an NDA. If you are unsure, don't agree to anything until the NDA has been examined by a legal advisor.

Always listen to what the customer has to say, and remember it is possible that he or she will be the risk owner and is therefore critical in this process.

## The six steps

As described earlier in this section, the Security Survey must be carried out in an organised manner, an approach that is logical and easy to follow, and it is generally agreed that there are six steps, which are:

1. Reasons for the survey.
2. Preliminary research.
3. Preparation.

4. Implementation of the survey (boots on the ground).
5. Post survey debrief.
6. The survey report.

> *Just a thought*
>
> What reasons might an organisation have for commissioning a Security Survey?

## Step 1: Reasons for the survey

Ideally, the Security Survey will be carried out as the result of a Security Risk Assessment, which in its report recommends further action. Ideally, the Executive Board or client should automatically authorise the survey, but that is perhaps unrealistic in practical terms because the Board generally tends to wait for something else to spur it on.

So, let's take a look at the main reasons for a Security Survey.

### *The Security Risk Assessment*

As mentioned, this is the ideal situation, and despite my previous remarks it should not be ignored or dismissed. If you recall, one of the Security Risk Assessment control measures is to reduce the level of risk, and that is achieved by the enhancement of physical and electronic security measures; all of which may be recommended as the result of a Security Survey. So, don't lose hope!

### *Insurance requirement*

Growing numbers of insurance brokers require enhanced security of a location before offering cover, and that of course makes a great deal of sense. Why would an insurance company offer cover against burglary, other than the fact that the security of the doors and windows, etc., is at an acceptable standard?

### *Organisational review*

Perhaps an organisational review is being carried out which necessitates a re-appraisal of operations, and maybe the location that requires the survey has moved from, let us say, an administrative building, to an archive containing sensitive commercial information or Research & Development data. The Board[1] has decided that current security support is lacking, and a Security Survey is required.

### *Laws and regulations*

Perhaps legislation, as the result of a terrorist attack, now demands that all public buildings are in need of a Security Survey. An example of this could be the forthcoming Martins Law, to be enacted after the Manchester Arena bombing in May 2017, during which 22 innocent people were killed by a suicide bomber, Salman Ramadan Abedi.[2]

### *New/changed threat(s)*

This is a common requirement for having a Security Survey carried out because the threat is never static, it is extremely dynamic. An example of this is the threat of a cyber-attack. Cybercrime has increased exponentially over the last decade, with cyber criminals being amongst the most potent offenders today. Prior to the increase in cybercrime, the onus would be for the owner of a location with ICT facilities to ensure that physical security was at an acceptable level, and that areas such as Human Resources, Cash Offices, etc., would be physically difficult to breach, but with the onslaught of cyber-crime, the threat has changed, and a Security Survey may be requested to ensure that all ICT facilities and networks are secured from a cyber-attack.[3]

### *As the result of crime*

Sadly, and of great concern is the fact that this is by far the most common reason for a Security Survey to be requested. Theoretically, it is difficult to understand why an organisation would wait until it has been attacked, before contemplating a Security Survey, but unfortunately, that is the harsh reality of business today. Perhaps those responsible for the safety and security of a location may not have the budget for a Security Survey, or maybe they disbelieve the evidence found in a Security Risk Assessment, or they may not trust the advice being given by the police. The most likely reason is the thought process which drives the argument that '*It will never happen to* me' or '*Why would anybody want to attack us? It's never happened before*. But whatever the reason is, far too often companies wait until they have been burgled or a member of staff has been attacked before they request a Security Survey.

Diplomacy warning!

> Never criticise your client for not having a Security Survey carried out until (in your opinion) it is too late, or after the event. They will have reasons for declining such a service, and that is their business, not yours!

## Step 2: Preliminary research

> *Reflection*
>
> Take a little time to reflect on how, and to what level you should research an organisation before you begin the Security Survey.

There is a famous military phrase, which is '*A day spent on recce (reconnaissance) is never wasted*', referring to the importance of research, and understanding what you are up against; research before a Security Survey is no different. Let us look at what we need to research before this leg of the Risk Journey.

Anybody who has ever attended a job interview will remember their stomach churning when asked the question '*What do you know about the company then?*' The worst case scenario is that you failed to research the organisation that you want to offer you employment! Even if you have carried out research, you still dread the thought of being asked that question, because you may have failed to investigate in sufficient detail, your hopefully new employer. Imagine being asked the question above, and your reply is, '*Sorry I haven't a clue*'. Interview finished; career short-lived. Certainly, with that company.

Security Auditors are in a similar position when they meet their potential clients because the first question to be asked will be, yep you guessed it'...*What do you know about the company then?*' Once again, if the auditor has failed to research the organisation that he/she is hoping to work with, the contract is terminated before it was signed, and the client will look for somebody more 'professional'. So once again I cannot overstate the importance of effective research, but where do you begin?

I began my involvement with security surveying at a time when there was an absolute reliance on public libraries, journals, and ...fax machines! So, the likelihood of carrying out any form of reliable research was extremely low; that is certainly not so today, as we live in an interconnected, globalised planet which, according to Schwab (2017) is undergoing the fourth industrial revolution, with digital communications being at the heart of this upheaval.

Today there are no excuses for not researching a potential client to the extent that we almost understand the organisation at an intimate level. But we still need to know where to start. So, let's take a look at a number of areas that should be on our research radar.

## *Aspects of research*

### *Company business operations*

Probably the most critical aspect of the Security Survey is understanding the company's business operations.

> *Pause for thought*
>
> Why is it important for the Security Auditor to have an early understanding of the organisations business operations?

This of course is all about risk and the risk appetite because risk acceptance will vary according to the nature and level of an organisations business operations.

For instance, as we have already discussed, British Utilities (BU) potential operations in Saudubai may be hampered because of the level of terrorist operations in the region. Naturally, BU wishes, indeed needs, to grow its business, particularly in light of the recent accident in Yemen; but the safety of its personnel must be an extremely high priority. Alternatively, a bank or other types of financial institution will accept relatively high levels of risk, because unless the risk is taken, business development will be extremely limited.

Retail is another sector, in a vaguely similar situation as financial institutes, that has a preponderance to put sales before security risk; without sales, there is no retail business.

## Scenario

### *Retail case study: the electrical retailer*

Several years ago, when I was a Regional Security Manager with a national electrical retail company, I was exposed to a sales tactic that I believed would end in disaster. Year on year sales for the retailer had been extremely unhealthy, and in what I believed was an act of sheer economic lunacy, the Sales Director issued an edict that would either make or break sales figures for quarter 4 of that year.

The Sales Director received permission to lead a sales drive in two regions of the UK that had recorded the highest crime rates in the country for that year: Liverpool and Newcastle upon Tyne.

It was decided that in all stores in the two regions, a total of eight outlets, live VCR boxes[4] would be placed just inside the main entrance/exit, with the rationale being that customers would pick up a live VCR box on their way into the shop and take it directly to the Point of Sale (PoS), pay for it and leave. The normal procedure was for the customer to identify the product of their choice, and a member of staff would retrieve it from the secure area to the rear of the shop and bring it to the PoS where it would be paid for and handed to the customer. It was envisaged by the sales team that the system of staff retrieving VCRs from the secure area and transporting it to the PoS would add to the time taken to achieve a sale while allowing customers to pick up the product as they entered the shop would actually increase sales. I was not convinced, and shop managers in the two regions referred to the system as 'pick and nick', alluding to the argument that of course theft of boxed VCRs would increase exponentially, and they were correct.

When an audit of the period was carried out during quarter 1, it was ascertained that shrinkage relating to theft had increased by 6%, mainly of course due to the theft of VCRs, and I was tasked with compiling a report about the increase in theft for the attention of, yes you have it, the Sales Director. The report was duly received at Board level, and the Sales Director had the courtesy of to reply directly to me a couple of weeks later.

In her letter, she expressed remorse at the increase in theft, which was about 6%, but she went on to inform me that sales over the same period, including VCRs, had increased by 23%.

Thank you very much.

### *Company background and the security culture*

The company background and security culture are often intertwined, and the Security Auditor needs to understand each one before he or she is confident that they appreciate the combination. Hope that makes sense. Let's look at a couple of examples.

- **The family business.**
  The family business is built on trust, and in general, that means an unwavering belief that within the family crime either doesn't exist, or the perpetrators will be 'outsiders', and will be swiftly apprehended and dealt with (whatever that means). For the Security Auditor, this can often be a problem because it is likely that the business owner (s) has requested a Security Survey because of the demands of their insurance broker, or perhaps on the advice of the local police Crime Reduction Officer. The Security Survey is likely to be seen as a necessary evil, *'....so the sooner it is over and done with, the better'*.

  It can often be an uphill struggle to convince this type of client, whose sole interest is the survival and growth of the family business, that the creation of a security culture throughout the business will be in his or her best interest, and that begins with an effective and transparent Security Survey. As always, trust is critical.

- **The corporate organisation.**
  The corporate organisation, whether it is a multi-site bank, or perhaps a global communications company, or an oil and gas corporation, such as BU is highly likely to have developed in size and operational capacity over a period in time. The organisation will be managed on a corporate scale, probably governed by an Executive Board of Directors, led by a Chief Executive Officer (CEO), and critical to the survival of the company will be a series of policies, plans, and procedures that will include Security Risk Management.

Company shareholders, aware of the importance of stable security will insist that the Executive Board instills a security culture within the organisation; a culture that will be led by the Senior Management Team and cascaded to all levels of the company.

So, whether the location to be security surveyed is a small family business, or a multinational corporation, one of your first tasks is to establish the lineage of the organisation and confirm that a security culture exists within the company. One means of achieving this is to investigate whether previous Security Surveys have taken place, and if they have, whether there are existing Security Survey Reports that can be examined.

It is by no means a certainty that previous Security Surveys have been carried out, and even if they have, there is no guarantee that subsequent reports exist, but if they do, they will be of great value to you.

So, let us assume that a previous Security Survey has been carried out, and perhaps if you are fortunate, within the last two years; your first task as a Security Auditor is to assure the client that releasing any subsequent reports will be of assistance to your current Security Survey endeavours. That it is in his or her best interests to discharge it to you.

The first thing you need to do once in possession of the report is, to establish the credibility of the author who carried out the previous Security Survey. Easier said than done I'm afraid, but a critical part of the process.

It may be that you know the author personally, and you have read his or her work in the past, or perhaps you belong to the same professional body as them, but you will still need to read the report in detail in order for you to decide if it is appropriate. It is possible that you may have to ask a colleague for a second opinion, but never forget the importance of client confidentiality.

Once you have established the credibility of the Security Survey Report, the next task is to decide if the recommendations made in the report are correct and if the client has agreed to and implemented them.

### *Reflection*

Think long and hard about this question. If the client has not agreed with, nor implemented what you believe to be credible recommendations, what should your line of thought be? Why do you think the recommendations have been ignored?

So, let us think about this.

Based on your personal and professional judgement, utilising whatever research means are available, you have decided that the author of the previous Security Survey Report has made a number of appropriate and sensible recommendations, which have not, however, been implemented by the client.

The first question you must ask yourself is '*why have the recommendations not been implemented?*'

### ⚠ Diplomacy warning!

Now you are going to require the skills of an international diplomat, because you have to approach the client and ask him or her why they decided to ignore, what in your professional opinion, are a series of recommendations that make a great deal of sense.

This is a time for cool heads and diplomatic reflection because there could be several reasons why previous recommendations have been ignored; let's examine a few.

## *Crime Pattern Analysis (CPA)*

This phase of preparedness is critical because the auditor and the client need to understand crime rates in the area of the survey; offences that may impact the business. For instance, the Operations Director at a distribution centre may not be particularly interested in bicycle theft, but he or she will need to know the rates of burglary and vehicle theft close to their location. In most developed countries, members of the public are likely to have access to law enforcement crime rates which will allow them to carry out a Crime Pattern Analysis (CPA) of their particular area. In the UK we are fortunate to have access to such statistics through www.police.uk Take a little time to feed your post code into the site, and you may be pleasantly surprised at the level of information available.

### *Cost*

Cost is likely to be the first reason why the client has chosen to potentially dismiss the recommendations made in a credible Security Survey Report, particularly during times when fiscal awareness is first on the agenda of every Board of Directors conversation. Every penny spent is scrutinised, and Heaven help the Chief Finance Officer who overspends. So cost is very often the first consideration.

Inevitably, when invited to comment on the cost of a Security Survey or its recommendations, the client having previously argued for quality is likely to scream '*What. How much?*', but that is almost a knee-jerk reaction requiring justification for spend. Equally, there is likely to be the argument that crime rates have historically been low, and why should the client believe the auditor; and anyway '*...we can't afford that much I'm afraid*'.

Once again this is a time for diplomacy. Let us deal with the two rebuffs one at a time.

**Crime rates have historically been low, and therefore why should the client believe the Auditor?**
Similar to the Security Risk Assessment, the Security Survey is heavily reliant on the provision of credible, corroborated evidence. The strategy is to use the compiled evidence from the Security Risk Assessment, and the research carried out prior to the Security Survey. It is quite futile advising the client that he or she should take your advice because '...I am an experienced security professional, and I know what I'm talking about.' A weak argument. It's all about evidence.

**'...we can't afford that much I'm afraid".**

This rebuff is a little more difficult to overcome because you won't have a full understanding of the financial resources of the client, but you must empathize with him or her.

Generally, the most effective approach to this problem after initial discussions about cost, and perhaps when the client says that he or she can't afford the survey, or its recommendations, is to be diplomatic with your response. Having explained the need for a Security Survey, and perhaps the consequences of an attack, it's always worthwhile asking the client to consider the impact on his or her organisation, and then ask them if they can afford NOT to have the survey or follow your recommendations.

Don't forget the need for diplomacy! Be aware that this is one of the most sensitive discussions you will ever have with your client or potential client, as nobody generally likes debating finance, and it is often the first barrier.

### *Time*

*Don't waste your time with explanations: people only hear what they want to hear.*

Paolo Coelho

*I couldn't find the time to read the Security Survey Report, I was far too busy, and my in tray was always full.*

Charles Swanson

When confronted with what you may see as an excuse, it is far too easy to dismiss it as nonsense, with phrases such as '*Well make time*' or '*Perhaps you should manage your diary better*', but remember that is not your role. If the client informs you that he or she has been pushed for time, I am not saying that you must believe them, but being professional dictates that once again, it is their business, not yours. I would never go as far as to say that the customer is always right, but I would argue vehemently that the customer is always the customer, who must be respected.

### *Disagreement*

From my experience this is a rarity, but of course if the customer decides that the recommendations made in the previous report lack credibility, then once again that is their opinion. However, as opposed to arguing that they should have sufficient funds to cover the cost of such recommendations, or they should make time to read them, in this instance you have the opportunity to convince the customer that the recommendations have been made in good faith, and actually (if you believe this to be the case) they are very sensible and worthy of his or her consideration.

Diplomacy warning!

Never be perceived to be taking sides against the client in favour of the previous surveyor. Don't risk being referred to as '*Bloody security, their all the same*' or '*Another consultant trying to make a quick buck*'. Diplomatic neutrality is the order of the day.

### *Criminal intent*

There is of course the possibility that your client has intentionally ignored all of the report recommendations, perhaps, unknown to you, because he or she is involved in some form of criminal activity. There are numerous reasons why this may be the case, but it isn't the responsibility of the Auditor to investigate any potential crimes. Rather, he or she, whilst being cognisant of the fact that criminal activity may have taken place, is there to survey, not criminally investigate.

*Reflection*

Here is a scenario for you to give some thought to.

During the Security Survey, the possibility of the client being involved in some form of criminality is brought to your attention. What will your actions be?

This is a dilemma that I hope you are never involved in, as there is no absolute solution, and it is not for me to advise you on the course of action to be taken. I can only say that integrity and principle are impossible to put a price tag on, and only you can decide what to do under such circumstances. I know what I would do because I've been there, but you must look at yourself in the mirror before taking what you believe to be the appropriate action.

As you can see, there are several reasons why your client may decide not to respond to the recommendations made in the previous survey report, and it isn't the responsibility of the Security Auditor to cast judgement, rather you should see it as one of many challenges that you must respond to in a professional manner. Once you are comfortable that you have carried out the appropriate levels of research required to continue with the survey process, the next step is for you to prepare.

## Step 3: Planning and preparation

*Give me six hours to chop down a tree and I will spend the first four sharpening the axe.*
Abraham Lincoln.[5]

There is also the six P's.

*Prior Planning and Preparation Prevents Poor Performance*[6]

If you were to put the following question to any professional "What is the most important part of your job", undoubtedly the answer would be "Planning and preparation".

The surgeon before carrying out an operation, the teacher prior to assembling her class, or the military officer contemplating some form of warfare; all must plan and prepare. Why should a security professional intending to carry out a Security Survey of a high-tech data centre or a power station be any different? Of course not.

The Security Auditor who arrives on site after *failing to plan… is planning to fail.*[7] The same Auditor should arrive at the data centre fully prepared for everything that he or she considers relevant. That of course is easier said than done, but experience tells me that there are certain activities that must be carried out before the Security Survey.

Think about the following considerations:

### *Maps and diagrams*

This I am sure must seem such a basic requirement; why wouldn't the professional Security Auditor ensure that he or she was armed with the appropriate maps/routes to the survey location and floor diagrams/schematics of the site? Of course, they would!

Unfortunately, experience tells me otherwise, and far too often this hasn't been a major consideration. Imagine the embarrassment of arriving late because you hadn't carried out a map appreciation of the route, and sat-nav sent you down a one-way street from which it was difficult to extricate yourself from, and you were forced to telephone the client and ask for the best way to his or her location!

Equally, because you had forgotten to ask the client to have floor diagrams available for you during the survey, you find yourself aimlessly wandering around a large oil refinery, constantly asking staff for directions.

### *Authorisation (crucial)*

Picture the scene at the Security Control Room of a sensitive data centre that you have just arrived at to carry out a critical Security Survey, and when you present yourself at the Reception Window, announcing who you are, and your reason for the visit, you are met with '*Sorry mate, your names not on the list*', and nobody from Head Office had informed the Site Security Manager of your intentions. Wow!

#### *Reflection*

What would you think if the Security Officer or Site Security Manager said "No worries pal, in you come, I'm sure there must have been a mistake? Where would you like to begin, the data halls?"

I have only experienced this once, and it had the potential to be very embarrassing. The Site Manager apologised profusely because he couldn't allow me access to the site as he had no authority, and my response was that it was my fault for not confirming and ensuring that the site was ready for me. I remember considering it at the time and explaining to the Site Manager that I would have been far more uncomfortable if the Site Manager had given me permission to enter without authority. What do you think?

### Changes in laws and regulations

Prior to the site visit, the Security Auditor must take into consideration any changes or developments in laws and regulations that may impact the survey. For example, and this is entirely feasible, there may be alterations to health and safety legislation, with the most common act being the Health & Safety at Work Act (1974), constantly evolving. Equally, and most recently the General Data Protection Regulations (GDPR) were enacted by law in 2016, and for all intents and purposes, this legislation replaced certain parts of the Data Protection Act (1998). Both pieces of legislation will of course impact the Security Survey, and therefore the professional Security Auditor must ensure that he or she is constantly updated in relation to changes in law and regulations.

### Social media

We live in an age where it could be argued that social media and social engineering have taken over our lives, whether it is Facebook, LinkedIn, Twitter, or whatever platform suits the individual or the organisation. We can learn a great deal about organisation individuals and corporate approaches by investigating social media platforms, not least when there have been promotions or changes of roles.

### Specific contacts

This may seem to be less important than other areas of preparation, but it is critical to identify key personalities, and then build a solid professional relationship with them; a relationship that develops during the course of the project, one that is built on reciprocal trust.

### Camera (smartphone)

I always advocate the use of a camera or smartphone to take photographs during the survey, but a word of caution. In the UK, most organisations are fairly relaxed about photos being taken at their location, except for sensitive areas such as data halls or R&D labs, but it is still critical to have permission to take photographs, preferably in writing. It may not be so easy in other countries, particularly in the US or the Middle East, where people tend to be a little more nervous than in the UK or most of Europe. Always be aware of local laws, and always ask permission to use your camera or smartphone.

### *Identification*

The UK can generally be counted in a minority of global countries where its citizens are not mandated by law to carry some form of photographic identity, and there are historical democratic reasons for this; Brits don't like being told what to do! However, my advice is to always carry some form of identity, such as a driving licence or a passport, because it can save a great deal of argument and debate when you appear on site.

### *Agreed visit times and dates*

Agreed visit times and dates will have been made during the early stages of the Security Survey, and it is important for such arrangements to be in place throughout the project. Remember that the client needs to trust the Auditor, and if appointments are constantly being postponed and re-arranged, such trust may be lost.

### *Transport arrangements (parking etc.)*

There is the possibility that the survey may take a number of days, and it is always to the advantage of the Auditor to ensure that he or she has arranged for a car parking space whilst on site.

Remember, time spent in preparation is never wasted!

## Step 4: Implementing the survey

### *The initial reconnaissance*

I can't overstate the importance of reconnaissance (recce), but I can repeat a very well-known military saying, which is:

*A day spent on recce is never wasted.*

The first comment to make is that the location to be security surveyed will look different when visited during daylight, as opposed to when examined during the hours of darkness.

Very often, sitting opposite the building, perhaps in a café having a cup of tea for twenty minutes, will offer the Security Auditor the opportunity to view the main entrance at which there may be Security Officers on duty. How efficient are they? Are they interacting with staff and visitors or are they merely in attendance without contributing to access control? You may see members of staff entering the building, using their access control cards. If access is Personal Identity Number (PIN) controlled, how easy is it for passersby or visitors to see the code being entered? Is there any form of piggyback occurring, when perhaps a member of staff has forgotten his or her card? Has no passback software been considered, or are staff using one card to allow multiples entrance to the building?

During the hours of darkness, the environment is different for a number of reasons. Very obviously lighting is less effective, perhaps because a number of lights are inoperative, offering the criminal a safer passage. The security team is often diluted during the night, and although there may have been three or four Security Officers on duty during the day, for some obscure reason, there is perhaps only one member of the security team available at night.

The reconnaissance is also the initial stage of an examination of the Defence in Depth concept, so, if possible, try to carry out a recce during the day and also during the hours of darkness. At this stage, thinking like a criminal is critical, because you will need an understanding of how easy it is to gain access to the premises.

## Physical penetration test

Diplomacy warning!

This is an incredibly sensitive phase of the Security Survey because naturally, the client needs the assurance that their premises are watertight but lurking in the background will be the realisation that in practical terms that is unlikely to be the case.

The initial stage of the penetration test is the discussion with the client, who may be reluctant, and that of course is his or her prerogative, so once again, diplomacy is critical.

If permission to carry out the penetration test is granted the first thing you must do is have it included in the signed scope of work.

In terms of the penetration test, your aim is to breach the access control protocols of the location, day and night, by any *subtle* means at your disposal, not by physically breaking a door or window to gain access. This is not a special forces operation; if challenged, you must explain the situation to ascertain the security awareness of whoever made the challenge, because very often, with a smile and an air of confidence the Security Auditor will be able to convince the member of staff or the Security Officer that they have lost their pass, and that they are just about to report it to security, or reception.

The worst case scenario is that you will have to attempt to breach a Defence in Depth strategy, so let's take a look at what you may need to do, stage by stage.

### Step 1

During the recce phase, carry out a 360-degree appreciation of either the perimeter fence or the outside of the building. This means discretely circumnavigating the first line of defence in an effort to discover a hole in the fence, or a fire exit held open to allow easy access and egress of staff, perhaps for a smoke break. This is very common, and if you are able to access the location by either breaching the fence or the fire exit, you are now illegally on your client's premises.

From here, the plan is to access an internal area of the location, one agreed with the client. This may be the ICT server room, the Security Control Room, or perhaps even the Executive Board Room. Wherever you have agreed to attempt a breach, it will be a restricted area, one that if attacked could cause considerable damage to the business and its operations.

### Step 2

If it impossible to access the location during stage 1, you will need to think about the robustness of the location access control system, and that means potentially challenging access control at either the main entrance or perhaps the goods inwards entrance.

In the first instance, it will be to your advantage to find a discrete location to observe the entrances, perhaps from a car to the rear of the building, looking at the goods inwards doors, or a café opposite the main entrance. This will give you the chance to appreciate operations and security at both entrances.

### *Goods inwards*

The goods inwards or goods in, as the entrance is often referred to, is an extremely busy area of the building, often operating on a 24/7 basis, with goods in staff focusing on deliveries that are often critical to the operations of the building.

The area is likely to be well lit, supported by CCTV, and very often the building security team, and because of such restrictions it may be difficult to breach, but it is always worth the effort.

### *Main entrance*

The business will focus most of its security attention on the main entrance because it is used by staff, management and visitors. Because it is a public entrance, it will be relatively simple to access the main reception area, which is likely to be robustly supported by good lighting, CCTV, and on-duty Security Officers. However, there will be times when the reception area is busy, and perhaps the Security Officer (s) will be away from the area for a number of reasons, and that may be the time to attempt penetration.

### ***Step 3***

Whether you have accessed the building via the goods in doors, or the main entrance, it is now likely (and this is the criminal thought process) that security standards will drop because staff believe that it is difficult to penetrate the outer security procedures, and their 'guard will be down'. This is a false sense of security which is quite common.

### ⚠ Diplomacy warning!

This is not a time for celebration, or self-achievement, because you have discovered a major flaw in the security defences of your client's building, rather, this is an opportunity to foster relations with him or her by proving your integrity.

### ***Step 4***

In a controlled fashion, your client must be informed of the results of the penetration test as soon as possible, particularly if you have been successful in your efforts to breach his or her defences.

The client is likely to request a formal penetration test report, and my recommendation is that you write it as a separate document to the Security Survey Report, and if possible, deliver it by hand yourself.

Keep the report factual, in chronological order, and as easy as possible to read and reflect upon.

Remember also that you may be asked to deliver a formal presentation to the Executive Board in relation to your findings.

Following the penetration test, you will begin the physical Security Survey by speaking to on-site personnel.

### *On site interviews of critical personnel*

The combination of effective interviews of a broad cross section of site/organisation personnel and a thorough examination of all security systems in situ will offer insight into the security culture of the organisation.

### ***Exercise "To be or not to be..."***

#### *Client A*

During the recce carried out on the night before the Security Survey was to take place, the Auditor made a note that the Duty Security Officer, as could be seen through the front window, was watching television, and paying little attention to movement in and out of the front entrance.

Whilst waiting in the reception area, the Security Auditor noticed that the access control barriers were not fitted with anti-passback facilities, because a number of staff had been seen passing their access control cards to colleagues behind them. It was also clear that a significant number of staff and management were not wearing their identity card lanyards, and this was being ignored by security staff.

Finally, although she was wearing a visitors pass, the Security Auditor was allowed to wander the building unchallenged.

**Verdict: Very weak security culture**

#### *Client B*

During the recce carried out during the night before the Security Survey was to take place, the Security Auditor was challenged on two occasions by extremely civil, but alert Security Officers.

Upon arrival at the site to be examined, the Security Auditor was asked if she could produce some form of identification at the entrance to the building. She was then shown to the reception area, where she was accompanied by a Security Officer until her escort arrived. She was escorted throughout the day, and upon speaking to a cross section of staff and management it was clear that territoriality was practised throughout the building.

**Verdict: A strong security culture.**

> *Pause for thought*
>
> Who are the most important people to speak to on-site?

This is an area too often ignored when Security Surveys are carried out; either ignored, or poorly approached. The keys to this phase are understanding who should be spoken to, in what order, and what questions should be asked.

Who, when, and what?

### *Who?*

Whilst the choice isn't limitless, it is likely that site personnel will want to speak to you, and you must identify personnel and appointments who will bring value to the survey. In reality, that is everyone from the contract Security Officer manning the main entrance to Executive Board members, all of whom will have something meaningful to say, but in what order?

### *When?*

This is now a matter of prioritisation, although in reality you will have to adhere to the diaries of those you wish to speak to, and that of course can be frustrating. The key to this stage is to plan well ahead, with an understanding that when the time comes to speak to Joe the Security officer, Andrea the Receptionist, or Sarah the Operations Director, you have an appropriate list of open-ended questions relating to who you are speaking to.

## *What?*

It is probably fair to say that Joe is unaware of the strategic planning of the organisation, or perhaps when the last security review took place, equally, Sarah will have no idea of the local crime patterns, or where the CCTV and lighting 'black spots' are. Andrea knows everybody who comes and goes, and that is where her main strengths lie. But what questions should be asked, and how should the interview be structured?

## *Questioning by type*

- **Semi-structured**

Allison Doyle in June 2020 explained that a semi-structured interview is a meeting in which the interviewer does not strictly follow a formalised list of questions. Instead, they will ask more open-ended questions, allowing for a discussion with the interviewee rather than a straightforward question-and-answer format.

The semi-structured interview allows for a modicum of structure, but not to the point where all questions are closed through the bureaucracy.

In this type of interview, the interviewer may prepare a list of questions but won't necessarily ask them all, or touch on them in any particular order, using them instead to guide the conversation. In some cases, the interviewer will prepare only a list of general topics to be addressed.[8]

- **Open ended questions**

The open-ended question allows for dialogue and discussion. For example, you may ask the on-site Security Officer what his role is and how long he has worked on that particular site. Or you may ask the ICT Manager when the network was last penetration tested, what was the procedure and how were the results measured.

- **Closed questions**

The closed question only requires a yes or no answer. For example, are you a licenced Security Officer, or is the network ISO 27001 certificated? It doesn't require any form of discussion or explanation. A simple yes or no is all that is required.

### *Security policies, plans, and procedures. Have they been adhered to?*

If you are given access to any site security policies, plans, and procedures from a previous survey, it will offer you a clear indication of the security culture of the organisations that have requested the survey.

Also, as described earlier in the book, if you agree with the observations made, and the advice given by your predecessor, and they have not been adhered to, it may be an indication that there are issues that need to be resolved. However, remember the importance of client confidentiality, and the criticality of the need for diplomacy.

### *Existing security systems in place*

Security Auditor. "*Who on earth chose these pretty worthless security systems?*"
Client. "*Me*"
Security Auditor. "Gulp…."

Diplomacy warning!

The easiest way of losing a contract is to criticise the client. The systems may not be perfect…but they are his or her systems.

There are two ways of examining the security systems in situ. You can paw over schematics and diagrams, whilst listening to the client or his/her operators, who are almost bound to defend every system down to its last working component.

Or you can ask about the limitations of the systems,[9] and then ask to see each component in action. Let's take a look at some of the systems and balance the pros and cons of each.

### *Policies, plans, and procedures*

If available, access to the relevant security policies, plans and procedures will afford you critical knowledge about the site, the organisation, and its security culture. Documentation such as the Site-Specific Assignment Instructions (SSAI's), which cover the requirements for contract manned guarding, Emergency Procedures, Evacuation Plans, and so on, if available should be read in detail prior to the Security Survey.

### Perimeter security

Perimeter security is the first line of defence for any location, and there are a number of areas that require examination during the Security Survey:

#### Type

The first consideration when examining the perimeter is whether either the fence, wall, or hedge line meets the needs of a Security Risk Assessment (SRA) and if it has been selected as the result of an Operational Requirement process.[10]

The range of perimeter security equipment is considerable, and as opposed to listing every option, you are advised to consult the CPNI Catalogue of Security Equipment, which may be found at https://www.cpni.gov.uk/cse-categories.

#### Maintenance and repair

Always walk the full length of the perimeter because it is only by applying that level of detail will you be able to decide if the equipment being examined is fit for purpose.

Think about the Ronseal paint analogy, *does it do what it says on the side of the tin?*

Of course, it is important to examine every aspect of the perimeter, whether it is a hole in the perimeter fence, a wall that is easy to climb, or a Security Officer who looks totally disinterested in his or her role on site. You have to establish, as with other items of equipment covered in this section, whether the perimeter is fit for purpose, but once again you must look at it from the perspective of the offender...*thinking like a criminal*...but why?

> *Just a thought*
>
> What will the criminal think if he or she sees a hole in the fence or a light that hasn't been operating for a number of days?

As security professionals, we examine analytics and analyse metrics...the criminal merely wants to know how he or she can successfully attack us. So, whilst you and I are spinning a business case that will, through our ingenuity and genius impress the Chief Finance Officer to the point where she graciously agrees to a 250-pounds budget alignment which will allow us to repair the 1-metre breach of the perimeter chain link fence, the criminal has carried out his risk assessment and decided to enter the premises through the hole; into an area that he believes (probably correctly) will be bereft of effective security.

You see the burglar looks at it this way; if sufficient funding hasn't been raised to repair a small hole, a week after it appeared, then it is likely that the security finance cupboard is empty, and the building will be easy pickings.

I am not so naive to think that funding can be raised overnight, but my argument is that any delay is music to the ears of the criminal; so, maintenance and repairs are critical, both in terms of securing the location, and the psychological signal sent to the criminal.

## Integrated security and perimeter security

> *Just a thought*
>
> What does the term integrated security mean?

Throughout the location to be security surveyed, the integration of security systems is important, but as the perimeter is the second layer of Defence in Depth, after the environment, and the location first line of defence, it is critical; but what does the term integrated security mean?

If you search for the term integrated security, you will find that the emphasis is on ICT platforms that support a number of security solutions, and that is fine. However, for the Security Survey we need to be a little more detailed, and a lot more flexible.

For example, without a doubt, the integration of CCTV, access control, intruder detection, lighting, and communication is far more effective when designed to be managed on a single platform, and through the use of one management system.

We are relating to a single end user in some form of Security Control Room who is able to control and manage all of those functions from one platform. For the Security Survey, such systems will need to be seen performing with synergy, that is to say, what happens if one of the named systems fails, is redundancy in place to ensure the failed system is compensated, and that there is no 'knock on effect'.

For example, should the lighting fail, is there back up illumination to allow for CCTV surveillance? If the Intruder Detection Systems (IDS) fails, will the access control systems compensate, and will the guard force be informed of the intruder detection failure?

The Security Auditor should examine the system under all circumstances, particularly when there are systems failures; what are plans b, c, d, etc.?

## *Access control*

As explained earlier in the book, access control is critical for the safety and security of any location, and it begins with the first line of defence and the first point of entry, which in this case is the perimeter, and access points therein.

## *External*

### The perimeter

After ascertaining the type of fence or wall in place, you must travel the length of the external boundary, because only by examining the entire perimeter will you be in a position to make a judgement about its levels of integrity, that is to say, the standards of maintenance and repair, and the operational effectiveness of all complementary systems. i.e., CCTV, lighting, PIDS, etc.

As with all other areas of the Security Survey, photography will be an excellent aid when explaining issues discovered, such as gaps in the fence line, a broken PIDS-taught wire, or inoperative lighting. There is every probability that the client and his or her staff will not be aware of flaws found in and around the perimeter.

A well-designed and implemented outer fence may consist of a 3-metre-high welded steel mesh construction, supported by a taught wire PID and roller spikes at the top. The inner fence is electrified and is also supported by a PID. Should pressure be brought to bear against either of the fences, the reaction time from the guard force was a maximum of thirty seconds.

## *Fence mounted*

The piezoelectric sensor cable is installed to the structure (the perimeter fence) that needs some form of protection. Audible signals and vibrations are generated during an intrusion, and they are transmitted to a seismic analyser for detection of activation. The analyser detection channels are programmed to detect penetration, pressure, cutting, breaking, climbing, and efforts to take out the system.

One of the main advantages of using any form of barrier-mounted PIDS is the presence of a barrier which provides a physical delay to the intruder's progress. Introducing a delay can assist in the verification and response processes which are initiated following an alarm. There are different advantages and disadvantages between the two generic categories of barrier-mounted PIDS – fabric-mounted PIDS and post-mounted PIDS. Within these two sub-categories, there are differences between systems using different technologies.

## *Ground-based PIDS*

The main advantage of ground-based PIDS is covertness, such that even a knowledgeable attacker should have no awareness of the presence of the system. This feature can make ground-based PIDS a good early warning system at the far perimeter of a site, giving security personnel additional time in which to apprehend any intruders Disadvantages of ground-based PIDS include high cost due to the ground works which must be undertaken to install most systems. Installation can cause considerable disruption, and together with the ground-settling and commissioning periods it may take quite some time to get a system fully up and running. Ground-based PIDS provides no delay or deterrence as there is no physical barrier. There are several different types of ground-based PIDS, each with its own strengths and weaknesses.

### *Radio frequency (RF) radiating field systems*

These systems can produce good overall performance. They have good discrimination between animal target sizes but are still susceptible to some false alarm causes, notably due to accumulated water following heavy rainfall.

### *Microphonic cable systems*

These PIDS offer reasonable performance at a modest price. Installation cost and disruption can be minimised for some systems by installing the cables directly into a small slot cut into the ground rather than requiring a wide trench. They can suffer false alarms from wildlife, and as with all systems that directly detect ground vibrations, microphonic cable PIDS can be vulnerable to heavy traffic in the vicinity and the pressure transmitted by the roots of trees and other vegetation that are moving in heavy wind.

### *Optical-Fibre cable systems*

The sensor cable of an Optical-Fibre (Fibre-Optic) system is immune to RF interference. As optical-fibre systems generally use one cable run for a whole perimeter, an installation can often require just one processing unit and power supply. However, the processing unit of such systems can be high cost, meaning that it can be an expensive solution for short perimeters. For longer perimeters, their price per linear metre can drop to an affordable level.

### *Balanced fluid-filled tube systems*

These systems can produce good detection and false alarm performance although covertness may be compromised by the requirement for access pits used to pressurise the tubes. This type of system tends to have a higher maintenance overhead as it is recommended that pressure checks are carried out at least annually.

### *Free-standing PIDS*

The main advantages of a free-standing PIDS system are reduced installation costs due to no requirement for a physical barrier, add to this is the fact that a lower level of groundwork is required. They do not hinder legitimate activity, such as the movement of vehicles, and if required, installations can be designed to be discreet/covert.

The main disadvantage however relates to the lack of a physical barrier offering delay to an intruder, meaning that a prompt response to alarms is required as an attacker can be well within the site within seconds.

However, free-standing PIDS can act as a first line of defence if they are constructed to surround and therefore offer cover to a perimeter fence/wall.

There are several different types of free-standing PIDS, with their own strengths and weaknesses.

### *Active Infrared Systems (AIS)*

The Active Infrared Detection system uses infrared light to activate an alarm. When the beam is severed, the systems can be installed to ensure reliable and accurate detection.

### *Passive Infrared Systems (PIR)*

These systems are not recommended for use as the primary detection solution for outdoor environments as their poor immunity to changing temperatures can result in either a very poor detection rate or a very high false alarm rate.

### *Doppler microwave systems*

Doppler microwave systems use one transmitter/receiver (transceiver) unit, and a maximum range can be defined, beyond which targets can move undetected. Such PIDS can be used to cover the dead zones of other free-standing PIDS or where activity beyond the required detection zone might cause false alarms, as is the case with other technologies (such as PIR)

### *Video-based detection systems*

Often referred to as ‘trip wires’, video-based detection systems (VBDS) are systems that analyse the video from CCTV systems and are designed to be able to automatically detect unusual activity within an imaged scene.[11]

The perimeter fence is supported by very effective high-pressure sodium security lighting, and digital CCTV which in itself is supported by movement detection software. This should include all access points.

By access points, I mean those entrances and exits used by staff, visitors and contractors. The single most important rule to follow here is that all access points should be kept to a minimum, with the maximum levels of protection being given.

Generally, the perimeter main access point will be controlled by a Security Officer, either manually, i.e., by opening the gate or lifting a barrier, or perhaps remotely from the Security Control Room.

The main access point should receive at least the same levels of security protection as any other section of the perimeter, and this should consist of an integrated security system with full electronic compatibility.

## Internal

Once you are content with the protection being afforded to the location perimeter, you should pay attention to the main building (s), which of course should be secure to the same level as the perimeter. The difference of course is the building (s) may consist of a number of internal locations and are likely to be several stories high. So let us take a look at the various aspects of the main building. This is where a robust and easy-to-manoeuvre Security Survey template is incredibly valuable. We will begin by examining a number of types of internal access control systems.

### *Keys*

Those were the days, when every Security Officer carried a bunch of keys on his (yes, generally his!) person, and physically checked all doors to make sure they were locked. And woe betide any Security Officer who lost or mislaid a key because that meant that all of the locks related to that key had to be replaced!

That is not to say that key and locking systems no longer exist, of course they do, but they are not as common as they once were. So let us take a look at the most common types of key and locking systems in use today.

### *Mortice locks*

A mortice key and locking system is designed to be installed inside of the door in order for it to work, and it provides a means of securing the door, and ultimately the building.

Generally, the choice is between a 3-lever mortice lock and a 5-lever mortice lock, the theory being that the more levers the lock contain, the more secure it is likely to be. Also, a 5-lever mortice lock is likely to meet the requirements for BS 3621, which is the standard most accepted by insurance companies.[12]

### *Multi-point locking systems*

A key-operated multi-point lock system is fitted into the body of the door and locks into the door frame.

When the lock is engaged multiple bolts will engage into the door frame, usually with a minimum of three points and sometimes four or five points

Multi-point locking systems are used domestically, normally at the front door, when the handle has to be manipulated before the lock is secure.[13]

### *Rim automatic deadlatch with key-locking handle*

A rim automatic deadlatch (night latch) is fitted on the inside of the door, with the key locking cylinder to insert the key to open the door located on the outside of the door. This type of lock is not as secure as a mortice locking system.

### *Digital locks*

Digital door locks are generally cost-effective, easy-to-install security solutions for the majority of buildings that require a reliable means of access control. The advantage is that numerous keys are not required, and the through flow is normally faster.

When installed, a PIN will be allocated, and it is recommended that the PIN is changed initially, and at regular intervals. This is an area that you should be aware of, and it should be part of the Security Survey.

### *Swipe cards*

Swipe cards operate by storing data in a magnetic layer placed on a card. The card is swiped through a magnetic reader to be able to confirm the data stored on it. This allows the card and its user to access the system the card is introduced to. The most common use is for access control purposes when the card is used to enter a room.

Originally it was believed that a sub-use of the card is to be able to audit where the card owner has been, but of course, that is impossible, as the owner may have allowed a colleague, who had perhaps forgotten their card, to use the card belonging to its lawful owner. So, the system can monitor card movement, but not necessarily card user movement. During the Security Survey, you should ask to see evidence of card auditing.

### *Proximity card readers*

Proximity card reader systems offer a greater level of security than swipe cards because the architecture and software installed are significantly more sophisticated than the magnetic strip found on the swipe card.

In terms of access control, a door access reader is the first security measure people encounter when trying to enter a space. In order to gain entry with a proximity card reader, the user needs to have an authorised proximity card on their person. Proximity cards and readers use RFID (radio frequency identification) to communicate wirelessly, with authorisation data encoded on the cards.

Proximity readers are a wise option for commercial building security, as they can be programmed to meet a wide variety of needs. Before installing an access control system with proximity card readers, it is important to understand the different types of readers available, and the potential benefits and drawbacks of a proximity card reader system.[14]

The majority of new commercial builds are protected by proximity card reader systems.

Auditing records should be examined during the Security Survey.

### *Biometrics*

Biometrics are body measurements and calculations related to human characteristics.

Biometric authentication (or realistic authentication) is used in computer science as a form of identification and access control. It is also used to identify individuals in groups that are under surveillance.

Biometric identifiers are the distinctive, measurable characteristics used to label and describe individuals. Biometric identifiers are often categorised as physiological characteristics, which are related to the shape of the body. Examples include, but are not limited to fingerprint, palm veins, face recognition, DNA, palm print, hand geometry, iris recognition, retina, and odour/scent.[15]

Biometric systems are generally installed to allow for an increased level of security, as measurable characteristics are deemed unique to individuals. There is of course a downside, and that is the fact that systems such as fingerprint readers can be distorted if the finger being examined has grease or dirt on it. So, the use of a biometric system, for example at a building site may not be ideal.

The greatest levels of security are normally achieved when a two-factor system has been installed, one that will require a PIN and biometric measurement.

Let us take a look at some of the different types of entrance that you will come across.

## Main entrance

In terms of footfall and movement the main entrance is likely to be the busiest area of the building, with staff, visitors, and contractors transiting this part of the location constantly. Depending upon the operational sensitivity of the building, the main entrance may be secure, or the company may have an open-door policy, allowing all personnel unhindered entrance through the main door.

You will first of all have to examine this entrance, which should be adequately lit and covered by video surveillance (CCTV). Whether the door is secure or otherwise, every person entering the building should be monitored, either through the use of video surveillance or perhaps being viewed by a Security Officer located immediately inside the entrance.

If the entrance is secure, all members of staff must be issued an appropriate access control card, which will serve them for all of their access needs throughout the building. The access control card should also have some form of 'no pass back' software installed so that once the card is used to enter a building, it cannot be used again until it has exited the location. There should be some form of communications system in place that will allow visitors and contractors access to the building.

### *Goods inward entrance (Goods in)*

Every commercial building is likely to have some form of goods in, normally located to the rear or side of the building. This is the entrance where products, and perhaps mail is delivered to the building, and very often it is the most vulnerable area.

If anything, this is the most vulnerable area of the building because it may be operational on a 24/7 basis, and there is a constant movement of staff and contractors, so naturally at some time, there is the potential for the security team to 'take their eye off the ball' so to speak. Goods should be afforded exactly the same level of security protection as any other area of the building, including CCTV, effective lighting, access control Security Officer attendance, and if secured during the hours of darkness, then of course monitored IDS.

### *Fire doors*

The greatest area of concern for fire door locations is the fact that they, certainly in the UK, by law cannot be secured from the inside. Everybody in the building has the right by law to have a safe evacuation route in the instance of a fire breaking out, and that is the reason why such exits cannot be secured from the inside. The Security Auditor when examining the fire door should ensure that it is not secured from the inside, and there should be some form of crash bar available to allow personnel to escape at speed. On too many occasions I have observed fire exits that have been secured by means of a robust padlock.

So, in terms of the outer face of the main building (s), the focus points are the main entrance, goods in, and all fire doors. Once inside the building, the first potential single point of failure is the reception area.

### *Reception area*

Looking at it from the perspective of the offender, and of course dependent on the size and configuration of the reception area, this is an ideal opportunity to hunker down and take stock of his next moves.

In a typical reception area of a large multi-occupied building in London, the reception desk is directly ahead when an entrance to the building is made, but there is 360-degree access, and if it is entered from the main road, once inside the visitor can turn to the left, where a staircase takes him or herself down to a small shopping mall, leading on to the main shopping area, and Transport For London rail link.

Although there is a heavy security presence in the reception area, it is relatively easy to blend in, whilst taking into account what other security infrastructures are in place.

When working at such a building, even if the reception area is smaller, you should take time to acquaint yourself with your surroundings, from a criminal point of view, in order to clarify if the CCTV cameras are located correctly, and if the access control barriers are operating efficiently i.e., is there a no pass back facility built in. Is lighting appropriate and are the Security Officers paying attention to the areas that are most vulnerable.

You should then approach the reception desk to gain an understanding of the effectiveness of this area of the building.

Figure 9 depicts a plan of a basic reception area in which it can be seen that once inside the building, the first barrier will be the reception desk itself, generally manned by skilled receptionists who may be supported by security staff. Once the credentials of the visitor have been verified, they may be escorted or perhaps given a temporary pass that will enable them to negotiate the access control turnstiles.

Once again, you should ensure that some form of no pass back facility has been included in the access control software, because once past the initial access control turnstiles, the visitor if unescorted, and that is not unusual he or she will have free reign throughout the public areas of the building. That is likely to include the basement and roof area.

At a time when the threat of a terrorist attack is extremely high, the Reception Area may contain some form of airport-style ex-ray system to visualise goods being carried into the building, and perhaps a metal detection archway operated by the security team. You should test both systems to ensure that they are operating effectively and are fit for purpose.

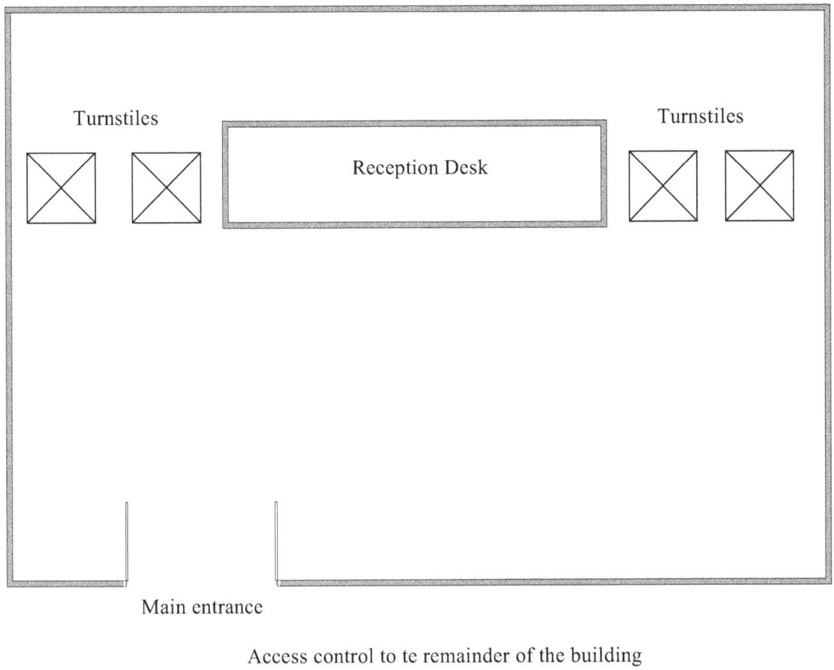


*Figure 9* The basic reception area.

## *Lift areas*

As mentioned, when discussing the reception area, once past the initial access control turnstiles, the visitor will be able to negotiate his or her way through the building via the normally insecure lift process. This is where you should be checking to ensure that the lift areas are covered by CCTV, which is monitoring and recording all movement.

If the building is multi-occupied, which is likely, certain floors may have been configured for staff access only. Should that be so, once again you should ensure that such a zoning process is in operation and is effective.

## *Floor security*

It is also likely that once the visitor disembarks the lift, he or she will be confronted with further access control by individual companies and organisations. Staff will have been issued access control cards, normally proximity reader cards, and visitors will be required to be afforded access control from an internal source, usually the receptionist.

Here you should ensure that once again, the lift area is supported by video surveillance (CCTV), that access control to the individual company is being managed, and that the communications systems enabling access are operational.

### *Sensitive or restricted areas*

Throughout the building, there will be a number of sensitive or resected areas, and in this section, I will identify them and explain how they should be protected.

### *Goods inwards area and mail room*

Very often, because space is at a premium, the Goods Inwards area contains the Mail Room, which may hold some form of x-ray process.

### *Communications/sever room*

It could logically be argued that the communications/server rooms are the most important areas of a building because they provide communications for the organisation, and generally hold very sensitive information and data. Therefore, it is imperative that they receive appropriate levels of security, proportional to the risk of them being attacked. Server rooms should also have a 'door open' alarm system, which activates if the door is left open for a preset length of time.

### *Location*

Ideally, the communications/server rooms should be located above the ground floor, and preferably in the centre of the working area. For ease of maintenance and repair, engineers will recommend that the communications/server rooms are located alongside an outer wall on the ground floor, and from their perspective, that of course makes sense. However, next to an outer wall on the ground floor also makes it easier for the room to be physically and digitally attacked.

- External protection

All surrounding walls to a communications/server room should be solid, floor-to-ceiling (often referred to as 'slab to slab') load-bearing in construction. The ceilings should be reinforced and if there is space above the communications/server room it should be alarmed. Equally, if there is a void below the room, where perhaps cables run, that space should be alarmed. The room should be supported by CCTV, and lighting should be at a level that will support video surveillance.

Access control should be two factors supporting, that is to say, there should be two means of controlling access, with the most common being a proximity card reader system, supported by a Personal Identification Number (PIN). If the levels of sensitivity are deemed critical, it may be necessary to increase access control protocols to include a biometric system. Once again, the best levels of physical security can be found on the CPNI website.

Only personnel vetted to work in the communications/server room should be given access to that part of the building, and the access control systems should be interrogated regularly to ensure that only those authorised to be in that room have accessed it.

- Internal protection.

Once again, CCTV and supporting lighting should be considered, with the room being covered by the building IDS

### *Private changing areas*

Staff may have access to a changing room with personal lockers. Access to the changing room should be secure, as should all individual lockers, and an examination of both should be included in the Security Survey.

### *Board room*

If there is a Board Room in the building under survey it should be afforded the same levels of security as those offered to the communications/server room. Also, the board room should be regularly counter surveillance examined to ensure there are no illegal listening devices that may have been planted by a competitor.

### HR/payroll

Finally, HR and Payroll should be examined to ensure that they are secure all times when not occupied, as they are likely to contain personal information that is of course overly sensitive.

### The Security Control Room

The Security Control Room is the nerve centre of all security, and occasionally Health & Safety systems in an organisation, and it is normally occupied on a 24/7 basis. However, before we look at how it functions, and the role it plays, it is important to understand that in itself it is, or should be classified as a Restricted Area, and as such should be accorded all of the security protocols related to such sensitive locations.

At the beginning of the Security Survey, or when the opportunity presents itself, you should examine the Security Control Room, and ask, probably the Security Supervisor or Senior Security Officers the following questions:

- Is the Security Control Room accessible on a 24/7 basis?
- What is the minimum number of Security Officers likely to occupy the room on a day and night basis?
- Outside of the Security Team, who has access to the room?
- What sensitive information and data is held? How is it secured?
- Who has access to the electronic systems?
- Is there a backup Security Control Room? If so, where is it, and how often is it manned, and are any systems in place tested?
- Is there a Daily Occurrence Book (DOB) available?
- The Security Control Room is also likely to be responsible for all of the following security and safety systems.

### Perimeter Intruder Detection Systems (PIDS)

The PIDS may consist of a taught wire system, an underground system or a line-of-sight configuration. Whichever it is, it should be tested during the course of the Security Survey. Whether it is somebody attempting to climb the fence, run across the ground that is protected, or break the infrared signal, the system should be tested to ensure that the alarm, if activated is responded to accordingly. All tests and activations should be recorded in an alarm activations log.

### *CCTV*

The CCTV system should first of all be inspected to ensure that it is fit for purpose, that is to say, all cameras are operational, and are covering the correct arcs and fields of vision. If any cameras are not operational, there should be a faults log in which the problems and their ultimate solutions will be recorded. Sit with the most experienced CCTV operator and ask him or her to take you through each camera setting, and the arcs and fields of vision designed for those cameras.

Check to ensure that all monitors are operating, and that the recording equipment is functioning correctly. If the system is fitted with Video Motion Detection software, have the operator show it to you in action, and ask them if it is adversely affected by the environment i.e., wind, rain, snow, etc.

### *IDS*

There may be Manned Guarding support 24/7, but restricted areas, such as the server/comms room should be fitted with an IDS. Ensure that the IDS s functional, and that upon activation it signals to the correct platform, i.e., the Security Control Room, or perhaps an Alarm Receiving Centre (ARC). Once again there should be an activation log that records all activations, including false alarms.

There may also be a 'door held open' alarm, and if there is, physically check to ensure it is operational and is being tested on a regular basis.

### *Automatic Access Control Systems (AACS)*

With technology being more attractive than ever, it is likely that all corporate locations will be equipped with some form of AACS. It may be a simple swipe card system, or perhaps a two-factor AACS comprising of a smart card coupled to a biometric system. However, if the AACS is configured, or whatever it consists of, it is likely that it will be managed by the Security Team from the Security Control Room. Once again, each system should be tested, and there should be a log or interrogation system that records all transactions and creates an alert every time there is a system denial i.e., somebody has tried to enter an area with the wrong privilege protocols.

### Communications Systems

It is extremely likely that there will be some form of communications system available to the Security Team and essential staff such as the Health & Safety Manager and the Facilities Manager. During the course of the Security Survey communications should be tested to ensure that all users of the system can speak to each other safely and that there are no weak communication areas, or 'black spots' at the location.

There should also be some form of network diagram showing the distribution of call signs, and the hierarchy of use i.e., security and safety take precedence over all users, with Health & Safety and the Security Team being issued their own channels. There should also be a dedicated Network Manager who ensures that network discipline is maintained in the interests of safety and security.

### Lone worker control systems

There is every likelihood that there will be single Security Officer cover, outside of the Security Control Room, particularly during the hours of darkness. If that is so, then particular attention must be paid to the safety and security of the lone Officer.

The organisation may invest in a lone worker system which allows the Security Officer to carry a piece of equipment that will alert the control room if he or she is in danger, and the controls for such a system will in all likelihood be installed in the Security Control Room.

### Patrol Management Systems

As previously explained, a Patrol Management System requires the patrolling Security Officer to connect with a certain number of points during his or her routine patrol. Within the Security Control Room will be an ICT-based platform that allows the information from the Patrol Management baton to be downloaded for interrogation. Such information will inform the reader, normally the client, of all patrol patterns, including when the Patrol Management points have not been connected, and that is normally a disciplinary offence.

### *First aid and defibrillation systems*

Because the Security Control Room is normally occupied 24/7, it is best practice to store first aid and mobile defibrillation equipment there.

### *Emergency grab bags*

Emergency grab bags are containers holding items of equipment that may be needed in an emergency and may consist of a first aid kit, a defibrillator, hand torches, spare radios and batteries, and anything that the Security Team believes may be needed in an emergency.

### *Key control*

Once again it is likely that all site or building keys will be held and secured in the Security Control Room. All keys must be signed out and signed back in at an appropriate time. There should be protocols in place to take into consideration a lost key.

### *Basement and roof areas*

The basement may comprise a couple of skips, and a few bicycles, or there may be a VIP car park there, an Uninterrupted Power Supply (UPS)/generator, and controls for the Building Management System (BMS).

The external roof area may contain only a couple of air condition vents, but perhaps also there is the Wi-Fi mast, air conditioning chillers, and Sky receivers. However, you will never know until you look.

Whether it is the basement or the external roof area, security must be proportionate to the risk, with systems such as CCTV, access control, IDS, and lighting being at a standard that will meet the operational requirement.

## Manned guarding

*I couldn't get a job, so I became a security guard.*[16]

A great deal has been written about manned guarding, everything from its evolution to its succession by technology, but I'm not going to repeat any of that. The aim of this section is to examine what you should be looking for when considering manned guarding as part of the defence of a location which is being security surveyed.

Security Officers far too often receive unnecessary bad press, the vast majority of which is unethical and immoral. For me, the Security Team is the beating heart of the security culture in an organisation, because it is easy to understand how senior managers accept security by the way they treat their Security Officers. If I enter a supermarket, and the duty Security Officer is collecting trolleys, or even standing to one side of the entrance totally immersed in his or her mobile phone, I immediately come to the conclusion that nobody really cares about security, and if that is what I think, how does the hardened criminal perceive that picture. It's his or her Christmas and birthday all rolled into one!

Ironically, a well-supported Security Team will pay dividends for the organisation that has faith in them and treats them as equals, so back to the survey.

At many locations, the Security Team is on duty 24/7, and so it naturally makes sense to approach the Security Officer first in relation to information needed about the building or area; it's their 'patch', and if you appear to be trustworthy, you have a credible and trusted ally.

I always ask the duty Security Officers the first questions about the location, and I generally end the survey in the Security Control Room or perhaps the canteen with either the Security Supervisor or the Senor Security Officer, and I'm sure you are now thinking, OK, what questions should we ask this font of all knowledge?

Well of course every survey is different, and the Security Officers that you may be speaking to will all have a different perspective on the questions being asked, and remember, this is not meant to be an exercise in divide and conquer. I am not for one second trying to persuade the Security Officer to tell tales out of school; quite the opposite, I am metaphorically saying that I trust his or her word, and I am aware that they will look at the security of the building or location in a different manner to let's say the CEO or the CFO.

They will tell you if they believe the access control system is effective, or when the CCTV was last maintained. They will also be trusted to confirm the real threats and vulnerabilities related to the site, what types of crime to expect, and realistically how long it takes for the police to arrive at the scene of the crime.

To me, the Security Team are the first and last defence of any location, and I repeat, if managed effectively they can be the fine line between a building being secure, or porous. Spending time speaking with the most junior and most experienced Security Officers will pay dividends for the Security Auditor. Junior managers may tell you what they think you want to hear; Security Officers will always say it how it is (thank goodness).

### *Building integrity*

It is pointless having a secure main entrance if the skylight on the top floor is vulnerable to attack, or the rear fire exit isn't covered by the building IDS. The standard of building integrity has to be consistent throughout, otherwise, as I have mentioned before, the weakness will be spotted by the criminal, and it will be exploited.

### *Doors and windows*

The rule of thumb is that all doors and windows must meet the minimum standards found throughout the buildings. Such entrances and exits must not be the weak link.

### *Roof*

I mentioned skylights earlier on, and they of course can be a significant vulnerability, but more common is the roof hatch which is used to access equipment such as air conditioning units and CCTV cameras. Far too often the hatch (s) will be insecure because it is easier for maintenance purposes. All such hatches should be secure, and they should be included in the building IDS, covered by the CCTV system.

## IDS

### *Internal*

Let's take a look at the most prominent systems on the market today.

### *Passive Infrared Motion Detection*

Probably the most common form of internal IDS used today is the Passive Infrared (PIR) system, and there is often confusion when comparing this to Active Infrared (AIR) systems (More about that later).

PIRs consist of a pyroelectric sensor, which can detect levels of infrared radiation (IR), particularly from human beings. It is known that every living species emits some form of low-level radiation, and basically, the hotter something is, the more radiation is emitted.

PIR systems are attenuated to search for an increase in IR when a human being enters the location that is being detected.

## *Active infrared detection (AIR)*

Active infrared detectors provide one or more beams of infrared that can be aligned to create a 'detection barrier' invisible to the human eye. If the beams are interrupted, for example by an intruder passing through them, the loss of infrared signal at the receiver is detected and an alarm is created.

As the name suggests, active infrared beams are an 'active' type of device meaning that they emit infrared energy, as opposed to passive infrared detectors that only receive infrared.

The operating wavelength is different too, typically in the 800–980 nm waveband, which is beyond the response range of the unaided human eye. Operating distances of AIR detectors intended for indoor use are available from 4 to 200 m and possibly greater.

Devices capable of operating distances greater than 5 m use collimating lenses and/or mirrors to intensify and focus the projected infrared beams. The electronic circuitry is generally in two parts; a transmitter that emits modulated bursts of infrared light and a receiver with optics and circuitry to collect and decode the modulated signal produced by the infrared light.

## *Microwave motion detection*

Microwave motion detectors emit electromagnetic 'radio' waves. When the microwaves come into contact with an object some of the waves are absorbed others are reflected and scattered in all directions and some are reflected back to the detector.

If movement is present, the frequency of the reflected waves is altered, and it is this change in frequency, known as 'Doppler shift,' that is used to determine the presence of an intruder. The shift in frequency is proportional to the velocity of the intruder.

The frequency of the microwaves reflected from stationary objects is unchanged, therefore ignored by the detector

Microwave detectors intended for use indoors usually have transmitter and receiver assemblies combined inside a single housing and are known as monostatic microwave detectors.[17]

### Combined detectors

Detectors incorporating two or more detection technologies in a single housing, e.g., passive infrared combined with microwave, have become popular because of their increased stability in the service environment. Commonly referred to as dual technology or 'Dual Tec' detectors, the combination of different technology types provides the benefit of increased resistance to false alarms compared with detectors of only a single technology.

The most common combined detector is the passive infrared combined with microwave, designed to operate in 'AND' configuration. Only when both detection technologies shall have sensed movement within a predetermined time window will an alarm output be generated.

### Passive infrared and microwave

The pairing of passive infrared with microwave detection technology can provide improved immunity to a false alarm, for example, the unwanted effects of heat sources, turbulent air, sun light reflections, etc. will not influence the microwave.

Similarly, the problems associated with the transmission of microwaves beyond the desired detection area, by penetrating glass, for example, are significantly reduced because the passive infrared is unable to 'see' through the glass.

Furthermore, the two different technologies are both sensitive to movement but in different directions (i.e., perpendicular). In theory passive infrared and microwave detection working together requires an element of movement in both directions for an alarm to be signalled, e.g., movement diagonally across the detection area.

This further increases the stability of the detector to unwanted disturbances in the service environment.[18]

### Door and window detection

Whilst PIR and dual tec systems will offer internal protection, there are also means of securing a location, which will detect intrusion before the intruder enters the building.

## Break glass detection

Piezoelectric glass break detectors comprise a piezoelectric element affixed to a metal or ceramic substrate, which during installation is glued to the surface of the glass inside the supervised area.

When the protected glass breaks the substrate and the piezoelectric element physically flex causing a minute electrical charge to be generated. The charge is amplified, and the resulting signal analysed to determine if an alarm is to be signalled.

## Vibration and shock detection

Vibration and shock detectors are used in applications where the expected intrusion attempt will result in the penetration of a planar surface (e.g. a wall) or other types of barrier, using techniques such as drilling, impacting with a sledge hammer, pick axe, or similar tool, cutting with a saw or grinder or oxyacetylene torch/rope, possibly even blasting with explosive

Seismic devices contain one or more piezo electric elements that produce an electrical charge when flexed physically. Attached to a suitable mechanism the piezo material's ability to generate electrical signals can be used to detect the presence of vibrations.

Modern types of inertia sensors use innovative designs to sense vibration, but the basic principles of operation can be explained by depicting a small metallic ball resting on a set of electrical contacts.

When the ball is at rest it completes an electrical circuit between the contacts. The continuous electrical circuit is interpreted by the electronic analyser circuitry as a quiescent non-alarm condition.

Because the ball is free to move with the inertia created by an impact on the substrate on which the detector is mounted, the ball jumps off the contacts, thereby interrupting the electrical circuit momentarily.

The interruption is of very short duration but is measurable by the analyser circuitry. A succession of multiple interruptions will be interpreted as an attack signature and an alarm condition generated.[19]

## Magnetically operated reed switches

Due to the relatively low cost of the standard types of magnetically operated reed switches, these types of protective switch have become the most popular.

However, some 'high security' models command higher prices due to the addition of in-built anti-tamper protection measures. Typically, the anti-tamper measures comprise two or more magnetically biased reed switches in addition to the alarm signalling reed switch. The additional reed switches are physically orientated in different positions to each other and to the alarm switch.

The selective positioning of the anti-tamper reed switches ensures that they only operate when a secondary external magnetic field is present, e.g. introduced by an attacker intent on interfering with the operation of the protective switch. The result is a tamper output from the protective switch signalling to the control equipment that a comprise attack has been attempted.

The reliability of magnetically operated reed switches is generally very good however, after many operations their electrical contacts will eventually wear out. Contact resistance measurements made as part of the scheduled maintenance checks should provide a warning of impending contact failure.[20]

### *Magnetic locking devices (Mag locks)*

A small metal plate is attached to the door and is positioned to come in direct contact with the electromagnet. When energised, the electromagnet will hold onto the metal plate to hold the door open. Whilst not part of an IDS, mag locks hold open devices are connected to the fire alarm system or life safety system.

#### *Key takeaway*

*Any alarm system is only as good as its design, installation, and maintenance.*

## Lighting

In many respects, lightning is the most effective deterrence in terms of crime prevention, because whilst the criminal is likely to try to circumnavigate security systems such as CCTV, access control, and intruder detection, the last thing he or she wants is to be seen in the open.

Of course, you can make the argument that the intruder is being seen if the CCTV system is operational, but the thought of being illuminated in an open space, where they can potentially be observed by either casual observers or Security Officers, is often enough to change the mind of the criminal who may decide to go elsewhere in order to evade apprehension. So as with other sections, we will now take a look at a range of lighting systems that you may come across during the Security Survey.

### *Light Emitting Diode (LED)*

Although LED lighting has been available for some time, it is only recently that it has been accepted as a feasible option for security lighting systems.

LED lighting, unlike older incandescent bulbs which use a frail filament, use a semiconductor that produces strong lighting immediately. Unlike other energy-saving lights, the LED is extremely efficient, using about 85% less energy, with a life span of twenty to thirty years! Although capital expenditure is costly, they are a return on investment and pay for themselves very quickly.

### *High- and low-pressure sodium lighting*

High-Pressure Sodium vapour (HPS) lights, similar to Low Pressure Sodium vapour (LPS) lights, are a specific type of gas-discharge light (also known as a high-intensity discharge, HID, or arc light). The principal difference between low- and high-pressure sodium lights is the operating pressure inside the lamp. As indicated by the name, "high" pressure sodium vapour lights operate at a higher internal pressure. The arc tube is made of aluminium oxide and the sodium metal is combined with several other elements like mercury which counterbalances the yellow glow with some white to light blue emissions.

Low-Pressure Sodium vapour (LPS) lights are a specific type of gas-discharge light (also known as a High-Intensity Discharge, HID, or arc light). The bulb principally contains solid sodium metal inside a borosilicate glass tube that vapourises once the lamp is turned on. During start (while the sodium is still in solid form) the lamp emits a dim reddish/pink glow. Once the metal is vapourised the emissions become the characteristic bright yellow associated with sodium vapour lamps. The spectrum of visible emissions from an LPS light is actually very close together (589 and 589.6 nm, virtually monochromatic) resulting in the colours of illuminated objects being nearly indistinguishable.[21]

Low-pressure sodium lights tend to be orange in colour, with a limit to colour identification of a description needed, whilst high-pressure sodium is far brighter, allowing better colour definition

### *Motion detection lighting*

An excellent lighting crime prevention strategy is to have motion detection lighting installed. To all intents and purposes, the area is unlit and perhaps insecure, until the potential criminal walks inside the motion detector field of vision and the light is activated. Under most circumstances, the criminal will make good his or her escape.

## Closed-circuit television (CCTV), often referred to today as video surveillance

It is probably fair to say that the introduction of CCTV, or video surveillance as it is now being referred to as, was a step change as far as the security industry is concerned. However, and this is often the downside, it would also be reasonable to argue that a significant percentage of non-security professionals believe that CCTV is the panacea to all crime-related issues.

Very often if crime rates increase, the answer is thought to be straightforward, install vast numbers of expensive cameras and the problem will disappear. If only that were true, life would be so much easier.

As an integral part of any security system, CCTV is an excellent tool; but that is exactly what it is, a tool; no more and no less. Used correctly CCTV can act as a deterrent, and as the detection system. Equally, if CCTV evidence is collated and used in a court of law effectively, it can be the difference between a guilty and a not guilty verdict when a crime has been committed, but…. it is not a silver bullet.

CCTV and video surveillance systems play an important role in the early identification of criminal or suspicious behaviour, and the investigation of crime and critical incidents including post-incident evidence gathering and forensic analysis. Such systems are also invaluable when investigating health and safety concerns and in the event of public liability claims.

The monitoring or regular reviewing of recorded images may assist in the identification of suspicious activity or 'hostile reconnaissance'. Hostile reconnaissance refers to the planning phase of a terrorist attack. In order to identify such activities, cameras should be placed in optimum positions across the site and offer clear images to the viewer. Should an intrusion or incident be detected, the CCTV system can then utilised to monitor and track the individual(s).

Such information would likely assist both the responding emergency services and any post-incident investigation.[22]

In this section, we will examine CCTV as part of an integrated security system, and we will look at its component parts.

However, from a user perspective, it is important to understand that a basic CCTV system is not particularly complicated, it is we who overcomplicate it by not fully understanding what CCTV is, and what its limitations are.

In extremely basic terms, here is how a CCTV system operates:

1. The intruder (s) breaches the perimeter.
2. If installed, he or she will be detected by Video Motion Detection (VMD) software.
3. The image of the intruder is then captured and stored.
4. The image is displayed on a monitor, probably in a security control room.
5. The image is sent to some form of recording device and is saved.
6. If necessary, a hard copy can be printed, or it can be burned to a DVD.

As with all systems covered in this book, the aim is not to explore technical specifications, rather it is for the security professional to be able to identify component parts before making recommendations.

So let us now begin to examine the component parts of a CCTV system.

## *Cameras*

It is outside the scope of this book to enter into detailed descriptions of the wide range of cameras on the market today, suffice it to say that the choices available are staggering, and the Security Auditor must make the correct decision, often on behalf of a client who may have no technical expertise whatsoever. This is where once again I emphasise the criticality of consulting a trusted Subject Matter Expert (SME)

However, it is reasonable to argue that the camera is at the heart of any CCTV system, and this should be the first priority when examining an Operational Requirement. It is also appropriate at this stage to discuss the use of what is too often referred to as 'dummy cameras'. Nonoperational cameras (dummy cameras) are often recommended by security consultants who are attempting to save their clients, and in their eyes, they are undue costs. The recommendation is based on the fact that in the opinion of the 'consultant', dummy cameras bare such a strong resemblance to operational units, and in his or her opinion, the potential burglar will not recognise the camera looking at them as anything less than an operational camera and will be deterred from attempting the crime.

There are a number of issues here.

In the first instance, insurance coverage for the client is likely to be null and void if such a practice is condoned. Second, the experienced criminal, and I would go as far as to say the street-wise opportunist, can identify a dummy camera as soon as he or she lays their eyes on it.

There are also a number of common-sense recommendations that the Security Auditor can make without consulting an SME.

### *Static or pan, tilt and zoom (PTZ)?*

The static camera, as the title suggests, is a camera that is used to monitor a single area, such as a fire exit, an entrance, or perhaps a corridor. It is a relatively simple concept, and of course, the static camera is costed at the lower end of the market. The PTZ on the other hand is a specialist piece of CCTV equipment, that is used for carrying out surveillance, generally of open grounds. Not only does a PTZ camera require training and practice, but it is also far more expensive than a static camera, and therefore the Security Auditor when specifying a system must be cognisant of the fact that his or her recommendations need to be cost-effective.

### *Lens type and definition levels*

If the camera is the heart of the CCTV system, the lens is the eyes of the camera, and its specification can mean the difference between an effective surveillance system, and a CCTV system that is vulnerable.

There is a huge array of camera choices on the market, but after consulting several CCTV SMEs, there is an agreement that in general terms, the auto iris lens[23] is multifunctional, and is the default recommendation for most CCTV systems.

### *Telemetry*

This is the process of transmitting data in one form or another, and in the case of CCTV, it is the transmission of imagery, from camera to capture and recording. There are three favoured means of transmission that you should be aware of.

## Coaxial

Coaxial cables are lengths of wire which consist of an inner insulated core of stranded or solid wire surrounded by outer insulated flexible wire braids. It is primarily used by cable TV companies to connect their satellite antenna facilities to customers' homes and businesses. It is also sometimes used by telephone companies to connect central offices to telephone poles near customers. It can be used for video surveillance, and there are a number of pros and cons.

- Pros.
    - Durability.

Because of their physical constitution, i.e., they are constructed from very robust material, this form of CCTV cable is quite long-lasting.

- Versatility.

The range of applications is quite unique and extremely versatile.

- Transmission distance.

This form of telemetry can be used for the transmission of CCTV signals over a relatively long distance.

- Reliability.

Because of their construction, and the robust insulating material surrounding the copper core, coax tends to be almost immune to electrical interference.

- Cons.
    - Cost.

Coax is relatively more expensive than other ordinary security cables owing to its seemingly high quality.

## Optical fibre cable

Optical fibre is a slim strand of glass, which acts as a waveguide for light over long distances. It has a core, which carries the actual light signal, and cladding, which is a layer of a glass surrounding the core. Most fibres operate in duplex pairs: one fibre is used to transmit, and the other is used to receive.

It is however feasible to transmit both signals over a single strand.

There are two main types of fibre optic cables: Single-Mode Fibre (SMF) and Multi-Mode Fibre (MMF). The difference is basically in the size of the core.

MMF has a much wider core, allowing multiple rays of light to propagate. SMF has a very narrow core which allows only a single mode of light to propagate. Each type of fibre has different properties with its own advantages and disadvantages.

- **Pros**
  - Speed

Fibre cables transmit information at extremely high speeds, and they are always preferable for systems that require fast transfer of data, with as few delays as possible.

  - Efficiency

Fibre transmits data with extreme efficiency because the signals being transmitted are not subject to electromagnetic interferences and very rarely need to be re-transmitted.

  - Capacity

Optical fibre quickly transmits more information and data than conventional copper wires.

  - Distance

There is almost no limit to the distance that fibre optical cable can carry data and information, without the need for a booster or amplifier.

- **Cons**
  - Labour intensive.

Optical fibre cable requires maximum physical labour for installation, maintenance, and repair.

  - Delicate.

The glass fibres require more protection through an outer cable, and the slightest scratch will usually reduce the ability of the cable to transmit signals effectively and efficiently.

  - Cost

Whilst optical fibre cable is the fastest and most efficient means of transmitting data and information, it is also the most expensive.

- **Cat 5**

Sometimes referred to as an Ethernet cable or LAN cable, a Cat 5 or category 5 is a network cable that consists of four twisted pairs of copper wire terminated by a particular plug known as an RJ-45 connector.

This form of cable is used in a variety of networks, delivering data transmission speeds of up to 100 Mbps. The maximum recommended length of a Cat 5 cable is 100 metres. More than this length without the aid of a bridge or other network device will probably cause network issues, including data packet loss and data transmission speed degradation.

- **Pros**
    - Costs

A serious advantage of Cat 5 cable over other forms of transmission is that Cat 5 is one of the most cost-effective options for networking cable. It is often used in cross-over cable work due to its affordability.

- Speed of transmission

Cat 5 cable offers high-transfer speeds, and it normally reaches high rates of transfer in relation to personal networks and older forms of cabling. The cable is also capable of transferring up to four signals concurrently.

- Versatility

Cat 5 cable has the advantage of versatility. This has two forms of the cable, with one form, referred to as a solid conductor. This form is rigid and is often used to connect wall sockets to the central control panel. The other form, which is the stranded conductor form, is often used to connect computers to wall outlets. Cat 5's versatility makes it ideal for a variety of applications, such as with computer networks and telephone wiring.

- **Cons**
    - Data transfer.

Cat 5 cable has a number of limitations, particularly in terms of technology. One of the main disadvantages of Cat 5 cable is the limited amount of data that can be transmitted through the cable. It is extremely limited in its top end for data transfer, and whilst the cable is still suited for home networking, it can only handle 100 Mbps, and is not as effective for larger corporate networks or for any process that requires large data streams such as in modern television transfers.

- Interference.

Another serious limitation of Cat 5 cable is its sensitivity to interference. The cable's effectiveness is often reduced by electrostatic disturbances from many handheld devices and other objects that project inductive interference.

The cable can also pick up interference from other Cat 5 cables that it is running parallel with. This is referred to as cross-talk. Cross-talk can cause serious problems with data transfers and signal strength, and it can also cause interference that will reduce transfer speeds.

So, the choice of telemetry is quite substantial, and as I have advised from the beginning of this section, always ensure that you liaise with an SME.

### Monitors

The CCTV Monitor is a critically important element within all CCTV systems. It provides real-time feedback not only from CCTV cameras but also from security surveillance equipment. The CCTV digital signal is converted into a visual picture which is shown on what is in effect a bespoke television set. Such screens are more than regular HDMI or VGA supporting systems, they are also fitted with BNC connectors that allow for camera-monitor connection.

Modern CCTV monitors are available in various types, such as:

- Light Emitting Diode (LED) monitors.
- Liquid Crystal Display (LCD) monitors.
- Thin Filmed Transistor (TFT) monitors.

The first thing to consider during procurement is the size of the monitor and its resolution. The large screen monitors up to 54" inches are ideal for monitoring centres, because they can easily display video material from several cameras at the same time.

### Recording and storage

Of course, the Video Cassette Recorder (VCR) was an amazing invention, and it was at the heart of early CCTV systems; then came digital recording.

Instead of scrolling through miles of stretched plastic tape trying to find an incident that occurred who knows when, the CCTV Operator today merely selects the date and time on the digital recorder, and he or she is able to 'burn' the incident onto a DVD, and the police investigator is in receipt of the evidence required to pursue a conviction through the courts of law.

## *Legal aspects of CCTV*

In the UK, CCTV is regulated by the Information Commissioner's Office (ICO). The ICO is the UK's independent body set up to uphold information rights.[24] The ICO covers legislation such as:

- General Data Protection Regulations (GDPR).
- Data Protection Act (DPA).
- Freedom of Information Act (FOI).
- Investigatory Act (2016)

The office is responsible for all matters CCTV and can be found at https://ico.org.uk/

It is safe to say that other countries and nation states will have offices that provide a similar service. The USA and EU certainly do.

## *Step 5*

### *Debriefing*

Once the physical security survey is complete, and all systems have been examined to ascertain if they are fit for purpose, you should then take the opportunity to debrief the client.

This is the time, in perhaps twenty minutes or so, that you will be able to give the client an overview of the Security Survey. Remember it is likely that the client will be nervous because he or she has opened up their operational heart to you, very likely exposing vulnerabilities that have been shared with nobody else; so, go easy on him or her. There are a number of issues that should be considered for the post-survey debrief.

- Thank you.
  Take the opportunity to thank the client for the time and support he or she has given you since the Security Survey began.

- A general overview of the survey.
  Just the relevant points of the survey, such as the areas you visited, and the people you spoke to. Don't avail too much information, rather inform the client that your report will be with him or her on an agreed date, in a manner convenient to him or her. Make sure you are compliant with that agreement, as your brand and reputation may come under scrutiny if you fail to comply with the agreement.
- Quick fixes.
  This is a good opportunity to build on the bond of trust. It may be that a light bulb isn't working in a particular room, or a CCTV camera is swinging on its hinges. Both problems can be solved in ten minutes, and it means that you will be seen as somebody to be trusted, as opposed to a bureaucratic ISO auditor who only wants to report nonconformity.
- Final arrangements.
  Come to a final agreement about how and when the report will be delivered, and in what format e.g., MS Word, PDF, and so on. Also, take the opportunity to ask if he or she will accept an initial draft version for the sake of brevity before the final report is written and delivered.

## Step 6

### *The report*

In the first instance, the report should be in a format agreed with the client, and like any other form of written report, it must be logical and easy to read and digest, containing evidence of the findings discovered during the Security Survey.

The Security Survey Report should be based on the Security Survey Template, and it should be written logically, following a number of recognised protocols, which are:

### *Who is the recipient?*

Understanding who the report is aimed at is crucial, because it may influence how it is written. For example, the recipient may have little or no understanding of security risk management and it my be necessary to reflect this in the report, potentially ensuring that it is not swayed by technical argument and language.

### *Sensitivities*

It may be that the report is sensitive, with a limited distribution list, and if that is the case it will need to have restricted levels of access. It may also be, and this is worthy of consideration for all reports, that the report is delivered by hand. If that isn't possible, it will need to be delivered with end-to-end encryption.

### *In what format is the report required?*

It may be that the preferred format is MS Word, or perhaps PDF. Whatever the preference, make sure that the request is adhered to.

### *When is it needed by?*

In agreement with the client, identify a date of delivery and ensure that you comply with the request. This is critical, because if your report is late, it may end up in file 13 (the waste paper bin)!

It is advised that the makeup of the report follows these guidelines.

- Front page.
  Subject of the report.
  When was it conducted and by who?
  Who was the report prepared by?
- Contents page.
  Introduction and background.
  Executive summary.
  Observations and recommendations.
  Conclusions
  Attachments.

### *Report top tips*

- Break up the paper into sections. Use clear paragraphs, but with spacing in between, as it is difficult to read an operational report unless you are offered the opportunity to take a break.
- Communicate clearly. Keep the wording as simple as possible. There is no requirement to use terminology or phrases that are designed to

impress the reader. Also, don't use abbreviations that have not been explained e.g., IDS.

- Number the pages and sections. This may seem to be a given, but if the report is extensive, it is easy to lose track if the pages are not numbered.
- Use an index. Use some form of index to the rear of the document, as this allows the reader to easily find different sections of the report.
- Source quotations. Although this is an operational report, if you use sources, perhaps Swanson (2021), it should be referenced as Swanson. C., (2021) *Professional Security Management: A Strategic Guide* Oxford, Routledge. This is known as the Harvard style of referencing.
- No slang. Don't use slang, as this is seen as unprofessional.
- Avoid jargon (where you can't avoid jargon, *explain it*). It is easy to slip into jargon, especially if you are from a police or military background.

### *Key takeaway*

*A Security Survey is only as good as the final report, so ensure that you leave sufficient time for the report to be proofread or peer-reviewed before submission to the client.*

## ***Security Survey Gap Analysis***

The Security Survey Gap Analysis is that stage in the process where the Security Surveyor has completed his or her examination of the security systems in place and is in a position to recommend actions to be taken that will enhance the security and risk management profile of the site under survey.

This is where we are, and this is where we need to be. See Figure 10.

*Figure* 10 The Security Survey gap analysis.

### *The Security Survey Template*

It is strongly advisable to use s Security Survey Template. There is an example of such a document to the rear of the book, and please feel free to use it and adjust it accordingly, in line with your personal approach and circumstances.

## The Security Survey report

The Security Survey Report will closely follow the structure of the template, but of course, no two locations are identical. That said, in this book, the report will be addressed as follows.

### *Survey details*

This will include such detail as:

- Name, address, and client point of contact.
- Location of the survey.
- Name and details of the surveyor.
- Date of the survey.

### *Initial stages of the survey*

The initial stages of the report will include:

- Description of the organisation, including business operations and business sector.
- Reason for the survey and asses to be protected.
- Initial research, planning, and preparation.

### *External factors*

External factors may include:

- Rural/urban environmental and employment rates.
- The Crime Pattern Analysis.
- The potential for CPTED.

- Location of nearest emergency (all) services.

### Perimeter protection

Perimeter protection will examine:

- Type and state of repair of any perimeter protection systems.
- Type and standards of PIDS if fitted.
- Type and standard of topping.
- Supporting security systems and their standards and state of repair.
- Entrances by type, numbers, and states of repair.
- Entrance access control systems by type and states of repair.
- Manned guarding coverage.
- Security Control Room operations.

### Main building (s)-external

Main building (s) external will look at:

- Description of buildings and access control to those buildings.
- CCTV by numbers, types, and standards/state of repair.
- IDS by numbers, types, and standards/state of repair.
- Lighting by numbers, types, and standards/state of repair.
- Distance from the perimeter.
- External utilities, areas of concealment and any aids to criminal activity.
- Restricted areas, such as garages, power plants, utilities etc.
- Parking arrangements.

### Main building (s)-internal

Once inside, the report will cover:

- Key personnel to speak to. Who, where and when?
- CCTV by numbers, types, and standards/state of repair.
- IDS by numbers, types, and standards/state of repair.
- Lighting by numbers, types, and standards/state of repair.
- Manned Guarding.

### *Internal specialist or restricted areas*

Internal specialist areas, such as server/comms rooms, HR, payroll, etc.

- Functions.
- Locations.
- Configuration and contents.
- Access control and authorisation.
- Electronic security systems in place e.g., CCTV, IDS, lighting, etc.
- Communications systems in place and used by whom.
- Operational hours.
- Back-up locations in place if they exist.

### *Conclusion*

The conclusion will contain the following information.

- Post survey debrief, to whom and by whom.
- Security Survey Report, in what format, and by when.
- Presentation. Is one required?
- Further work discussions.
- Client verdict.
- Will a Security Audit be required?

The Security Survey concludes what will generally have been an extremely complicated process in which the Security Auditor will have exhausted hours, days, and probably weeks to carry out an extensive examination of the security systems in place. The Security Survey however is only as good as the report written and delivered (securely and on time) to the client.

Corners must not be cut, and there has to be reliance on quality. Consider the following final four pieces of advice:

- Take your time, as it is pointless rushing if you are only going to produce a poor report.
- Have the report proofread by a trusted colleague.

- Gain buy-in from the client by asking him or her if you can send a draft for their initial perusal and comments.
- Deliver it securely on time, or it may end up in file 13!

## Security Survey – unique sectors

As with the Security Risk Assessment, we have now reached that part of the book where, by use of the Security Survey Template, we will test the theory of security surveying against a series of particular, but fictitious security environments, beginning with corporate security.

The following Security Surveys will not contain the levels of information to be found in an operational Security Survey, rather they will offer advice and guidance on what should be covered as a baseline.

Equally, although the template will be used, there will be differences between each sector, and throughout each Security Survey, the book examples will refer to site expectations, and what has actually been discovered during the survey.

## Corporate Security

**TXT Canada Way, Pegasus Wharf, London. E14 5DY**

| Document owner | Reference number | Proof-reader | 1st check | 2nd check |
|---|---|---|---|---|
| John Horrigan | Sec Surv/CW/01/22 | | | |
| | | | | |

1. **Survey details.**
2. **Initial stages of the survey.**
3. **External factors.**
4. **Perimeter protection.**
5. **Main building (s)-external.**
6. **Main building (s)-internal.**
7. **Internal specialist or restricted areas.**
8. **Conclusion.**

## Section 1: Survey details

Name and appointment of the client.

| |
|---|
| Mr John Horrigan. Chief Operating Officer. |

Address (s)

| |
|---|
| 50 Canada Way, Pegasus Wharf, London. E14 5DY. |

Point of Contact.

| |
|---|
| Mr Mark Baker. Chief Security Officer (CSO) |

E mail.

| |
|---|
| m.baker@pegasus.com |

Telephone.

| |
|---|
| 02061366543 |

Web address.

| |
|---|
| www.canadaway.com |

Location of Survey.

| |
|---|
| 50 Canada Way, Pegasus Wharf, London. E14 5DY. |

Name of Security Auditor.

| |
|---|
| Charles Swanson MSc FSyI |

Organisation.

| |
|---|
| STC |

Date of Survey.

| |
|---|
| S21 February 2022 |

## Section 2: Initial stages of the survey

### *Section 2.1 General description and business operations*

50 Canada Way is a 35 story, multi-occupied corporate building in the centre of one of the busiest financial areas in the world. It is the location of BU Head Office, which occupies floors 1 to 5, and floor 35. Floors 6 to 34 are occupied by other businesses that are not within the scope of this Security Survey. BU also has space in the basement for its Uninterruptible Power

Supply (UPS), a backup diesel generator, and twelve car parking spaces for the Senior Management Team.

BU is a gas and oil exploration company, with a global footprint, and it employs approximately 75,000 members of staff worldwide. The Head Office operates on a 24/7 basis, and whilst its primary aim is to manage the day-to-day running of its global empire, there is also a research and development arm on the second floor, and a large data hall containing extremely sensitive data and information on the third floor.

The building has access from an adjacent road, and from an underground shopping mall. 50 Canada Way has open access on a 24/7 basis and is protected by Security Officers contracted from Pegasus Security. At any one time, there will be up to 2,000 occupants of the building.

### Section 2.2 Reasons for the survey

As the results of the Security Risk Assessment are based on intelligence and evidence presented, it has been decided by Subject Mater Experts (SME) that the likelihood of an attack against the ICT network is *High* with the impact being *Very high*. The next stage is to present the findings to the risk owner (CEO) for consideration, and hopefully, a decision will be made about the appropriate risk treatment required.

The CEO fully accepts the results of the Security Risk Assessment, and he has decided that all aspects of physical security require attention, because he quite correctly realises that poor physical security may allow a breach, and that may lead to an attack against the ICT system. Therefore, he has decided that the most effective option is for a full Security Survey of 50 Canada Way to be carried out.

> *Pause for thought*
>
> What is the first step in the Security Survey journey?

### Section 2.3 Assets to be protected

#### *People*

50 Canada Way is a high-rise building, with multi occupancy requirements, and to that extent, it is a people-attracted location. This exemplifies

the argument that the first and most critical asset here are people, ranging from visitors to the building and the underground retail environment, to management and staff, and any contractors carrying out essential repair and maintenance work.

### *Brand and reputation*

The building, with its incredibly attractive underground retail appendage, is seen as a beacon of prosperity at Pegasus Wharf in London, with annual growth being a constant. Through its commercially driven brand, it has a reputation second to none in the South of England, and that must be protected.

### *Data and information*

Data and information are the life blood of any commercial organisation, and 50 Canada Way is no exception. From exclusive retail sales information to data research and development, the building is totally reliant on one of its most crucial assets, data, and information.

### *ICT systems*

Huge investments have been made in the ICT infrastructure and digital network within 50 Canada Way, and a variety of systems, including security frameworks managing CCTV, IDS, etc. are critical. ICT within the location is an extremely important asset, one known by criminals, and as such it requires protection.

### *Infrastructure*

It would be impossible for the location to function effectively without its current infrastructure of power provision, ICT support, lighting, and so on. Once again this is an asset that requires maximum protection.

### *Retail*

The retail services located below 50 Canada Way are the subject of a separate Security Survey Report but suffice it to say that the shopping area is a massive asset that requires protection.

## Section 2.4 Initial Research

Remember this:

There is a famous military phrase, "*A day spent on recce (reconnaissance) is never wasted*", referring to the importance of research, and understanding of what you are up against; research before a Security Survey is no different. Let us look at what we need to research before this leg of the Risk Journey.

### Company background and security culture

It is relatively straight forward to investigate the background of a company because most of the information required will be open-source material. As far as BU is concerned, it has always been a forward-thinking, ethically operating organisation, but it was involved in a major environmental accident some years ago, which cost the company a great deal of money, and it was a huge blow to its brand and reputation. Because of this, the focus is now on sales and business growth, with security perhaps being placed, in the short term, on the back burner.

### Unemployment rates in the area

Unemployment rates in and around Pegasus Way are far lower than the national average, and indeed lower than anywhere else in London.

### Previous criminal incidents

Historically, there have been minor crimes committed in and around Pegasus Way, but there is no record of any major crime.

### Previous Security Surveys

A Security Rick Assessment and Security Survey were carried out five years ago, and the reports were handed over to the then CEO, Mark Lipton. They were produced in hard copy and electronic format, so you will need to discover their where abouts, and thinking about the section which discussed previous reports, take the necessary action as discussed in the section covering the basic Security Survey.

### Crime Pattern Analysis (CPA)

Critical to any Crime Pattern Analysis is an understanding of what crime impacts the location being surveyed. The Security Manager or CEO of a corporate institute is unlikely to be too worried about anti-social behaviour or bicycle theft, as example, but he or she will obviously be concerned if levels of theft and assault are high.

As a refresher, it is worth thinking about how we gather information about crimes being committed in the area that we are paying attention to, and in this case, we are looking at the post code E14 5DY, which we are going to feed into www.police.uk

From August 2020 to July 2021, June has been the most prominent, with approximately 240 crimes being committed.

During the last twelve-month period, the most prominent three crimes have been anti-social behaviour (c1100), violence and sexual offences (c600), and shoplifting (c200). For the Security Manager and CEO at BU, of most concern will be violence and sexual offences, burglary (c150), and robbery (c75).

Broadly speaking, if you examine crime statistics during the last month, or over the last three years, the figures will largely be the same.

### *Key takeaways*

*The research element of the security will, to a certain extent, be dependent on the client and location, but a word of advice, the Security Auditor can never research too much.*

Next comes planning and preparation.

## Section 2.5 Planning and preparation

Remember what Lincoln had to say:

*'Give me six hours to chop down a tree and I will spend the first four sharpening the axe'.*

As with research, there are a number of areas that must be taken into consideration, and to a certain extent, they will change in accordance with the type of location being surveyed.

### *Maps and diagrams*

It is extremely likely that corporate buildings will be located in high-profile areas, and the BU building is no exception. Because of this, maps of the general area of Pegasus Wharf will be readily available, particularly online. However, obtaining detailed diagrams and schematics of the building may not be so straightforward. Such documentation will probably be in the possession of the Building or Facilities Manager, but whether he or she will release them for the purposes of the Security Survey is difficult to say. Very often a compromise is made, with the surveyor being offered a copy of the building/location fire diagram.

### Authorisation and specific points of contact

It is likely, although not guaranteed that access to a corporate location will be more difficult than most other locations, simply because of the operations carried out at that particular building. It is therefore critical that the Security Auditor identifies a single point of contact and uses that relationship for authorisation in terms of access to and around the building under survey. It is also worth noting, for the purpose of the survey, whether the Auditor is escorted around the building during the survey. If he or she isn't, the alarm bells should start to ring.

As noted, the British Utility building at 50 Canada Way is the company's Head Office, and there is also the facility to hold extremely sensitive information and data. As such the highest levels of authorisation will be required for all visitors.

### Changes in laws and regulations

It is unlikely that there will be major alterations or changes in law and regulations at 50 Canada Way, but by virtue of the fact that it is a corporate building, the Security Auditor must make every effort to remain vigilant to any changes in circumstances.

### Social media

All corporate entities will have a high profile on social media, and BU is no exception, as its primary function is oil and gas exploration, which are contentious operations. Therefore, by the very nature of its profile, the company will have a range of social media visitors, and it will be to the advantage of the Security Auditor to remain vigilant to all social media communications.

### Photography

Photography is a significant tool when the Security Survey Report is being written, and of course, a picture paints a thousand words, but a note of caution. In the UK taking photographs during a Security Survey is unlikely to be a major issue, if permission has been granted that is. However, globally it is probably not as straightforward, with a number of countries such as Iran and Turkey being very reluctant as far as 'foreigners' taking photographs is concerned, particularly at military or corporate locations; so, authorisation is critical.

Ensure that when you apply to take photographs, you receive written authority, drafted by the person responsible, in a language that can be understood by all involved.

### *Identification*

This is tricky, and fraught with complexities, because unlike most other countries, the population of the UK is not mandated to carry any form of identification, and that can be a problem. Very often, when entering a corporate building visitors will be required to produce some form of identification. An identity card, a passport, or perhaps a photographic driving licence, and the absence of such documentation may determine whether access will be granted. My advice is to always carry some form of identification on your person as it will save embarrassment and potential loss of face.

### *Agreed visit times and dates*

If you were to stand and watch reception areas in busy corporate buildings, you would realise very quickly that people are coming and going constantly, and the receptionist is often deluged with visitors who are early or late for appointments. Once again, my advice is to always be punctual, because in a corporate environment time is critical.

### *Transportation arrangements*

Corporate buildings are normally found in the middle of busy city centres, and 50 Canada Way is no exception. Car parking is extremely limited, and my advice is to plan your travel arrangements as early as possible, using the mode of transport that is likely to be most convenient.

Once you have an understanding of why the Security Survey is required, and you have carried out the necessary research and preparation it is now the time to consider the actual physical survey.

## Section 3: External factors

### *Section 3.1 Environment*

*Rural/urban*

50 Canada Way is located in the centre of an extremely busy financial district in the middle of the City of London.

### *Section 3.2 Crime Pattern Analysis*

See Section 2.

### *Section 3.3 Employment rates*

There are approximately 120,000 people in full-time employment in Pegasus Wharf.

### *Section 3.4 Potential for Crime Prevention Through Environmental Design (CPTED) using the acronym MAINT*

**M**aintenance: Standards of repair and maintenance at the site under survey are extremely high.

**A**ccess Control: Access control in and around the target building is well thought out, matching any CPTED expectations.

**I**mage: 50 Canada Way is iconic in terms of image, and whilst it may be a target for the criminal or terrorist, it also stands for pride and self-belief.

**N**atural surveillance: There is an abundance of natural light external to, and within the building, which has also been designed to make the most of straight lines and open spaces.

**T**erritoriality: There are tables and chairs outside of the building for use by staff and the general public, and there is a shopping mall below, enhancing a feeling of territoriality.

### *Section 3.5 Nearest police station*

The nearest police station, belonging to British Transport Police (BTP) can be found at 55 Alan Hocken Way, London E15 3AT.

### *Section 3.6 Nearest hospital*

The nearest medical facility can be found at 2 Upper Bank St, London E14 5EE.

### *Section 3.7 Nearest fire and rescue*

The nearest fire station can be found at 168 E India Dock Rd, London E14 0BP.

## Section 4: Perimeter protection

There is no perimeter at the location under survey.

## Section 5: Main building (s) external

### *Section 5.1 Key personnel*

As with all other sector Security Surveys, this is one of the most critical sections of the survey, and it is imperative that as many key personnel as possible are spoken to.

#### *Who?*

50 Canada Way is a very high-profile target location, and it is imperative to speak with the following personnel.

- John Horrigan. COO.
- Mark Baker. CSO.
- Debbi Harrison. HR Director.
- Elly Dolan. CFO.
- Mark Chappel. ICT Manager.
- John Beck. Senior Security Supervisor.
- Security Officers.
- Receptionists.
- Contractors.

It is important to speak to as many and varied site personnel as possible, in order to achieve a rounded approach at the interview stage.

### *When?*

There is no definitive means of ascertaining or calculating when the best time is to speak to key personnel. There are operations being carried out on a 24/7 basis, so the emphasis is on you adapting your schedule to speak to as many relevant people as possible.

### *What?*

With such a divergent range of key personnel being spoken to, with potentially tight time margins you are advised to preselect the questions to be asked before each interview, ensuring that all questions are appropriate, and adding knowledge gained during the Security Risk Assessment.

## *Section 5.2 Description of building (s)*

The building in question is a 35-story unit, constructed of reinforced concrete, steel, and glass. There is also an underground car park, and a multi-occupied shopping mall.

## *Section 5.3 Number of access points and how are they secured.*

Access points to the building, and how they are secured are as follows:

### *Main entrance*

The main entrance, which is a double leaf glass and steel door is insecure during trading hours, with access to members of the public and staff. The main entrance is secured at 2000hrs and is made remotely accessible by either the Security Officer occupying the main reception desk or from the Security Control Room. People wishing to enter the building after trading hours are required to show some form of identity to the CCTV camera above the main entrance.

### *Goods inwards*

There is a goods inwards entrance located within the basement, which is occupied and operational on a 24/7 basis, and anybody wishing to enter the building by this means must prove a form of identity and the reason for their visit.

*Observations*

There is no CCTV coverage supporting the goods inwards room.

*Recommendations*

The goods inwards entrance is operational on a 24/7 basis, and once entered there is the potential for access to the remainder of the building. It is therefore recommended that the building CCTV system is extended to provide cover for this area.

*Fire exits*

There are four fire exits located on the ground floor, all of which are controlled from within. The fire exits are linked to the automated fire control system, and should the fire alarm sound, all fire exits will be released. This allows unopposed access to the building from outside.

*Observations*

Whilst there is CCTV support immediately inside the building covering the fire exits, there is no camera coverage externally.

*Recommendations*

Although ultimately it is the building owner's responsibility, it is recommended that the site CCTV is extended to include coverage externally at every fire exit. This may mean a series of negotiations with the building owner, and this is likely to be the responsibility of the Facilities Manager

### Section 5.4 CCTV

There is a single CCTV camera external to the main entrance to the building. The camera is a digital colour unit that is in a good state of repair and is fit for purpose. The camera signals back to the Security Control Room via Cat 5 cabling and images are captured and recorded on a Digital Network Video Recording (DNVR) system.

*Observations*

The provision of only a single CCTV camera above the main entrance means that the building is vulnerable to an external attack, which may not be detected.

### *Recommendations*

It is recommended as a matter of some urgency that the building CCTV system is extended to cover 360 degrees, with a static camera being installed on each corner. The extra cameras will then signal to the building (Not BU) Security Control Room.

## Section 5.5 IDS

When the building is secured, the main entrance, goods inwards doors, and fire exits are protected by an IDS (door contacts), which if breached will activate a silent alarm signal, received at the building Security Control Room.

During the Security Survey, it was observed that the IDS was operational and fit for purpose.

## Section 5.6 Lighting

The building is protected by external LED street lighting and building wall-mounted LED lighting units. Lighting is activated by photocell technology, which senses the reduced natural light, and will activate the street and building external lights accordingly.

### *Observations*

During the course of the Security Survey, it was observed that two of the lighting units above the front entrance, and a single lighting unit covering the goods inwards door were inoperative.

### *Recommendations*

It is, once again, recommended as a matter of urgency that the building owner/manager is contacted to have the unserviceable lighting units replaced.

## Section 5.7 Distance from the perimeter

N/A

## Section 5.8 External utilities

Nil.

### *Section 5.9 Areas of concealment*

Nil.

### *Section 5.10 Items to help the criminal*

Nil.

### *Section 5.11 Restricted areas*

There is an underground area that houses a VIP car park for BU vehicles, an Uninterruptible Power Supply (UPS), and space for a standby diesel generator. At the time of the Security Survey, all three areas were secure and well lit. The same areas are also subject to irregular patrols, carried out by duty Security Officers.

### *Section 5.12 Parking arrangements*

The only staff car park is located underground, and it is for use by the BU Senior Management team (see above).

## Section 6: Main building (s) internal

### *Section 6.1 Access control*

#### *Access to and within the building*

This is where an effective Security Survey Template reflects its true value, as it should comply with the Defence in Depth concept, detailing the areas to be examined during the survey, and in what order. An example copy of a Security Survey Template can be found at the rear of the book. As far as this section is concerned, you may be operating at a site quite unlike 50 Canada Way, in that there may be some form of perimeter protection, and that is taken into consideration in the Security Survey Template. There will also be examples of sites that are protected by a robust perimeter fence or wall.

Back to 50 Canada way.

This is a standalone building, with three main entrances. There is a South Entrance, an East Entrance and a West Entrance, and all must be examined as part of the Security Survey. The South Entrance is the main means of entering the building and that must be examined first, but what are we looking for.

Well once again it will be to your advantage if you were to position yourself a short distance from the entrance and observe access control for ten or fifteen minutes. During this period, you should try to blend in, and not be too conspicuous, whilst watching how people are entering and leaving the building. This particular type of building which allows access to members of the public is relatively easy to observe because from the outside there is no overt access control.

You will be able to judge how security staff are operating, and perhaps make observations about anything suspicious, in and around the entrance. If a reconnaissance the previous night has been carried out, you will have been able to gauge the levels of lighting.

This should be repeated for the other two entrances (nobody said it was going to be easy!)

At the same time, you should be able to examine ground floor fire exits, and perhaps a Goods Inwards (goods in) entrance, and you will be able to gauge if security at those locations is being taken seriously. Perhaps the fire exit is being wedged open, probably by a fire extinguisher, or the pneumatic bollards in front of the goods inwards doors are never raised.[25]

## *The ground floor*

Although there are three entrances to this building, there is a single reception desk, see Figure 11.

Having made observations, and recorded notes relating to access to the building, once inside the reception area, you will have the opportunity to maintain a low profile whilst carrying out observations of this part of the building.

In the first instance, you should try to 'get a feel for the area', which I understand is neither tangible nor scientific. However, you should examine the footfall of people entering the building, how busy it is, and where people are going. Are they mulling about, speaking to colleagues, waiting for escorts or acquaintances; what are they doing? Are there Security Officers on duty in the reception area, and if there are, what are they doing? Do they appear to be alert, 'switched on', or are they speaking to the receptionist, checking their mobiles, leaning against a wall looking completely bored?

Are there CCTV cameras in the reception area, if so, where are they installed, and in your opinion, at first glance, are they located correctly?

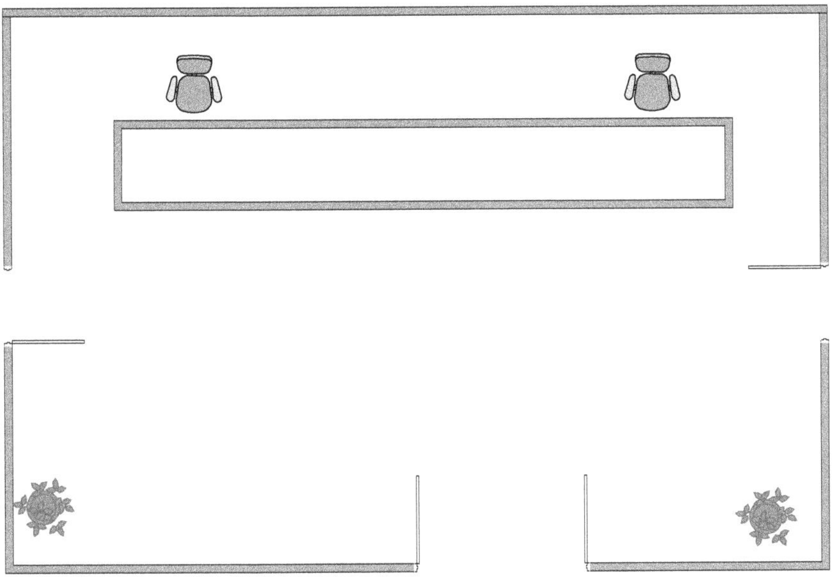

Figure 11 Three entrances and one reception desk.

You should have the opportunity to examine their arcs and fields of vision from the Security Control Room later during the survey.

It would not be a great idea to take any photographs at this stage, as you are only likely to bring attention to yourself unnecessarily. Leave photos for later on.

If you have yet to be challenged, now is the time for you to introduce yourself to the receptionist, requesting they call the point of contact/escort.

It is also worthy of note at this stage to record whether you are expected or not, and if you have been asked to produce some form of identification.

Assuming you are expected, your point of contact/escort will arrive, and template in hand, beginning with the basement it will be time to start the physical Security Survey. During this part of the Security Survey, try to ensure that your escort (s) are familiar with all aspects of the building/location. If there are areas, such as the Server/Comms Room, that you will have to ask questions about, ensure the relevant Subject Matter Expert (SME) is at hand.

Once inside, all members of staff will access the lift area by means of a proximity card which, when introduced to the reader will allow movement through the turnstiles. You observe that the system is supported by a no pass back facility, which means that individual cards cannot be reused for entrance purposes until they have exited the area. That is not to say that cards cannot be used by personnel other than the authorised holder.

### *Observations*

Other than carrying out random or spot checks, there is no way of confirming who is using what card.

### *Recommendations*

It is recommended that a photographic identity/access control card system is considered, meaning that personnel attempting to enter the lift area will have their photograph identification confirmed before being granted access.

## Section 6.2 CCTV

There are currently thirty static CCTV cameras installed across the six floors occupied by BU, allocated as follows:

### *Floors 1–5*

There are two cameras focussing on the lift entrances, two cameras inside the office space, and one camera covering the server/communications room.

### *Floor 35*

There are two cameras focussing on the lift entrances, two cameras inside the office space, and one camera covering the sever/communications room.

All cameras are in a good state of repair and are fit for purpose. The CCTV system utilises Cat 5 cabling which signals to the BU Security Control Room, with all images being recorded onto a Network Video Recording (NVR) platform.

### *Observations*

There is only one camera external to the building, and there are two areas on each floor where there is no camera coverage. The Executive Boardroom on the 35$^{th}$ floor currently receives no camera coverage.

### *Recommendations*

The following recommendations should be given consideration.

Once again, although ultimately it is the building owner's responsibility, it is recommended that the building CCTV is extended to include an extra four external cameras to afford the building 360-degree support.

It is further recommended that two extra cameras are installed on each floor and that two cameras are installed in the Executive Boardroom.

## Section 6.3 IDS

### *Ground floor*

The main entrance, the goods inwards door, and all fire exits have internal door contacts fitted, and should any of the entrances be forced, the IDS will raise an alarm in the building Security Control Room.

### *Floors 1–5*

All entrances to BU office space have door contacts, and the server/communications rooms are protected by internal dual technology IDS sensors.

### *Floor 35*

The entrance to BU office space is protected by door contacts. Internally, all Senior Management Team offices are protected by a dual technology IDS sensor, as is the Executive Boardroom.

If the IDS is activated on any BU floors, it will signal to the BU Security Control Room.

At the time of the Security Survey, all elements of the IDS were fit for purpose.

## Section 6.4 Lighting

Lighting across all of the BU floor space is movement activated, with a manual override. There is also emergency battery-powered lighting should the mains supply fail.

During the Security Survey, it was observed that all internal lighting was operational and fit for purpose.

## *Section 6.5 Manned guarding*

The entire Security Team is employed by BU.

### *Duty hours*

0600hrs to 1800hrs, Monday to Friday (inclusive) there is a Security Supervisor and five Security Officers on duty.

1800hrs to 0600hrs, and Saturday/Sunday there is a Security Supervisor and three Security Officers on duty.

### *Duties carried out e.g., patrolling, Security Control Room duties, and FM support*

Security Officers carry out the following duties, day, and night.

- Security Control Room Management.
- Alarm response
- Patrolling (internal).
- Search duties.
- Static security.
- FM support.[26]
- Security incident management.
- Investigations.
- Report writing.

### *Training and licencing*

Although there is presently no legislative or regulatory requirement for 'in-house' Security Officers to hold a front-line SIA licence, BU have invested in the process, ensuring that all of their Security Team members are trained and licenced appropriately.

### *Extra curriculum qualifications e.g., Fire Wardens, Health and Safety, and so on*

All members of the BU security team hold the following qualifications:

- First aid
- Fire and evacuation.

- Health & Safety.
- Level 3 Security Management certificate.

### *Site Assignment Instructions (SAI's).*[27]

There is a set of Site Assignment Instructions (SAIs) which have been drawn up by the company Security Manager. The SAIs are reviewed every six months.

At the time of the Security Survey, there were no issues surrounding manned guarding.

## Section 7: Internal specialist or restricted areas

There are a number of specialist or restricted areas at the location under survey, in no particular order.

### *Section 7.1 Uninterruptible Power Supply (UPS) room*

The UPS is located in the basement, in a single, secure room with one point of access. The room contains a battery-powered Uninterruptible Power Supply that is used, for a limited period, in an emergency to power the ICT network.

The UPS is only accessed by Facilities Management engineers, network engineers, and the security team. Access is by means of a proximity card reader system, and it is supported by CCTV and the building IDS.

There is a land line telephone inside the UPS room which is used to communicate with the Security Control Room.

During the Security Survey, it was observed that the UPS was operational and fit for purpose.

### *Section 7.2 Standby diesel generator room*

The standby generator is also located in the basement, in a secure space next to the UPS room. It has one point of access.

As with the UPS, the standby generator is only accessed by Facilities Management engineers, network engineers, and the Security Team. Access is also by means of a proximity card reader system, and it is supported by CCTV and the building IDS.

There is a land line telephone inside the generator space which is used to communicate with the Security Control Room.

During the Security Survey, it was observed that the generator was operational and fit for purpose.

### Section 7.3 Senior Management Team (SMT) car parking

There are six SMT car parking bays located in the basement. Access to the basement car park is by means of the building proximity card reader system, and the area is supported by the building CCTV system, with very good movement detection lighting.

The car park is patrolled three times per day, and three times per night by duty Security officers.

Every car space occupant (driver) is issued with a remote opening device to allow access to, and egress from the car park.

### Section 7.4 Security control room

The BU Security Control Room is located on the ground floor, and it is responsible for the operations and management of the following security and safety systems.

- **CCTV**

  The CCTV system having been examined was deemed to be fit for purpose. That is to say, all cameras were operational, covering the correct arcs and fields of vision. There is a Faults Log, and at the time of the Security Survey, it was up to date. The Security Auditor sat with the most experienced CCTV operator and was taken through each camera setting and the arcs and fields of vision designed for all cameras.

  All monitors were operating, and the recording equipment was functioning correctly. The system is not fitted with Video Motion Detection software.
- **IDS**

  There is Manned Guarding support 24/7, and all Restricted Areas, such as the server/comms room should are fitted with an IDS. The IDS is functional, and upon activation, it signals to the correct platform, i.e., the Security Control Room. There is an activation log that records all activations, including false alarms, and at the time of the Security Survey, it was up to date.

There is also a 'door held open' alarm, which was tested and found to be operationally functional.

- **Automatic Access Control Systems (AACS)**
  There is a functioning Automatic Access Control system which was tested during the Security Survey and was found to be operationally functional and fit for purpose.
  There is a hierarchy of permissions allowing authorised personnel only into areas such as server/comms rooms, UPS/generator rooms, the Executive Board Room, and so on.
- **Communications Systems**
  Because of the complexity of the building, and the fact that there is a 24/7 Security Team, there is a handheld radio system, and during the Security Survey, it was checked to ensure that all radios were in good working order and were being managed correctly. There is also a covert radio system in situ. That was functioning and was being used correctly.
- **Lone worker control systems**
  There is no lone worker control system in use.

### *Observations*

During the Security Survey it was observed that throughout the night, Security officers are expected to carry out external patrols alone.

### *Recommendations*

It is strongly recommended that a lone worker control, the system is initiated to offer cover to the vulnerable Security Officers.

- **Patrol Management Systems**
  There is no Patrol Management system in place.
- **First aid and defibrillation systems**
  There are first aid and defibrillations systems in place. They are in good working order and are secured. There is also a log which records when they were last used, for what purpose, and by whom.
  At the time of the Security Survey, the log was up to date, and the defibrillation systems were fit for purpose.

- **Emergency grab bags**
  There are emergency gran bags in the control room, and they are appropriately managed and stored correctly. Once again there is a log which identifies when they were last used and by whom.
  At the time of the Security Survey, the log was up to date, and the defibrillation systems were fit for purpose.
- **Key control**
  There is a key press, and at the time of the Security Survey, all keys were accounted for.

## *Section 7.5 Server/communications*

There is a server/communications room located in the centre of floors 1–5. Each room contains communications and ICT controls for the business unit being supported on that floor. Access is restricted to ICT engineers, and the security team, and is achieved by the use of a two-factor access control system consisting of a proximity card reader system and individual PIN.

The server/communications room is protected by four load-bearing walls and a solid floor. Cabling enters from a false ceiling, which is supported by the building IDS, an internal/external CCTV.

There is an internal communications land line with a direct connection to the Security Control Room, and the location is visited three times per day, and three times per night by the duty Security officer.

### *Observations*

There is no reserve server/communications room.

There is the possibility that the server/communications room could be disabled by either physical or electronic (cyber) attacks.

### *Recommendations*

It is recommended that as a matter of urgency, a reserve server/communications room is identified. The room should be fitted out with equipment and systems that allow the Business Unit to continue operations after an attack.

### *Section 7.5 Executive boardroom*

There is an Executive Boardroom located on floor 35. The room contains low level security data and information. Access is restricted to the Senior Management Team, and security personnel, and is achieved by the use of a two-factor access control system consisting of a proximity card reader system and individual PIN.

The Boardroom is protected by four load-bearing walls, and a solid floor. Cabling enters from a false ceiling, which is supported by the building IDS, and internal/external CCTV.

There is an internal communications land line with a direct connection to the Security Control Room, The location is visited three times per day, and three times per night by the duty Security Officer.

## Section 8: Conclusions

### *Section 8.1 Post survey de brief*

A post survey debrief was arranged, during which Mr Baker was informed of a number of 'quick fixes', and an agreement was reached in relation to the Security Survey Report. Mr Baker requested the report to be delivered to him by hand within 14 working days.

There is a requirement for a security presentation, and future talks will take place in relation to other work throughout the UK.

The client concluded by declaring that he was very satisfied with the Security Survey, and how it was carried out.

### *Key takeaways*

*As previously mentioned, a Security Survey is only as good as the written report.*

# Publicly accessible locations (PAL)

## Liverport Arena, Liverpool Docklands, LE1 2BB

| Document owner | Reference number | Proof-reader | 1st check | 2nd check |
| --- | --- | --- | --- | --- |
| Sue Beck | SecSurv/LA/02/22 | | | |

1. **Survey details.**
2. **Initial stages of the survey.**
3. **External factors.**
4. **Perimeter protection.**
5. **Main buildings-external.**
6. **Main buildings-internal.**
7. **Internal specialist or restricted areas.**
8. **Conclusion.**

## Section 1: Survey details

Name and appointment of the client.

| |
| --- |
| Mrs Sue Beck. CEO |

Address (s)

| |
| --- |
| Liverport Arena, Liverpool Docklands, LE1 2BB. |

Point of Contact.

| |
| --- |
| Mr Steve Watts. Security Manager. |

E mail.

| |
|---|
| s.watts@larena.com |

Telephone.

| |
|---|
| 015112346487 |

Web address.

| |
|---|
| www.LiverpoolArena.com |

Location of Survey.

| |
|---|
| Liverport Arena, Liverpool Docklands, LE1 2BB. |

Name of Security Auditor.

| |
|---|
| Charles Swanson MSc CSyP |

Organisation.

| |
|---|
| STC |

Date of Survey.

| |
|---|
| 23 December 2021 |

## Section 2: Initial stages of the survey

It was decided that because of the unique operations of the arena, the Security Survey would be carried out whilst no event was taking place, with a further visit, at a later stage during an event.

### *Section 2.1 General description and business operations*

The Liverport Arena is a multi-functional, covered stadium that holds a variety of events including pop concerts, conferences, exhibitions, and indoor sports activities such as basketball, volleyball, badminton, and so on.

By virtue of the fact that the arena is covered, and there is a variety of events means that it is accessible to businesses on a 24/7 basis throughout the year. Timings do of course depend on the nature of the event, and the requirements of the client.

### *Section 2.2 Assets to be protected at the location under survey include*

#### *People*

There are approximately seventy-five full and part-time staff working at the arena, not including contractors and cleaning staff. When an event is being held, there are also sports persons, pop stars, commerce, and industry leaders, and at times high ranking national and international government ministers and their protection teams. From a conference that may have a hundred or so delegates, to a pop concert where several thousand people are likely to be in attendance.

People are therefore considered a top priority in terms of asset protection.

#### *Sensitive information and data*

Sensitive information and data are assets that are very attractive to a variety of criminals and may consist of sales information, security data, classified information about individual events and their participants, and information relating to future events. They are critical assets to the arena management team.

#### *Infrastructure*

The infrastructure of the arena refers to the facilities and systems that support the functions of the building, including ICT, Building Management

Systems, power supply, water, and gas. All of which are critical to the functionality of the premises, and should they be attacked, the impact could be catastrophic, particularly if the arena is occupied at the time of the attack.

### *Brand and reputation*

The Liverport Arena, like so many stadia, relies on its brand and reputation to gain sales and grow the business. The name of the arena is associated with safety, security, and excellent customer service. Any negative connotations would be critical for the future of the location, and to that end, brand and reputation are assets that must be protected at all costs.

## *Section 2.3 Reasons for the Security Survey*

It is planned to hold a very high-profile music festival in the arena, and it will be the first of its kind since the Manchester Arena attack.

Table 37 has been lifted directly from the arena Security Risk Assessment, and it can be seen that the likelihood of a terrorist attack against the arena is *medium*, but the impact of such an event would be *catastrophic*.

Historically, the events team have been more than able to cope with a music festival or a pop concert, and as is standard procedure, the team sought advice from the local Counter Terrorism Security Advisor (CTSA). Advice received from the police specialist has been that although procedurally it appears the arena is prepared to engage with the public, subject matter expert advice should be listened to, and a formal Security Survey of the arena should be carried out by a competent Security Auditor.

*Table* 37 Likelihood and impact of a terrorist attack against the Liverport Arena *after* mitigation

| | **Impact** | *1 (Very low)* | *2 (Low)* | *3 (High)* | *4 (Very high)* | **5 (Catastrophic)** |
|---|---|---|---|---|---|---|
| **Likelihood** | | | | | | |
| 1 (Very low) | | | | | | |
| 2 (Low) | | | | | | |
| **3 (Medium)** | | | | | | **15/25** |
| 4 (High) | | | | | | |
| 5 (Very high) | | | | | | |

## Section 2.4 Initial research

### Company background and security culture

The Liverport Arena was commissioned in January 2005, as the result of funding from the European Commission, and it was opened in January 2008 by Her Majesty Queen Elizabeth II, to be used as a multi-functional stadium for all types of events.

On 07 July 2005, four young men from Leeds carried out the first suicide attack against the United Kingdom, killing 79 passengers on the London transport system, and injuring almost 800. As the result of what is now referred to as 7/7, the security infrastructure of the Liverport Arena was designed into the architectural planning for the building.

Furthermore, it was decided by the owners of the building, Liverport City Council, that going forward, all members of staff, security or otherwise would receive security training on a regular basis, endearing itself to the local population.

During the Security Survey, evidence of staff security training was examined, and as the result of a great deal of hard work by the security team, HR, and the Training Manager, there is a good level of security training delivered to all members of staff, full and part-time.

### Unemployment rates

Unemployment in the general area is higher than the national average, with circa 14% of all adults currently seeking employment.

### Previous criminal incidents

There is a history of minor crimes in and around the arena, but since the commission of the survey, there have been no serious crimes recorded.

### Previous Security Surveys

Although Security Risk Assessments are carried out on a regular basis, at least once per year, this is the first Security Survey to be commissioned at the location. Copies of all Security Risk Assessment Reports have been made available for scrutiny.

### *Crime Pattern Analysis (CPA) – LE1 2BB*

The postcode LE1 2BB indicates an area of Liverport that is devoted to hospitality and entertainment. Although cybercrime and terrorism are not covered in this form of CPA, it is safe to say that they will be classified as two of the most serious threats to any community. In terms of general crime, the greatest fear for this area is related to robbery and burglary, which are in fact relatively minimal.

From January 2020 to December 2021, the greatest levels of crime originate from anti-social behaviour, violence and sexual offences, and theft (in its many forms).

## *Section 2.5 Planning and preparation*

Having carried out initial research in relation to the arena, there was then focus on planning and preparation. As with all other sectors covered in this book, there are a number of similarities, but equally, there are unique areas that require particular preparation.

### *Maps and diagrams*

The Liverport Arena is located in the city centre, adjacent to the river Mertees, and is easily located. There are ample maps of the area, easily accessed from local retail outlets. In terms of diagrams, they were acquired from the Security Manager.

### *Authorisation and specific points of contact*

The Security Survey was authorised by Liverport City Council, and the direct point of contact is the Security Manager. It was also important to make contact with the local CTSA and then maintain communications with both parties throughout the survey process.

### *Changes in laws and regulations*

All security professionals should constantly stay abreast of new laws and regulations, and in terms of event security, probably the most critical piece of legislation being planned is a proposed Act of Parliament called Protect Duty.[28] The law is intended to be a legal requirement for all public places to ensure preparedness for and protection from terrorist attacks. This piece of legislation is referred to as Martyn's Law.

### *Social media*

The events team at the Liverport Arena are, to a certain extent reliant on social media to increase public awareness and sales. Therefore it was important to constantly monitor all social media platforms such as Facebook, Instagram, Twitter, and so on, to have a full understanding of how the arena is publicising itself because research is one of the many instruments in the professional criminal or terrorist's toolbox.

### *Photography*

Photography is a very important tool and should certainly be included in the final report, and permission to take photographs in and around the arena was granted. Although there is no legal requirement to have permission to take photographs outside, it will always save time, effort, and embarrassment if written permission is granted for internal and external photography.

### *Identification*

In the United Kingdom, unlike most developed nations there is no requirement to carry proof of identification. However, as with photography, in order to save time and avoid unnecessary delay, the Security Auditor was advised to carry his driving licence or passport to show if required for entry to the arena.

### *Agreed visits, times, and dates*

This may be seen as minutia, but the client and their team are always extremely busy, particularly when preparing for a major event, and it was beholden on the Security Auditor to ensure that all appointments made were honoured, and that visit times and dates were adhered to. This was achieved throughout the Security Survey.

### *Transportation arrangements*

There is ample parking space in and around the arena, and Liverpool boasts one of the most efficient public transport systems in the UK. Transportation was not an issue.

## Section 3: External factors

### *Section 3.1 Environment*

#### *Rural/Urban*

The Liverpool Arena is located in the centre of a very busy city, and adjacent to a thriving water leisure area.

### *Section 3.2 Crime Pattern Analysis*

See Section 2.

### *Section 3.3 Employment rates*

There are approximately 1,000 people employed in the local area, including the water and leisure facilities.

### *Section 3.4 Potential for Crime Prevention Through Environmental design (CPTED) using the acronym MAINT*

**M**aintenance: Standards of repair and maintenance at the site under survey are extremely high.

**A**ccess Control: Access control in and around the target building is well thought out, matching any CPTED expectations.

**I**mage: The Liverpool Arena is iconic in terms of image, and whilst it may be a target for criminals or terrorists, it also stands for pride and self-belief.

**N**atural surveillance: There is an abundance of natural light external to, and within the building, which has also been designed to make the most of straight lines and open spaces.

**T**erritoriality: There are tables and chairs outside of the building for use by staff and the general public, and there is a shopping mall below, enhancing a feeling of territoriality.

### Section 3.5 Nearest police station

The nearest police station can be found at Lord Street, Liverport, LE1 7BS. It is accessible to the public from 0900 to 1700hrs, Monday to Friday, and the telephone number is 0152 928 0990. Should an emergency require reporting, members of the public are advised to call 999.

### Section 3.6 Nearest hospital

The nearest hospital, with an A&E facility, is located at North Road, Liverport, LE1 11DZ. The telephone number is 0152 924 2615. Should an emergency require reporting, members of the public are advised to call 999.

### Section 3.7 Nearest fire and rescue

The nearest fire and rescue station is located at Glendale Road, Liverport, LE112VC. The telephone number is 0152 924 5963. Should an emergency require reporting, members of the public are advised to call 999.

## Section 4: Perimeter protection

There is no perimeter at the Liverport Arena.

## Section 5: Main building (s) external

### Section 5.1 Key personnel

As with all other sectors' Security Surveys, this is one of the most critical sections of the survey, and it is imperative that as many key personnel as possible are spoken to.

#### *Who?*

The Liverport arena is an extremely high-profile target location, and it was imperative to speak with the following personnel.

Sue Beck. CEO.
Steve Watts. Security Manager
Paul Hilliard. HR Director.
Bill Giles. CFO.
Mark Chappel. ICT Manager.

John O Rourke. Senior Security Supervisor.
Security Officers.
Receptionists.
Stewards.
Contractors.

It is important to speak to as many and varied site personnel as possible, in order to achieve a rounded approach to the interview stage.

### *When?*

There is no definitive means of ascertaining or calculating when the best time is to speak to key personnel. The arena is open at irregular times, so the emphasis is on you to adapt your schedule to speak to as many relevant people as possible.

### *What?*

With such a divergent range of key personnel being spoken to, with potentially tight time margins you are advised to preselect the questions to be asked before each interview, ensuring that all questions are appropriate, and adding knowledge gained during the Security Risk Assessment.

## Section 5.2 Description of building (s)

The building in question is of very modern design and is constructed of concrete, steel, and glass. It consists of a basement, a ground floor which includes the concert area, and an upper floor for overstage sitting. The building conforms with all current building regulations and has been Security Risk Assessed.

## Section 5.3 Number of access points and how are they secured

Number of access points and how they are secured are as follows:

### *Main entrance*

The main entrance, which consists of five double-leaf glass and steel doors is secure when no events are taking place. One of the five doors offers access to the box office, and is open Monday to Saturday, from 0900 to 2000hrs, with a Security Officer or member of staff being located immediately inside the door.

All main entrance points are secured at 2000hrs, and the arena IDS is set by the duty Security Officer. The building is then vacated, with all alarm systems (and CCTV) being remotely monitored at an Alarm Receiving Centre (ARC), from which a response can be despatched if an alarm is activated.

At the time of the Security Survey, all alarm systems were fit for purpose.

### *Goods inwards*

There is a goods inwards entrance located to the rear of the building, which is occupied and operational whilst the venue is open. Deliveries must be confirmed in advance, and persons requiring entrance must prove identity. The entrance is protected by the building IDS which is set once the arena is secured.

### *Observations*

The goods inwards entrance is covered by the building CCTV system, although at the time of the Security Survey two cameras were unserviceable.

### *Recommendations*

CCTV is critical to the security of the arena, and the two faulty cameras should be repaired or replaced as a matter of urgency.

### *Fire exits*

There are eight fire exits located on the ground floor, all of which are controlled from within. The fire exits are linked to the automated fire control system, and should the fire alarm be activated, all fire exit locking mechanisms will be released. This allows unopposed access to the building from outside. The fire exits are covered by the building CCTV system, and all exits are covered by the building IDS, being active on a 24/7 basis. If one or more of the fire exits are opened from the inside of the building, the silent IDS will activate and during operational hours there will be a reaction from the arena Security Control Room. Once the building is secure at 2000hrs, an IDS activation will be responded to from the ARC.

At the time of the Security Survey, all fire exits were protected by an IDS that was fit for purpose.

### Section 5.4 CCTV

There are twelve CCTV cameras external to the building, in the following locations:

- Two static cameras covering the main entrance.
- A single static camera covers each of the eight fire exits.
- There are two static cameras supporting the goods inwards area.

The cameras are digital colour units that are all in a good state of repair and are fit for purpose.

During operational hours the cameras signal back to the Arena Security Control Room via Cat 5 cabling, with images captured and recorded on a Network Video Recording (NVR) system. Whilst the arena is secured, the CCTV system is remotely monitored by the ARC.

At the time of the Security Survey, all cameras were functional and fit for purpose.

### Section 5.5 IDS

When the building is secured, the main entrance, goods inwards doors, and fire exits are protected by an IDS (door contacts), which if breached will activate a silent alarm, received at the ARC. At the time of the Security Survey, the IDS was fit for purpose.

At the time of the Security Survey, all IDS elements were functional and fit for purpose.

### Section 5.6 Lighting

The arena and surrounding area are protected by external LED street lighting and building wall-mounted LED lighting units. Lighting is activated by photocell technology, which senses the reduced natural light, and will activate the street and building external lights accordingly.

### *Observations*

During the Security Survey, it was observed that two of the wall-mounted LED lighting units illuminating the main entrance were unserviceable.

### *Recommendations*

Effective lighting is critical to the security of the arena, and it is recommended that the two faulty lights are replaced as a matter of urgency.

## *Section 5.7 Distance from the perimeter*

N/A

## *Section 5.8 External utilities*

There is a National Grid power substation to the rear of the building, and there is a gas supply inspection port located adjacent to the goods inwards door. Security of both utilities is the responsibility of the suppliers, and at the time of the Security Survey, both utilities were secure.

## *Section 5.9 Areas of concealment*

There is a recessed section of the wall connecting the goods inwards door, and it is of sufficient depth to conceal a full-sized human being.

### *Observations*

The recess is large enough to conceal a full-sized human being, and at the time of the Security Survey, the recessed area was not covered by the CCTV system.

### *Recommendations*

It is recommended that the arena's external CCTV system is re-calibrated to offer cover in relation to the described recessed area. If that is not possible, it is recommended that an extra camera is installed to cover the recessed area.

It is further recommended that in the interim period, all security patrols cover the area of concern.

### *Section 5.10 Items used to help a criminal*

At the time of the survey, no such items were observed.

### *Section 5.11 Restricted areas*

With the exception of the aforementioned electricity and gas utilities, which are the responsibility of the power and gas suppliers, there are no external restricted areas.

### *Section 5.12 Parking arrangements*

There are five parking areas that support traffic flow at the Liverport Arena.

Four of the car parks are located external to the arena and are covered by the site CCTV system, and the fifth car parking area is located below the arena being reserved for VIP parking. When not in use, the underground car park is secured by means of a single steel roller shutter door, connected to the arena IDS and CCTV system.

During an event, the car park is controlled by a static Security Officer who is in possession of a list of expected guests. Once the Security Officer confirms the identity of the guest, a single-arm barrier will be raised, and the driver of the vehicle will be advised of the parking bay to be used. The car park CCTV cameras are also configured as Automatic Number Plate Recognition (ANPR) units, and still images of all vehicles entering the car park will be held on file for thirty days.

## Section 6: Main building (s) internal

### *Section 6.1 Access control*

#### *Access to and within the building*

This is a detached building, with one main entrance area, a goods inwards door, and eight fire exits, and as with the Security Survey carried out at 50 Canada Way, the first task was to establish the security regime in terms of staff and visitors accessing the building.

Figure 12 is a simple floor plan of the arena, in which all of the entrances and exits are displayed.

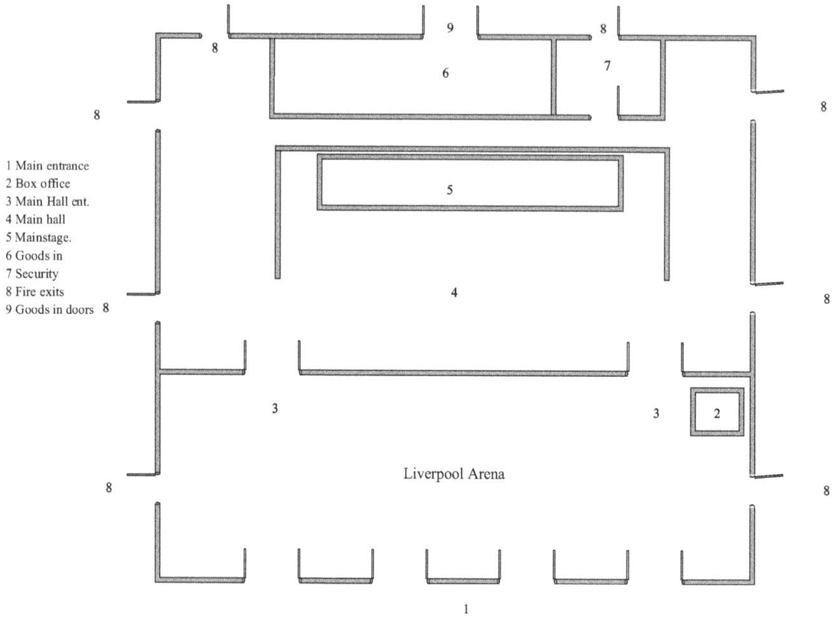


*Figure 12* Liverport Arena floor plan.

The arena is surrounded by retail outlets, cafeterias, and restaurants, and the Security Auditor was able to blend in quite naturally, observing how staff and members of the public accessed the building. He was also able to monitor the activities and reactions of the Duty Security Officers.

Whilst carrying out external observations, the Security Auditor also had the opportunity to observe the security of the goods inwards doors.

## *Observations*

Whilst observing the fire exits, it was noted that one of the fire escape doors was wedged open by the use of a fire extinguisher. The IDS activation did not signal to the alarm monitor in the Security Control Room.

## *Recommendations*

During observations, the Security Auditor brought the open door to the attention of a Security Officer, and the door was secured.

However, it is recommended that the building IDS is examined to discover why it didn't activate when the fire exit was opened, or if it did activate, why no positive action was taken in response.

## *Section 6.2 Access control-inside*

### *Staff*

Once inside, all members of staff access secure areas of the arena by means of a proximity card which, when introduced to the reader allows access to a particular area. The system is supported by a no pass back facility, which means that individual cards cannot be reused for entrance purposes until they have exited the area. That is not to say that cards cannot be used by personnel other than the authorised holder.

### *Observations*

Other than carrying out random or spot checks, there is no way of confirming who is using what card.

### *Recommendations*

It is recommended that a photographic identity/access control card system is considered, meaning that personnel attempting to enter the lift area will have their photograph identification confirmed before being granted access.

### *Visitors/contractors*

All visitors and contractors report to the Security Control Room, where they are issued with a temporary pass. The pass must be displayed at all times, and it has to be surrendered upon leaving the building.

All rooms within the arena are linked to the site proximity card reader access control system, which is managed and audited by the Security Team, from within the Security Control Room.

### *Search*

Everybody entering the arena is made aware of the search policy which states that their bags may be searched on entry, as a condition of entry. This is carried out in an irregular manner, meaning that when no event is taking place, the onus is on security staff to decide who is to be searched.

When an event is due to take place, all carried luggage is searched before entrance is authorised.

### *Observations*

During the Security Survey, it was observed that none of the security team were search qualified. That is to say, nobody had attended a formal search training course.

### *Recommendations*

It is recommended that all Security Officers and a percentage of arena staff attend a formal search training course that on completion awards a search qualification.

## *Section 6.3 CCTV*

In total there are currently 14 CCTV cameras installed within the arena, at the flowing locations:

- Main building entrance. Two cameras.
- Main hall entrance. Two cameras.
- Main hall. Four cameras.
- Corridors. Three cameras.
- Goods inwards. One camera.
- Security Control Room. Two cameras.

The CCTV system utilises Cat 5 cabling which signals to the Arena Security Control Room, with all images being recorded onto a Network Video Recording (NVR) platform. When the arena is closed, the CCTV system is monitored form the Alarm Receiving Centre.

All cameras are in a good state of repair and are fit for purpose.

### *Observations*

There is currently no CCTV coverage in the box office, nor are there any cameras installed on the stage area.

### *Recommendations*

It is recommended that cameras are installed within the box office and on either side of the stage.

## Section 6.4 IDS

When the building is secure, all fire exits have internal door contacts fitted, and should any of the entrances be forced, the IDS will alarm in the building's Security Control Room.

Internal dual technology IDS sensors are installed at the following locations.

- Main entrance covering the entrance doors,
- All internal corridors.
- Waiting area adjacent to the box office.
- Inside the box office.
- Main Hall.
- Goods inwards.
- Security Control room.

When the building is secure, any alarm activation will be monitored and managed by the Alarm Receiving Centre, and a security patrol will be despatched to investigate.

At the time of the Security Survey, all IDS elements were functional and fit for purpose.

## Section 6.5 Lighting

Lighting across the arena floor space is movement activated, with a manual override. There is also emergency battery-powered lighting should the mains supply fail.

At the time of the Security Survey, all lighting units were functional and fit for purpose.

## Section 6.6 Manned guarding

The entire Security Team is employed by Liverport City Council.

Duty hours – When there are no events taking place.

0800 to 1800hrs – Monday to Friday: One Security Supervisor and four Security Officers.

1800 to 0800hrs – Monday to Friday: Three Security Officers.

Duty hours – When an event is taking place.

0800 to 1800hrs: One Security Supervisor and four Security Officers.

1800hrs until the arena is clear: One Security Officer and six Security Officers.

1800hrs until the arena is clear: The security tam will be supplemented by 12 Security Stewards responsible for car parking and bag searching.

### *Observations*

The complementary stewards are not SIA Front-Line licenced.

### *Recommendations*

It is recommended that all security staff deployed at the arena hold Front-Line SIA licences.

### *Duties carried out*

Security Officers carry out the following duties, day, and night.

- Security Control Room Management.
- Alarm response
- Patrolling (internal).
- Search duties.
- Static security.
- FM support.[29]
- Security incident management.
- Investigations.
- Report writing.

### *Extra curriculum qualifications*

All Liverpool Arena Front-Line Security Officers hold the following qualifications:

- First aid
- Fire and evacuation.
- Health & Safety.
- Search.

### *Observations*

During the Security Survey, it was observed that none of the stewards tasked with carrying out bag searches were search qualified.

It was also observed that none of the Security Control Room CCTV operators hold an SIA Public Space Surveillance (PSS) licence. The CCTV system looks at public space outside of the arena.

### *Recommendations*

In the first instance it is critical that all stewards tasked with carrying out search procedures are search trained and qualified. Effective search is one of the first lines of defence, and it must be carried out to the highest possible standards.

In terms of Public Space Surveillance, it is likely, although not definite that the Arena Senior Management Team may be in breach of the Security Industry Act (2001), and it is therefore imperative that all CCTV operators hold the necessary SIA PSS licence.

### *Site Specific Assignment Instructions (SSAI's)*[30]

There is a set of Site-Specific Assignment Instructions (SSAI's) which have been drawn up by the Arena Security Manager. The SSAI's are reviewed every six months, and there is a contractual requirement for the review to be formally recorded and authorised by the Arena Security Manager.

### *Observations*

At the time of the Security Survey, it was observed that the SSAIs had not been signed by the Arena Security Manager for two years.

### *Recommendations*

Unrecorded SSAI reviews may lead to contractual issues, but perhaps more importantly, they could reflect security issues at the arena that have not been remedied. It is recommended that the SSAIs are formally reviewed, recorded, and signed off at the earliest opportunity.

## Section 7: Internal specialist or restricted areas

### *Section 7.1 Box office*

The box office is located inside the main hall, and it is deemed a restricted area because it holds sensitive information, and at times cash.[31] The box office is protected by the arena CCTV system, also the building IDS. Selected access to the room is by means of a proximity card reader system.

### *Section 7.2 Uninterruptible Power Supply (UPS) room*

The UPS is located to the rear of the building, in a single, secure building with one point of access. The room contains a battery-powered Uninterruptible Power Supply that is used, for a limited period, in an emergency to power the ICT network.

The UPS is only accessed by Facilities Management engineers, network engineers, and the Security Team. Access is by means of a proximity card reader system, and it is supported by CCTV and the building IDS.

There is a land line telephone inside the UPS room which is used to communicate with the Security Control Room.

### *Section 7.3 Standby diesel generator room*

The standby generator is also to be found at the rear of the building, in a secure location next to the UPS room. It has one point of access.

As with the UPS, the standby generator is only accessed by Facilities Management engineers, network engineers, and the Security Team. Access is also by means of a proximity card reader system, and it is supported by CCTV and the building IDS.

There is a land line telephone inside the generator space which is used to communicate with the Security Control Room.

### *Section 7.4 The security control room*

The Liverpool Arena Security Control Room is located on the ground floor and manages all of the following security and safety systems.

- **CCTV**
  During the Security Survey it was observed that the CCTV system was fit for purpose, that is to say, all cameras are operational, and are

covering the correct arcs and fields of vision. If any cameras are not operational, there is a faults log in which the problems and their ultimate solutions will be recorded.

During the Security Survey, the Security Auditor sat with the most experienced CCTV operator and was taken through each camera setting and the arcs and fields of vision designed for that camera.

All monitors were operating, and the recording equipment was functioning correctly. The system is fitted with Video Motion Detection software.

During the Security Survey, all cameras and software were operating correctly and were fit for purpose.

- **IDS**

  There is Manned Guarding support, and restricted areas are fitted with an IDS. The IDS is functional, and upon activation, it signals to the correct platform, i.e., the Security Control Room, or perhaps an Alarm Receiving Centre (ARC). Once again there is an activation log that records all activations, including false alarms.

  There is also a 'door held open' alarm, and it is periodically physically checked to ensure it is operational and is being tested on a regular basis.

  During the Security Survey, the IDS was operating correctly and was deemed fit for purpose.

- **Automatic Access Control Systems (AACS)**

  The Liverport Arena has advanced access control systems installed, and during the Security Survey, the system was examined to ensure it was fit for purpose, and that it was being controlled and managed in accordance with the policies and procedures of the location. There is a hierarchy of permissions to allow authorised personnel only into areas such as server/comms rooms, UPS/generator rooms, the Executive Board Room, and so on.

  During the Security Survey, the AACS was operating correctly and was fit for purpose.

- **Communications systems**

  The communications system at the arena consists of a number of handheld radios, monitored and managed from the Security Control Room. There should be a formal radio network that is conformed to by all users, and there must not be any 'black spots', where radio communications are poor, or even nonexistent.

During the Security Survey, all radios were operational, radio discipline was being adhered to and there were no black spots.

- **Lone worker control systems**
  There is no lone worker control system in use.
- **Patrol Management Systems**
  There is no Patrol Management system in place.
- **First aid and defibrillation systems**
  There are first aid and defibrillations systems in place, and during the Security Survey, they were in good working order and are secured. There was also a log in place to record when they were last used, for what purpose, and by whom.
- **Emergency grab bags**
  There are emergency gran bags in the control room, and during the Security Survey, it was observed that they were appropriately managed and stored correctly. There is a log identifying when they were last used and by whom.
- **Key control**
  There is a key press, and at the time of the Security Survey all keys were present, and those not in storage had been signed out.

### *Section 7.5 Server/communications*

There is a server/communications room located in the Security Control Room, which is occupied whilst the arena is open. When the arena is closed, the server/communications room is protected by the building's CCTV and IDS. All server data is backed up to a cloud server and managed from the Alarm Receiving Centre.

During the Security Survey, the Security Auditor found the Server/Communications Room secure.

## Section 8: Conclusion

### *Section 8.1 Post survey de brief*

A post-survey debrief was carried out, during which the Arena Security Manager was informed of a number of 'quick fixes', and an agreement was reached in relation to the Security Survey Report. The Security Manager requested the report be delivered to him by hand within thirty working days.

There is a requirement for a survey presentation, and future talks will take place in relation to other work at other publicly accessible locations within the United Kingdom.

The Security Manager concluded by declaring that he was very satisfied with the Security Survey and how it was carried out.

## *Key takeaways*

*Remember the Manchester Arena attack and let's pray that lessons have been learned*

## Retail security

### Security Survey: Tescaldi Supermarket, 50 Canada Way

| Document owner | Reference number | Proof-reader | 1st check | 2nd check |
|---|---|---|---|---|
| Alan Youngblutt | SecSurv/TS/03/22 | | | |

1. **Survey details.**
2. **Initial stages of the survey.**
3. **External factors.**
4. **Perimeter protection.**
5. **Main buildings-external.**
6. **Main buildings-internal.**
7. **Internal specialist or restricted areas.**
8. **Conclusion.**

## Section 1: Survey details.

Name and appointment of the client.

| |
|---|
| Mr Alan Yougblutt. |

Address (s)

| |
|---|
| Tescaldi Supermarket, 50 Canada Way. Pegasus Wharf, London. E14 5DY. |

Point of Contact.

| |
|---|
| Mr Steven Halpin. |

E mail.

| |
|---|
| ayoungblutt@tescaldi.com |

Telephone.

| |
|---|
| 020706754432 |

Web address.

| |
|---|
| www.tescaldi.com |

Location of Survey.

| |
|---|
| Tescaldi Supermarket, 50 Canada Way. Pegasus Wharf, London. E14 5DY. |

Name of Security Auditor and date of survey.

| |
|---|
| Charles Swanson. 21 November 2021. |

Organisation.

| |
|---|
| STC |

## Section 2: Initial stages of the survey

### *Section 2.1 Genera description and business operations*

Tescaldi is a major retail outlet, located below 50 Canada Way, in the heart of the shopping area. From a security perspective, as with all other stores in the national chain, the Tescaldi outlet in Canada Way operates on a self-assessment basis, with the Store Manager completing a Self-Assessment Report twice per year.

Although there is no significant data set to confirm, it is likely that a percentage of theft at the retail outlet will have been committed by staff and management, and from a security culture perspective, that is of concern.

As with all other sectors, the retail Security Survey will meet certain criterion, based on the recognised six steps of the Security Survey.

### Section 2.2 Reasons for the survey

The shop has suffered a number of criminal incidents in the last six months, and there has been an increase in shrinkage.

#### Shrinkage

Shrinkage is the term used to cover the difference between recorded and actual stock.

It is the discrepancy between the value of stock held and the value of stock sold, and takes two forms: Known and Unknown

Known shrinkage:

- Price reductions
- Wastage
- Discovered theft

Unknown shrinkage:

- Unrecorded waste
- Undiscovered theft
- Undeclared reductions

As a result of the above, the Tescaldi Regional Security Manager secured funds for a Security Survey to be carried out.

### Section 2.3 Assets to be protected

The assets to be protected at the location under survey are as follows:

### *People*

In a retail environment, people are generally divided into three groups.

- **Staff**
  At Tescaldi, Canary Way there are 75 full and part-time members of staff.
- **Customers**
  Approximately 3,400 customers shop in the supermarket daily. This is known as footfall.
- **Delivery staff**
  The store receives seven deliveries per week, and quite often the goods being received are high-value produce; and that of course places delivery drivers under a certain amount of danger from robbery.

### *Stock*

The Tescaldi store accepts and sells stock ranging from inexpensive household goods to extremely expensive clothing and electronics equipment. Almost all of the stock held from a criminal perspective conforms with the criminological CRAVED theory, which stands for:

**C**oncealable.
**R**emovable.
**A**ccessible.
**V**aluable.
**E**njoyable.
**D**isposable.

All of the above pointing to the fact that the store, once again from a criminal point of view, is a legitimate target.

### *Sensitive sales information and data*

The store has its own HR department, meaning that here will be sensitive information relating to staff, which must be protected for GDPR reasons.[32] Equally, sensitive commercial information is held on the store ICT system, which is connected to the group ICT network.

### *Brand and reputation*

The Tescaldi Group is an FSTE 100 member, and as such its brand and reputation impact the share price, with the knock-on effect which sees shareholders potentially suffering. Also, it has a reputation for ensuring safe shopping, and the health and safety of its staff. If there is an impression, and that is all it may take, that standards are falling, the brand and reputation of the group and the store will be negatively impacted.

## ***Section 2.4 Initial research***

### *Company background and security culture*

The Tescaldi store at Canada Way is part of the Tescaldi Group which has been trading since 1892. The store has been in existence since Canada Way opened in 2001, and has continued to grow physically, and in terms of business development. As mentioned, there has been an increase in shrinkage during the last twelve months, but the Group Security Function has been forward-thinking in arranging for a Security Survey.

### *Unemployment rates in the area*

Unemployment rates in the area are lower than the national average and lower than in the remainder of London.

### *Previous criminal incidents*

No serious previous criminal incidents have been reported.

### *Previous Security Surveys*

Throughout the group, there is a reliance on the Store Security Self-Assessment (SSA), which is convenient and allegedly more cost-effective. Therefore, there has never been a Security Survey carried out at this particular store, and SSSA reports will have to suffice in terms of learning from past incidents and assessments.

### *Crime Pattern Analysis (CPA)*

As mentioned previously, critical to any Crime Pattern Analysis is an understanding of what crime impacts the location being surveyed. The Store

Manager of a large internal bespoke outlet is unlikely to be too worried about anti-social behaviour or bicycle theft, as examples, but he will obviously be concerned if levels of theft and assault are high.

Once again, as with the Security Survey carried out in a corporate environment, it is worth thinking about how we gather information about crimes being committed in the area that we are paying attention to, and in this case, we are looking at the post code E14 5DY, which we are going to feed into www.police.uk

From August 2020 to July 2021, June has been the most prominent, with approximately 240 crimes being committed.

During the last twelve-month period, the most prominent three crimes have been anti-social behaviour (c1100), violence and sexual offences (c600), and shoplifting (c200). For the Tescaldi Store Manager, of most concern will be violence and sexual offences, burglary (c150), and robbery (c75).

Broadly speaking, if you examine crime statistics during the last month, or over the last three years, the figures will largely be the same.

Next comes planning and preparation.

## Section 2.5 Planning and preparation

"*A man who does not plan long ahead will find trouble at his door.*" – Confucius[33]

As with research, there are a number of areas that must be taken into consideration, and to a certain extent, they will change in accordance with the type of location being surveyed.

### Maps and diagrams

In terms of maps and diagrams, there is still a necessity to be able to effectively navigate around the store, which has a ground floor and three levels above. As with most other locations, it may be difficult to access detailed maps and schematics but having the ability to find your way around the store is critical.

### Authorisation and specific points of contact

In this particular scenario, authorisation has come from the Store Manager because of the relatively high levels of shrinkage, which may of course include theft. The point of contact in this instance is the Senior Security Supervisor, Mr Steven Halpin.

### *Changes in laws and regulations*

As with the corporate building at 50 Canada Way, it is unlikely that there will be major alterations or changes in law and regulations at Tescalsi. However, because it is people reliant, and therefore heavily dominated by health and safety legislation and regulations, the Security Surveyor must make every effort to remain vigilant to any changes in circumstances.

### *Key takeaways*

*I may have said this before. Although this is not a Health & Safety Survey, the Security Auditor must always bear in mind that safety is paramount, particularly in a people-dominated environment, and therefore, any safety issues identified during the survey must be reported to the risk owner.*

### *Social media*

The demography of retail staff is generally quite young, and therefore it is likely that store staff will engage with social media. I am not for one minute advocating the interrogation of individual accounts, but you are likely to learn about the culture of the store and its staff by observing social media.

### *Photography*

As I have mentioned previously, photography is a significant tool when the Security Survey Report is being written, and of course, a picture paints a thousand words, but a note of caution. Taking photographs in a retail environment is likely to draw attention to your efforts, but on balance, it is worthy of the extra attention. However, ensure that you have permission to take photographs, and capture images of shoppers as that may have all kinds of data protection issues.

### *Identification*

The need, or perhaps advice to carry some form of identity applies to the retail sector, just as it does with any other area where a Security Survey is carried out. It may be inconvenient, and it may go against your views of civil rights in the UK, but it will however be to your advantage in the long term.

### *Agreed visit times and dates*

The Tescaldi store, just as with any other retail outlet, is always busy, because staff prioritise customer service very highly in their daily activities. It is therefore beholden to you to ensure that you adhere to the times and dates agreed for your visit (s).

## Section 3: External factors

### *Section 3.1 The environment*

The Tescaldi Supermarket is located within an extremely busy shopping centre, located in the basement of 50 Canada Way, which is found in one of the most crowded areas of London. Road and rail communications are excellent, and the business is growing year on year.

### *Section 3.2 Crime Pattern Analysis*

See Section 2.4.

### *Section 3.3 Employment rates*

There are approximately 120,000 people in full-time employment in Pegasus Wharf.

### *Section 3.4 Potential for Crime Prevention Through Environmental Design (CPTED) using the acronym MAINT*

Maintenance: Standards of repair and maintenance at the site under survey are extremely high.

Access Control: There is public access to the store during trading hours only.

Image: Tescaldi is a prestigious retail outlet, and the image is extremely important.

Natural surveillance: There is an abundance of natural light external to, and within the building, which has also been designed to make the most of straight lines and open spaces.

Territoriality: Regular training takes place to ensure that all members of staff are aware of their responsibilities in terms of protecting the store and themselves.

### *Section 3.5 Nearest police station*

The nearest police station, belonging to British Transport Police (BTP) can be found at 55 Alan Hocken Way, London E15 3AT.

### *Section 3.6 Nearest hospital*

The nearest medical facility can be found at 2 Upper Bank St, London E14 5EE.

### *Section 3.7 Nearest fire and rescue*

The nearest fire station can be found at 168 E India Dock Rd, London E14 0BP.

## Section 4: Perimeter protection

The Tescaldi store is located in the underground area of 50 Canada Way, and as such, there is no perimeter.

## Section 5: Main building (external)

### *Section 5.1 Key personnel*

*Who?*

The Tescaldi supermarket is a thriving retail outlet, with a number of key personnel who needed to be spoken. They were.

| | |
|---|---|
| Alan Youngblutt. | Store Manager. |
| Elaine Brown. | Store Deputy Manager. |
| Jake Gill. | Regional Security Manager. |
| Gill O Rourke. | Marketing Manager. |
| Steven Halpin. | Senior Security Supervisor. |
| Security Officers. | |
| Store staff. | |

It is important to speak to as many and varied store personnel as possible, in order to achieve a rounded approach to the interview process.

### *When?*

There is no definitive means of ascertaining or calculating when the best time is to speak to key personnel. The store is open seven days per week, so the Security Auditor has to ensure he or she is flexible in meeting the needs of the survey.

### *What?*

Theft and the potential for burglary are prevalent, so the Security Auditor had to be focussed on those particular crimes when he sought the opinions and views of his interviewees.

## *Section 5.2 Description of the building*

The store is located in the middle of the Canda Way Shopping Center. It is adjoined by two similar units, consists of four floors, and is in a good state of repair.

Opening hours are as follows.

Monday-Saturday: 0900–2000hrs.

Sunday (and Bank Holidays): 1000–1600hrs.

## *Section 5.3 Number of access points, and how are they secured?*

### *Front entrance*

The front entrance is a double-leaf steel and glass door that is accessible to members of the public during shopping hours. Whilst the store is open for trading, a Security Officer is situated immediately inside, monitoring the entrance, and the store CCTV system.

There is also an Electronic Article Surveillance (AES) system installed, which is designed to alarm if a Radio Frequency Identification (RFID) tag moves between the AES antennae.

There are two cameras linked to the store CCTV system, installed externally, overlooking people entering and exiting the store. At the time of the Security Survey, both cameras were fit for purpose.

External lighting, provided by the shopping centre management team is very effective.

When the store is closed for business, an IDS, in the form of ground contacts is set, signalling to an off-site Alarm Receiving Centre (ARC).

There are two plate glass windows on either side of the main entrance, and both are protected by break glass detection devices, which are set when the store closes.

### *Observations*

It was observed during the Security Survey, that whilst the duty Security Officer is monitoring the store CCTV system, he or she could not carry out observations on the entrance.

During the Security Survey the store AES constantly alarmed, but the activations were ignored by staff and the duty Security Officer, as in their words '*It is always going off, and we have no trust in it*'.

### *Recommendations*

It is recommended that either a second Security Officer is deployed to the store front entrance, or the CCTV is monitored from a central location, perhaps the ARC currently being used for monitoring purposes.

It is also recommended that the AES system is examined for any prevailing faults, and that staff and the Security Team receive training related to how an activation should be responded to.

### *Goods inwards entrance*

The goods inwards entrance, or 'goods in' is to the rear of the store and is used for acceptance of all stock deliveries, with the entrance consisting of a galvanised steel roller shutter door. The entrance is used for deliveries only during trading hours, with access being managed by two members of the store team.

There is a single CCTV camera overlooking the goods inwards entrance, which at the time of the Security Survey was fit for purpose.

When the store is closed for business, an IDS, in the form of ground contacts is set, signalling to an off-site Alarm Receiving Centre (ARC).

External lighting is provided by the shopping centre management team.

### *Observations*

At the time of the Security Survey, two of the three external LED lighting units were inoperative. Not only does this fail to provide adequate lighting for CCTV, but it also introduces an element of danger to the safety of staff who may be in that area. This is very much a critical health and safety issue.

### *Recommendations*

As a matter of urgency, it is strongly recommended that the two inoperative lighting units are replaced by the Building Management Team as soon as possible.

### *Fire exit*

The fire exit is to the rear of the store and is used only for emergency evacuations. The exit consists of an outward swinging single-leaf steel door, with a three-point locking mechanism. The door is connected to the store IDS and is set on a 24/7 basis. It can only be opened from the inside, and once open, the IDS will signal to the Security Control Room and the ARC.

There is a single CCTV camera overlooking the fire exit, which at the time of the Security Survey was fit for purpose.

External lighting is provided by the shopping centre management team.

For observations and recommendations, see comments about the goods inwards door, as it is adjacent to the fire exit.

## Section 5.4 CCTV

External CCTV coverage consists of two cameras protecting the front entrance, one camera over the fire exit, and a single camera supporting the Goods In entrance. All cameras signal to the main Security Control Room inside 50 Canada Way, and at the time of the Security Survey, all cameras were fit for purpose.

## Section 5.5 IDS

There are Reed Contacts protecting the front entrance, the fire exit, and the Goods In doors. The IDS signals to the main Security Control Room at 50 Canada Way and should one of the alarm points be activated there will be an immediate response from the security team. At the time of the Security Survey, the IDS was deemed fit for purpose.

### Section 5.6 Lighting

External lighting in the form of wall and ceiling mounted LED units are supplied by the centre management team, and at the time of the Security Survey lighting was fit for purpose.

### Section 5.7 Distance from the perimeter

N/A.

### Section 5.8 External utilities

Nil.

### Section 5.9 Distance from perimeter

N/A.

### Section 5.10 Areas of concealment

Nil

### Section 5.11 Items to assist a criminal

Nil

### Section 5.12 Restricted areas

Nil

### Section 5.13 Parking arrangements

There are no particular parking areas for the store, other than outside of the goods inwards area during deliveries.

## Section 6: Main building (internal)

Having discussed the external areas of the Tescaldi store, we will now focus on the inside.

### Section 6.1 Access control

There are two; types of access control used at the store.

### *Keys*

Five lever Mortice locking devices are used to secure the main doors and the goods inwards doors. The same locking devices are used to secure the payroll office and the manager's office.

### *Card access*

Throughout the remaining areas of the store, a proximity card reader system is deployed. Every member of staff is issued with a proximity identity card that allows access to common areas of the store. Selected members of the management team and the security team are issued high-level security cards that allow them access to all areas of the store.

### *Observations*

During the course of the Security Survey, the following observations were made:

Although there is a key press for securing all store keys, there is no record of key movement. That is to say, there is no evidence of who signed the keys out or in.

There is no audit trail to confirm the management of proximity cards. The access control administrator was unable to confirm how many cards had been issued, and how many had been returned by members of staff who have left employment.

### *Recommendations*

It is recommended, as a matter of some urgency, that a key register is deployed, and all key movement is recorded continuously.

It is also recommended that an audit procedure is introduced in order to understand exactly where all proximity cards are at any one time.

## *Section 6.2 CCTV*

There are 108 static digital cameras located in the following locations:

- Main shopping floors 80 cameras.
- Goods inwards storage area 4 cameras.

- ICT server room 4 cameras.
- Manager's office 2 cameras.
- HR/payroll 2 cameras.
- Lifts and stairwells16 cameras.

Cameras signal to the Alarm Receiving Centre (ARC), and the Security Officer at the front entrance has the capability to monitor all cameras on a 16-split quad monitor. All images are recorded and stored on a Digital Video Network (DVN) at the ARC.

At the time of the Security Survey, all CCTV equipment was fit for purpose.

## Section 6.3 IDS

The store is protected by an IDS consisting of the following elements.

### Doors and windows

All doors and windows capable of opening are protected by Reed Contacts that activate when separated after setting.

### Store internal space

Internal space is protected by dual technology sensors that activate and silently alarm when there is a breach after setting. The alarm is set by a member of the store management team when the store closes at the end of a working day. Alarm activation is received at the main Security Control Room which is occupied on a 24/7 basis. The IDS is tested weekly, and at the time of the Security Survey was deemed to be fit for purpose.

## Section 6.4 Lighting

External lighting provided by the centre management and internal lighting is excellent, and at the time of the survey was deemed fit for purpose.

## Section 6.5 Manned guarding

Manned Guarding is provided by the shopping centre management, and during the Security Survey, the service was deemed fit for purpose.

### *Section 6.6 Internal specialist or restricted areas*

Nil.

## Section 7: Conclusions

### *Section 8.1 Post survey de brief*

A post survey de brief was arranged, during which Mr Youngblutt was informed of a number of 'quick fixes', and an agreement was reached in relation to the Security Survey Report. Mr Youngblutt requested the report to be delivered to him by hand within fourteen working days.

There is a requirement for a security presentation, and future talks will take place in relation to other work throughout the UK.

The Store Manager concluded by declaring that he was very satisfied with the Security Survey, and how it was carried out.

## Critical national infrastructure

**Critical national infrastructure security-50 Canada Way, Pegasus Wharf, London. E14 5DY**

| Document owner | Reference number | Proof-reader | 1st check | 2nd check |
|---|---|---|---|---|
| Kevin Gill | SecSurv/CNI/04/22 | | | |

1. **Survey details.**
2. **Initial stages of the survey.**
3. **External factors.**
4. **Perimeter protection.**
5. **Main buildings-external.**
6. **Main buildings-internal.**
7. **Internal specialist or restricted areas.**
8. **Conclusion.**

## Section 1: Survey details

Name and appointment of the client.

| |
|---|
| Mr Kevin Gill. CEO. |

Address (s)

| |
|---|
| 50 Canada Way, Pegasus Wharf, London. E14 5DY. |

Point of Contact.

| |
|---|
| Mr Mike Downs. CISO |

E mail.

| |
|---|
| m.downs@pps.com |

Telephone.

| |
|---|
| 01253674449 |

Web address.

| |
|---|
| www.pps.com |

Location of Survey.

| |
|---|
| 50 Canada Way, Pegasus Wharf, London. E14 5DY. |

Name of Security Auditor and date of survey.

| |
|---|
| Charles Swanson. 15 November 2021. |

Organisation.

| |
|---|
| STC |

Date of Security Survey

| |
|---|
| 03 November 2021 |

## Section 2: Initial stages of the survey

It is important to note that in the UK, CPNI are responsible for all aspects of critical national infrastructure security, but there are very occasional circumstances when expert evidence is required for balance or validation. It is also worth pointing out that CPNI recognise Chartered Security status and will often be prepared to share information and intelligence that is not open source. 50 Canada Way has already been security risk assessed, and that will be reflected in this Security Survey Report.

### *Section 2.1 General description and business operations*

The data centre at 50 Canada Way is a Telecoms Data Centre which is owned and operated by Britel.[34] It requires very high connectivity and is responsible for driving content delivery, mobile services, and cloud services.

The data centre is located on the 35th floor of Canada Way and is separated from the remainder of the building by virtue of the fact that the 34th floor is unoccupied and secure. There are circa 100 members of staff and management, and it is not accessible to members of the public.

The building is located in the centre of Pegasus Wharf, London, and is easily accessible by road, rail, and air services.

The data centre is operational on a 24/7 basis, and in terms of security, it is overseen by CPNI.

Figure 13 illustrates the Data Centre on the 35th floor of 50 Canada Way, whilst Figure 14 depicts the Data Halls.

### *Section 2.2 Reasons for the survey*

A Security Risk Assessment was carried out on 26 November 2021, and it was estimated by network subject matter experts that the likelihood of an attack against the data centre is very high, with an impact that is also very high, giving a risk measurement of 20/25 (4×5). This measurement must be reduced. The Senior Management team, after liaison with CPNI, decided that a physical Security Survey of the location would be commissioned.

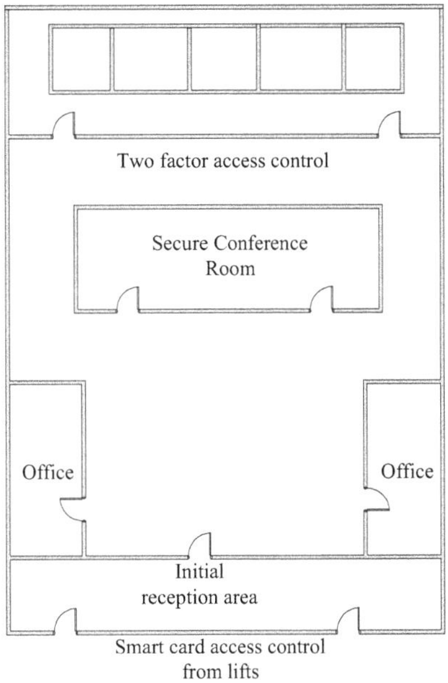


Figure 13 35th floor Data Centre, with the Data Halls to the north of the diagram.

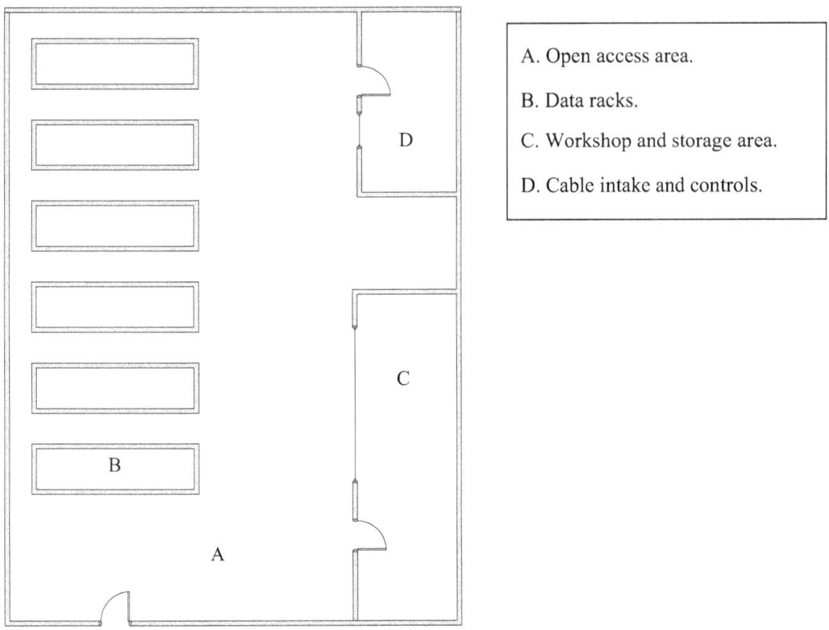


Figure 14 50 Canada Way Data Halls.

## Section 2.3 Assets to be protected

### People

A common theme running through other Security Surveys is the importance of human beings, and the Data Centre is no different. Although there is no access to the public, there are approximately 100 members of management and staff, and there are also deliveries and contractors who need access.

### Brand and reputation

In terms of asset protection, brand and reputation are critical, because although the Data Centre is potentially part of the UK's critical national infrastructure, it is also a commercially dependent operation.

### Data and information

The Data Centre holds commercially sensitive and publicly critical data and information, and this form of communication is a critical asset. There will also be personal and personnel information that is required to be held secure in terms of GDPR.

### ICT systems

The ICT systems at the Data Centre require very high connectivity and are responsible for driving content delivery, mobile services, and cloud services. Such services and systems constitute critical ICT assets.

### Infrastructure

The Data Centre infrastructure is critical as it allows all data containment and transference on a 24/7 basis and is therefore a critical asset to the location.

## Section 2.4 Initial research

As with all other Security Surveys, the initial research is extremely important, and the culture of the Data Centre must be taken into account.

### *Company background and security culture*

50 Canada Way as a building was completed in 2001, and the Data Centre was integral in the design of the host location, meaning that security was designed in, and crime was designed out at the architectural stage.

Initially, the Data Centre was categorised as a Tier-II operation which meant that it included systems, power, and cooling redundancy, with a guarantee of at least 99.741% uptime. However, requirements for CPNI status meant that it had to be upgraded to Tier IV. Such classification data must be able to guarantee 99.995% uptime, or no more than 26.3 minutes of downtime per year, including full fault tolerance, system redundancy, and 96 hours of outage protection.

For very obvious reasons, the security culture at the Data Centre has to be of the highest level, and this is audited by on-site management and CPNI on a regular basis.

### *Unemployment rates in the area*

Because of the success of Pegasus Wharf, unemployment rates in the area are significantly lower than the national average, with only 2% of all adults in the area seeking full-time employment.

### *Previous criminal incidents*

There have been no previous criminal incidents at the Data Centre.

### *Previous Security Surveys*

Notwithstanding the fact that CPNI regularly reviews all security aspects at the Data Centre, there has never been a formal physical Security Survey carried out.

### *Crime Pattern Analysis (CPA)*

The postcode E14 5DY illustrates the Pegasus Way area that is devoted to high-rise corporate buildings.

Although cyber crime and terrorism are not mentioned in this form of CPA, it is safe to say that they will be classified as two of the most serious threats to any community.

In terms of general crime, it can be seen that anti-social behaviour, violence and sexual offences, and vehicle crime are the three highest profile offences, but the Security Manager is more likely to be concerned about burglary, robbery, and the possession of offensive weapons.

### *Key takeaways*

*The nature of the building being surveyed will always firstly be associated with cybercrime, and this must be taken into consideration during the Security Survey.*

## Section 2.4 Planning and preparation

> *There are no secrets to success. It is the result of preparation, hard work, and learning from failure.*
>
> Colin Powell[35]

### *Authorisation and specific points of contact*

The point of contact is Mr Mike Downs, who is the Chief Information Security Officer (CISO), but it must be remembered that the location is a potential critical national infrastructure node, and therefore authorisation for all visits is critical.

### *Maps and diagrams*

Maps of the general area won't be an issue, as they will be readily available at most newsagents, but drawings and diagrams of the Data Centre will be sensitive and therefore confidential, so Mr Downes will have to be approached as early as possible in order that authorisation may be granted. It is highly unlikely that authorisation will be granted to remove such documentation from the premises.

### *Changes in law and regulation*

All national critical infrastructures are covered by normal UK legislation, and new measures to protect the nation's critical infrastructure and digital services from cyber-attacks and computer network failure came into force on 10 May 2018.

Firms in health, water, energy, transport, and digital infrastructure will now be expected to have robust safeguards in place against cyber threats and report breaches and network outages to regulators within 72 hours or they face fines of up to £17 million.

The National Cyber Security Centre, set up by the government in October 2016 as part of GCHQ, has already responded to more than 950 significant incidents, including WannaCry.

It will also give new regulators powers to assess critical industries and make sure plans are in place to prevent attacks.

The regulator will have the power to issue legally-binding instructions to improve security, and – if necessary – impose significant fines.

The legislation will also cover other threats affecting IT such as hardware failures and environmental hazards.[36]

The Security Auditor must ensure that they are aware of all pertinent legislation and regulation, with the two web sites most likely to be of assistance being:

- The National Cyber Security Centre – https://www.ncsc.gov.uk/
- The Centre for the Protection of National Infrastructure – https://www.cpni.gov.uk/

### *Social media*

Unlike most other Security Survey locations, the Data Centre at 50 Canada Way is unlikely to have a strong social presence. Nevertheless, the Security Auditor should investigate in detail to assess any potential infringements or attacks.

### *Photography*

With this being an extremely sensitive location, more so than ever, permission will be needed before any photographs are taken, particularly from an internal, perspective. It is also likely that all photographs will be censored before the publication of the report.

### *Identification*

It is extremely likely that some form of photographic evidence will be expected before access to the Data Centre is allowed.

### *Agreed visits, times, and dates*

As with all other sectors covered in the book, agreed visits, times and dates must be adhered to as everybody involved is incredibly busy, with time schedules being tight.

## Section 3: External

### *Section 3.1 Environment*

50 Canada Way is situated in an extremely busy part of the capital, and it is the epicentre of all corporate establishments within that area. The location is close knit, and in many ways, the area is operational on a 24/7 basis. Road and rail communications are excellent, and it is extremely easy to access air and sea passage.

### *Section 3.2 Crime Pattern Analysis*

See Section 2.4.

### *Section 3.3 Employment rates*

Employment rates in the area are very high, and 50 Canada Way is responsible for a significant percentage, currently employing circa 2,000 people.

### *Section 3.4 Potential for Crime Prevention Through Environmental Design (CPTED), using the acronym MAINT.*

**M**aintenance: 50 Canada Way is well maintained, and in an excellent state of repair.

**A**ccess Control: Access control to the building is very good, and the same concept when applied to the 34th and 35th floors is excellent.

**I**mage: 50 Canada way is iconic, and this is an area for concern, because on several occasions, 9/11 being an excellent example, criminals and terrorists have attacked such buildings because of their image.

**N**atural surveillance: Internally and externally, straight lines, natural, light and reception sitting design allow for very good natural surveillance.

**T**erritoriality: There is an excellent security culture throughout the building, and during the Security Survey it was clear that staff and management have positive attitudes in terms of territoriality.

### *Section 3.5 Nearest police station*

The nearest police station, belonging to British Transport Police (BTP) can be found at 55 Alan Hocken Way, London E15 3AT.

### *Section 3.6 Nearest hospital*

The nearest medical facility can be found at 2 Upper Bank St, London E14 5EE.

### *Section 3.7 Nearest fire and rescue*

The nearest fire station can be found at 168 E India Dock Rd, London E14 0BP.

## Section 4: Perimeter protection

There is no perimeter protection at the site under survey.

## Section 5: Main building (s) external

As with all other sectors' Security Surveys, this is one of the most critical sections of the survey, and it is imperative that as many key personnel as possible are spoken to.

#### *Who?*

50 Canada Way is a very high-profile target location, and it is imperative to speak with the following personnel.

- Mr Kevin Gill. CEO.
- Mr Mike Downs. CISO.
- Debbi Jones. HR Director.
- John Dolan. CFO.
- John Beck. Senior Security Supervisor.
- Security Officers.
- Receptionists.
- Contractors.

It is important to speak to as many and varied site personnel as possible, in order to achieve a rounded approach to the interview stage.

### *When?*

There are no definitive means of ascertaining or calculating when the best time is to speak to key personnel. There are operations being carried out on a 24/7 basis, so the emphasis is on flexibility, with the Security Auditor adapting his or her schedule to speak to as many relevant people as possible.

### *What?*

With such a divergent range of key personnel being spoken to, particularly in such a sensitive location, with potentially tight time margins you are advised to preselect the questions to be asked before each interview, ensuring that all questions are appropriate, adding knowledge gained during the Security Risk Assessment.

## *Section 5.2 Description of building (s)*

The building in question is a thirty-five-story unit, constructed of re-enforced concrete, steel, and glass. There is also an underground car park, and a multi-occupied shopping mall.

## *Section 5.3 Number of access points and how are they secured*

Access points to the building, and how they are secured are as follows:

### *Main entrance*

The main entrance, which is a double leaf glass and steel door is insecure during trading hours, with access to members of the public and staff.[37] The main entrance is secured at 2000hrs and is made remotely accessible by either the Security Officer occupying the main reception desk or from the Security Control Room. People wishing to enter the building after trading hours are required to show some form of identity to the CCTV camera above the main entrance, and id authorised they will be afforded access by the Duty Security Officer.

### *Goods inwards*

There is a goods inwards entrance located within the basement, which is occupied and operational on a 24/7 basis, and anybody wishing to enter the building by this means must prove identity, and the reason for their visit.

### *Observations*

There is no CCTV coverage supporting the goods inwards room.

### *Recommendations*

The goods inwards entrance is operational on a 24/7 basis, and once entered there is the potential for access to the remainder of the building. It is therefore recommended that the building CCTV system is extended to provide cover for this area.

### *Fire exits*

There are four fire exits located on the ground floor, all of which are controlled from within. The fire exits are linked to the automated fire control system, and should the fire alarm sound, all fire exits will be released. This allows unopposed access to the building from outside.

### *Observations*

Whist there is CCTV support immediately inside the building covering the fire exits, there is no camera coverage externally.

### *Recommendations*

Although ultimately it is the building owner's responsibility, it is recommended that the site CCTV system is extended to include coverage externally at every fire exit. This may mean a series of negotiations with the building owner, and this is likely to be the responsibility of the Facilities Manager

## *Section 5.4 CCTV*

There is a single CCTV camera external to the main entrance to the building. The camera is a digital colour unit that is in a good state of repair and is fit for purpose. The camera signals back to the Security Control Room via Cat 5 cabling and images are captured and recorded on a Digital Network Video Recording (DNVR) system.

### *Observations*

The provision of only a single CCTV camera above the main entrance means that the building is vulnerable to an external attack, which may not be detected.

### *Recommendations*

It is recommended as a matter of urgency that the building CCTV system is extended to cover 360 degrees, with a static camera being installed on each corner. The extra cameras will then signal to the building's Security Control Room.

## *Section 5.5 IDS*

When the building is secured, the main entrance, goods inwards doors, and fire exits are protected by an IDS (door contacts), which if breached will activate a silent alarm signal, received at the building Security Control Room.

During the Security Survey, it was observed that the IDS was operational and fit for purpose.

## *Section 5.6 Lighting*

The building is protected by external LED street lighting and building wall-mounted LED lighting units. Lighting is activated by photocell technology, which senses the reduced natural light, and will activate the street and building external lights accordingly.

### *Observations*

During the course of the Security Survey, it was observed that two of the lighting units above the front entrance, and a single lighting unit covering the goods inwards door were inoperative.

*Recommendations*

It is, once again, recommended as a matter of urgency that the building owner/manager is contacted to have the unserviceable lighting units replaced.

### *Section 5.7 Distance from the perimeter*

N/A

### *Section 5.8 External utilities*

Nil.

### *Section 5.9 Areas of concealment*

Nil.

### *Section 5.10 Items to help the criminal*

Nil.

### *Section 5.11 Restricted areas*

There is an underground area that houses a VIP car park for BU vehicles, an Uninterruptible Power Supply (UPS), and space for a standby diesel generator. At the time of the Security Survey, all three areas were secure and well lit. The same areas are also subject to irregular patrols, carried out by duty Security Officers.

### *Section 5.12 Parking arrangements*

The only staff car park is located underground, and it is for use by the BU Senior Management team (see above).

## Section 6: Main building (s) internal[38]

### *Section 6.1 Access control*

*Lift access*

Access to floors 34 and 35 is restricted to authorised personnel. Normal lift activity will cease on floor 33.

### *Floor 34*

Floor 34 is secure, with access limited to authorised personnel only.

### *Floor 35*

There are two lifts giving access to floor 35, and upon exit from a lift, a proximity (smart) card is required to enter the main office space. The data halls are protected by two-factor access control, consisting of a proximity (smart) card and fingerprint biometric access control.

## *Section 6.2 CCTV*

Once again, this section will cover floors 34 and 35 only.

### *Floor 34*

Static digital cameras, signalling to a Digital Network Video Recording Systems in Security Control Room are located in the following positions.

- Lift area: 2 cameras.
- Covering the inside of the entrance: 1 camera.
- Covering the fire exit stairway: 1 camera.

### *Floor 35*

Static digital cameras, signalling to a Digital Network Video Recording Systems in Security Control Room are located in the following positions.

- Lift area: 2 cameras.
- Covering the inside of the entrance: 2 cameras.
- Each office (internal): 1 camera.
- The secure conference room: 2 cameras.
- Outside of the Data Hall: 2 cameras.
- Inside the Data Hall: 4 cameras.

At the time of the Security Survey, all CCTV elements were operational and fit for purpose.

### *Section 6.3 IDS*

The IDS is configured in the following manner.

#### *Floor 34*

The main door and fire exit are protected by Reed contacts.

Internal space is supported by Dual Technology Volumatic sensors.

#### *Floor 35*

The main door and fire exit are protected by Reed contacts.

Internal general space is supported by dual technology volumetric sensors.

Both offices are protected by door contacts and internal dual technology sensors.

The secure conference room is protected by door contacts and internal dual technology sensors.

The Data Halls are protected by door contacts and internal dual technology sensors. The data hall doors are also protected by a 'door held open' system which silently alarms in the Security Control Room if the door is held open for more than 120 seconds.

All alarms are tested weekly, with the results being recorded. At the time of the Security Survey, all ID systems were operational and fit for purpose.

### *Section 6.4 Lighting*

All internal lighting consists of individual strip lighting units which are manually controlled. At the time of the Security Survey, all lights were fit for purpose.

## Section 7: Internal specialist or restricted areas

This section refers to restricted areas with specialist applications, which if successfully attacked would negatively impact the Data Centre.

### *Section 7.1 Floor 34*

Floor 34 is permanently secure and unoccupied in order to create a buffer zone below the Data Centre. If that floor was breached it would leave floor 35 vulnerable to attack from below.

## *Section 7.2 Floor 35*

There are two restricted areas on floor 35.

### *The Secure Conference Room*

The Secure Conference Room is a restricted area because of the nature of business carried out therein. Extremely sensitive meetings related to the Data Centre and its operations are held there, and should the contents of such meetings be compromised, the integrity of the Data Centre would be threatened.

### *The Data Halls*

The Data Halls are restricted areas because of the nature of their existence. Within the Data Halls are a number of data server racks. A server rack is an open frame structure designed for accommodating technical or electronic equipment including routers, network switches, hubs, servers, etc. The server rack makes it possible to securely hold multiple pieces of equipment in one area and is typically going to be used by businesses and kept either in data centres or communications closets.[39]

The Data Hall is constructed from load-bearing brick and steel walls, and a solid ceiling. There is an underground void for cable access, and that is protected by the site IDS. Access to the server room is by two-factor access control, consisting of a proximity reader card, and biometric fingerprint software. Entrance to the room is restricted to the ICT Team, and government representatives.

The room is supported internally and externally by CCTV which is monitored from the Security Control Room, the lighting is excellent, and the room is protected by an IDS when secure. The ICT Team has access to a communications land line, a cell phone, and a Personal Attack button has been installed.

The integrity of the Data Hall is checked by a Security Officer every hour when it is not occupied.

The room is operational on a 24/7 basis, and twice per day all data is backed up to an encrypted cloud. This means that should the Data Hall be destroyed, or the servers taken out of action, all data is secure.

## Section 8: Conclusion

Survey debrief was carried out, during which Mr Gill was informed of a number of 'quick fixes', and an agreement was reached in relation to the Security Survey Report. Mr Gill requested the report to be delivered to him by hand within thirty working days.

There is no requirement for a formal presentation at this stage, and Security Survey will not be replicated at any other critical infrastructure site in the foreseeable future.

Mr Gill concluded by declaring that he was satisfied with the Security Survey and how it was carried out.

## Maritime security

### Security Survey: Liverport Container Terminal

| Document owner | Reference number | Proof-reader | 1st check | 2nd check |
|---|---|---|---|---|
| John Jones | SecSurv/LCT/05/22 | | | |

1. **Survey details.**
2. **Initial stages of the survey.**
3. **External factors.**
4. **Perimeter protection.**
5. **Main buildings-external.**
6. **Main buildings-internal.**
7. **Internal specialist or restricted areas.**
8. **Conclusion.**

## Section 1: Survey details

Name and appointment of the client.

| |
|---|
| Mr John Jones. CEO |

Address (s)

| |
|---|
| Liverport Container Terminal<br>Alfred Dock<br>Liverport |

Point of Contact.

| |
|---|
| Mr Brian Mc Farlane. PFSO |

E mail.

| |
|---|
| MB@liverportct.com<br>www.liverportct.com |

Telephone.

| |
|---|
| 015512347654 |

Web address.

| |
|---|
| Location and date of Survey.<br>Liverport Container terminal. 21 December 2021 |

Name of Security Auditor and date of survey.

| |
|---|
| Charles Swanson. 29 September 2022. |

Organisation.

| |
|---|
| SCT |

## Section 2: Initial stages of the survey

Notwithstanding the fact that Liverport Container Port holds a UK certificated Port Facility Security Plan (PFSP), as a result of a Security Risk

Assessment, it was decided by the executive to have a Security Survey carried out by an independent security professional.

### *Section 2.1 General description and business operations*

The Liverport Container Terminal is located on the Northwest coast of England and is serviced by a first-class rail service, and direct road communications from the M62. The terminal operates on a 24/7 basis, and currently handles 1.5 million containers per year, with a workforce of approximately 5,000 full and part-time staff and management.

Containers arrive from, and depart to all four corners of the world, with a significant number carrying very high-value products, such as computer chips and high-value ICT hardware. Figure 15 illustrates the operations at the port facility. To the south can be seen containers that have been delivered and are awaiting loading. Containers to the north await vehicle pick up. To the west is the ship/port interface, with a number of cranes used for loading/unloading. The entrance is via the southern controlled barrier and bollards, managed from the Security Control Room. Vehicle exit is via the northern egress point.

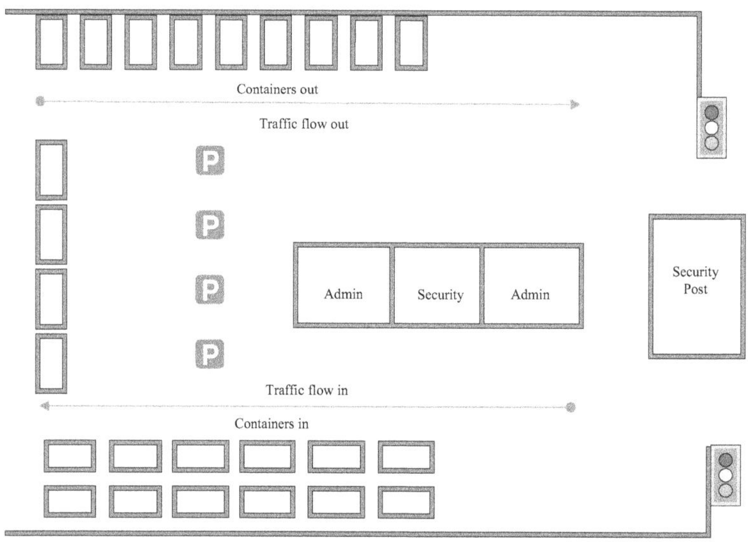


*Figure* 15 Liverport Container Terminal.

## *Section 2.2 Reasons for the survey*

The terminal is technology dependant, with all container movement being ICT automated. Crime levels at the terminal are low, but crime intelligence received from the local police is vague.

The Board of Directors has decided, as a result of the Security Risk Assessment, that in order to ensure people feel safe, and that all assets are protected, a physical Security Survey of the container terminal is needed.

## *Section 2.3 Assets to be protected*

As with every other Security Survey carried out so far, people actually located or visiting the Container Terminal are the number one priority in terms of asset protection, followed by:

### *Brand and reputation*

During a period of twenty years of maritime trading, the Liverport Container Terminal has earned a first-class reputation as one of Europe's busiest and most efficient operators in the maritime industry. The owners of the terminal have recently invested £2 billion in a new technical framework that is ready to accept 5G, and any future upgrades that may be required. A loss of, or a tarnished reputation would be devastating for future growth.

### *Data and information*

The container port, as mentioned in its PFSP will hold a great deal of sensitive data and information, particularly in respect of future container movement, which would be attractive to criminals and terrorists alike. There will also be personal, and personnel information held, which is required to be protected in accordance with the General Data Protection Regulations (2016).

### *ICT systems*

As mentioned earlier in this section, Liverport Container has recently invested £2 billion in a new technical framework that is ready to accept 5G, and the ICT network will be one of the most advanced systems in the UK maritime industry. However, the sophistication of the terminal ICT network may make it more attractive to criminals and terrorists who see it as a challenge, and of course, if the network is compromised, it would mean maximum disruption to the terminal.

### *Infrastructure*

The terminal infrastructure is a significant asset, as it allows container operations to continue on a 24/7 basis, and should the infrastructure be attacked, it would likely bring all operations to a standstill.

### *Vessels and their cargo*

Vessels and their cargo are one of the most critical assets to any port facility, particularly the Liverport Container Terminal, as they are the life blood of business expansion. In terms of this facility, where the cargo consists of 40-foot containers carrying high-value contents, the combination of the ship and her cargo is crucial and must be protected.

## *Section 2.4 Initial research*

Culturally, maritime security is a different prospect from most of the other sectors, but undeniably, a port facility is a land-based location with a partial water perimeter.

## *Section 2.5 Company background and security culture*

As mentioned earlier, Liverport Container terminal has been a very successful operation for at least the last twenty years, with positive business growth year on year. It is now one of the most technologically advanced container terminals in Europe, if not on a global standing, and it is very likely that this growth will continue exponentially. However, after 9/11, and the inception of the International Ship and Port Facility (ISPS) Code, the Board of Directors at Liverport has instilled a culture of security risk management awareness, and even though the terminal holds a UK Port Facility Security Plan, the land-based Security Survey was commissioned to ensure that the security culture is maintained, and indeed where possible, improved.

### Section 2.6 Unemployment rates in the area

Unemployment in the general area is higher than the national average, with circa 14% of all adults currently seeking employment.

### Section 2.7 Previous criminal incidents

There is a history of minor crimes in and about the facility, but since its ISPS Code certification, there have been no recorded serious crimes that have taken place.

### Section 2.8 Previous Security Surveys

The only other survey that has been carried out is the Port Facility Security Assessment (PFSA) leading to the Port Facility Security Plan (PFSP), but both documents are protected and cannot be released for inspection.

### Section 2.9 Crime Pattern Analysis (CPA) – LE14 4CD

The postcode LE1 4CD indicates an area of Liverport that is devoted to maritime activities. Although cybercrime and terrorism are not covered in this form of CPA, it is safe to say that they will be classified as two of the most serious threats to any community. In terms of general crime, the greatest fear for this area will be related to robbery and burglary, which are in fact relatively minimal.

Through research, it appears that the greatest levels of crime originate from anti-social behaviour, violence and sexual offences, and theft (in its many forms).

#### Key takeaways

*Whilst maritime locations may be dominated by the ISPS Code, there will always be gaps that must be filled in by the Security Survey.*

### Section 2.10 Planning and preparation

> *You can't plow a field simply by turning it over in your mind.*
>
> Gordon B. Hinckley[40]

As with all other sectors covered in this book, planning and preparation are critical for the success of any Security Survey, and the maritime sector is no different. So let us take a look at what planning and preparation is needed before the Security Survey at the Liverport Container Terminal.

### *Authorisation and specific points of contact*

Authorisation once again is critical, and the point of contact will be the Port Facility Security Officer (PFSO), Mr. Brian McFarlane.

### *Maps and diagrams*

As with every other sector covered in this book, relevant maps and diagrams are critical for the maritime security survey. Maps of the area will be freely available, and the terminal PFSO should be able to assist with diagrams and schematics of the container terminal.

### *Changes in laws and regulations*

The maritime sector is a global phenomenon, and there is always the potential for new legislation and regulation, with the most striking piece of legislation enacted on 01 July 2004. That was the ISPS Code, which was introduced globally as a direct result of 9/11. It will be to the advantage of all Security Officers to be in possession of the document, which can be found at https://www.imo.org/en/OurWork/Security/Pages/SOLAS-XI-2%20ISPS%20Code.aspx.

### *Social media*

The Liverport Container Terminal is likely to be prominent on a number of social media platforms such as Facebook, Twitter, etc., and it will be to the advantage of the Security Auditor to monitor the said platforms before carrying out the Security Survey.

### *Photography*

The location is a large and complex piece of real estate, with a number of operations taking place concurrently, consequentially photography is essential in support of the final documentation. However, once again, a word of caution, the Security Auditor must have permission to take photographs within the boundary of the terminal.

### *Identification*

As discussed throughout this section of the book, although proof of identification is not a lawful requirement in the UK, it is recommended that the Security Auditor is in possession of either a valid passport or photographic driving licence.

### *Agreed visit times and dates*

Brian McFarlane, like all other PFSOs throughout the UK, is an extremely busy person, and it is therefore imperative that you adhere to all dates and times agreed.

> Charles Swanson. 29 September 2022

### *Key takeaways*

*As simple as this may sound-failing to prepare is preparing to fail.*

## Section 3: External factors

### *Section 3.1 Environment*

The Liverpool Container Terminal is located within an extremely busy waterfront, surrounded by a very large urban sprawl.

### *Section 3.2 Crime Pattern Analysis*

See Section 2.

### Section 3.3 Employment rate

Unemployment rates in Liverport are higher than the national average, and the container terminal is one of the most important employers in the area, currently employing approximately 5,000 full and part-time staff.

### Section 3.4 Potential for Crime Prevention Through Environmental Design (CPTED) using the acronym MAINT

**M**aintenance: Maintenance and standards of repair are of a very high standard.
**A**ccess Control: Access control is being effectively managed.
**I**mage: Liverport Container Terminal is iconic in terms of image, and whilst it may be a target for the criminal or terrorist, it also stands for pride and self-belief.
**N**atural surveillance: There is scope for natural surveillance.
**T**erritoriality: Staff and management must be accountable for the security of the terminal.

### Section 3.5 Nearest police station

The nearest police station is located at Brown Street, LE 6 21FC, and is accessible to the public on a 24/7 basis. To call the police in an emergency situation, dial 999. For non-emergency issues dial 101.

### Section 3.6 Nearest hospital

The closest hospital is the Liverport Teaching Hospital, Dove Lane, LE1 24DX. To call for emergency assistance call 999. For non-emergency help dial 119.

### Section 3.7 Nearest fire and rescue

There is a fire and rescue station located at Galsworthy Road, LE22 7FH. This is the closest medical facility, and to call it in an emergency dial 999. For non-emergency assistance call 01551 926 0566.

## Section 4: Perimeter protection

### *Section 4.1 Type*

To the North, East, and South of the perimeter, the container terminal is protected by a 3-metre heavy gauge galvanised welded mesh fence. The western side of the container terminal is the ship/port interface, and there is no perimeter protection.

### *Section 4.2 PIDS by type*

Although the perimeter fence is relatively new, it is unsupported by any form of PIDS.

#### *Observations*

During the course of the Security Survey, it was observed that the perimeter fence is bare of any form of PIDS.

#### *Recommendations*

It is recommended that a fabric PIDS is installed. The sensor will be an Optical-Fibre cable system. The sensor cable of an Optical-Fibre (Fibre-Optic) system is immune to RF interference. The Optical-Fibre system will only require one cable run for a whole perimeter, and it will need just one processing unit and power supply.[41]

### *Section 4.3 PIDS activation and response*

It is recommended that an attempted breach will transmit a silent signal to the Security Control Room, and upon receipt of the alarm activation, there should be an immediate response from the Manned Guarding Security Team.

### *Section 4.4 Topping*

There is a low-voltage electric fence installed above the welded mesh perimeter fencing, designed to deliver a non-lethal electric shock to the intruder.

## Section 4.5 State of repair

The perimeter fence and supporting topping are in a very good state of repair, and at the time of the Security Survey, both were fit for purpose.

## Section 4.6 Supporting security systems

The perimeter fence is supported by CCTV, LED lighting, and Manned Guarding. During the Security Survey, all supporting systems were deemed fit for purpose.

## Section 4.7 Supporting security systems specifications

During the course of the Security Survey, the following security systems specifications were observed.

## Section 4.8 Closed Circuit Television (CCTV)

There are sixteen static digital CCTV cameras installed to support the perimeter of the container terminal, affording 360-degree cover, including the ship/port interface and the entrance/exit area. Although every camera is a switchable unit, allowing it to operate under varying flux conditions, the CCTV system is supported by LED lighting units. The CCTV system is also supported by Video Movement Detection (VMD) software, allowing every camera to be able to send pre-notification of any movement within its field of vision. The camera's signal to the Security Control Room, where all images are recorded and stored on a Network Digital Video Recording System (NDVR).

## Section 4.9 Security lighting

Perimeter security lighting consists of sixteen 1,000-watt LED units, including the ship port interface and the entrance/exit areas.

## Section 4.10 Manned guarding

See the section covering manned guarding.

## Section 4.11 Supporting systems state of repair

During the Security Survey, the following observations and recommendations were made.

### *Observations*

Two of the perimeter LED units were nonoperational, and one of the CCTV cameras was not signalling to the Security Control Room.

### *Recommendations*

As a matter of urgency, the following recommendations are made.

The two light units need to be replaced, and the CCTV camera requires to be either repaired or replaced.

## *Section 4.12 Entrances*

There are two entrances that are designed for either vehicular or pedestrian entry.

There is also the ship/port interface which is used for ships crews to disembark for land-based purposes.

## *Section 4.13 Entrance types*

As mentioned above, there are two front (Eastern) entrances, and there is the ship/port interface, specified as follows.

## *Section 4.14 Front (Eastern) entrances/exits*

The front (Eastern) entrances/exits have three pneumatic stainless-steel bollards, specified to PAS 68, as recommended by CPNI,[42] protecting each entrance. Behind the bollards, there is a steel single-arm barrier and communications system, controlled by the Security Control Room.

## *Section 4.15 The ship port interface*

This is the area where the vessel is berthed, generally for loading/unloading purposes, but through the use of the ship's gangways, and dependent on the ISPS Code Security Level,[43] it offers the vessel's crew and officers the opportunity to embark and disembark the ship.

### *Observation*

During the Security Survey, it was observed that on three occasions, during night operations, two gangways on a container vessel were not manned or secured. This poses a threat to the terminal.

### *Recommendation*

It is recommended that the PFSO, Mr. Mc Farlane, liaises with all shipping lines to ensure that the ISPS Code is adhered to at all times, emphasising the point that poor security on an ISPS certificated ship, can increase the threat to the servicing Port Facility.

## *Section 4.16 Entrance (s) state of repair*

During the course of the Security Survey, it was observed that all entrances were fit for purpose.

## *Section 4.17 Entrance access control systems*

This section relates purely to the front entrances/exits, which are configured as follows.

### *Staff*

All members of staff are issued a photo identification card, which is configured as a single-factor proximity card. Staff will show their cards to the reader installed in the Security Control Room, and the system will acknowledge and record their movements in and out.

### *Visitors and contractors*

All visitors and contractors are instructed to report to the Security Control Room, where they are issued a temporary visitors pass that must be surrendered on leaving the terminal.

### *Container vehicle drivers*

When container vehicles arrive at the terminal, the RFID tag installed on the vehicle chassis will communicate with the RFID reader at the Administration Section, which will verify all required details of the vehicle, the container, and its movements. All container movements will be pre-arranged, and without such an arrangement, the container will not be authorised to enter the terminal.

### *Observations*

It was observed, that by the time the vehicle reaches the Proximity Card Reader, the bollards will have been lowered, and the barrier raised, removing all physical protection.

### *Recommendations*

It is recommended that the pneumatic barriers are replaced by PAS rising blockers, as pneumatic bollards are not designed to be constantly raised and lowered. It is further recommended that the RFID reader is re-located forward of the blocker on a free-standing post, thus ensuring that vehicle and container identification are confirmed before allowing entrance. The driver should then confirm his or her company identification with the Duty Security Officer at the Security Control Room Reception Area.

There is an on-site container x-ray scanner available, and a percentage (Depending on availability and traffic volume) of all containers will be x-rayed to ensure they contain no contraband, weapons, and explosives, or people.

## ***Section 4.18 Entrance access control systems state of repair***

During the Security Survey, it was observed that the entrance access control systems were fit for purpose.

## ***Section 4.19 Manned guarding***

All information relating to the Security Team will be found in the Site Assignment Instructions (SAI), which are confidential, and are located in electronic format on the company IT network.

There is manned guarding support on a 24/7 basis, which includes the following details.

### *In house-licenced*

The 'in house' Security Team who all hold SIA Front-Line Licences, consist of the following.

One Senior Security Supervisor who reports to the PFSO.

Four Security Supervisors.

Twenty Security Officers.

### *Shifts availability*

The Senior Security Supervisor works Monday to Friday: 0800hrs to 1800hrs.

The four Security Supervisors operate on a shift roster consisting of the following hours.

0600–1400hrs.

1400–2200hrs.

2200–0600hrs.

### *Duties and roles*

The duties and roles of the Security Team can be found in the Site Assignment Instructions, but an abridged version is as follows.

### *Security Control Room duties*

- Access control.
- Visitors pass management.
- Alarm management and response.
- CCTV monitoring.
- Communications management.
- Patrolling.
- Search.
- Incident response.
- Investigation and reporting.
- Facilities Management patrols.
- Escort duties.

### *Specialist qualifications*

All Security Officers hold the following qualifications.

- Front-line Security Officer licence.
- First aid.
- Fire Wardens.
- Public Space Surveillance (PSS)
- Search procedures.

## *Section 4.20 Security Control Room*

The Security Control Room is located to the east of the container terminal and is to be found in the same building as the administration departments.

### *Security Control Room manning times*

The Security Control Room is manned and operational on a 24/7 basis, throughout the year.

### *Security Control Room duties*

The Security Control Room, primarily because it is occupied and operational 24/7, 365 days per year, is at the heart of the container terminal.

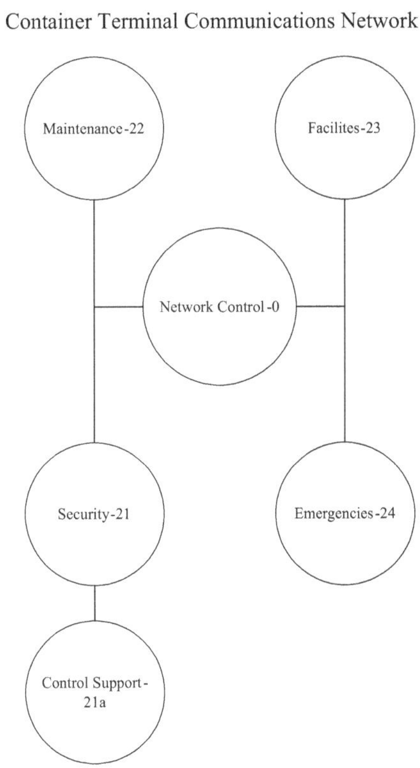


Figure 16 The Communications Network, and individual call signs.

Arguably the most important task carried out by the team in the Security Control Room is access control, with all entrants to the terminal being processed by one of the Duty Security Officers.

All alarm activations signal to the Security Control Room, and the CCTV system is managed from here.

Sensitive documentation in hard and electronic form is held in the control room.

The Security Control Room is also the Crisis Control Room when needed.

There is no reserve Security Control Room.

The Security Control Room serves as the Communications Centre for the terminal, with the communications network being managed from here. See Figure 16, which is the communications network.

### *Observations*

It was observed during the Security Survey that there is no reserve Security Control Room.

### *Recommendations*

It is recommended as a matter of urgency that a reserve Security Control Room is identified and fitted out accordingly.

### *Key takeaways*

*Any Security Control Room is very often seen as the nerve centre of the site, and there has to be flexibility to coordinate usage, in order that the control room can be used for other purposes. A functioning reserve Security Control is critical.*

## Section 5: Main building (s) external

### *Section 5.1 Key personnel*

As mentioned earlier, during the Security Survey it is imperative that all key personnel are spoken to in regard to the security and risk management of the location. This is the first opportunity available for the Security Auditor to begin research from the inside, and it is imperative that he or she chooses correctly.

### *Who?*

In a maritime situation, it is always advantageous to speak to the PFSO, in this instance Brian Mc Farlane, and if a vessel is berthed, it will help if you can speak to the Ship Security Officer (SSO).

It is also important to speak to staff involved in operations, such as the Security Team, Crane Drivers, Stevedores, contractors, and so on.

The aim of such conversations is for the Security Auditor to receive an all-round set of opinions about current issues relating to the container terminal.

### *When?*

There is no right and wrong about when people should be spoken to, there is no template, this is where professional judgement will be required, with the Security Surveyor fitting into the timetable of his or her interviewees.

### *What?*

As with all other sectors, questions asked in a maritime environment, particularly a bespoke port facility such as a container terminal, must be appropriate, and they have to add to the knowledge gained during the Security Risk Assessment.

### *Key takeaways*

*The container terminal is operational on a 24/7 basis, meaning the Security Surveyor will need to be available day and night.*

## ***Section 5.2 Description of buildings***

There are two buildings at the container terminal, and they are:

### *The Administration/Security Control Room building*

The Administration/Security Control Room building is a relatively new single-story unit, of brick, steel, and glass construction. The building is in a very good state of repair, and at the time of the Security Survey, it was deemed fit for purpose.

### *The x-ray scanning facility*

The x-ray scanning facility is also a new single-story unit, of brick, steel, and glass construction. The building is in a very good state of repair, and at the time of the Security Survey, it was deemed fit for purpose.

## Section 5.3 Number of access points and how they are secured

### *The Administration/Security Control Room building*

The Administration/Security Control Room building has three access points, all of which are secured by means of a proximity card reader system. The administration elements of the building are occupied Monday to Friday, 0800–1800hrs.

### *The x-ray scanning facility*

The X-ray scanning facility has roller shutters for container vehicle entrance/exits at each end of the building, which is secured from the inside, when not in use. There is also a single leaf pedestrian door which is secured by means of a proximity card reader system.

## Section 5.4 CCTV

### *The Administration/Security Control Room building*

There are seven static digital cameras installed external to the Administration/Security Control Room building. All of the cameras are supported by effective lighting, signalling to the Security Control Room where images are recorded and stored on the site Network Digital Video Recording system. The cameras are located at each corner of the building, allowing 360-degree cover, and there is also a camera above each of the entrances, which also serve as fire exits.

### *The x-ray scanning facility*

There are seven static digital cameras installed external to the x-ray scanning facility. All of the cameras are supported by effective lighting, signalling to the Security Control Room where images are recorded and stored on the site

Network Digital Video Recording system. The cameras are located at each corner of the building, allowing 360-degree cover, and there is also a camera above each of the entrances. The pedestrian entrance serves as a fire exit.

At the time of the Security Survey, all building external cameras were fit for purpose.

## *Section 5.5 IDS*

### *The Administration/Security Control Room building*

All doors and windows are fitted with Reed contacts, offering protection against any unauthorised breach via those points of entrance. The door and window contacts on the administration section of the building are set when the doors are secured, and should there be an attempted unauthorised entry, there will be a silent activation of the IDS in the Security Control Room.

The doors and window contacts fitted to the Security Control Room are not set, unless there is the unlikely event of the control room being unoccupied.

### *The x-ray scanning facility*

The three doors found on the x-ray scanning facility are fitted with Reed door contacts, which are set after the last container has been x-rayed, normally at 2200hrs. Should there be an attempted breach, there will be a silent activation of the IDS in the Security Control Room.

At the time of the Security Survey, all building external IDS elements were fit for purpose.

## *Section 5.6 Lighting*

LED flood lighting is installed at the Administration/Security Control Room building and at the x-ray scanning facility.

At the time of the Security Survey, all building external lighting was fit for purpose.

## *Section 5.7 Distance from the perimeter*

The X-ray scanning facility is located adjacent to, and approximately 20 metres from the southern perimeter fence line, and approximately 20 metres from the berthing area.

The Administration/Security Control Room building is located approximately 5 metres from the main terminal entrance and is equidistant between the north and south perimeter lines.

## Section 5.8 External utilities

The following external utilities can be found within the container terminal.

### Electricity supply

There is a step-down National Grid substation supplying electrical power to the container terminal. The substation is protected by a 2-metre brick wall and electrified fencing above the wall. Lighting, CCTV, and an IDS are also provided by National Grid. All systems are monitored from the Security Control Room.

### Gas

The Liverport Container Terminal is supplied by the United Kingdom's National Transmission System (NTS), which is the network of gas pipelines that supply gas to about forty power stations and large industrial users from natural gas terminals situated on the coast.[44]

### Water

Water is supplied directly from Northwest Water, by means of underground pipe networks.

## Section 5.9 Areas of concealment

There are no areas of concealment in the proximity of the two buildings, however, because of the 24 hours of operations, and the movement of vehicles and containers the situation is fluid, meaning that there may be areas of concealment in the terminal.

### Recommendations

Notwithstanding the CCTV coverage afforded to the perimeter and the two buildings, there are another 22 cameras, combining digital static, and pan, tilt and zoom units that offer full coverage of the terminal.

It is recommended that a separate CCTV survey takes place to ensure that adequate cover is provided.

It is further recommended that all container terminal patrols by the security team take into consideration the feasibility of concealment.

## Section 5.10 Items to aid a criminal

Adjacent to the X-ray scanner building is a small tool store building, approximately 5 metres by 10 metres, containing mainly hand tools, ladders, paint, etc.

### Observations

During the Security Survey, it was observed that the tool shed was insecure, in that the only entrance to the building, a single leaf, in swinging wooden door was unlocked, with no sign of any occupant.

### Recommendations

It is recommended that when unoccupied, the tool shed is secure, and it should be visited by the security patrol on a regular basis.

## Section 5.11 Restricted areas

The following locations and structures have been categorised as Restricted Areas, and as such will require extra vigilance and surveillance by the Security team.

- The Security Control Room.
- All external utilities.
- The x-ray scanning facility.
- The Administration Building.
- All vessels.
- The IT server room.
- The vehicle park.
- Container waiting areas.

## Section 5.12 Parking arrangements

There is a central parking area for staff car parking only.

## Section 6: Main building (s) internal

### *Section 6.1 Access control*

Other than the external access control measures mentioned, there are no other forms of access control.

### *Section 6.2 CCTV*

Internal CCTV is as follows:

#### *The Administration/Security Control Room building*

On grounds of health & Safety, there is one digital static CCTV camera located in each of the administration areas, and there are three cameras in the Security Control Room covering the reception area, the CCTV controls, and the search area.

#### *The x-ray facility*

There are three digital static CCTV cameras in the x-ray facility, one on either end of the inside of the building, and for health and safety reasons there is a single camera in the Operations Room, where the X-ray facilities are housed.

### *Section 6.3 IDS*

Internal Intruder Systems is as follows:

#### *The Security Control Room*

The Security Control Room has elements of the IDS installed (Dual Technology sensors), but it will only be set in the unlikely event of the control room being unoccupied.

#### *The Administration*

Internally, the Administration Rooms are protected by a number of Dual Technology IDS devices, which consist of PIR and Microwave sensors. This form of IDS combination is known to reduce false alarms.

### *The x-ray facility*

Internally the x-ray facility is protected by a number of Dual Technology IDS devices, which consist of PIR and Microwave sensors.

All IDS activations are received at the Security Control Room, and there will be an immediate response.

## Section 7: Internal specialist or restricted areas

This section refers to restricted areas with specialist applications, which if successfully attacked would negatively impact the container terminal.

The following internal restricted areas will be explained.

### *Section 7.1 The Security Control Room*

The Security Control Room is located close to the eastern entrance/exit and is equidistant from north and south perimeter fences.

It serves as the terminal Security Control Room, and when necessary, as a Crisis Command and Control Centre, and it is equipped and manned appropriately.

There are two entrances to the Security Control Room, to the east and west facings of the building.

Access to the Security Control Room is restricted to security personnel and Senior Management who may require access for operational reasons. Access is gained by means of a proximity card reader systems, with smart cards being issued on a need-to-have basis.

The Security Control Room is supported by internal and external CCTV coverage, which is monitored from within and is also signalled to an Alarm Receiving Centre (ARC), and although the room is occupied on a 24/7 basis, there is an IDS installed, which in the event of an evacuation, can be set and monitored from the ARC.

At any one time, there will be a minimum of three Security Officers (including the Security Supervisor) on duty in the control room. Duty officers have access to a telephone land line, handheld radios, and cell phone network, and three Personal Attack buttons have been installed.

### *Observations*

Currently there is no control room back up facility.

### *Recommendations*

It is strongly recommended that a Security Control Room backup facility is identified, fitted with sufficient fittings and systems[45] should it be required to be manned operationally.

## *Section 7.2 The X-ray scanning facility*

The X-ray scanning facility is a single-story unit located in the south-east corner of the terminal, and by the very nature of the sensitive and extremely expensive equipment contained in the building must be declared a Restricted Area.

Access is by means of the site proximity card reader system, and once again access is only authorised for the security team and members of the X-ray operations and management function.

The building is supported internally and externally by CCTV which is monitored from the Security Control Room, the lighting is excellent, and the facility is protected by an IDS when secure. The X-ray operator has access to a communications land line, a handheld radio, and a cell phone, and a Personal Attack button has been installed.

The X-ray facility is included on the Security Officers' patrol route, and it is checked every hour, occupied, or otherwise.

The facility is operational on a 24/7 basis if needed. Operations depend on the movement of vessels and containers.

There is a mobile X-ray facility held in reserve should it be required as back up.

## *Section 7.3 The Administration Building*

The Administrative Building is a single-story unit located directly behind the main entrance to the terminal, and it sits on either side of the Security Control room. The building primarily holds sensitive personal, and personnel information and data, and that is why it has been classified as a Restricted Area.

Access is by means of the site proximity card reader system, and once again access is only authorised for the security team and members of the Administration Team.

The building is supported internally and externally by CCTV which is monitored from the Security Control Room, the lighting is excellent, and the facility is protected by an IDS when secure. The Administration Team has access to a communications land line, and a cell phone and a Personal Attack button has been installed.

The Administration Building is included on the Security Officers' patrol route, and it is checked every hour during hours of non-occupation.

The building is operational from 0900hrs to 1700hrs, Monday to Friday, and is closed over the weekend. Operations depend on the movement of vessels and containers, and for that reason, the Administration Building may be occupied if required because of operational necessity.

Should the Administration Building be evacuated for any length of time, administration operations can be carried out from the Security Control Room.

### *Section 7.4 The ICT server room*

The ICT server room is located within the Administration Building. The room holds a number of computer terminals that store extremely sensitive commercial and personal information and data, and it also holds information relating to Operational Technology (OT), and for that reason, it has been classified as a Restricted Area.

The ICT server room is constructed from load-bearing brick and steel walls, and a solid ceiling. There is an underground void for cable access, and that is protected by the site IDS. Access to the server room is by two-factor access control, consisting of a proximity reader card, and biometric fingerprint software. Entrance to the room is restricted to the ICT Team and Security Supervisors.

The room is supported internally and externally by CCTV which is monitored from the Security Control Room, the lighting is excellent, and the room is protected by an IDS when secure. The ICT Team has access to a communications land line, a cell phone, and a Personal Attack button has been installed.

The integrity of the ICT server room is checked by a Security Officer every hour when it is not occupied.

The room is operational on a 24/7 basis, and twice per day all data is backed up to an encrypted cloud. This means that should the ICT room be destroyed, or the servers taken out of action, all data is secure.

### *Key takeaways*

*The container terminal is heavily dependent on ICT, and to that end, the network must receive the maximum amount of security attention.*

## Section 8: Conclusion

### *Post survey debrief*

A post-survey debrief was carried out, during which the PFSO, Mr Brian McFarlane was informed of a number of 'quick fixes', and an agreement was reached in relation to the Security Survey Report. Mr Mc Farlane requested the report be delivered to him by hand within 30 working days.

There is a requirement for a survey presentation, but future talks will take place in relation to other work at other container terminals within the UK.

The PFSO concluded by declaring that he was very satisfied with the Security Survey and how it was carried out.

## Aviation security

### Security Survey: Birmingpool (BPL) International Airport Departures Building

| Document owner | Reference number | Proof-reader | 1st check | 2nd check |
|---|---|---|---|---|
| Bill Seppings | SecSurv/BPL/06/22 | | | |

1. **Survey details.**
2. **Initial stages of the survey.**
3. **External factors.**
4. **Perimeter protection.**
5. **Main buildings-external.**
6. **Main buildings-internal.**
7. **Internal specialist or restricted areas.**
8. **Conclusion.**

## Section 1: Survey details

Name and appointment of the client.

| |
|---|
| Mr Bill Seppings. CEO. |

Address (s)

| |
|---|
| Birmingpool (BPL) International Airport Departures Building, Birmingpool, B26 3QR. |

Point of Contact.

| |
|---|
| Mr Paul Brown. Airport Head of Security. |

E mail.

| |
|---|
| p.brown@birmingpool.com |

Telephone.

| |
|---|
| 012213456753 |

Web address.

| |
|---|
| www.birmingpool.com |

Location and date of Survey.

| |
|---|
| Birmingpool (BPL) International Airport Departures Building, Birmingpool, B26 3QR. |

Name of Security Auditor and date of survey.

| |
|---|
| Mr Charles Swanson. 01 December 2021. |

Organisation.

| |
|---|
| STC |

## Section 2: Initial stages of the survey

As the result of a recent Security Risk Assessment, and after liaising with Birmingpool Constabulary Counter Terrorism Unit, it had been decided that thought must be given to the overall security of the Departures Building which appeared to be extremely vulnerable.

### *Section 2.1 General description and business operations*

Birmingpool (BPL) International Airport is located in the Northwest England, and under normal circumstances, has a daily footfall of between 7,000 and 10,000 passengers. The airport is also an international hub, with large commercial airliners flying to and from all corners of the globe.

The location selected for the Security Survey is the Departures Building, an area with complete access to the general public on a 24/7 basis, and it is a department that has been identified as the fastest growing and busiest function of the airport.

### *Section 2.2 Reasons for the survey*

The Board of Directors has decided, as a result of the recent Security Risk Assessment based on the likelihood and impact of a marauding terrorist attack at Birmingpool International Airport, prior to any risk treatment, that in order to ensure people feel safe, and that all assets are protected, a physical Security Survey of the Departures Building is needed.

### *Section 2.3 Assets to be protected*

#### *People*

As with every other Security Survey carried out so far, people operating in or visiting the Departures Building are the number one priority in terms of asset protection, followed by:

#### *Brand and reputation*

Due to its growth as an international hub, global airlines are ferociously competing to establish themselves as a partner to the airport, and as such its brand and reputation are one of its most prized assets.

#### *Data and information*

The Departures Building holds a vast amount of sensitive data and information, particularly in respect of passenger and aircraft movement, which would be attractive to criminals and terrorists alike. There will also be personal, and personnel information held, which requires protection in accordance with the General Data Protection Regulations (2016).

### *ICT systems*

As with all other international airports, Birmingpool International Airport is heavily reliant on Information Communication Technology (ICT), in areas such as Air Traffic Control Systems, passenger movement, aircraft management, and security controls. ICT is a major asset, without which today, any airport would struggle to operate, let alone compete.

### *Infrastructure*

The Departures Building infrastructure is a significant asset, as it allows all air movement operations to continue on a 24/7 basis, and should the infrastructure be attacked, it would likely bring all operations to a standstill.

### *Aircraft*

From a micro perspective aircraft are not necessarily a departures asset, there is of course a symmetry, as an attack against an aircraft would impact all departure movement.

## *Section 2.4 Initial research*

From a cultural and operations perspective, aviation security is quite unique, and as the repercussions of the 9/11 attacks in the United States still continue to reverberate, the Security Auditor must ensure that all research possible is carried out before a Security Survey, in order that no detail is missed. He or she must not present the criminal or terrorist with a target that should have been better protected.

### *Company background and security culture*

The original site for Birmingpool International Airport began its operational existence as a small cargo service airport in 1951, with inaugural flights being restricted to within the UK. In 1995 it was purchased by the LFC group, and it was transformed into a passenger airport serving the UK and Europe; before receiving a huge private investment in 2010, which completely altered its business approach, allowing it to act as an international and global hub for all major airlines.

The attacks against the World Trade Center in New York on 11 September 2001 altered the security culture, or perhaps should have altered the security culture of all international airports. Birmingpool is a positive exemplar, and the fact that it is constantly security risk assessed and is now about to have a high-level Security Survey carried out is a testament to the devotion to safety and security of the Executive Board.

### *Unemployment rates in the area*

Unemployment in Birmingpool is slightly higher than the national average, and employment rates in the area of the airport are amongst the highest in the UK.

### *Previous criminal incidents*

As mentioned, the footfall at the airport is between 7,000 and 10,000 daily, and it would be quite surprising if no general crime was committed. However, as mentioned, to date the security culture is robust, and there has been no recorded serious crime or acts of terrorism against the location.

### *Previous Security Surveys*

The Government will be publishing all UK aviation laws (including retained EU law) on legislation.gov.uk in due course. In the meantime, the Civil Aviation Authority (CAA) has developed this website[46] to support the industry in understanding its rights and obligations under UK law, now that the UK has left the European system. The CAA is continuing to work with its suppliers to improve the format and structure of the documents.

Currently, all UK aviation must adhere to Commission Implementing Regulation (EU) 2015/1998 of 5 November 2015 laying down detailed measures for the implementation of the common basic standards on aviation security (Text with EEA relevance) (Retained EU Legislation).[47]

The vast majority of global nation states will conform to similar legislation, but there will always be the potential for an independent Security Survey.

To date, this will be the first independent physical Security Survey of Birmingpool International Airport.

### *Crime Pattern Analysis (CPA) – B26 3QR*

The postcode B26 3QR refers to an area of the city devoted to Birmingpool International Airport, and although cybercrime and terrorism are not covered in this form of CPA, it is safe to say that they will be classified as two of the most serious threats to any community. In terms of general crime, the greatest fear for this area will be related to robbery and burglary, which are in fact relatively minimal.

In 2022, the three greatest types of crime are violence and sexual offences, shoplifting, and anti-social behaviour. However, the offences likely to concern the Airport Security Manager are vehicle crime, burglary, robbery, and the possession of weapons.

### *Key takeaways*

*The Crime Pattern Analysis (CPA) is an indication of a crime previously committed, and it has limited value when considering future offences.*

## Section 2.5 Planning and preparation

An international airport is geographically and strategically extremely complicated, and any Security Survey carried out will require distinct levels of professionalism and detail. Therefore, planning and preparation are critical.

### *Authorisation and specific points of contact*

A contract covering the scope of work was agreed before work began, and that was authorisation to carry out the work. The point of contact has been identified as the Head of Security, Mr Paul Brown.

### *Maps and diagrams*

The airport is geographically a high-profile facility in the area where it is located, and by using a search engine it was simple to find all relevant maps of the area. As with all other Security Surveys covered in the book so far, floor plans and fire diagrams were readily available from Mr Brown.

### *Changes in laws and regulations*

Aviation security is extremely high profile, and after 9/11 it is also very dynamic, in that because of the terrorist threat, laws, and regulations could change very quickly. As with all other sectors, the Security Auditor will need to stay abreast of all aviation legislation and national/international regulations. This was researched by the Security Auditor before the work began.

### *Social media*

As with all other sectors covered so far, Birmingpool International Airport is accessible on all major social media platforms, and once again this is an opportunity to see it from a customer perspective.

### *Photography*

Taking photographs at any international airport is often fraught with danger, because of the sensitivities within that location. In a number of countries, photography is illegal, often carrying a prison sentence. Whilst that is not so at Birmingpool International Airport, the Security Auditor was strongly advised to seek permission through his point of contact before taking photographs. Authority to take essential photographs was given.

### *Identification*

As discussed throughout this section of the book, although proof of identification is not a lawful requirement in the UK, the Security Auditor was advised to be in possession of either a valid passport or photographic driving licence. During the Security Survey, he was challenged on a number of occasions.

### *Agreed visit times and dates*

Mr Brown is an extremely busy person, and it was therefore imperative that both parties adhered to all dates and times agreed.

### *Key takeaways*

*A professional Security Auditor can never be too prepared!*

## Section 3: External factors

### *Section 3.1 Environment*

Birmingpool International Airport is set in grounds some distance from an urban environment, but road and rail communications are excellent.

### *Section 3.2 Crime Pattern Analysis*

See Section 2.

### *Section 3.3 Employment rate*

Unemployment rates in Birmingpool are higher than the national average, and the airport is one of the most important employers in the area, currently employing approximately 2,000 full and part-time staff.

### *Section 3.4 Potential for Crime Prevention Through Environmental Design (CPTED) using the acronym MAINT*

**M**aintenance: The departures building is very well maintained.
**A**ccess Control: There is the potential for access control throughout the airport?
**I**mage: The airport is iconic in terms of image, and whilst it may be a target for criminals or terrorists, it also stands for pride and self-belief.
**N**atural surveillance: The departure lounge been designed with natural surveillance in mind?
**T**erritoriality: Staff and management have demonstrated ownership and territoriality?

### *Section 3.5 Nearest police station*

The nearest police station is located at Bishop Street, BE 6 21MX, and is accessible to the public on a 24/7 basis. To call the police in an emergency situation, dial 999. For non-emergency issues dial 101.

### *Section 3.6 Nearest hospital*

The closest hospital is the Birmingpool Teaching Hospital, Walton Lane, BE21 7DX. To call for emergency assistance call 999. For non-emergency help dial 119.

### *Section 3.7 Nearest fire and rescue*

There is a fire and rescue station located at Captains Lane, BE11 7GY. This is the closest medical facility, and to call it in an emergency dial 999. For non-emergency assistance call 01551 926 0566.

## Section 4: Perimeter protection

There is no perimeter protection supporting the Departures Building, but there is a perimeter fence surrounding the airport, which was taken into consideration for the Security Survey.

### *Section 4.1 Type*

Surrounding the entire airport estate is a 2.3-metre-high security welded mesh, and 6mm vertical line fencing. The fence has been designed and installed to the standards recognised by CPNI.

### *Section 4.2 PIDS by type*

PIDS at the airport are fabric-mounted systems, where the sensor is attached to the fabric of the fence in the form of a tamper-resistant taught wire system which detects pressure against the fabric. When activated, the PIDS will transmit a silent signal to the Security Control Room. The levels of false alarms are extremely low.

At the time of the Security Survey, the PIDS was deemed fit for purpose.

### *Section 4.3 PIDS activation and response*

An attempted breach will transmit a silent signal to the Security Control Room, and upon receipt of the alarm activation, there will be an immediate response from the Manned Guarding Security Team. Such a response will be included in the KPI[48] and Service Level Agreement (SLA) and should be regularly tested.

### Section 4.4 Topping

There is a 600-millimetre low voltage electric fence installed above the welded mesh perimeter fencing, designed to deliver a non-lethal electric shock to the intruder. For aesthetic reasons, there are sections of the perimeter fence not covered by the electric fence.

#### Observation

There is an obvious weakness at those points where there is no electric fence.

#### Recommendations

If it is inappropriate to install electric fencing, those areas where the vulnerability has been identified will need to be supported by other means. e.g., Enhanced CCTV and manned guarding cover.

### Section 4.5 State of repair

The perimeter fence and supporting topping are in a very good state of repair, and at the time of the Security Survey, both were fit for purpose.

### Section 4.6 Supporting security systems

The perimeter fence is supported by CCTV, LED lighting, and Manned Guarding.

### Section 4.7 Supporting security systems specifications

During the course of the Security Survey, the following security systems were observed.

### Section 4.8 Closed Circuit Television (CCTV)

There are ninety-six static and PTZ digital CCTV cameras installed in support of the perimeter of the airport, affording 360-degree cover, including the two main entrances. Although every camera is a switchable unit, allowing it to operate under varying flux conditions, the CCTV system is supported by LED lighting units. The CCTV system is also supported by Video Motion Detection (VMD) software, allowing every camera to be able to send pre-notification of any movement within its field of vision. The cameras signal the Security Control Room, where all images are recorded and stored on a Network Digital Video Recording System (NDVR).

### *Observations*

During the Security Survey, it was observed that three static cameras covering the western side of the perimeter fence were non-operational and had been for two weeks.

### *Recommendations*

CCTV is a critical function in terms of Defence in Depth (DiD), and it is strongly recommended that the units are repaired or replaced as a matter of urgency.

## Section 4.9 Security lighting.

Perimeter security lighting consists of one hundred and twenty 1,000-watt LED units, including coverage of both entrances to the airport.

At the time of the Security Survey, all lighting units were fit for purpose.

## Section 4.10 Manned guarding

See Section 4.19

## Section 4.11 Security supporting systems state of repair

During the Security Survey, a number of observations and recommendations were made. See this section.

## Section 4.12 Entrances

There are two entrances, and two emergency exits at the airport; all are designed for vehicular access.

### Section 4.13 Main entrance

The main entrance is to the south of the airport and is used for general access.

Physically the main entrance consists of the following.

### Section 4.14 Main gate

The main gate is a steel double-leaf sliding unit, which is controlled from the Security Control Room, and it is permanently open unless it is required to be secure in the event of an emergency.

Forward of the sliding gate is single-arm steel barrier, which is controlled by the site Automatic Number Plate Recording (ANPR) CCTV system which lifts the barrier once a photograph of the vehicle has been taken. This is also used for payment when the vehicle is leaving the airport.

Behind the barrier is a Hostile Vehicle Mitigation (HVM) vehicle blocker rising kerb, designed to CPNI specifications[49] which is flush with the surface of the road unless needed to prevent entrance by an unauthorised vehicle.

### Section 4.15 Goods inwards gate

The goods inwards gate, or goods in gate, as it is usually referred to, is to the north of the airport.

The goods in gate is a single steel electric sliding unit, also controlled by the Security Control Room. This entrance is permanently closed, and only open from inside when a vehicle with a prior appointment requires access.

There is also a pedestrian entrance for use by staff, and it is accessed by means of the site proximity card reader system.

### Section 4.16 Emergency exits

Both of the emergency exits are for pedestrian use only and are controlled by a crash bar system on the inside of the perimeter gate. The emergency gates are also connected to the site IDS system, and when they are opened, an alarm is registered at the Security Control Room which must be investigated.

### *Observations*

During the Security Survey, both emergency exits were covertly opened, and neither opening activated the IDS. Upon investigation by the Airport Security Manager, it was deduced that the IDS had been decoupled during maintenance work.

### *Recommendations*

It is recommended that the emergency exits are re-connected to the site IDS at the earliest opportunity.

## Section 4.17 Entrance state of repair

During the course of the Security Survey, it was observed that all entrances were in a good state of repair.

## Section 4.18 Entrance access control systems

See the previous section relating to entrance specifications.

## Section 4.19 Entrance access control systems state of repair

With the exception of the emergency exit IDS, all access control systems are fit for purpose.

## Section 4.19 Manned guarding

All information relating to the Security Team will be found in the Site Assignment Instructions (SAI), which are confidential, and are located in electronic format on the company ICT network.

There is manned guarding support on a 24/7 basis, which includes the following details.

### *In house-licenced*

The ‘in house’ Security Team who all hold SIA Front-Line Licences, consists of the following.

- One Senior Security Supervisor who reports to the Airport Security Manager.
- Four Security Supervisors.
- Twenty Security Officers.

### *Shifts availability*

The Senior Security Supervisor works Monday to Friday: 0800hrs to 1800hrs.

The four Security Supervisors operate on a shift roster consisting of the following hours.

- 0600hrs to 1400hrs.
- 1400hrs to 2200hrs.
- 2200hrs to 0600hrs.

### *Duties and roles*

The duties and roles of the Security Team can be found in the Site Assignment Instructions, but an abridged version is as follows.

- Security Control Room duties:
    - Access control.
    - Visitors pass management.
    - Alarm management and response.
    - CCTV monitoring.
    - Communications management.
- Patrolling.
- Search.
- Incident response.
- Investigation and reporting.
- Facilities Management patrols.
- Escort duties.

### *Specialist qualifications*

All Security Officers hold the following qualifications.

- Front-line Security Officer licence.
- First aid.
- Fire Wardens.
- Public Space Surveillance (PSS)
- Search procedures.

## *Section 4.20 Security Control Room*

The Security Control Room is located adjacent to the Main Entrance, and there is a reserve option in the Departures Building. Birmingpool Constabulary also occupies the Security Control Room, and there are three police officers attending for duty on a 24/7 basis.

### *Security Control Room manning times*

The Security Control Room is manned and operational on a 24/7 basis, throughout the year.

### *Security Control Room duties*

The Security Control Room, primarily because it is occupied and operational 24/7, 365 days per year, is at the heart of the airport.

- Arguably the most important task carried out by the team in the Security Control Room is access control to the Goods in entrance, with all entrants being processed by one of the Duty Security Officers.
- All alarm activations signal to the Security Control Room, and the CCTV system is managed from here.
- Sensitive documentation in hard and electronic form is held in the control room.
- The Security Control Room is also the Crisis Control Room when needed.
- There is a reserve Security Control Room in the Departures Building.
- The Security Control Room serves as the Communications Centre for the airport, with the communications network being managed from here. See Figure 17, which is the communications network.

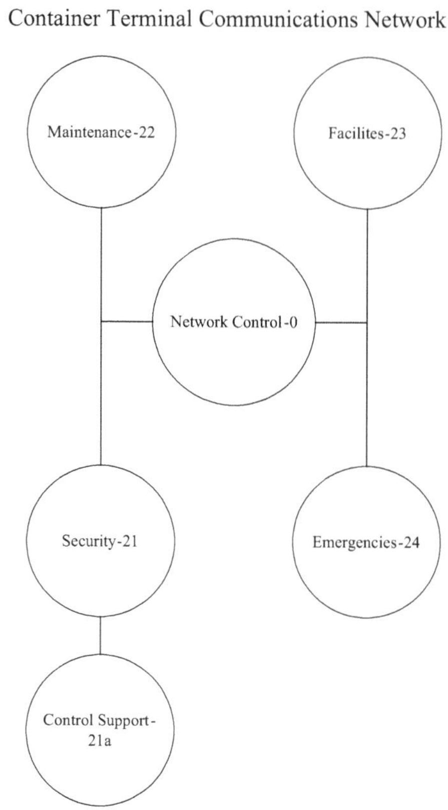


*Figure 17* The Communications Network (2), and individual call signs.

### *Key takeaways*

*Any Security Control Room is very often seen as the nerve centre of the site, and there has to be flexibility to coordinate usage, in order that the control room can be used for other purposes. A functioning reserve Security Control Room is critical.*

## Section 5: Main building external

### *Section 5.1 Key personnel*

It is imperative that all key personnel are spoken to in regard to the security and risk management of the location. This is the first opportunity available for the Security Auditor to begin research from the inside, and it is imperative that he or she choose correctly.

### *Who?*

It is critical to interview the following key personnel.

Mr Bill Seppings. CEO
Mr Paul Brown. Head of Security.
Ms Sue O Brian. HR Manager.
Mr Pete Hilliard. Operations Manager.
Inspector Maria Brown. British Transport Police.
Mr Charlie Green. Senior Security Supervisor.

### *When?*

There is no ideal time to speak to airport key personnel because operations are carried out over a 24/7 period, and therefore, those who have volunteered to be interviewed should be spoken to at their convenience.

### *What?*

As with all other sectors, questions asked in an aviation environment, particularly in an international airport, must be appropriate, and they have to add to the knowledge gained during the Security Risk Assessment.

### *Key takeaways*

*The airport is operational on a 24/7 basis, meaning the Security Auditor will need to be available day and night.*

## *Section 5.2 Description of the building*

The Departures Building is a single-story building of brick, glass, and steel construction. It is in a very good state of repair, and at the time of the Security Survey, it was deemed to be fit for purpose. Figure 18 illustrates the southern public entrances, east, and west fire escapes, and Departure Longe exits.

The building contains the following sections as seen in the diagram index.

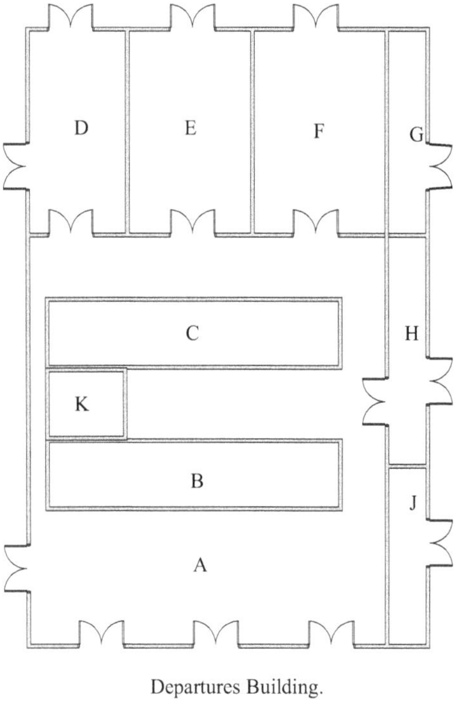


Index.

A. Public area.

B. Baggage and ticketing.

C. Security

D-F. Departure lounges

G. Security Control Room

H. Storage.

J. HR Department.

*Figure 18* The departures building.

## Section 5.3 Number of access points and how they are secured

The following access points are to be found at the building being security surveyed.

### Main entrance

There are three main entrances to the south of the Departures Building. All are permanently open for access by members of the public and travellers, but there is the option of securing the doors should there be a requirement. Once secure the entrances will be protected by the building IDS.[50] During the Security Survey, it was observed that they were fit for purpose.

### *Fire exits*

There are four fire exits located on the east and west of the building. All fire exits are steel, double-leaf outward swinging doors, all of which are opened from the inside by use of a crash bar system. The exits are protected by the building IDS, and during the Security Survey, it was observed that they were fit for purpose.

### *Departure lounge exits*

The Departure Lounge exits allow passengers access to the airport tarmac, and consequentially the aircraft they are authorised to enter. The exits are protected by the building IDS, and during the Security Survey, it was observed that they were fit for purpose.

## *Section 5.4 CCTV*

There are fourteen static digital cameras installed external to the Departures Building. All of the cameras are supported by effective lighting, signalling to the Security Control Room where images are recorded and stored on the site Network Digital Video Recording system. The cameras are located at each corner of the building and are also installed to cover all entrances and exits, allowing 360-degree cover.

At the time of the Security Survey, all building external cameras were fit for purpose.

## *Section 5.5 IDS*

By virtue of the fact that the Departures Building is accessible to members of the public, passengers, air crew, and contractors on a 24/7 basis, the IDS is permanently unset. However, should the need arise, the building can be protected by the site IDS, consisting of perimeter protection in the form of door and window contacts.

As with the perimeter PIDS, should the Departure Building activate, the alarm will be received at the Security Control Room from where it will be investigated.

At the time of the Security Survey, all building external IDS elements were fit for purpose.

## Section 5.6 Lighting

LED flood lighting is installed externally at the Departure Building affording 360-degree cover.

At the time of the Security Survey, all building external lighting was fit for purpose.

## Section 5.7 Distance from the perimeter

The Departure Building is located approximately 100 metres from the southern perimeter fence line.

## Section 5.8 External utilities

The following external utilities servicing the Departure Building can be found at the airport.

### Electricity supply

There is a step-down National Grid substation supplying electrical power to the Departure Building. The substation is protected by a 2-metre brick wall and electrified fencing above the wall. Lighting, CCTV, and an IDS are also provided by National Grid. All systems are monitored from the Security Control Room.

### Gas

Gas for Birmingpool Airport is supplied by the UK's National Transmission System (NTS), which is the network of gas pipelines that supply gas to about forty power stations and large industrial users from natural gas terminals situated on the coast.[51]

### Water

Water is supplied directly from Northwest Water, by means of underground pipe networks.

## Section 5.9 Areas of concealment

There are no areas of concealment.

### *Section 5.10 Items to aid a criminal*

Adjacent to the Security Control Room is a small tool store, approximately 5 metres by 10 metres, containing mainly hand tools, ladders, paint, etc.

#### *Observations*

During the Security Survey, it was observed that the tool store was insecure, in that the only entrance to the store, a single leaf, in swinging wooden door was unlocked, with no sign of any occupants.

#### *Recommendations*

It is recommended that when unoccupied, the tool store is secure, and it should be visited by the security patrol on a regular basis.

### *Section 5.11 Restricted areas*

The following locations and structures have been categorised as Restricted Areas, and as such will require extra vigilance and surveillance by the Security team.

- The Security Control Room.
- All external utilities.
- The IT server room.
- The HR Department.
- Staff leisure rooms.
- The tool store.

### *Section 5.12 Parking arrangements*

There is a central parking area to the rear of the building for staff car parking only.

## Section 6: Main building (s) internal

Unlike other sectors covered so far in the book, travellers using the Departures Building will be embarking on a distinct route, from entering the building to boarding an aircraft, with Figure 19 illustrating that journey.

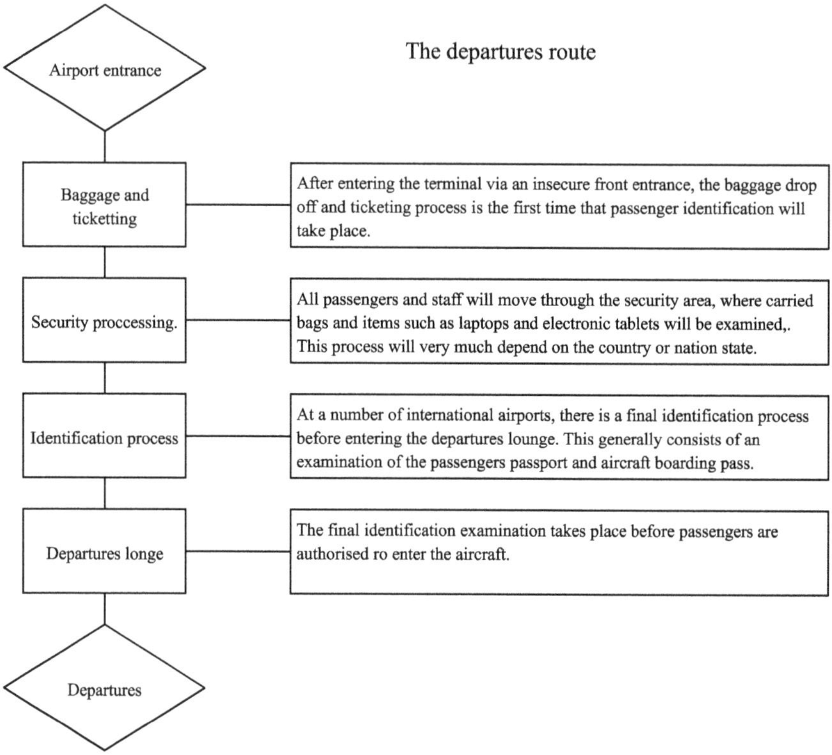


*Figure 19* The departures route.

## *Section 6.1 Access control*

The following restricted areas are protected by distinct automatic access control systems.

### *Baggage handling/movement areas*

From the moment baggage is dropped off until it reaches the loading vehicle, all bags and surrendered cases will travel through a secure area, and during the Security Survey, it was observed that the entrance to the restricted areas is controlled by the site proximity card reader system.

### *The security inspection area*

As with baggage handling/movement, the security inspection area is a restricted location, and it is also protected by the site proximity card reader system.

### *The ICT server room*

The ICT server room is arguably the most sensitive location within the airport as it manages all technical aspects of the airport's operations. Access is by means of the site proximity card reader system, and a biometric fingerprint operation is restricted to vetted security personnel, and ICT network management personnel.

### *The HR department*

The HR department holds extremely sensitive information and data relating to airport personnel, and as such, it is a restricted area protected by the airport proximity card reader system.

### *The Security Control Room*

The Security Control Room is occupied and operational on a 24/7 basis and can be legitimately described as the nerve centre of airport security operations. As such it is critical that access to the location is secure, and with that in mind, access control management must meet the same levels as the ICT server room, with two-factor access control. Proximity card reader and biometric systems are in place.

### *Departure lounges*

Whilst passengers enter all departure lounges via the public entrance, staff will have secure access to other areas of the lounges and will be required to use a proximity smart card.

### *Land/airside interfaces*

This is the final access-controlled exit from the landside area of the airport, and staff must use their smart cards to allow passengers access to the aircraft.

During the Security Survey, it was observed that all access control systems within the Departures Building were fit for purpose.

## *Section 6.2 CCTV*

Static digital CCTV cameras, signalling to the Security Control Room have been installed at the following locations.

- Public area.
- Two cameras covering the three main entrance doors.
- Baggage and ticketing.
- Four cameras covering the front of the baggage and ticketing area, and four cameras to the rear covering staff on duty.
- Security check area.
- Four cameras covering the front of the security check area, and four cameras to the rear covering staff on duty.
- Departure lounges
- Four cameras covering the front entrances to the departures lounge, and two in each lounge.

### *The Security Control Room*

There is one camera covering the outside of the Security Control room, and three inside.

### *Storage*

One camera covering the length of the storage are:

### *HR Department*

There is one camera covering the outside of the Security Control room, and three inside.

### *IT Server Room*

There is one CCTV camera covering the external facing of the IT Server Room, and two cameras inside.

### *Fire exits*

Every fire exit is covered by a CCTV camera.

As mentioned, all cameras signal to the Security Control Room where they are monitored, with images being captured and recorded on the airport Network Video Recording Network. The footage is backed up onto a remote cloud.

### *Section 6.3 IDS*

As with the building's external IDS, all sensors in the Departures Building are unset, with the following exceptions.

- The ICT Server Room.
- The door to the ICT Server room is protected by contacts, and a door held open alarm.[52] Internally the room is protected by a number of Dual Technology sensors, which if activated will alarm the Security Control Room.
- The HR department.
- As with the ICT Server Room, the door to the HR Department is protected by contacts, and internally the room is protected by a number of Dual Technology sensors, which if activated will alarm the Security Control Room.
- The storage area.
- The door to the HR Department is protected by contacts, and internally the room is protected by a number of Dual Technology sensors, which if activated will alarm the Security Control Room.

All IDS activations are received at the Security Control Room, and there will be an immediate response.

At the time of the Security Survey, the IDS protecting the Departures Building was fit for purpose.

## Section 7: Internal specialist or restricted areas

This section refers to restricted areas with specialist applications, which if successfully attacked would negatively impact the airport.

The following internal restricted areas will be explained.

### *Section 7.1 The Security Control Room*

The Security Control Room is located in the eastern part of the building, adjacent to one of the Departure Lounges, and north of the central storage facility.

It serves as the airport Security Control Room, and when necessary, as a Crisis Command and Control Centre, and it is equipped and manned appropriately.

There is one entrance to the Security Control Room.

Access to the Security Control Room is restricted to security personnel and Senior Management who may require access for operational reasons. Access is gained by means of a proximity card reader system, with smart cards being issued on a need-to-have basis.

The Security Control Room is supported by internal and external CCTV coverage, which is monitored from within and is also signalled to an Alarm Receiving Centre (ARC), and although the room is occupied on a 24/7 basis, there is an IDS installed, which in the event of an evacuation, can be set and monitored from the ARC.

At any one time, there will be a minimum of three Security Officers (including the Security Supervisor) on duty in the control room. Duty officers have access to a telephone land line, handheld radios, and cell phone network, and three Personal Attack buttons have been installed.

### *Observations*

Currently, there is no control room backup facility.

### *Recommendations*

It is strongly recommended that a Security Control Room backup facility is identified, and equipped with sufficient fittings and systems[53] in the event that it should be required to be manned operationally.

## *Section 7.2 The ICT server room*

The ICT server room is located centrally, in between the ticketing/baggage area and the Security Check area. The room holds a number of computer terminals that store extremely sensitive commercial and personal information and data, and it also holds information relating to Operational Technology (OT), and for that reason, it has been classified as a Restricted Area.

The ICT server room is constructed from load-bearing brick and steel walls, and a solid ceiling. There is an underground void for cable access, and that is protected by the site IDS. Access to the server room is by two-factor access control, consisting of a proximity reader card, and biometric fingerprint software. Entrance to the room is restricted to the ICT Team and Security Supervisors.

The room is supported internally and externally by CCTV which is monitored from the Security Control Room, the lighting is excellent, and the room is protected by an IDS when secure. The ICT Team has access to a communications land line, a cell phone, and a Personal Attack button has been installed.

The integrity of the ICT server room is checked by a Security Officer every hour when it is not occupied.

The room is operational on a 24/7 basis, and twice per day all data is backed up to an encrypted cloud. This means that should the ICT room be destroyed, or the servers taken out of action, all data is secure.

## Section 8: Conclusion

### *Post survey de brief*

A post-survey debrief was carried out, during which the Airport Security Manager, Paul Brown was informed of a number of 'quick fixes', and an agreement was reached in relation to the Security Survey Report. Mr Brown requested the report be delivered to him by hand within thirty working days.

There is no requirement for a survey presentation, but future talks will take place in relation to other work at other airports within the United Kingdom.

The Security Manager concluded by declaring that he was very satisfied with the Security Survey and how it was carried out.

## Hostile environment security

### Security Survey: BU drilling operations in the Kingdom of Saudubai (KoS)

| Document owner | Reference number | Proof-reader | 1st check | 2nd check |
|---|---|---|---|---|
| Bob Clark | SecSurv/KoS/07/22 | | | |

1. **Survey details.**
2. **Initial stages of the survey.**
3. **External factors.**
4. **Perimeter protection.**
5. **Main buildings-external.**
6. **Main buildings-internal.**
7. **Internal specialist or restricted areas.**
8. **Conclusion.**

## Section 1: Survey details

Name and appointment of the client.

| |
|---|
| Mr Bob Clark. CEO. |

Address (s)

| |
|---|
| Greater Safaniya, Kingdom of Saudubai. |

Point of Contact.

| |
|---|
| Mr John Beck. CSO. |

E mail.

| |
|---|
| j.beck@bu.com |

Telephone.

| |
|---|
| 020513456753 |

Web address.

| |
|---|
| www.bu.com |

Location of Survey.

| |
|---|
| Greater Safaniya, Kingdom of Saudubai. |

Name of Security Auditor and date of survey.

| |
|---|
| Charles Swanson. 05 January 2022. |

Organisation.

| |
|---|
| STC |

### *Case study – In Amenas*

Although the attack by al Qaeda against the site at In Amenas, Algeria on the 16 of January 2013, was an assault against a gas drilling platform, the lessons that should have been learned apply to any such drilling location, in what must have been assessed as a hostile area.

39 foreign hostages, and a local Security Officer, were killed when the site was attacked after a prolonged stand-off. After the attack, it is believed that 685 Algerian workers and 107 foreigners were released.

According to the Algerian Prime Minister at the time, Abdelmalek Sellal, the terrorists, numbering around 40, had inside intelligence and detailed plans of the important site.

In the first phase of the operation, the terrorists attacked two buses carrying workers on their way off the site to In Amenas airport. Three foreigners who tried to escape the bus attack were believed to have been shot as they ran through the sand. Two others, a former British soldier and an Algerian Security Officer were killed as they challenged the militants.

The Al Qaeda operatives then stormed the accommodation holding local workers, mainly Algerian and Filipino, but it was clear that the target was American, French, and British ex-patriots, who were by now either fleeing or hiding.

On 17 January, Algerian Special Forces attacked the site, killing several dozen terrorists, and freeing an unconfirmed number of hostages.

Of course, the questions that should have been asked after the event were how it was allowed to happen, what level of risk assessment had been carried out, and what mitigation strategies were in place to tear the risk.

Answers that were never released to the public.

## Section 2: Initial stages of the survey

### *Section 2.1: General description and business operations*

BU have signed a Joint Venture agreement with the government of the Kingdom of Saudubai to drill for heavy crude oil at a location 50 kilometres west of Greater Safaniya. It is estimated that the field will yield 120,000 barrels per day, with an estimated oil reserve of 37,000 million barrels.

### Section 2.1 Reason for the survey

Based on corroborated intelligence from the UK and KoS security services, Table 38 shows the likelihood and impact of a VBIED and marauding terrorist attack, prior to any risk treatment. This reflects the fact that because of the assets, threats, and vulnerabilities involved in the equation, the likelihood is high (4), and the worst-case impact could be catastrophic (5) giving a risk measurement of 20/25.

### Summary

*The threat of a terrorist attack against BU drilling operations in Saudbei was deemed to be High, with an impact that was estimated to be Catastrophic (15/25). The BU Senior Management Team after consultation with the Security Risk Assessor and relevant stakeholders decided that the most effective means of mitigation was to reduce the risk. After risk treatment was complete it was decided by all parties that the risk of a terrorist attack had been reduced to a low likelihood (10/25) which means it still has a Catastrophic impact should an attack be successful.*

As a result of the Security Risk Assessment, the Executive Board of BU commissioned an independent security professional to carry out a physical Security Survey of the proposed drilling site.

An important international document related to overseas travel is ISO ISO31030 (2021).

*Table* 38 Likelihood and impact of a terrorist attack against the Liverpoort Arena *before* mitigation

| **Impact** | 1 (*Very low*) | 2 (*Low*) | 3 (*High*) | 4 (*Very high*) | **5 (*Catastrophic*)** |
|---|---|---|---|---|---|
| **Likelihood** | | | | | |
| 1 (Very low) | | | | | |
| 2 (Low) | | | | | |
| 3 (Medium) | | | | | |
| **4 (High)** | | | | | **20/25** |
| 5 (Very high) | | | | | |

This document offers guidance to organisations on how to manage the risk(s), to the organisation and its travellers, as a result of undertaking travel.

This document provides a structured approach to the development, implementation, evaluation, and review of:

- Policy.
- Programme development.
- Threat and hazard identification.
- Opportunities and strengths.
- Risk assessment.
- Prevention and mitigation strategies.

## Section 2.2 Assets to be protected

### People

Taking into consideration the Security Risk Assessment, and the fact that a terrorist attack is the most likely threat, and with over 50 UK personnel and 200 local employees being present, the critical asset to be protected is the followed by: brand and reputation.

### Brand and reputation

You will recall that in 2020, the organisation recorded a turnover of $275.4bn, with profits after tax amounting to just over $4bn.

However, since a drilling accident in the Gulf of Aden during 2015, when nineteen employees were killed, with an oil spillage consisting of 4.6 million barrels, and with litigation and clean-up charges of over $45bn, BU has struggled to regain market share and is currently aggressively attempting to recall past glories.

Brand and reputation are therefore critical to the Board and shareholders of BU, and it is an asset that must be protected at all costs.

### Data and information

The heavy oil drilling site will hold a great deal of sensitive data and information, particularly with respect to future production and sales, which would be attractive to criminals and terrorists alike. There will also be personal, and personnel information held, which is required to be protected in accordance with the General Data Protection Regulations (2016).

### *Produce*

There is a potential to lift 37,000 million barrels of heavy oil from the ground, with a price of approximately $80 per barrel ($296bn).

### *ICT/OT systems*

Oil production levels are likely to grow exponentially during the first couple of weeks of the drilling process, and ICT/OT systems will be required on a 24/7 basis. ICT/OT systems are critical to the drilling and production processes and are therefore crucial assets.

### *Infrastructure*

The site infrastructure is a significant asset, as it allows drilling operations to continue on a 24/7 basis, and should the infrastructure be attacked, it would likely bring all operations to a standstill.

## Section 2.4 Initial research

This particular Security Survey is like no other carried out so far, in that the greatest threat is loss of life, followed by damage to brand and reputation, and potentially a loss of produce.

### *Company background and security culture*

The company background has already been explored in the Security Risk Assessment, and because of the unique circumstances surrounding this operation, it will be advantageous for the Security Auditor to carry out SWOT analysis.

### *External factors*

External factors are disparate and diverse, and for those reasons, a PESTLE analysis should also be carried out.

### *Unemployment rates in the area*

No official or credible figures relating to unemployment in either Saudubai or the region of Greater Safaniya are available, but it is probably safe to assume that levels of employment in the area of the BU drilling operations are greater than the national average.

### *Previous criminal incidents*

In general, national levels of crime are extremely low, probably because of the legal sanctions and punishments delivered by an extreme government. There have been no previous criminal incidents because operations are only due to begin in the near future.

### *Previous Security Surveys*

Other than the Security Risk Assessment, there has been no attention paid to security and risk at the site.

### *Crime Pattern Analysis*

Because of a lack of corroborated evidence-based statistics, it was impossible to carry out a Crime Pattern Analysis.

However, the most prevalent crimes committed in the region are Kidnap & Ranson, Cybercrime, and Terrorism.

## Section 2.5 Planning and preparation

*To be prepared against surprise is to be trained. To be prepared for surprise is to be educated.*
*James P. Carse*

As with all other sectors covered in this book, planning and preparation is critical for the success of any Security Survey, and the hostile environment sector is no different. So let us take a look at what planning and preparation is needed before the Security Survey at the BU oil exploration site.

### *Authorisation and specific points of contact*

Authorisation is critical, particularly in a country that can best be described as a police state, and the point of contact here will be the Regional Security Manager, Mr Mike Bluestone BEM.

### *Maps and diagrams*

Maps of the country, and in particular maps of Greater Safaniya will be in short supply, so it is advisable to seek assistance from Mr Bluestone. Because of the extremely high levels of health and safety requirements, there should be an abundance of fire/floor diagrams and various schematics.

### *Changes in laws and regulations*

As mentioned earlier, the Kingdom of Saudubai may best be described as a police state, with laws and regulations changing on an almost daily basis. There are also high levels of corruption at every level of the local and national government. This is something that the Security Surveyor must be cognisant of at all times.

### *Social media*

Although social media platforms such as Facebook, Instagram, etc. are partially controlled by the Saudubai government, there is still merit in monitoring the media for local chatter.

### *Photography*

The location is a large and complex piece of real estate, with a number of operations taking place concurrently, consequentially photography is essential in support of the final documentation. However, once again, a word of caution, the Security Auditor must ensure that permission is granted to take photographs within the boundary of the exploration site. He or she must not take photographs outside of the site as this may compromise activities, particularly if brought to the attention of local or national law enforcement agencies.

### *Identification*

As discussed throughout this section of the book, although proof of identification is not a lawful requirement in the UK, it will be to the advantage of the Security Auditor to be in possession of either a valid passport or photographic driving licence. He or she must be prepared to be stopped by the police who may demand proof of identity

### *Agreed visit times and dates*

John Beck, like all other members of the security team, is an extremely busy person, and it is therefore imperative that the Security Auditor adheres to all dates and times agreed.

### *Key takeaways*

It is impossible to prepare too much.

## Section 3: External factors

### *Section 3.1 Environment*

The BU exploration site is 50 kilometres west of Greater Safaniya, in a desert environment. Water and gas are supplied from the national grid supply system, with electricity being generated by UK-provided AC diesel generators which are kept on site.

The workforce is accommodated on site, with lessons learned from the In Amanas incident, i.e., the accommodation and canteen are inside a protected area. See Figure 20.

Food and spares replenishment occurs on a daily basis, being delivered by armed escorted vehicle convoys.

### *Section 3.2 Crime Pattern Analysis*

See Section 2.4.

### *Section 3.3 Employment rate*

Employment at the drilling site is significantly higher than in other areas of the country, and it is therefore critical, for local economic reasons, that operations continue.

### *Section 3.4 Potential for Crime Prevention Through Environmental Design (CPTED) using the acronym MAINT*

**M**aintenance: The site is very well maintained.

**A**ccess Control: There is a good level of access control be maintained?

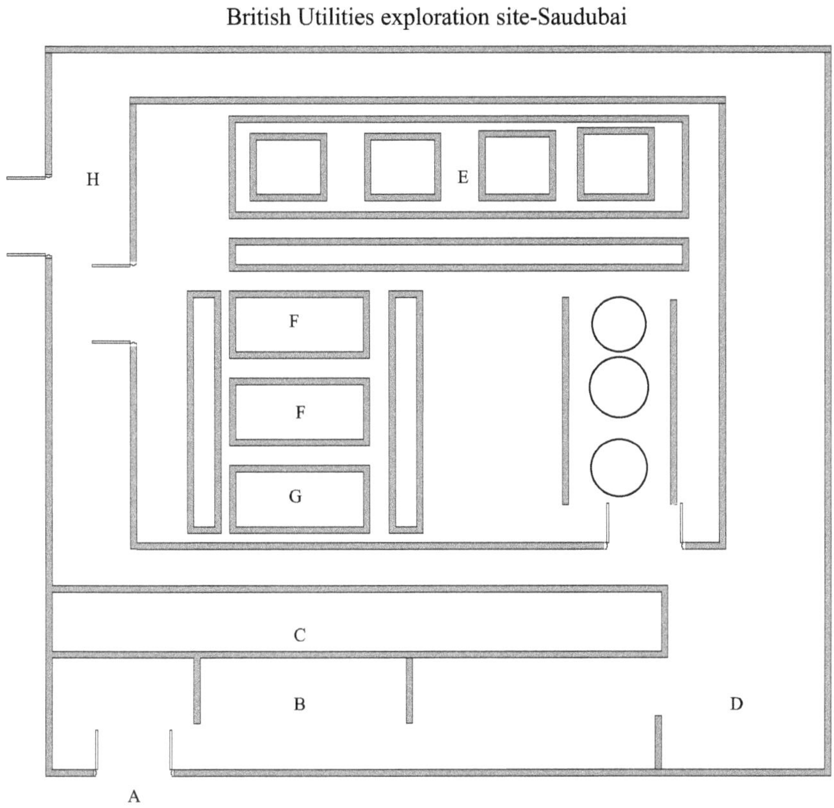


*Figure* 20 British Utilities plan.

**I**mage: The exploration site is iconic in the area, and whilst it is critical for positive public relations, it also attracts criminal and terrorist attention.

**N**atural surveillance: There is an abundance of natural lighting, straight lines, and effective vision, so natural surveillance should easily be achieved.

**T**erritoriality: Can the UK and local workforces be persuaded to take control of their place of work?

## Section 3.5 Nearest police station

The nearest police station is in Greater Safaniya, but communications are extremely poor, and there is a reliability question in terms of police response.

### Section 3.6 Medical treatment

There is the equivalent of a UK military field hospital adjacent to the site. The hospital is managed by a combination of the UK and local medical teams.

### Section 3.7 Firefighting

There is a well-equipped firefighting facility on site. Once again this is managed by a combination of former UK firefighters and local responders.

## Section 4: Perimeter protection

To add context to the size and complexity of the Security Survey, there are two perimeters; an outer security line, and an inner perimeter. The outer perimeter is 5 kilometres in length, and the inner perimeter is 2 kilometres long.

### Section 4.1 Type

As mentioned above, there are two perimeter lines.

- Outer perimeter.

This is the first line of defence and consists of a 3-metre-high welded mesh fence, with one single entrance.

- Inner perimeter.

The second line of defence consists of a 3-metre-high welded mesh fence, with two entrances/exits.

At the time of the Security Survey, both perimeter fence lines were fit for purpose, and in a good state of repair.

### Section 4.2 PIDS by type

#### *Outer perimeter*

A fabric PIDS is installed. The sensor is an Optical-Fibre cable system which is immune to RF interference. The Optical-Fibre system will only require one cable run for a whole perimeter, and it will need just one processing unit and power supply.[54] Should pressure be brought to bear against the fence, the PIDS will silently activate, and it will alarm the Security Control Room.

The perimeter fence is also protected by a ground-based system. One of the advantages of ground-based PIDS is covertness, such that even a knowledgeable attacker should have no awareness of the presence of the system. This is ideal for Defence in Depth, as it will offer the response force time and distance to challenge and apprehend intruders before they are within close proximity to their target (s).

### *Inner perimeter*

The inner perimeter fence line PIDS replicates the outer perimeter system, but for operational reasons, it is limited to the fabric-installed sensors, with no ground-based system because of legitimate movement within the perimeter fence.

## *Section 4.3 PIDS activation and response*

An attempted breach of either of the fence lines will transmit a silent signal to the Security Control Room, and upon receipt of the alarm activation, there will be an immediate response from the Manned Guarding Security Team.

## *Section 4.4 Topping*

There is no topping in support of the outer fence.

There is a low-voltage electric fence installed above the welded mesh inner perimeter fencing, designed to deliver a non-lethal electric shock to the intruder.

## *Section 4.5 State of repair*

The perimeter fence, and supporting electric fence are in a very good state of repair, and at the time of the Security Survey, both were fit for purpose.

## *Section 4.6 Supporting security systems*

The perimeter fence is supported by CCTV, LED lighting, and Manned Guarding.

## Section 4.7 Supporting security systems specifications

During the course of the Security Survey, the following security systems specifications were observed.

## Section 4.8 Closed Circuit Television (CCTV)

There are fifty-five static digital CCTV cameras installed to support the outer perimeter of the site, and twenty-five cameras covering the inner perimeter, affording 360-degree cover. Although every camera is a switchable unit, allowing it to operate under varying flux conditions, the CCTV system is supported by LED lighting units.

The CCTV system is also supported by Video Movement Detection (VMD) software, allowing every camera to be able to send pre-notification of any movement within its field of vision. Each section of the PIDS is covered by the CCTV system, and should there be an attempted breach, there will be visual verification.

All cameras signal to the Security Control Room, where images are recorded and stored on a Network Digital Video Recording System (NDVR).

At the time of the Security Survey, the CCTV system was in good working condition and deemed to be fit for purpose.

## Section 4.9 Security lighting

There are one hundred outer perimeter 1,000-watt LED security lighting units, and forty-five inner perimeter 1,000-watt LED units giving overlapping support.

At the time of the Security Survey, all lighting units were operating, and the system was deemed fit for purpose.

## Section 4.10 Manned guarding

See Section 4.16.

## Section 4.11 Entrances

### *Outer perimeter*

There are two entrances (north and south) that are permanently secured unless authorised access is required.

### *Inner perimeter*

There is the southerly main entrance, and two fire exits at the western perimeter.

## Section 4.12 Entrance types

### *North and south outer perimeter entrances*

The north and south outer perimeter entrances consist of an inward swinging 3-meter steel gate that is opened manually when required.

### *South and eastern inner perimeter entrances*

The main entrance is an electronically controlled, in swinging double-leaf steel gate, which is 6 metres wide and 3 metres high.

## Section 4.13 Entrance (s) state of repair

During the course of the Security Survey, it was observed that all entrances were fit for purpose.

## Section 4.14 Entrance access control systems

### *North and south outer perimeter entrances*

The gates are interlocking, with two suited locks towards the top and bottom of the gate, and they are manually opened and closed.

### *Inner perimeter entrances*

The main entrance is linked to the site access control system, and the fire exits are secured from inside, with crash bar exit systems.

### *Observations*

During the Security Survey, it was observed that the keys for locking and unlocking the outer perimeter gates were not accounted for. It was further observed that when the same gates are locked or unlocked, the procedure was not recorded in the Security Control Room Daily Occurrence Book (DOB).

### *Recommendations*

In terms of accountability, it is recommended that all keys are signed out of the central key press and signed back in when returned. Consideration should be given to the installation of an electronic key press. It is further recommended, that whenever the outer perimeter entrance is attended to it should be entered into the DoB.

## Section 4.15 Entrance access control systems state of repair

During the Security Survey, it was observed that the entrance access control systems were fit for purpose.

## Section 4.16 Manned guarding

The Manned guarding Security Team consists of ex-patriots and locally employed Security Officers.

All information relating to the Security Team will be found in the Site Assignment Instructions (SAI), which are confidential, and are located in electronic format on the company ICT network.

There is manned guarding support on a 24/7 basis, which includes the following details.

### *In house*

The 'in house' Security Team consists of the following:

- One Senior Security Supervisor (UK ex-patriot, former police officer), who reports to the Site Security Manager.
- Four Security Supervisors (UK ex-patriot former HM Forces).
- Twenty Security Officers (locally employed).

### *Shifts availability*

The Senior Security Supervisor works Monday to Friday: 0800hrs to 1800hrs. He is on stand-by at all times.

The four Security Supervisors and their teams operate on a shift roster consisting of the following hours.

- 0600hrs to 1400hrs.
- 1400hrs to 2200hrs.
- 2200hrs to 0600hrs.

### *Duties and roles*

The duties and roles of the Security Team can be found in the Site Assignment Instructions, but an abridged version is as follows.

- Security Control Room duties:
  - ccess control.
  - isitors pass management.
  - larm management and response.
  - CTV monitoring.
  - ommunications management.
- Patrolling.
- Search.
- Incident response.
- Investigation and reporting.
- Counter Terrorism patrols.
- Escort duties.
- Armed Quick Reaction Force.

### *Specialist qualifications*

All Security Officers hold the following qualifications.

- First aid.
- Fire Wardens.
- Public Space Surveillance (PSS) CCTV operations.
- Search procedures.
- Fluid speakers in Arabic and English.
- Advanced weapons trained.[55]

## ***Section 4.17 Security Control Room***

The Security Control Room is located within the main office complex, which is located north of the accommodation blocks.

### *Security Control Room manning times*

The Security Control Room is manned and operational on a 24/7 basis, throughout the year.

### *Security Control Room duties*

The Security Control Room, primarily because it is occupied and operational 24/7, 365 days per year, is at the heart of the exploration site.

- Arguably the most important task carried out by the team in the Security Control Room is access control, with all entrants to the site being processed by one of the Duty Security Officers. Every vehicle will enter the search bay where it will be searched for contraband, weapons, and explosives, before being released for entrance via a single-arm barrier, and an internal gate. Both of which are manned by duty Security Officers.
- All alarm activations signal to the Security Control Room, and the CCTV system is managed from here.
- Sensitive documentation in hard and electronic form is held in the control room.
- The Security Control Room is also the Crisis Control Room when needed.
- There is no reserve Security Control Room.
- The Security Control Room serves as the Communications Centre for the terminal, with the communications network being managed from here.
- All arms and ammunition are held separately within a secure area of the Security Control room.

## Section 5: Main building (s) external

### *Section 5.1 Key personnel*

It is imperative that all key personnel are spoken to in regard to the security and risk management of the location. This is the first opportunity available to you to begin research from the inside, at it is imperative that you choose correctly.

### *Who?*

It is critical to interview the following key personnel.

Bob Clark CEO
John Beck CSO
Charlie Taylor Operations Manager
Jack Simson H&S Manager
Andrew Nixon Logistics and Communications Manager
Andrew Miller ICT/OT Manager

### *When?*

There is no ideal time to speak to airport key personnel because operations are carried out over a 24/7 period, and therefore, those who have volunteered to be interviewed should be spoken to at their convenience.

### *What?*

As with all other sectors, questions asked in a hostile environment must be appropriate, and they have to add to the knowledge gained during the Security Risk Assessment.

## *Section 5.2 Description of buildings*

There are four buildings at the drilling site, and they are:

### *The office complex*

The office complex building is a new single-story unit, of brick, steel, and glass construction. The building is in a very good state of repair, and at the time of the Security Survey, it was deemed fit for purpose. The Security Control Room is contained within the office complex.

### *The drilling complex control room*

The drilling complex control room is also a new single-story unit, of brick, steel, and glass construction. The building is in a very good state of repair, and at the time of the Security Survey, it was deemed fit for purpose.

### *The accommodation blocks*

The accommodation blocks are new single-story units, of brick, steel, and glass construction. They are also protected from incoming small arms fire. There are two accommodation blocks, one serving ex-patriots, and the other reserved for locally employed personnel. The buildings are in a very good state of repair, and at the time of the Security Survey, they were deemed fit for purpose.

### *The canteen*

The canteen is a new single-story unit, of brick, steel, and glass construction. The catering block serves food for all site personnel and operates on a 24/7 basis, in order that hot and cold food may be supplied at all times. The buildings are in a very good state of repair, and at the time of the Security Survey, it was deemed fit for purpose.

## *Section 5.2 Number of access points and how they are secured*

### *The office complex*

The office complex has two access points, both of which are secured by means of a proximity card reader system. There is also a fire exit to the rear of the block, which is secured from within, and exit may be gained by pushing the crash bar. The administration elements of the building are occupied Monday to Friday, 0800hrs to 1800hrs. There are two other areas within the office block.

### *The Security Control Room*

The Security Control Room has one access point, with authorised entry only. Access is by means of a proximity card reader system, and there is also a fire exit.

### *The site ICT/OT server room*

The ICT/OT server room is also to be found in the office block, with access being gained by means of a proximity card reader system, and an iris scanning biometric access control system.

### *The drilling complex control room*

The drilling complex control room is a free-standing building inside the main drilling area.

The control room has one access point, which is secured by means of a proximity card reader system. There is also a fire exit to the rear of the block, which is secured from within, and exit may be gained by pushing the crash bar.

The control room is occupied on a 24/7 basis, and in accordance with Site Standing Instructions, it must be permanently secured.

### *Observations*

Smoking is prohibited in and around the control room and for security reasons the building is secured on a twenty-four seven basis.

During the Security Survey, it was observed that although the main entrance was secure, the rear fire exit was held open by means of a fire extinguisher, and two members of staff were stood outside smoking cigarettes

### *Recommendations*

It is recommended that the control room rear fire exit is alarmed, and when it is opened, the alarm will signal to the main operations centre of the control room, and an audible sounder will activate.

Further, it is recommended that sanctions should be taken against any person smoking in that area.

### *The accommodation blocks*

Both accommodation blocks have two main entrances that are controlled by the site proximity card reader system, and a single fire exit that is released from the inside when pressure is brought to bear on the door crash bar.

### *Canteen*

The canteen has two main entrances that are controlled by the site proximity card reader system, and a single fire exit that is released from the inside when pressure is brought to bear on the door crash bar.

During the Security Survey, access control measures applied to the four buildings were operating correctly and were deemed to be fit for purpose.

## Section 5.3 CCTV

There are fifty-five static digital CCTV cameras installed to support the outer perimeter of the site, and twenty-five cameras covering the inner perimeter, affording 360-degree cover. Although every camera is a switchable unit, allowing it to operate under varying flux conditions, the CCTV system is supported by LED lighting units.

The CCTV system is also supported by Video Movement Detection (VMD) software, allowing every camera to be able to send pre-notification of any movement within its field of vision. Each section of the PIDS is covered by the CCTV system, and should there be an attempted breach, there will be visual verification.

All cameras signal to the Security Control Room, where all images are recorded and stored on a Network Digital Video Recording System (NDVR).

At the time of the Security Survey, the CCTV system was in good working condition and deemed to be fit for purpose.

### The office complex

The office complex, which is relatively exposed, is supported by seven CCTV cameras, giving it 360-degree protection, with both entrances and the fire exit also being covered.

### The drilling complex control room

In a similar manner to the office complex, the drilling complex control room has 360-degree protection, with the single entrance and fire exit also being covered by the site CCTV system.

### The accommodation blocks

The two accommodation blocks are individual free-standing buildings that are fully covered by the CCTV system, including cameras above the entrances and fire exits.

### *The canteen*

#### *Observation*

There is no CCTV coverage of the canteen.

#### *Recommendations*

As the canteen is operational on a 24/7 basis, it is recommended the site CCTV system is developed to include all aspects of the building. This will include a full 360-degree cover, with the entrances and fire exits being supported.

## Section 5.4 IDS

### *The office complex*

All doors and windows are fitted with Reed contacts, offering protection against any unauthorised breach via those points of entrance. The door and window contacts on the administration section of the building are set when the doors are secured, and should there be an attempted unauthorised entry, there will be a silent activation of the IDS in the Security Control Room.

### *The drilling complex control room*

The doors found in the drilling complex control room are fitted with Reed door contacts, which are only set if the building has to be evacuated.

At the time of the Security Survey, all building external IDS elements were fit for purpose.

### *The canteen*

The doors and windows found in the canteen are protected by Reed switches, which are only set if e canteen has to be secured. Under normal circumstances, the canteen is operational on a 24/7 basis.

## Section 5.5 Lighting

LED flood lighting is installed to protect all buildings and at the time of the Security Survey, all building external lighting was fit for purpose.

### *Section 5.6 Distance from the perimeter*

All four buildings are located approximately 20 metres from the perimeter fence.

### *Section 5.7 External utilities*

The following external utilities can be found within the container terminal.

- **Electricity supply**
  Electrical power is supplied by two 100kva diesel generators that are secured in their own compound, which is supported by CCTV, lighting, and the site IDS.
- **Water**
  Water is supplied directly from underground manmade reservoirs, which are replenished on a weekly basis.

### *Section 5.8 Areas of concealment*

There are no areas of concealment in the proximity of the four buildings, however, because of the 24 hours operations, and because of the movement of vehicles, the situation is fluid, meaning that there may be areas of concealment in the terminal.

#### *Recommendations*

Notwithstanding the CCTV coverage afforded to the perimeter and the four buildings, there are another twenty-two cameras, combining digital static, and pan, tilt, and zoom units that offer full coverage of the site.

It is recommended that a separate CCTV survey takes place to ensure that adequate cover is provided.

It is further recommended that all patrols by the security team take into consideration the feasibility of concealment.

### *Section 5.9 Items to aid a criminal*

Adjacent to the canteen building is a small tool store building, approximately 5 metres by 10 metres, containing mainly hand tools, ladders, paint etc.

### *Observations*

During the Security Survey, it was observed that the tool shed was insecure, in that the only entrance to the building, a single leaf, in swinging wooden door was unlocked, with no sign of any occupant.

### *Recommendations*

It is recommended that when unoccupied, the tool shed is secure, and it should be visited by the security patrol on a regular basis.

### ***Section 5.10 Restricted areas***

The following locations and structures have been categorised as Restricted Areas, and as such will require extra vigilance and surveillance by the Security team.

- The Drilling Complex Control Room.
- The office complex.
- The accommodation block.
- The power plant.
- The IT server room.
- The vehicle park.

### ***Section 5.11 Parking arrangements***

There is a central parking area for staff car parking only.

## Section 6: Main buildings (s) internal

### ***Section 6.1 Access control***

#### *The office complex*

Access to, and internally is driven by the site proximity card reader system, with no unauthorised personnel having access to the building.

#### *The drilling complex control room*

The drilling complex control room is accessed by means of a proximity card, but internally, access to the ICT functions is by means of a fingerprint biometric system which is restricted to ICT personnel only.

### *The accommodation blocks*

All individual accommodation rooms are protected by the proximity card reader system.

### *The canteen*

Although there is a fresh and frozen food store, there is no internal access control.

### *Recommendations*

It is recommended that the fresh and frozen food stores are protected by the site access control system, and that only catering staff are allowed access.

## Section 6.2 CCTV

Internal CCTV is as follows:

### *Office complex*

On grounds of health and safety, there are two internal fixed cameras capturing the working areas and entrances/exits.

### *Drilling complex control room*

There are five internal fixed cameras capturing the three monitored working areas and entrances/exits.

### *Accommodation blocks*

On grounds of privacy and civil liberties, there are no cameras inside the accommodation blocks.

### *Canteen*

On grounds of health and safety, there are two internal fixed cameras capturing the working areas and entrances/exits.

At the time of the Security Survey, the CCTV system was operational and fit for purpose.

### 6.3 IDS

Of the four buildings in question, only the office complex and the drilling complex control room are supported by internal dual technology IDS. Should either of the buildings be breached, a silent alarm signal will be sent to the Security Control Room, from where there will be an immediate response. The office complex IDS s set at the end of the day,[56] whilst the IDS in the drilling complex control room is only set if the building has to be evacuated in the event of an emergency.

At the time of the Security Survey, the IDS was operational and fit for purpose.

### 6.4 Lighting

All internal illumination consists of individual strip lighting units which are manually controlled. At the time of the Security Survey, all lighting units were operational and fit for purpose.

## Section 7: Internal specialist or restricted areas

This section refers to restricted areas with specialist applications, which if successfully attacked would negatively impact the drilling site.

### Section 7.1 The Drilling Complex Control Room

The Drilling Complex Control Room is located in the northern area of the site.

It serves as the overall control room for all drilling operations and is therefore highly sensitive.

There is one entrance to the Drilling Complex Control Room.

Access to the Drilling Complex Control Room is restricted site engineers, security personnel and Senior Management who may require access for operational reasons. Access is gained by means of a proximity card reader system, with smart cards being issued on a need-to-have basis.

The Control Room is supported by internal and external CCTV coverage, which is monitored from within, and although the room is occupied on a 24/7 basis, there is an IDS installed, which in the event of an evacuation, can be set and monitored from the site Security Control Room.

At any one time, there will be a minimum of three Drilling Technicians on duty in the control room. There is access to a telephone land line, hand-held radios, a cell phone network, and three Personal Attack buttons have been installed.

## Section 8: Conclusion

### *Post survey debrief*

A post-survey debrief was carried out, during which the site Security Manager was informed of a number of 'quick fixes', and an agreement was reached in relation to the Security Survey Report. The Security Manager requested the report be delivered to her by hand within thirty working days.

There is no requirement for a survey presentation, but future talks will take place in relation to other work of a similar nature.

The Security Manager concluded by declaring that he was very satisfied with the Security Survey and how it was carried out.

## Close protection

**Security Survey: The Brambles, Little Ivy, Porchester. PE217DX**

| *Document owner* | *Reference number* | *Proof-reader* | *1st check* | *2nd check* |
|---|---|---|---|---|
| | SecSurv/CP/08/22 | | | |

1. **Survey details.**
2. **Initial stages of the survey.**
3. **External factors.**
4. **Perimeter protection.**
5. **Main buildings-external.**
6. **Main buildings-internal.**
7. **Internal specialist or restricted areas.**
8. **Conclusion.**

## Section 1: Survey details

Name and appointment of the client.

| |
|---|
| Mr Adam Friedman CEO BU. |

Address (s)

| |
|---|
| The Brambles, Little Ivy, Porchester. PE217DX. |

Point of Contact.

| |
|---|
| Mr Adam Freidman |

E mail.

| |
|---|
| N/A |

Telephone.

| |
|---|
| 07986122345 |

Web address.

| |
|---|
| N/A |

Location of Survey.

| |
|---|
| The Brambles, Little Ivy, Porchester. PE217DX. |

Name of Security Auditor and date of survey.

| |
|---|
| Ian Hall. 20 December 2021 |

Organisation.

| |
|---|
| Close Protection Team |

## Section 2: Initial stages of the survey

The Brambles is the country residence of a newly appointed Chief Executive Officer, Adam Friedman, who is employed by BU. The Brambles sits on its own secluded plot of land, just outside of the small village of Little Ivy, which is three miles from Porchester in the Midlands.

### Section 2.1 General descriptions of business operations

The Brambles is a fifteen room, three story Victorian detached house, set in 10 acres of mainly grass land, with a 360-degree perimeter. Whilst the house is used on a permanent basis for the principal, his wife, and two young children (Charlie who is eight, and Elly who is nine), Mr Friedman has a large study on the third floor from which he occasionally dedicates to working from home.

The house has state of the art ICT communications, with its own end to end encrypted communications server located on the third floor, adjacent to the principal's study. There is back up cloud cover for the server, and Mr Friedman is prohibited from storing company business on his home server.

Added to the Security Survey, it has been agreed that a safe room will be identified and fortified accordingly.

### Section 2.2 Reason (s) for the survey

Because of extensive drilling operations in the Middle East, the British security services believe that BU may be targeted by an Islamic fundamentalist terrorist organisation, and the Porchester Police Counter Terrorism Unit (CTU) has further identified terrorist threats against Mr Friedman. Specifically the offence of kidnap and ransom, either en route, but more likely from his home in Little Ivy.

The Executive Board of BU, supported by the Board of Shareholders has commissioned a highly respected security company to carry out close protection duties, and you are the Team Leader.

After consultation with the CTU and the principle, Mr Friedman, it has been decided that as a matter of urgency, the Brambles requires a full physical Security Survey and you, who both hold a level four qualification in Managing Security Surveys have been commissioned to carry out the work.

### Section 2.3 Assets to be protected

By virtue of the fact that Mr Friedman is protected by a team of six bodyguards on a 24/7 basis, he is the main asset, and this is where politics too often intervenes.

> *Just a thought*
>
> In your opinion, should Mr Friedman's family be treated as assets, and therefore be protected by the CP team? Tough one!

BU provides three executive Jaguar saloons, which Mr Friedman is allowed to use for personal and business reasons. They are of course a major asset, as they are critical to the safety of the principle.

As mentioned earlier, there is an encrypted IT server in the house, and although he may be in breach of company procedures, it is likely that Mr Friedman has downloaded sensitive commercial data.

Finally of course there is the CP team, who are critical to the safety of the principal (and his family perhaps.).

## Section 2.4 Initial research

Unlike other Security Surveys, where the Security Auditor is likely to be unfamiliar with the organisation, he or she is tasked with protecting, for this particular Security Survey, you as Team Leader, and your deputy have a strong understanding of the principle, his movements, and the building to be security surveyed.

However, there are still a few areas that need research.

### Security Risk Assessment

The Close Protection Security Risk Assessment carried out earlier in the project focused on the likelihood and impact of an attack against a principal moving from his or her vehicle to a location, perhaps the office or accommodation, when the principal is at their most vulnerable. The context of this scenario is completely different because the threat is believed to be either an attack against the occupants of the house or an attempted kidnap situation. So the first piece of research that was needed was a Security Risk Assessment of the house, considering the likelihood and impact of such a risk. The methodology can be found in Section 1 of this book.

### Criminal intelligence

The problems with criminal and counter terrorism intelligence, is that the source must be credible, and the intelligence corroborated. Walsh, cited in Gill

(2014) when describing intelligence argues that it is a service industry whose sole aim is to interpret a threat environment for a decision maker, and that of course is common sense, but how is it achieved in practical terms.

In the first instance, remember that the initial intelligence in relation to the current threat originated from the Counter Terrorism Unit (CTU), so that should be your first line of enquiry. That can also be supplemented by commissioning a credible crime intelligence company, of which there are many. Also, Interpol has produced a good online fact sheet titled *Criminal intelligence analysis*.[57]

## *Key takeaways*

*Criminal intelligence is an excellent tool which offers another dimension to the threat assessment, but remember, it is only that, a tool. Never rely totally on criminal intelligence alone, because if it is flawed, it can be more of a hindrance than a help.*

## *Technology*

At some stage of the survey, you will need to consider either the introduction of new security technology or perhaps upgrading systems already in place. The level four qualification and this book will have equipped you with the knowledge required to specify a basic security system, however, remember that very few people are masters of all trades. It is therefore strongly advised that you, in the first instance, consider the Operational Requirement, before seeking technical assistance from a credible Subject Matter Expert (SME). Trust is key.

## *Alternative accommodation*

Whether it is whilst The Brambles is being refurbished, having systems installed, or in the event of an emergency, you must consider alternative accommodation for the family. This will be a difficult task, but it is one which cannot be ruled out on grounds of cost or time, because if the principal (and his family) is forced to evacuate at short notice, they need to move to a secure location, complete with communications and Internet access.

## *Reserve transportation*

In this instance the principal has been provided with three top-of-the-range Jaguars which are precisely suited to his needs; however, arrangements must be made for alternative transportation should any element of the current fleet fail.

### *Safe room*

A safe room has been requested, and at this stage, you will need to begin to plan for its specification, thinking about location, access, communications, evacuation, and so on. The design of the room will be covered later in this section of the book.

### *Previous criminal incidents*

The Brambles is located in a very quiet location, and to date, there have been very few minor crimes recorded.

### *Previous security surveys*

There have been no previous Security Surveys carried out.

### *Crime Pattern Analysis (CPA) – SO224AA*

You would be forgiven for thinking that because Little Ivy is a small village, with little or no apparent crime to speak about, a Crime Pattern Analysis is a waste of time and resources. Wrong!

Porchester, which is only three miles away, and is a medium-sized town, does in fact have worrying levels of criminality. A similar-sized property to The Brambles was burgled three months ago, and it is believed that the criminals came from Porchester.

Research demonstrates the three most serious crimes committed during the last twelve months are violence and sexual offences, anti-social behaviour, and criminal damage/arson. However, the Porchester constabulary has informed you that there has been an increase in vehicle crime, burglary, and the possession of weapons, all of which are extremely concerning for the principal and his family.

## ***Section 2.5 Planning and preparation***

In a similar vein to the research phase of the Security Survey, final preparations were required before the 'boots on the ground' stage, so let's look at what preparations were required.

## The Security Survey Template

A template is critical, and there is an example of that document in this book. However, whilst in terms of process, a template is extremely helpful, don't be restricted, or two-dimensional. Always use the template, but if you need to adapt it to the singular requirements of whatever sector you are involved in, then do so. Creativity is an important skill when carrying out a Security Survey, best exemplified by adopting a criminal approach. As I have advised so many times, don't gloat or polish your ego, instead think about how you can circumnavigate the systems in place, and any upgrades.

How you complete the template is of course your choice and it will be based on individual skills and preferences, but one option is to use some form of a recording device, as this will make it easy from a practical perspective.

## Timelines

At the earliest opportunity, ensure you have some form of project chart illustrating the timelines for all aspects of the Security Survey, from the initial meeting with the client to the final engagement when the Security Survey Report is accepted and signed off.

Remember (and I'm not sure who said this but...) *failing to plan is planning to fail.*

## The risk assessment

If a Security Risk Assessment has been carried out, ensure you read it, and if possible, have a copy with you during the Security Survey, because you will be examining systems to confirm that they are fit for purpose, have an operational requirement, and ensure that it is one that has been designed and commissioned to meet all identified risks. How can you possibly specify a security system or systems if you are unaware of the risk they are designed to mitigate against?

For example, if the risk is burglary, and the CCTV system has not been installed to cover the perimeter fence, what use is it?

### *SME/Specs*

Remember the importance of the Subject Matter Expert (SME) when considering specifications. Even though you may hold a level 4 qualification in security surveying, your technical knowledge is likely to be fairly rudimentary. Make provisions to call on, when necessary, the skills and technical capability of a credible SME who is able to offer the correct levels of technical advice and guidance. Credibility and trust are critical.

### *Drawings*

Ensure that you are in possession of the latest versions of all drawings and schematics in relation to the property and systems therein.

### *Equipment-Cameras etc.*

Probably the most important piece of equipment for you to be equipped with is either a digital camera or a smartphone. Photographs definitely have their place in a Security Survey Report, but even though you are the CP Team Leader, ensure that the principle (and his family) are aware that you will be taking internal and external photographs.

### *Clothes-weather/day-night*

This may seem a minor issue, but you will be walking the grounds day and night, sun and rain. Plan your clothing accordingly.

## Section 3: External factors

### *Section 3.1 Environment*

As previously mentioned, the building that has been security surveyed is located in a semi-rural environment, with no close adjacent neighbours.

### *Section 3.2 Crime Pattern Analysis*

See Section 2.4.

### *Section 3.3 Employment rate*

Employment in the near vicinity is lower than the national average.

### *Section 3.4 Potential for Crime Prevention Through Environmental Design (CPTED) using the acronym MAINT*

**M**aintenance: The buildings and grounds are very well maintained and are in an exceptional state of repair.
**A**ccess Control: Access control is managed very well by the CP Team and domestic staff.
**I**mage: The buildings and grounds are attractive, and whilst it is critical for local positive public relations, it may also attract criminal and terrorist attention.
**N**atural surveillance: There is an abundance of natural lighting, straight lines, and effective vision, so natural surveillance should easily be achieved.
**T**erritoriality: The CP Team and domestic staff definitely assume a posture of territoriality.

### *Section 3.5 Nearest police station*

The nearest police station is in Porchester High Street, and it accessible from 0900hrs to 1700hrs, Monday to Friday. In an emergency, it is advised to call 999 for assurance.

### *Section 3.6 Nearest hospital*

The closest hospital is the Porchester Training Hospital, Field Lane, Porchester. The hospital is accessible 24/7, and it is advisable to call 111, or in an emergency, 999.

### *Section 3.7 Nearest fire station*

The nearest fire station is also to be found at Porchester High Street, and it is accessible from 0900hrs to 1700hrs, Monday to Friday. In an emergency, it is advised to call 999 for assurance.

## Section 4: Perimeter protection

### *Section 4.1 Type*

The house is part surrounded by a 2.5 natural stone wall, with a 1-metre steel fence running along the southern boundary.

### *Observations*

During the Security Survey, it was observed that there was a 2-metre gap on the northern side of the wall. It appears that it was an area being repaired, which the workforce for some reason failed to complete.

### *Recommendations*

Although the perimeter wall is well lit, and the gap can be seen from the main house, it is recommended that the gap is closed at the earliest opportunity, otherwise, it will continue to send negative signals that may encourage criminal elements.

## *Section 4.2 PIDS*

### *Observations*

During the Security Survey it was observed that there are no PIDS supporting the perimeter wall. When questioned about this obvious vulnerability, the Principle, Mr Friedman admitted that he never considered such an increase in physical security, and in his defence, it has to be admitted that PIDS had never been discussed when his security was spoken about with the local Crime Prevention Officer.

### *Recommendations*

It is recommended that a ground based PIDS is considered. The system will offer 360-degree cover, should be attenuated to human downward pressure, and should signal to the main house if breached. Once installed and commissioned, it should be tested on a regular basis. It is further recommended that Porchester police are approached to ascertain if some form of police response to an activation could be agreed.

## *Section 4.3 PIDS activation and response*

See Section 4.2.

## *Section 4.4 Topping*

N/A.

### *Section 4.5 State of repair*

See Section 4.1.

### *Section 4.6 Supporting security systems*

The perimeter wall is supported by CCTV and lighting.

### *Section 4.7 Supporting security systems specifications*

During the course of the Security Survey, the following security systems specifications were noted.

### *Section 4.8 Closed Circuit Television (CCTV)*

There are sixteen static digital CCTV cameras installed to support the outer perimeter of the site, affording 360-degree cover. This includes the single point of entry. Although every camera is a switchable unit, allowing it to operate under varying flux conditions, the CCTV system is supported by LED lighting units.

All cameras signal to the main house, where images are recorded and stored on a Digital Video Recording System (DVR).

At the time of the Security Survey, the CCTV system was in good working condition and deemed to be fit for purpose.

### *Section 4.9 Security lighting*

Perimeter security lighting consists of sixteen 300-watt LED PIR movement detection and flood lights.

There are also two 300-watt LED flood lights on either side of the main entrance, which are activated in accordance with natural lighting conditions.

At the time of the Security Survey, all lighting units were operational, and the system was fit for purpose.

### *Section 4.10 Manned guarding*

There are no Security Officers deployed at the sight under survey.

### Section 4.11 Supporting systems state of repair

During the Security Survey, it was observed that all supporting systems were fit for purpose.

### Section 4.12 Entrances

There is a single point of entry for either vehicular or pedestrian access.

### Section 4.13 Entrance by type

Entrance to the grounds is via an inward swinging, 3-metre, ornate steel gate. There are two CCTV cameras overlooking the gate, and there is a two-way communications system connecting the entrance to the main house. Vehicles and pedestrians are only allowed access once their identity and the reason for visiting have been verified from within the main house.

### Section 4.14 Entrance state of repair

The entrance and supporting systems are in an excellent state of repair, and at the time of the Security Survey, all systems were fit for purpose.

### Section 4.15 Entrance access control systems

See Section 4.13.

### Section 4.16 Manned guarding

There are no Manned guarding provisions, but there is a four-person Close Protection (CP) Team that resides with the principal and his family.

A member of the Close Protection Team is responsible for monitoring alarms, CCTV, and communications from the premises Operations Room.

### Section 4.17 Operations Room

The Operations Room is located on the first floor of the building, adjoining the ICT suite.

### Section 4.18 Operations Room manning times and duties

Whilst the principal is in residence, the Operations Room is permanently manned by a member of the CP team, and when Mr Friedman is away from home, all controls are managed by the in-house domestic team.

The Operations Room carries out the following functions.

- CCTV monitoring and management.
- Alarm monitoring and response.
- Communications (internal and external).
- Equipment storage.
- Incident response and recording.

If the Operations Room is disabled, all functions can be carried out from within the safe room.

See Section 6.

## Section 5: Main buildings external

### *Section 5.1 Description of buildings*

There are two buildings located on the estate.

#### *The main building*

The Brambles is a fifteen room, three story Grade 2 listed Victorian detached house, set on 10 acres of mainly grass land, with a 360-degree perimeter.

#### *The vehicle compound*

The vehicle compound is a single-storey building constructed from brick and steel and is located 50 metres from the main building.

### *Section 5.2 Number of access points and how they are secured*

#### *Main building*

There are two access points, and windows as follows.

#### *Main entrance*

The main entrance is a solid hardwood, double-leaf inward swinging door, with reinforced steel surrounding. It is secured by means of a seven-lever mortice locking system, and inside there are two sliding steel security bolts which support the main locking system.

Keys to the main building are held by:

- The family – One key each.
- The CP team – Keys held by the Team Leader and Deputy Team Leader.
- Operations room – One key held in a secure key press.[58]

### *Rear entrance*

The rear entrance, used by non-family members is a solid hardwood, single leaf inward swinging door, reinforced by steel surroundings, and secured by means of a seven-lever mortice locking system. There are two sliding steel security bolts.

### *Ground floor windows*

There are twelve ground floor windows, all of which are wooden framed, single glazed hung casement windows. Because the building is a Grade 2 listed building, it has been impossible to replace the windows, except with like for like. The windows can be mechanically secured from the inside, and every window is further protected by internal Reed contact switches. Should a window be forced once secure, the Reed switch will signal to the Operations Room.

### *First-floor windows*

As with the ground floor windows, they are not protected by the house IDS.

### *Second-floor windows*

As with the first-floor windows.

### *The vehicle compound*

There are two vehicle access/egress points and a single pedestrian entrance. There are no windows.

### *Vehicle access/egress points*

Both points are accessed by means of a remotely controlled roller shutter door, which has a manual override. Remote cards for the door are held by the CP Team, and there is a spare card held in Operations Room.

### *Pedestrian entrance*

The pedestrian entrance is a solid hardwood, single-leaf inward swinging door. The door is secured by means of two seven-lever locking systems, with keys held by the CP team, and with a spare key being held in the Operations Room.

## ***Section 5.3 CCTV***

Both buildings are covered by the location CCTV system.

### *Main building*

The main building is supported by the presence of six static digital cameras, including four covering the corners of the building, and one over each door. Every camera signals to the building Operations Room, with images being stored on a Digital Video Recording system, that is only accessed by the CP team.

### *Vehicle compound*

As with the main building, the vehicle compound receives full CCTV coverage, with a camera installed on each corner, and with all three access/egress points being protected.

### *Observations*

During the Security Survey, it was observed that two of the cameras covering corner sections of the main building were unserviceable. As was the camera covering the pedestrian entrance to the vehicle compound.

### *Recommendations*

It is recommended that the three unserviceable CCTV cameras are repaired or replaced as a matter of urgency, as this vulnerability threatens the safety of the principal and that of the CP vehicle fleet.

## *Section 5.4 IDS*

### *Main building*

All ground floor doors and windows are protected by Reed contact switches which are linked to the building IDS.

### *Vehicle compound*

The three entrances are protected by Reed switches, which are linked to the location IDS.

At the time of the Security Survey, all IDS components were fit for purpose.

## *Section 5.5 Lighting*

### *Main building*

There is low-level stainless-steel bollard lighting surrounding the main building which is activated when natural light drops to a pre-set lux level. Over each door, there is a Passive Infrared (PIR) motion detection light. There is also a low-voltage safety light installed on every wall.

### *Vehicle compound*

As for the main building.

## *Section 5.6 Distance from the perimeter*

Both buildings are approximately 50 metres from the northern perimeter, 100 metres from the eastern and western perimeters, and approximately 300 metres from the southern perimeter. There is open ground between the buildings and all sections of the perimeter allowing for ideal observations of the grounds.

## *Section 5.7 External utilities*

There is an Uninterruptable Power Supply (UPS)[59] and a standby 50 kilo volt amps (KVA) generator immediately behind the vehicle compound. The UPS and the generator are contained in individually secured compounds that are supported by the site CCTV, IDS, and lighting systems, and at the time of the Security Survey, all systems were deemed fit for purpose.

### *Section 5.8 Areas of concealment*

There are no areas of concealment.

### *Section 5.9 Items to aid a criminal*

There are no items to aid a criminal.

### *Section 5.10 Restricted areas*

The only restricted areas are:

- The main building.
- The vehicle compound.
- The power supplies.[60]

### *Section 5.11 Parking arrangements*

There is limited parking space in front of the house for visitors, and all family vehicles are parked in the vehicle compound.

## Section 6: Main buildings internal

### *Section 6.1 Building descriptions*

#### *Main building*

As mentioned, the Brambles is a fifteen-room, three-story Grade 2 listed Victorian detached house, set in 10 acres of mainly grass land, with a 360-degree perimeter.

#### *Ground floor*

As can be seen from Figure 21 the ground floor consists of five rooms or areas, connected by a single passageway and two doors (front and rear). The principal and his family predominantly congregate in this area of the house.

### *First floor*

Figure 22 illustrates the first floor which consists of five rooms or areas, connected by a single passageway.

As can be seen from the illustration, the first floor is dedicated to operations, with the inclusion of a safe room.

### *Safe room*

The safe room was identified and fitted out as the result of the Security Risk Assessment, in which the threat of an attack against the house was believed to be likely. The safe room is easily accessible, and the principal, his family, and the CP Team can exist in the safe room for up to 24 hours if required.

### *Second floor*

Figure 23 illustrates the second floor which consists of five rooms or areas, connected by a single passageway.

### *The vehicle compound*

The vehicle compound is a single-story building constructed from brick and steel and is located 50 metres from the main building. It is large enough to hold three Jaguar saloon vehicles, two family hatchback vehicles, and there is a small workshop. It has two vehicle entrances and one pedestrian door.

## **Section 6.2 Access control**

Internal access control of the two buildings is configured as follows.

### *Main building – ground floor*

The only room on the ground floor that is access controlled is the study because it contains a safe holding sensitive hard copy information. Access is by means of a proximity card reader system, with only the principal and the CP Team Leader/Deputy holding smart cards for access purposes.

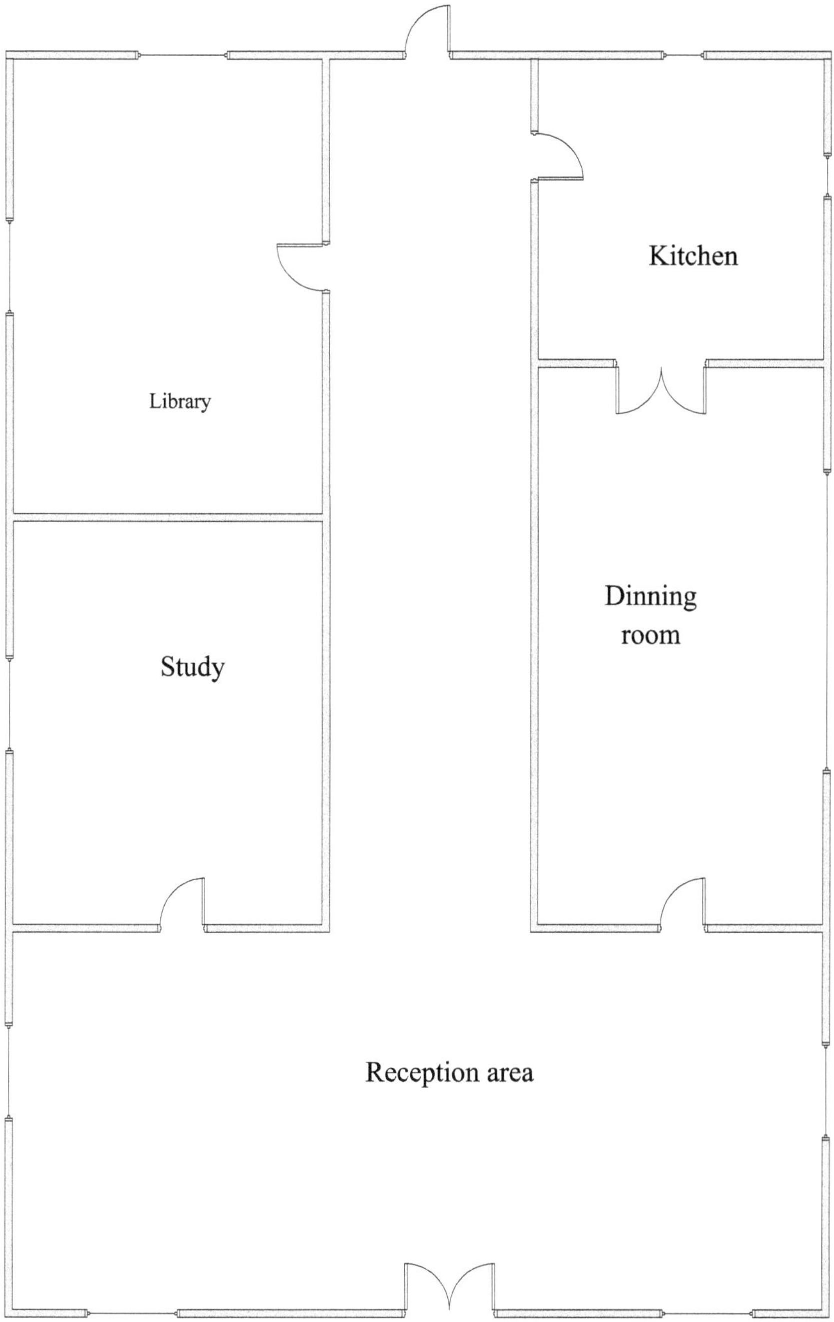


*Figure 21* CP main building ground floor.

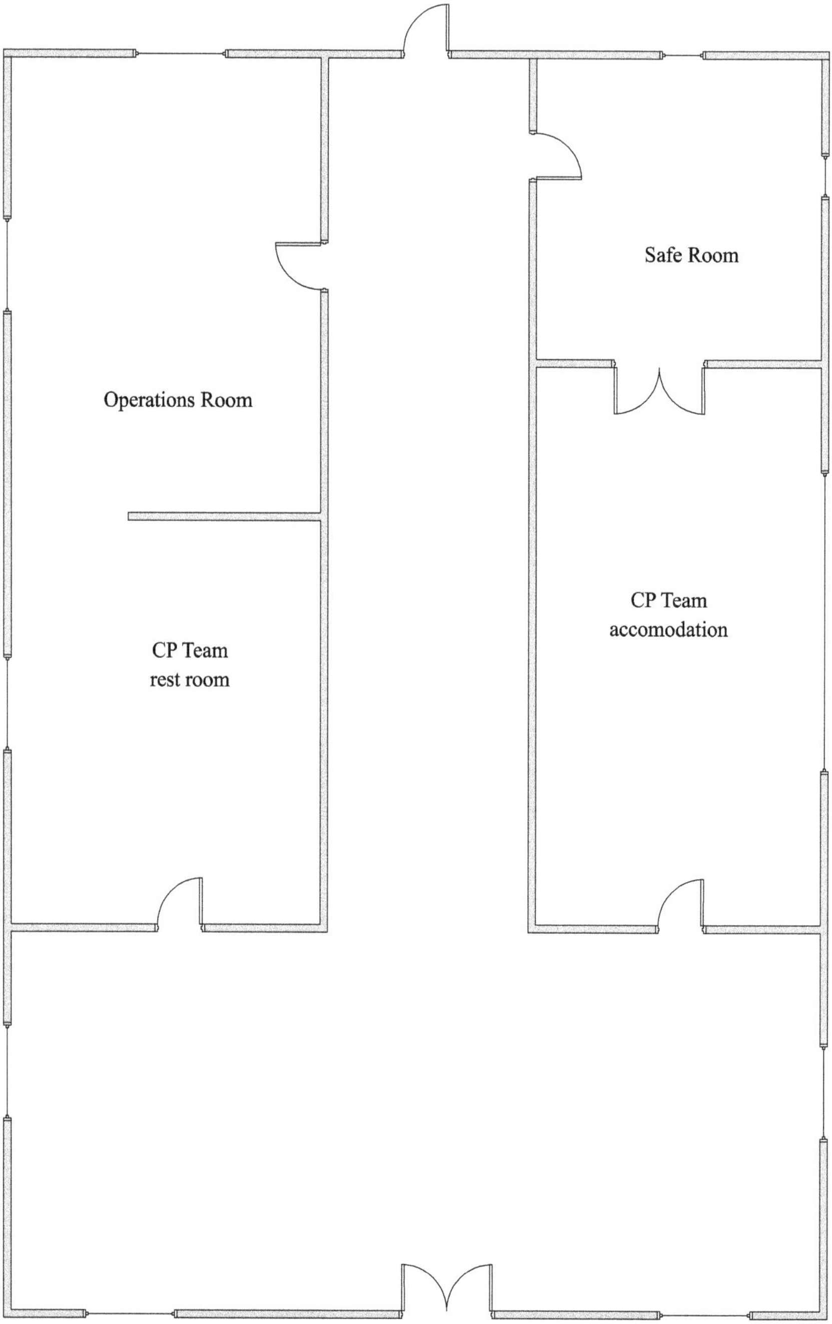


Figure 22 CP main building first floor.

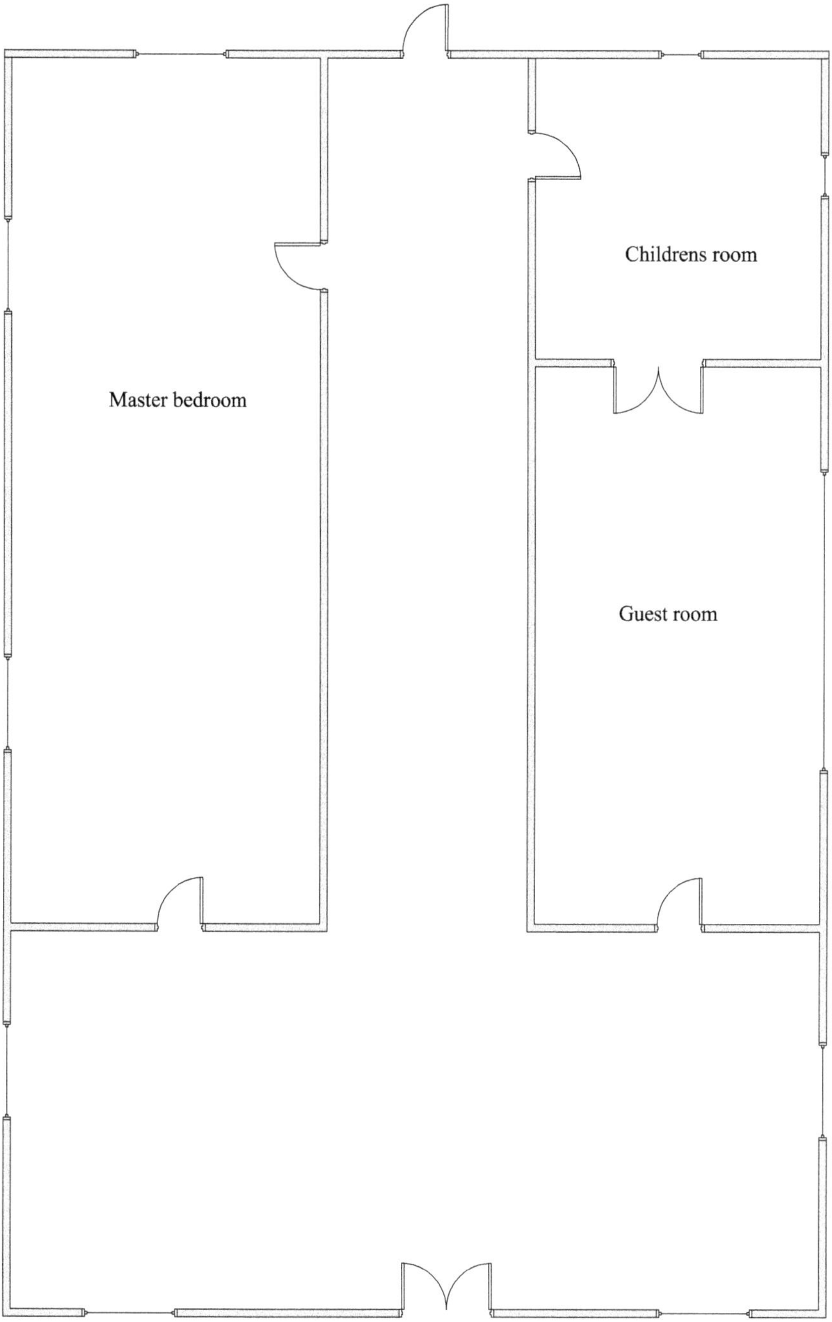


Figure 23 CP main building second floor.

### *Main building – first floor*

As mentioned, the first floor is the operations floor, with all rooms being subject to access control protocols by means of the proximity card reader system. The Operations Room is double factored, with a PIN complementing the card reader system. Only members of the CP Team and the principal have access to the rooms on this floor.

### *Main building – second floor*

Only the master bedroom and the guest room are access controlled, also by means of the proximity card reader system.

### *The vehicle compound*

The internal workshop is protected by the proximity card reader system, with only members of the CP Team having access to that area.

## *Section 6.3 CCTV*

Internal CCTV is configured as follows.

### *Main building – ground floor*

There are internal digital static CCTV cameras in the following positions:
Reception area:
One camera covering the front entrance.
One camera covering the main passageway and rear door (Figure 24).

### *Main building – first floor*

There are internal four digital static CCTV cameras in the following positions:
Operations Room:
One camera covering the door from the inside.
Safe room:
Two cameras covering both doors from the inside (Figure 25).
Central passageway:
One camera.

Figure 24 CP main building ground floor CCTV.

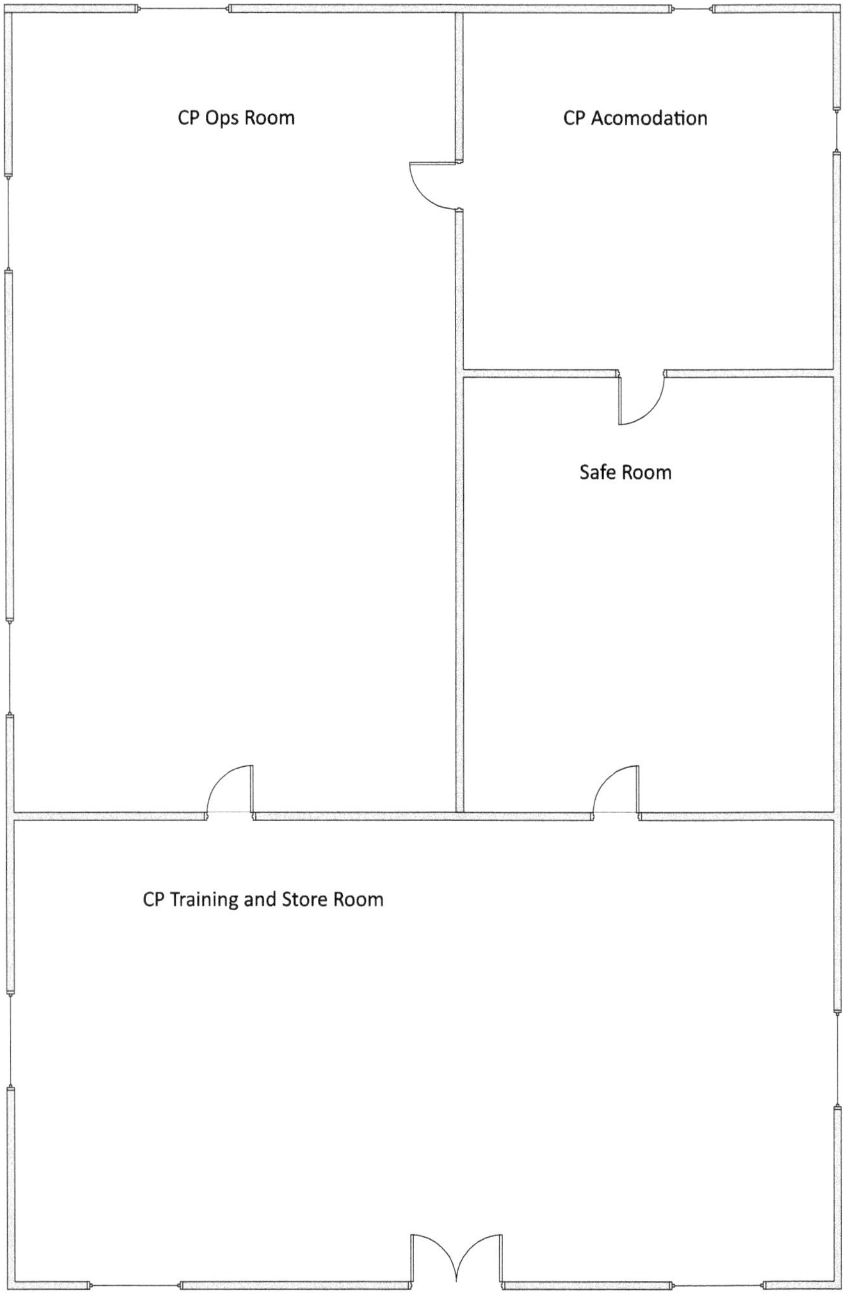


Figure 25 CP main building first floor CCTV.

Figure 26 CP main building second floor CCTV.

### *Main building – second floor*

There are no internal CCTV cameras on this floor (Figure 26).

### *Vehicle compound*

There are two CCTV cameras in the main body of the building. And one camera protects the workshop.

During the Security Survey, it was observed that the internal CCTV system was fit for purpose.

## Section 6.4 IDS

Internal IDS s configured as follows:

### *Main building – ground floor*

There are Dual Detection IDS sensors in the following locations.

- The reception area.
- The study.
- The dining room.
- The library.
- The kitchen.
- The central passageway.

The ground floor IDS is set by the duty CP Team member when the family retires for the evening. Should it activate, a silent signal will be transmitted to the Operations Room. There are Personal Attack Buttons in every room. If struck thee will be a reaction from the CP Team and the local constabulary.

### *Main building – first floor*

There are Dual Detection IDS sensors in the following locations.

- The Operations Room.
- The safe room.[61]
- The CP accommodation.
- The CP rest room.

The first floor IDS is only set when the floor is unoccupied.

There are Personal Attack (PA) Buttons in every room. If struck thee will be a reaction from the CP Team and the local constabulary.

### *Main building – second floor*

There are Dual Detection IDS sensors in the following locations.

- The master bedroom.
- The children's bedroom.
- The guest room.

The second floor IDS is only set when the floor is unoccupied.

There are Personal Attack Buttons in every room. If struck thee will be a reaction from the CP Team and the local constabulary.

### *Vehicle compound*

There is a Dual Technology sensor in the main body of the building and a similar unit in the workshop.

There are two Personal Attack Buttons in the vehicle compound. If struck thee will be a reaction from the CP Team and the local constabulary.

During the Security Survey, it was observed that the internal IDS system was fit for purpose.

### *Section 6.5 Lighting*

Internal lighting in both buildings consists of fluorescent ceiling lights, and in the main building, chandeliers, and wall lighting units.

During the Security Survey, it was observed that the internal lighting system was fit for purpose.

## Section 7: Internal specialist or restricted areas

This section refers to restricted areas with specialist applications, which if successfully attacked would negatively impact the target locations.

## *Section 7.1 The Operations Room*

The Operations Room is located on the first floor of the main building, adjacent to the CP Team accommodation, and opposite the Safe Room.

It is occupied on a 24/7 basis whilst the principal is in situ and is responsible for the following tasks.

### *CCTV and IDS*

One of the priorities of CP Team members on duty in the Operations Room is the management of the location CCTV and IDS systems. All CCTV cameras signal back to and are stored on the site DVR network, with CP Team members having authority to 'burn' incidents onto a DVD for evidential purposes, before handing them over, on signature to the police. Should the IDS indicate a breach, it will also signal to the Operations Room, from where a response shall be immediate.

### *Communications*

All communications are monitored from the Operations Room, with the Duty CP Team member acting as the network supervisor. This includes CP Team members' one-to-one communications when on foot, and mobile communications when the team has been deployed.

### *Intelligence*

One of the tasks for on-duty CP Team members is the collation and dissemination of local, national, and international criminal intelligence. To that end, extremely sensitive information is held in electronic and hard copy format, secure in the Operations Room.

## *Section 7.2 The safe room*

The safe room is located on the first floor adjacent to the CP Team accommodation quarters and opposite the Operations Room.

The safe room has been reinforced to withstand a physical attack, with the door and walls meeting CPNI standards in terms of resistance to attack.

The safe room has been located and designed to make it relatively simple for the principal, his family, and the CP Team to reach and be secure.

Because of the sensitivity of the safe room and its contents, all details are disclosed on a separate document for selected eyes only.[62]

### *Section 7.3 The vehicle compound*

The vehicle compound is a standalone building, designed, and constructed to garage the CP team fleet, and private vehicles owned by the principal and his wife. To that end, it has been declared a Restricted Area.

## Section 8: Conclusion

A post survey debrief was carried out, during which the principal was informed of a number of 'quick fixes', and an agreement was reached in relation to the Security Survey Report. The principal requested the report be delivered in writing as soon as possible.

The principal concluded by declaring that he was very satisfied with the Security Survey and how it was carried out.

## Bibliography

Abraham Lincoln quote (77) https://www.projectmanager.com/blog/planning-quotes Accessed on 13 April 2021.

Aviation Legislation (117) https://info.caa.co.uk/uk-regulations/ Accessed on 28 December 2021.

Biometric measurements (81) https:/en.wikipedia.org/wiki/Biometrics Accessed on 21 August 2021.

Broder. J. F., Tucker. E., (2012) *Risk Analysis and the Security Survey* Amsterdam, Elsevier.

CCTV monitoring (88) https://www.gov.uk/government/publications/crowded-places-guidance/cctv Accessed on 10 February 2022.

Colin Powel quote (104) https://www.azquotes.com/quotes/topics/preparation-and-planning.html Accessed on 22 March 2022.

CPNI PAS 68 Standards (112) https://www.cpni.gov.uk/sites/default/files/citvsb_catalogue/CSE%20HVM%20-%20Impact%20Rated%20-%20Rating%20System%20Explained%20-%2020210201_0_0.pdf Accessed on 25 November 2021.

Critical Infrastructure Regulations (105) https://www.gov.uk/government/news/tough-new-rules-to-protect-uks-critical-infrastructure-come-into-force Accessed on 22 March 2022.

Guide to PIDS (112) CPNI Guide to Perimeter Intrusion Detection Systems (PIDS) https://www.cpni.gov.uk/system/files/documents/2c/80/Guide-to-PIDS.pdf Accessed on 24 November 2021.

High and Low Pressure Sodium Lighting Detection (88) StouchLighting https://www.stouchlighting.com/blog/led-vs-hps-lps-high-and-low-pressure-sodium Accessed on 23 August 2021.

ICO Legal Responsibilities (91) https://ico.org.uk/about-the-ico/who-we-are/ Accessed on 21 March 2022.

Jeffrey. C. Price. M. A. C. Jeffrey. S., (2009) *Practical Aviation Security: Predicting and Preventing Future Events* Amsterdam Elsevier.

Mac Caulay. T., (2009) *Critical Infrastructure: Understanding its Component Parts, Vulnerabilities, Operating Risks, and Interdependencies* London, CRC Press.

Magnetically Operated Reed Switches (87) CPNI intrusion detection systems guidance for security managers July 2013 file:///C:/Users/cswan/Downloads/IDS-Guidance-for-security-managers.pdf Accessed on 19 August 2021.

Martin. G., (2006) *Unextending Terrorism* London, Sage Publications.

Microwave Motion Detection (84) CPNI intrusion detection systems guidance for security managers July 2013 file:///C:/Users/cswan/Downloads/IDS-Guidance-for-security-managers.pdf Accessed on 19 August 2021.

Momboisse. R. B., (1977) *Industrial Security for Strikes, Riots and Disasters* London, Charles C Thomas Publishers.

Mortice Locks (78) Master Locksmiths Association (MLA) https://www.locksmiths.co.uk/faq/door-lock-types-guide/ Accessed on 21 August 2021.

Murphy. M. N., (2010) *Small boats, weak states, dirty money* London, C Hurst & Co.

Natural Gas Supply (115) https://en.wikipedia.org/wiki/National_Transmission_System Accessed on 27 November 2021.

Natural Gas Supply (112) https://en.wikipedia.org/wiki/National_Transmission_System Accessed on 27 November 2021.

Organisational Review (68) https://democracy.manchester.gov.uk/documents/s13150/Appendix%201%20-%20Martyns_Law_Final_Report.pdf Accessed on 28 June 2021.

Passive Infrared and Microwave Detection (85) CPNI intrusion detection systems guidance for security managers July 2013 file:///C:/Users/cswan/Downloads/IDS-Guidance-for-security-managers.pdf Accessed on 19 August 2021.

Protect Duty (97) https://www.gov.uk/government/news/government-sets-out-plans-to-protect-public-places-from-terrorist-attacks Accessed on 06 November 2021.

Royal Society, (1992) *Risk: analysis, perception, management.* London, The Royal Society Publishing.

Schwab. K., (2017) *The Fourth Industrial Revolution* World Economic Forum.

Semi Structured Interviews (75) https://www.thebalancecareers.com/what-is-a-semi-structured-interview-2061632 Accessed on 10 July 2021.

Server Rack Details (108) https://community.fs.com/blog/different-types-of-server-rack-used-in-data-center.html Accessed on 24 March 2022.

Three-point locking systems (79) Master Locksmiths Association (MLA) https://www.locksmiths.co.uk/faq/door-lock-types-guide/ Accessed on 21 August 2021.

UK and EU aviation legislation (118) https://publicapps.caa.co.uk/docs/33/Law%202015-1998%20(30Mar2021).pdf Accessed on 28 December 2021.

Vibration and shock detection (86) CPNI intrusion detection systems guidance for security managers July 2013 file:///C:/Users/cswan/Downloads/IDS-Guidance-for-security-managers.pdf Accessed on 19 August 2021.

Video based detection systems (83) The Home Office Guide to Perimeter Intrusion Detection Systems (PIDS) https://www.cpni.gov.uk/system/files/documents/2c/80/Guide-to-PIDS.pdf accessed on 17 August 2021.

## Notes

1 You may have to brief the Board to explain exactly what a Security Survey is.

2 https://democracy.manchester.gov.uk/documents/s13150/Appendix%201%20-%20Martyns_Law_Final_Report.pdf Accessed on 28 June 2021.

3 This is absolutely an area where most Security Surveyors will be in need of specialist advice and guidance.

4 That is to say, boxes containing Video Cassette Recorders (VCR).

5 https://www.projectmanager.com/blog/planning-quotes.

6 There is also the seven P's which former military veterans may remember!
7 I don't take credit for that quote, but it absolutely worthwhile and in context.
8 https://www.thebalancecareers.com/what-is-a-semi-structured-interview-2061632 Accessed on 10 July 2021.
9 If anybody attempts to convince you that their systems have no limits, take that advice with a Kilogram of salt. Every system ever designed has limitations.
10 The Security Risk Assessment has been covered earlier in this book, and it is recommended that due consideration be given to the CPNI OR1 and OR2 approach to the Operational Requirement. See www.cpni.gov.
11 The Home Office Guide to Perimeter Intrusion Detection Systems (PIDS) https://www.cpni.gov.uk/system/files/documents/2c/80/Guide-to-PIDS.pdf accessed on 17 August 2021.
12 Master Locksmiths Association (MLA) https://www.locksmiths.co.uk/faq/door-lock-types-guide/ Accessed on 21 August 2021.
13 Master Locksmiths Association (MLA) https://www.locksmiths.co.uk/faq/door-lock-types-guide/ Accessed on 21 August 2021.
14 Open path https://www.openpath.com/blog-post/proximity-card-readers-for-access-control Accessed on 21 August 2021.
15 https://en.wikipedia.org/wiki/Biometrics Accessed on 21 August 2021.
16 Part of a conversation heard by me a few years ago.
17 CPNI intrusion detection systems guidance for security managers July 2013 file:///C:/Users/cswan/Downloads/IDS-Guidance-for-security-managers.pdf Accessed on 19 August 2021.
18 CPNI intrusion detection systems guidance for security managers July 2013 file:///C:/Users/cswan/Downloads/IDS-Guidance-for-security-managers.pdf Accessed on 19 August 2021.
19 CPNI intrusion detection systems guidance for security managers July 2013 file:///C:/Users/cswan/Downloads/IDS-Guidance-for-security-managers.pdf Accessed on 19 August 2021.
20 CPNI intrusion detection systems guidance for security managers July 2013 file:///C:/Users/cswan/Downloads/IDS-Guidance-for-security-managers.pdf Accessed on 19 August 2021.
21 StouchLighting https://www.stouchlighting.com/blog/led-vs-hps-lps-high-and-low-pressure-sodium Accessed on 23 August 2021.

22 https://www.gov.uk/government/publications/crowded-places-guidance/cctv Accessed on 10 February 2022.

23 An auto iris is part of a motorised lens and has the ability to automatically adjust to keep a constant level of light in the video image – this is useful for environments where the light levels change, for example outdoors. https://www.techcube.co.uk/blog/cctv-cameras-explained/ Accessed on 20 February 2022.

24 https://ico.org.uk/about-the-ico/who-we-are/ Accessed on 21 March 2022.

25 This is quite a common occurrence.

26 Facilities Management (FM) support requires patrolling Security Officers to be aware of any electrical or mechanical issues that may require attention by the FM Manager.

27 Site Assignment Instructions relate to all security aspects of the British Utilities (BU) floor space, and they are designed to ensure that the Security Team is fully aware of all duties required to be carried out.

28 https://www.gov.uk/government/news/government-sets-out-plans-to-protect-public-places-from-terrorist-attacks Accessed on 06 November 2021.

29 Facilities Management (FM) support requires patrolling Security Officers to be aware of any electrical or mechanical issues that may require attention by the FM Manager.

30 Site Specific Assignment Instructions relate to all security aspects of the Liverport Arena floor space, and they are designed to ensure that the Security Team is fully aware of all duties required to be carried out.

31 Cash from the box office is retrieved twice a week, at irregular intervals, and is transported to a nearby high street bank where it is deposited.

32 General Data Protection Regulations (2016).

33 https://www.projectmanager.com/blog/planning-quotes Accessed on 08 October 2021.

34 British Telecommunications PLC.

35 https://www.azquotes.com/quotes/topics/preparation-and-planning.html Accessed on 22 March 2022.

36 https://www.gov.uk/government/news/tough-new-rules-to-protect-uks-critical-infrastructure-come-into-force Accessed on 22 March 2022.

37 The 34th floor is unoccupied and secure, and there is no access to the 35th floor by members of the public.

38 This section will cover floors 34 and 35 only.

39 https://community.fs.com/blog/different-types-of-server-rack-used-in-data-center.html Accessed on 24 March 2022.
40 https://www.goodreads.com/quotes/tag/planning Accessed on 18 November 2021.
41 CPNI Guide to Perimeter Intrusion Detection Systems (PIDS) https://www.cpni.gov.uk/system/files/documents/2c/80/Guide-to-PIDS.pdf Accessed on 24 November 2021.
42 https://www.cpni.gov.uk/sites/default/files/citvsb_catalogue/CSE%20HVM%20-%20Impact%20Rated%20-%20Rating%20System%20Explained%20-%2020210201_0_0.pdf Accessed on 25 November 2021.
43 There are three ISPS Code Security Levels. Level 1 covers normal operations. Level 2 means enhanced security, and level 3 is the highest level, entailing maximum security procedures. A vessel will normally leave port if she is operating at Level 3.
44 https://en.wikipedia.org/wiki/National_Transmission_System Accessed on 27 November 2021.
45 CCTV and alarm monitoring, communications etc.
46 https://info.caa.co.uk/uk-regulations/ Accessed on 28 December 2021.
47 https://publicapps.caa.co.uk/docs/33/Law%202015-1998%20(30Mar2021).pdf Accessed on 28 December 2021.
48 Key Point Indicators (KPI) are measurements of contractual conformance and are agreed by the service provider and the client at the beginning of the contract.
49 HVM-Hostile Vehicle Mitigation, conforming to PAS 68 specifications.
50 Covered later in this section.
51 https://en.wikipedia.org/wiki/National_Transmission_System Accessed on 27 November 2021.
52 If the ICT Server Room is held open for more than 180 seconds, the silent alarm will activate in the Security Control Room.
53 CCTV and alarm monitoring, communications etc.
54 CPNI Guide to Perimeter Intrusion Detection Systems (PIDS) https://www.cpni.gov.uk/system/files/documents/2c/80/Guide-to-PIDS.pdf Accessed on 24 November 2021.
55 All Security Officers receive regular weapons handling training and must be aware of the current rules of engagement.
56 Times can vary dependant on work and drilling schedules.

57 file:///C:/Users/cswan/Downloads/27_CAS01_05_2014_EN_web%20(1).pdf Accessed on 01 December 2021.
58 Signed out by cleaning and catering staff when required.
59 For use in the event of the ICT system being denied electrical power. The UPS will run for one hour before the generator begins to supply power.
60 UPS and standby generator.
61 The safe room also has a personal alarm button that if struck will signal to the Operations Room.
62 The principle, the CP Team and the local police.

# 3

# THE SECURITY AUDIT

Part 2 of the chapter will see a number of Security Audit reports that have been generated within a number of diverse environments, once again, mirroring the locations chosen for the Security Risk Assessment and the Security survey.

As far as I am aware, there is no Security Audit process or template readily available. That is not to say that a number of organisations don't have their own audit protocols in use, but that is the exception rather than the rule. The template that I have provided was devised by me as a baseline document, and as with the other two available templates in the book, it can of course be adjusted to individual organisational needs.

Figure 27 re-introduces you to the Risk Journey, in which the Security Audit is the final element, and once again I re-emphasise the argument that this is the only logical approach to any form of organisational security review, and that there is an absolute symbiotic relationship between the three elements.

DOI: 10.4324/9781003186335-4

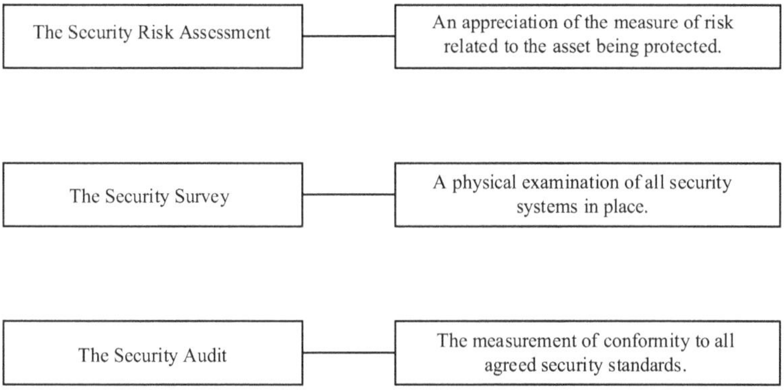


*Figure 27* The Risk Journey.

## The Security Audit

Auditing typically refers to financial statement audits or an objective examination and evaluation of a company's financial statements – usually performed by an external third party.[1] However, for the purposes of this book, we will be looking at Security Auditing which encompasses assets that are not purely financial.

## Security

### *We must learn from experience!*

In 2017 on behalf of one of my clients, I led a ten-person Project Team to carry out three Security Surveys at petroleum refineries, all of which were listed as part of the country's critical national infrastructure. During the surveys a number of critical vulnerabilities were identified, each being described in detail as part of the post-Security Survey Report.

Observations about each vulnerability were detailed in the report, as were the corresponding recommendations. One of the observations related to a serious flaw in the Perimeter Intruder Detection System (PIDS), and it was recommended that for the sake of the integrity of the plant, remedial action was to be taken immediately.

In December 2021 during a conversation with the same client, out of curiosity, I asked when the follow-up or Security Audit had taken place, and what were the results. I received a vague look, and a shrug of the shoulders, which informed me that no such follow-up visit had taken place, and to all intents and purposes, the PIDS could still be unfit for purpose.

Unlike the Security Risk Assessment and the Security Survey which both, to a certain extent, rely on investigated empirical evidence, the Security Audit is dependent on agreed standards that have generally been identified earlier in the process. It is recommended that the Security Audit is carried out six to twelve months after the Security Survey, dependent upon local circumstances, and the severity of any vulnerabilities identified during the survey.

Whilst the Security Risk Assessment and the Security Survey are readily (at least to a certain extent) accepted processes designed to identify and mitigate risk to an individual or an organisation, the Security Audit, and its functions are less clear.

During the Security Risk Assessment and the Security Survey, certain standards will either have been identified,[2] or perhaps introduced for the first time, and the idea behind the Security Audit, much as with any other form of audit is to ensure those standards are maintained.

Today, more than ever, organisations are favouring formal accreditation and certification, with British and ISO standards being pre-emptive. The most common standards are highlighted in Table 39.

*Table 39* International Organisation Standards (ISO)

| | |
|---|---|
| ISO 9001 | Quality Management Systems |
| ISO 14000 | Environmental management |
| ISO 18000/1 | Information Technology |
| ISO 18788 | Management Systems for Private Security Operations |
| ISO 22301 | Business Continuity Management |
| ISO 22320 | Security Resilience, Emergency Management, Guidelines for Incident Management |
| ISO 27001 | Information Security Systems Management |
| ISO 27032 | Information Technology, Security Techniques, Guidelines for Cyber Security |
| ISO 28000 | Supply Chain Security |
| ISO 28007 | Guidelines for private maritime security companies (PMSC) that provide privately contracted armed security personnel (PCASP) on board ships. |
| ISO 31000 | Risk Management |
| *British Standards* | |
| BS 11200 | Crisis Management |

## The Security Auditor

Earlier in the book I wrote that I am of the opinion that the title most likely to be recognised throughout the security sector, and probably other business sectors is that of the Security Auditor.

Auditors are recognised in most sectors as professionals who can be relied upon to accurately measure competency and compliance levels, and that of course can be applied to the security sector. As you will have seen throughout the book, the Security Auditor is responsible for carrying out the Security Risk Assessment, the Security Survey, and now the Security Audit.

## The Security Audit process

If an organisation wishes to be audited against its Quality Management System (QMS), or to seek certification of its Information Security, it will approach auditors to investigate conformity of ISO 9001 (Quality Management) or ISO 27001 (Information Security Management). A system that is relatively straightforward.

Conversely, if the same organisation requires confirmation of its security systems being fit for purpose, it is unable to audit for conformity, because at present, relative British or International Standards don't exist.

My proposal and argument are that such an imbalance needs to be rectified, and this is where security auditing asserts itself in the overall process that I have named the Risk Journey.

In reality, the Security Audit begins at the end of the Security Survey, when standards have either been clarified or identified. There will have been agreement steps between the Security Auditor and his or her client in terms of the process, and preliminary dates can be set for follow-up actions.

### *The Security Audit gap analysis*

As mentioned, during the Security Survey, it is likely that a number of vulnerabilities will have been highlighted by the Security Auditor in their report, accompanied by observations and recommendations; and this is key. This will inform client of the steps required to meet his or her expectations about the levels of security they wish to achieve. This is the Security Audit gap.

## *Internal Security Audit*

Based on the findings form the Security Survey, and prior to the agreed follow up by the external Security Auditor, an internal Security Manager will carry out a review or Self-Assessment of the organisations levels of security in order to understand what is required to be done, if anything, before the Security Audit.

On the agreed date, the external Security Audit will take place.

### *Case study: A Data Centre*

A Data Centre in the South of England has been subject to a Security Survey as the result of a Security Risk Assessment which has identified high-level risks of a physical attack, and the penetration of its ICT network.

During the Security Survey, the following observations and recommendations were made.

**Observation 1:**

The retractable bollards to the front of the main entrance were deemed not fit for purpose.

**Recommendation (s):**

It was recommended that the bollards be replaced with a system conforming to PAS 68 specifications.

**Observation 2:**

The ICT network was overdue for a software upgrade.

**Recommendation (s):**

It was recommended that the ICT network be certificated to ISO 27001 standards.

**Observation 3:**

The Crisis Management Plan (CMP) had not been upgraded or tested for three years.

**Recommendation (s):**

It was recommended that the organisation CMP be rewritten to meet BS 112000 standards.

Note:

All of the above are to be audited twelve months after the date of the Security Survey.

## The Security Audit report

Unlike the Security Survey, which is the result of an on-site examination of all systems, using a recognised template, a formal written report is produced and submitted; the Security Audit is the document produced at the time of the audit.

In the following part of this section, we shall transpose the observations made during a series of sector Security Surveys covered in the book, and they will act as Security Audit examples, beginning with Corporate security.

## Unique sectors

## Corporate security

Security Audit

| | |
|---|---|
| Name and location of audit. | Mr John Horrigan. Chief Operating Officer.<br>British Utilities<br>50 Canada Way<br>Pegasus Wharf<br>London<br>E145DY |
| Date of audit. | 29 January 2022 |
| Audit lead. | John Beck |
| Reference number. | SecAud/CW/01/22. |

| | |
|---|---|
| **Security Audit Management summary.**[3] | As the result of a Security Survey carried out at British Utilities on 20 July 2021, during which a number of vulnerabilities were identified, it was decided by the Senior Management Team to commission a Security Audit.<br>The majority of vulnerabilities identified during the Security Survey have been rectified, but there are still issues surrounding the lack of a reserve server/communications room. |

**Observations from the Security Survey.**

1. There is no CCTV coverage supporting the goods inwards the room.
2. Whilst there is CCTV support immediately inside the building covering the fire exits, there is no camera coverage externally.
3. During the course of the Security Survey, it was observed that two of the lighting units above the front entrance, and a single lighting unit covering the goods inwards door were inoperative.
4. During the Security Survey it was observed that throughout the night, Security officers are expected to carry out external patrols alone.
5. **There is no reserve server/communications room. There is the possibility that the server/communications room could be disabled by either physical or electronic (cyber) attacks.**

| |
|---|
| **Audit observations.**<br>1. There is now CCTV coverage supporting the goods inwards room, and externally above all fire exits.<br>2. Lighting at the location is now fit for purpose.<br>3. Security Officers are no longer carrying out external patrols alone.<br>4. ***Although there is the possibility of the server/communications room being disabled by either physical or electronic (cyber) attack, at the time of the Security Audit it was observed that there is still no reserve server/communications room.*** |

| | |
|---|---|
| **Non-Conformities and actions required.** | The lack of actions taken with respect to the server/communications room constitutes a non-conformity, which must be resolved before the Security Audit is complete.<br><br>It is once again recommended that a reserve server/communications room be identified at the earliest opportunity. |

| | |
|---|---|
| **Auditors' final remarks.** | It is clear that the Management Team at British Utilities has invested heavily in terms of time, effort, and financial support to meet the requirement of the majority of theSecurity Audit requirements, but attention must be paid to the server/communications room and its reserve support.<br><br>During the course of the audit, the Security Auditor was afforded the assistance needed, reflecting a positive security culture at the site audited. |

| *Auditor details* | *Auditor signature* | *Date.* |
|---|---|---|
| John Beck | Online | 07 February 2022 |
| | | |

## Publicly accessible locations

| | |
|---|---|
| Name and location of audit. | Ms Debbi Beck.<br>Liverport Arena<br>Liverport Docklands<br>LE1 2BB |
| Date of audit. | 01 February 2022 |
| Audit lead. | Charles Swanson |
| Reference number | SecAud/LA/02/22 |

| | |
|---|---|
| **Security Audit Management summary.**[4] | As the result of a Security Survey carried out at the Liverport Arena, on 16 July 2021, during which a number of vulnerabilities were identified, it was decided by the Senior Management Team at the arena to commission a Security Audit.<br><br>The majority of vulnerabilities identified during the Security Survey have been rectified, but there are still issues surrounding the site AIs that require resolution. |

**Observations from the Security Survey.**

1. The goods inwards entrance is covered by the building CCTV system, although at the time of the Security Survey two cameras were unserviceable.
2. During the Security Survey it was observed that two of the wall-mounted LED lighting units illuminating the main entrance were unserviceable.
3. Whilst observing the fire exits, it was noted that one of the fire escape doors was wedged open by the use of a fire extinguisher. The IDS activation did not signal to the alarm monitor in the Security Control Room.
4. During the Security Survey it was observed that none of the security team was search qualified. That is to say, nobody had attended a formal search training course.
5. There is currently no CCTV coverage in the box office, nor are there any cameras installed on the stage area.
6. It was also observed that none of the Security Control Room CCTV operators hold an SIA Public Space surveillance (PSS) licence. The CCTV system looks at public space outside of the arena.
7. ***At the time of the Security Survey it was observed that the AIs had not been signed off by the Arena Security Manager for two years.***

**Audit observations.**

1. The site CCTV system is now fully fit for purpose, with all cameras being operational.
2. The site lighting system is now fully fit for purpose, with all lights being operational
3. During the Security Audit it was observed that all fire exits were secure, and when tested the IDS was fully fit for purpose.
4. The Site Search Team is now fully search qualified.
5. The Box Office and stage are now covered by the site CCTV system.
6. All Security Control Room CCTV operators now hold an SIA Public Space surveillance (PSS) licence.
7. ***At the time of the Security Audit it was observed that the AIs had still not been signed off by the Arena Security Manager.***

| | |
|---|---|
| Non-Conformities and actions required. | The lack of actions taken with respect to the site AIs constitutes a non-conformity, which must be resolved before the Security Audit is complete.<br><br>It is once again recommended that the AIs are signed off by the Arena Security Manager, and that the procedure is included in the site compliance plans. |

| | |
|---|---|
| Auditors' final remarks. | It is clear that the Management Team at the Liverport Arena has invested heavily in terms of time, effort, and financial support to meet the requirement of the majority of the Security Audit requirements, but attention must be paid to the Site Assignment Instructions.<br><br>During the course of the audit, the Security Auditor was afforded the assistance needed, reflecting a positive security culture at the site audited. |

| *Auditor details* | *Auditor signature* | *Date.* |
|---|---|---|
| Charles Swanson | Online | 28 February 2022 |

## Retail security

| | |
|---|---|
| Name and location of audit. | Mr Jim Dolan<br>Tescaldi Supermarket, 50<br>Canada Way.<br>Pegasus Wharf<br>E145DY |
| Date of audit. | 10 March 2022 |
| Audit lead. | Charles Swanson |
| Reference number | SecAud/TSCW/03/22 |

| | |
|---|---|
| **Security Audit Management summary.**[5] | As the result of a Security Survey carried out at Tescaldi Supermarket, on 12 September 2021, during which a number of vulnerabilities were identified, it was decided by the Senior Management Team to commission a Security Audit.<br><br>The majority of vulnerabilities identified during the Security Survey have been rectified, but there are still issues surrounding the issue of smart card credibility. |

| **Observations from the Security Survey.** |
| --- |
| 1. It was observed during the Security Survey, that whilst the duty Security Officer is monitoring the store CCTV system, he or she is unable to carry out observations on the entrance.<br>2. During the Security Survey, the store EAS constantly raised alarm, but the activations were ignored by staff and the duty Security Officer.<br>3. Although there is a key press for securing all store keys, there is no record of key movement. That is to say, there is no evidence of who signed the keys out or in.<br>4. **There is no audit trail to confirm the management of proximity cards. The access control administrator was unable to confirm how many cards had been issued, and how many had been returned by members of staff who have left employment.** |

| **Audit observations.** |
| --- |
| 1. An extra Security Officer has been recruited to focus solely on the CCTV system.<br>2. Since the Security Survey was carried out the EAS system has been replaced with a system that is more reliable.<br>3. An electronic RFID secure key press has been installed, and an audit is created as soon as a key is removed.<br>4. **There is still no audit trail to confirm the management of proximity cards. The Access Control Administrator is still unable to confirm how many cards have been issued, and how many had been returned by members of staff who have left employment.** |

| | |
| --- | --- |
| **Non-Conformities and actions required.** | The lack of actions taken in respect of the issuing of smart cards constitutes a non-conformity, which must be resolved before the Security Audit is complete.<br><br>It is once again recommended that the Access Control Administrator is given support to assist her in what is an onerous task because of staff turnover, which is very high. |

| | |
| --- | --- |
| **Auditors' final remarks.** | It is clear that the Management Team at Tescali Supermarket Services has invested heavily in terms of time, effort, and financial support to meet the requirement of the majority of the Security Audit requirements, but the issue relating to smart cards requires attention.<br><br>During the course of the audit, the Security Auditor was afforded the assistance needed, reflecting a positive security culture at the site audited. |

| *Auditor details* | *Auditor signature* | *Date.* |
| --- | --- | --- |
| Charles Swanson | Online | 17 March 2022 |
| | | |

## Critical national infrastructure security

| | | |
|---|---|---|
| Name and location of audit. | Kevin Gill<br>50 Canada Way<br>Pegasus Wharf<br>London<br>E145DY | |
| Date of audit. | 01 March 2022 | |
| Audit lead. | John Beck | |
| Reference number | SecAud/CW/04/22 | |

| | |
|---|---|
| **Security Audit Management summary.**[6] | As the result of a Security Survey carried out at 50 Canada way, on 22 September 2021, during which a number of vulnerabilities were identified, it was decided by the Senior Management Team to commission a Security Audit.<br><br>All of the vulnerabilities identified during the Security Survey have been rectified. |

| |
|---|
| **Observations from the Security Survey.**<br>1. There is no CCTV coverage supporting the Goods Inwards door.<br>2. There is no external CCTV coverage supporting the fire exits.<br>3. There is only a single CCTV camera covering the outside of the building.<br>4. Two external, lighting units were non-operational. |
| |

| |
|---|
| **Audit observations.**<br>1. There is now a static CCTV camera covering the Goods Inwards door.<br>2. There are now external CCTV static cameras covering the fire exits.<br>3. There are now seven CCTV cameras covering the outside of the building.<br>4. All external lighting is now serviceable. |

| | |
|---|---|
| **Non-Conformities and actions required**. | All non-conformities have been attended to. |

| | |
|---|---|
| **Auditors' final remarks.** | It is clear that the Management Team at the Data Centre has invested heavily in terms of time, effort, and financial support to meet the requirement of the majority of the Security Audit requirements, but the issue relating to smart cards requires attention.<br><br>During the course of the audit, the Security Auditor was afforded the assistance needed, reflecting a positive security culture at the site audited. |

| *Auditor details* | *Auditor signature* | *Date.* |
|---|---|---|
| Charles Swanson | Online | 14 March 2022 |
| | | |

## Maritime security

| | |
|---|---|
| Name and location of audit. | Liverport Contained Terminal<br>Alfred Dock<br>Liverport |
| Date of audit. | 02 April 2022 |
| Audit lead. | Charles Swanson |
| Reference number | SecAud/LCT/05/22 |

| | |
|---|---|
| **Security Audit Management summary.**[7] | As the result of a Security Survey carried out at the Liverport Container terminal, on 21 October 2021, it was decided by the Senior Management Team to commission a Security Audit. |

**Observations from the Security Survey.**

1. During the course of the Security Survey it was observed that the perimeter fence is bare of any form of PIDS.
2. Two of the perimeter LED units were nonoperational, and one of the CCTV cameras was not signalling to the Security Control Room.
3. ***It was observed, that by the time a vehicle reaches the Proximity Card Reader, the bollards will have been lowered, and the barrier raised, removing all physical protection.***
4. ***It was observed during the Security Survey that there is no reserve Security Control Room.***

**Audit observations.**

1. The perimeter fence is now fitted with fabric taught wire PIDS.
2. Lighting and CCTV systems are now fit for purpose and are fully functional.
3. ***It was observed during the Security Audit, that by the time a vehicle reaches the Proximity Card Reader, the bollards still will have been lowered, and the barrier raised, removing all physical protection.***
4. ***There is still no reserve Security Control Room.***

| | |
|---|---|
| **Non-Conformities and actions required.** | There are two non-conformities that require attention.<br><br>1. It was observed during the Security Audit, that by the time a vehicle reaches the Proximity Card Reader, the bollards still will have been lowered, and the barrier raised, removing all physical protection.<br><br>2. There is still no reserve Security Control Room. |

| | |
|---|---|
| **Auditors' final remarks.** | Although the majority of observations have been attended to, there are still two non-conformities<br>It is formally noted that staff and management have worked very hard to achieve the status quo. |

| *Auditor details* | *Auditor signature* | *Date.* |
|---|---|---|
| Charles Swanson | Online | 10 April 2022 |

## Aviation security

| | |
|---|---|
| Name and location of audit. | Mr Bill Seppings CEO<br>Birmingpool (BPL) International Airport Departures Building, Birmingpool, B26 3QR |
| Date of audit. | 02 April 2022 |
| Audit lead. | Charles Swanson |
| Reference number | SecAud/BPL/06/22 |

| | |
|---|---|
| **Security Audit Management summary.**[8] | As the result of a Security Survey carried out at Birmingpool International Airport, on 21 October 2021, it was decided by the Senior Management Team to commission a Security Audit. |

**Observations from the Security Survey.**

1. During the Security Survey it was observed that three static cameras covering the western side of the perimeter fence were non-operational and had been for two weeks.
2. During the Security Survey, both emergency exits were covertly opened, and neither breach activated the IDS. Upon investigation by the Airport Security Manager, it was deduced that the IDS had been decoupled during maintenance work.
3. During the Security Survey it was observed that the tool store was insecure, in that the only entrance to the store, a single leaf, in swinging wooden door was unlocked, with no sign of any occupants.
4. **Currently there is no Security Control Room backup facility.**

**Audit observations.**

1. The airport CCTV system is now fit for purpose, with all equipment being fully functional.
2. All fire exit IDS units are now fit for purpose and operationally functional.
3. **During the Security Audit it was observed that the tool store was still insecure.**
4. **Currently there is still no Security Control Room backup facility.**

| | |
|---|---|
| **Non-Conformities and actions required.** | There are two non-conformities that require attention.<br>1. The tool store is insecure<br>2. There is still no reserve Security Control Room. |

| | |
|---|---|
| **Auditors' final remarks.** | Although the majority of observations have been attended to, there are still two non-conformities.<br>It is formally noted that staff and management have worked very hard to achieve the status quo. |

| *Auditor details* | *Auditor signature* | *Date.* |
|---|---|---|
| Charles Swanson | On-line | 10 April 2022 |

# Hostile environment security

## Aviation security

| | |
|---|---|
| Name and location of audit. | Bob Clarke CEO<br>Greater Safaniya, Kingdom of Saudubai. |
| Date of audit. | 10 April 2022 |
| Audit lead. | Charles Swanson |
| Reference number | SecAud/KoS/07/22 |

| | |
|---|---|
| **Security Audit Management summary.**[9] | As the result of a Security Survey carried out at the British Utilities' site, Greater Safaniya, Kingdom of Saudubai on 12 October 2021, it was decided by the Senior Management Team to commission a Security Audit. |

**Observations from the Security Survey.**

1. During the Security Survey it was observed that the keys for locking and unlocking the outer perimeter gates were not signed for. It was further observed that when the same gates are locked or unlocked, the procedure was not recorded in the Security Control Room Daily Occurrence Book (DOB).
2. During the Security Survey it was observed that although the main entrance was secure, the rear fire exit was held open by means of a fire extinguisher, and two members of staff were stood outside smoking cigarettes.
3. There is no CCTV coverage of the canteen.
4. During the Security Survey it was observed that the tool shed was insecure, in that the only entrance to the building, a single leaf, in swinging wooden door was unlocked, with no sign of any occupant.

| |
|---|
| **Audit observations.**<br>1. During the Security Audit it was observed that the keys for locking and unlocking the outer perimeter gates were still not being signed for. It was further observed that when the same gates are locked or unlocked, the procedure was not recorded in the Security Control Room Daily Occurrence Book (DOB).<br>2. During the Security Audit it was observed that all exits and entrances were secure, and that staff were adhering to Standing Instructions relating to smoking on site.<br>3. There is still no CCTV coverage of the canteen.<br>4. During the Security Audit it was observed that the tool shed is now secure. |

| | |
|---|---|
| **Non-Conformities and actions required.** | There are two non-conformities that require attention.<br>1. Keys are not being signed for and locking/unlocking of the perimeter gates are not being recorded in the DOB.<br>2. The canteen is not protected by the site CCTV system. |
| **Auditors' final remarks.** | Although the majority of observations have been attended to, there are still two non-conformities.<br>It is formally noted that staff and management have worked very hard to achieve the status quo. |

| *Auditor details* | *Auditor signature* | *Date.* |
|---|---|---|
| Charles Swanson | Online | 17 April 2022 |

## Close protection

| | |
|---|---|
| Name and location of audit. | The Brambles, Little Ivy, Porchester. PE217DX. |
| Date of audit. | 10 April 2022 |
| Audit lead. | Charles Swanson |
| Reference number | SecAud/CP/08/22 |

| | |
|---|---|
| **Security Audit Management summary.**[10] | As the result of a Security Survey carried out at The Brambles on 21 November 2021, it was decided by the client to commission a Security Audit.<br><br>All of the vulnerabilities identified during the Security Survey have been rectified. |

| |
|---|
| **Observations from the Security Survey.**<br>1. During the Security Survey it was observed that two of the cameras covering corner sections of the main building were unserviceable. As was the camera covering the pedestrian entrance to the vehicle compound. |

| **Audit observations.** |
|---|
| 1. The CCTV system is now fit for purpose, with all elements functioning correctly. |

| | |
|---|---|
| Non-Conformities and actions required. | There are no non-conformities that require attention. |

| | |
|---|---|
| **Auditors' final remarks**. | There are no non-conformities that require attention<br>It is formally noted that staff and management have worked very hard to achieve the status quo. |

| *Auditor details* | *Auditor signature* | *Date.* |
|---|---|---|
| Charles Swanson | Online | 17 April 2022 |

That is the end of the final section, and by reaching this point you have paused, reflected, and researched a process that I believe will be to your professional advantage. All I have to do now is conclude.

## Bibliography

Auditing (134) Auditing. https://corporatefinanceinstitute.com/resources/knowledge/accounting/what-is-an-audit/ Accessed on 19 September 2021.

## Notes

1 Auditing https://corporatefinanceinstitute.com/resources/knowledge/accounting/what-is-an-audit/ Accessed on 19 September 2021.
2 Perhaps British or International standards.
3 This will include sight of the Security Survey and its overall findings.
4 This will include sight of the Security Survey and its overall findings.
5 This will include sight of the Security Survey and its overall findings.
6 This will include sight of the Security Survey and its overall findings.
7 This will include sight of the Security Survey and its overall findings.
8 This will include an overview of the Security Survey and its overall findings.
9 This will include an overview of the Security Survey and its overall findings.
10 This will include an overview of the Security Survey and its overall findings.

# CONCLUSION

This is by far the most difficult part of the book because several hundred pages have to be summarised, and that is far from easy.

Looking back to the period before I began writing, I consulted a number of extremely professional colleagues and friends (see acknowledgements), who offered me advice, guidance, and inspiration, without which I would have struggled. However, the dialogue and engagement with genuine Subject Matter Experts spurred me to realise what I was trying to achieve in the publication of my second book, and I hope that I haven't let anybody down.

In my first book, *Professional Security Management: A Strategic Guide*, my aim was *to examine exactly what is required of the professional security manager in a demanding and fast changing business orientated sector*, and I believe that by and large I achieved that. Taking that one step further, the aim of this book is *to assist security and other professionals in carrying out the Security Risk Assessment, the Security Survey, and the Security Audit, in that order; what I refer to as the Risk Journey.* Only time, and my revered readers will confirm if I have achieved my second aim.

One thing that I am absolutely convinced of, and I hope that I have argued this effectively, is that the Risk Journey is the correct approach when a Security Review of an organisation is required. Assess, Survey and Audit.

I am also resolute in my opinion that we as an industry require single-minded governance, and we need to identify a professional individual, one that is recognised by all sectors, and I hope this will start a debate. I have called that professional the Security Auditor, for the reasons and arguments I have offered in this book, arguments that I am sure will be discussed, and probably challenged; and that of course is extremely healthy.

Researching for and writing this publication has probably been the most difficult task that I have completed in a career that spans far too many decades, but if it generates dialogue and debate about the industry uniformity required going forward, then I can take a breath before researching for my next project.

Thank you. I hope you have enjoyed reading my/your book, and further, I wish you good luck and good fortune in all of your professional endeavours.

Charles Swanson.
31 March 2022.

# Annexe A

## SECURITY RISK ASSESSMENT TEMPLATE

## Security Risk Assessment (SRA) template (example)

The Risk Journey

### Introduction

The Security Risk Assessment is the first stage in the Risk Journey, and as such the data from this process is critical for the next two stages.

The risk assessment is by no means a straightforward process, and whereas when surveying and auditing there are clear guidelines relating to performance and conformance, the Security Risk Auditor, without such guidelines or standards is expected to gather and collate reliable evidence relating to risk, before presenting it to the risk owner. However, let us not hold any illusion that the risk assessment, security, or otherwise, is 100% reliable. The risk assessment is just that; it is an assessment, an assumption, even a calculated guess; and it is not 100% accurate.

It is important to understand that this is a baseline Security Risk Assessment (SRA) template, and you are advised to be aware that organisations will produce templates perhaps more in tune with their needs. However, using this or some other form of base line template will offer the Security Auditor a level of uniformity; but don't be afraid to be flexible.

Take a look at the following format and the example information used, and decide if it suits you; but remember, flexibility is critical.

## Contents

1. **The SRA details**
2. **Rationale behind the assessment**
3. **Assets**
4. **Threats**
5. **Vulnerabilities.**
6. **Likelihood evaluation.**
7. **Impact assessment.**
8. **Risk assessment pre-mitigation**
9. **Risk assessment post-mitigation.**
10. **Summary**

## Section 1: SRA details (Example)

Name and appointment of client.

| |
|---|
| Mr John Beck. CEO. |

Address (s)

| |
|---|
| British Utilities. Pegasus House, Liverport. LE217DX |

Point of Contact.

| |
|---|
| Mr Ian Kelly. CSO. |

E mail.

| |
|---|
| Ian.kelly@bu.com |

Telephone.

| |
|---|
| 01519280566 |

Web address.

| |
|---|
| www.bu.com |

Location of and date of SRA.

| |
|---|
| Pegasus House, Liverport. LE217DX |

Name of Security Auditor.

| |
|---|
| Charles Swanson MSc CSyP |

Organisation.

| |
|---|
| STC |

## Section 2: Rational

Separate to the cover page, this is the opportunity for the Security Auditor to clarify who is involved in the project, what the reasons are for the assessment, exactly what location and operations are involved, and what are the time scales.

Example.

> As a result of liaison with Liverpool police, it was agreed that a Security Risk Assessment of Pegasus House, Liverpoort, LE217DX will be carried out as soon as possible.

## Section 3: Assets

This is the first step in the Security Risk Assessment process, and it is critical for the Security Auditor to have a firm understanding of exactly what in the organisation requires protection. The list below is not in order of criticality, but that can change, depending on the needs and priorities of the organisation.

> After taking instructions from the client, it is clear that the following assets require protection.
>
> - Personnel.
> - Brand and reputation.
> - ICT hardware and software.
> - Data and information.
> - Buildings and infrastructure.
> - Intellectual Property (IP).

## Section 4: Threat analysis

After asset identification, the process of threat analysis is extremely important because it will give the assessor and his or her client an understanding of where the most likely threats will emanate from, and in what form.

As with a number of other sections of the Security Risk Assessment the Security Auditor may request advice from independent Risk Analysis Subject Matter Experts.

## Section 5: Vulnerability analysis

The criminal will use recognised vulnerabilities, or weaknesses to expose and attack the asset, and it is therefore crucial for the Security Auditor to identify individual/organisational vulnerabilities and attend to them at the earliest opportunity.[1]

Example.

Pegasus House is the corporate Head Office for British Utilities, and through research and conversation with key personnel, it is clear that the following vulnerabilities exist at the site being assessed.

- Physical access control to the building.
- Physical security systems are aged, and may not be fit for purpose:
  - CCTV.
  - Access control.
  - Lighting.
  - Intruder Detection Systems (IDS).
- ICT integrity.
- Security training and awareness.
- Security policies, plans and procedures.
- Vetting and screening of key personnel.

## Section 6: Likelihood evaluation

This is by far the most complicated phase of the Security Risk Assessment because, in reality, the Security Auditor is attempting to forecast the future. Inevitably, security practitioners at this stage will rely on the analysis of past incidents, and that is an important component in the process, but the likelihood evaluation requires significantly more evidence than just historical data. Consider the following when carrying out a likelihood evaluation, and always remember to consult a Subject Matter Expert (SME) if the topic e.g., ICT, terrorism etc., is outside of your particular skills.

- The attractiveness of the asset (s) to the attacker.
- Where does the threat originate?
- What weaknesses may attract the attacker e.g., Poor access control, weak lighting, etc.?
- Would the impact of a successful attack be to the benefit of the criminal?
- Is there corroborated intelligence to support the likelihood of an attack?
- Is there historical statistical evidence of previous attacks?

## Section 7: Impact assessment

This phase of the Security Risk Assessment is perhaps more straightforward than the likelihood assessment because it can be calculated in tangible quantitative values. For example, in terms of cost, how will it impact the organisation, or as the result of an attack, will lives be lost? Once again, consider the following when carrying out an impact assessment, and always remember to consult a Subject Matter Expert (SME) if the topic e.g., ICT, terrorism, etc., is outside of your particular skills.

- Loss of life.
- Financial cost.
- Loss of brand and reputation.
- Share value.
- Sector credibility

## Section 8: Risk assessment (pre-mitigation)

This is an accumulation of the evidence gathered during the SRA research phase..[2] Assets, threats, vulnerabilities, and likelihood calculations will have been carried out, potentially with the assistance of credible intelligence and SME advice.

Example

*Table A1* The Security Risk Assessment before mitigation.

| | **Impact** | 1. very low | 2. Low | 3. High | **4. Very high** | 5. Catastrophic |
|---|---|---|---|---|---|---|
| **Likelihood** | | | | | | |
| 1. Very low | | | | | | |
| 2. Low | | | | | | |
| 3. Medium | | | | | | |
| **4. High** | | | | | **16/25** | |
| 5. Very high | | | | | | |

The completed risk assessment will be handed to the risk owner for a decision. Should it be accepted, avoided, reduced, or shared?

Table A1 illustrates a risk assessment, pre-mitigation, when the likelihood of a cyber-attack is deemed to be High (4), and the impact is believed to be very high (4) giving a risk level score of 16/25.

## Section 9: Risk assessment (post-mitigation)

This is the point when after liaising with the risk owner a decision is made[3] about how the risk is to be treated. In this instance, the owner of the risk has decided that acceptance, avoidance, and sharing are inappropriate, and a decision to reduce the risk has been taken, meaning that a number of mitigation measures will be required. Once again, if this particular risk (the cyber-attack) is beyond the skill sets of the assessor, advice from the relevant SME should be sought. Once mitigation measures have been implemented, there should be a reduction in the risk factor (Figure A1).

Table A2 shows that as the result of mitigation measures introduced, the likelihood is believed to be Low (2), with an impact score, as the result of a successful attack, of Very High (4), giving an overall score of 8/25.

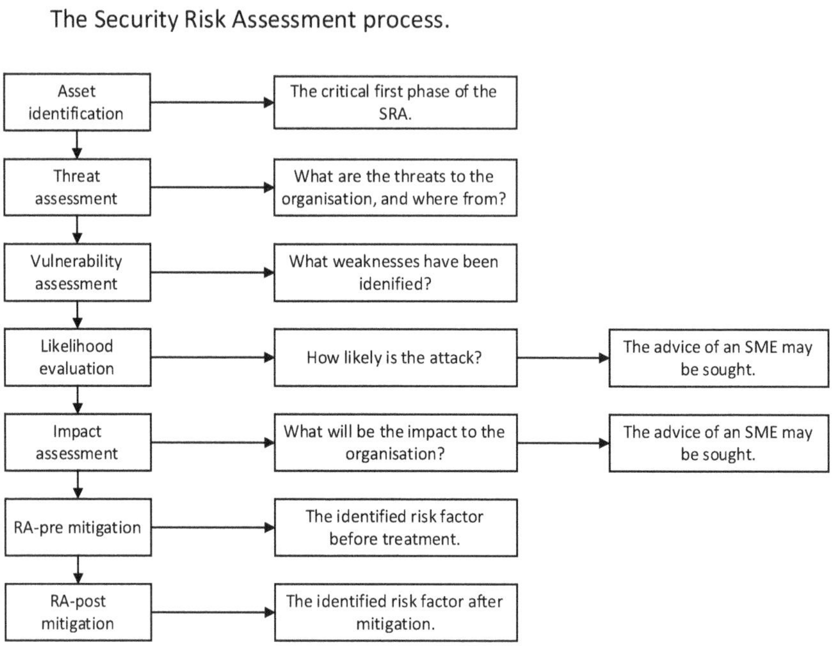


*Figure A1* illustrates the Security Risk Assessment in terms of a basic flow diagram.

*Table A2* The Security Risk Assessment after mitigation.

| | **Impact** | *1. Very low* | *2. Low* | *3. High* | ***4. Very high*** | *5. Catastrophic* |
|---|---|---|---|---|---|---|
| **Likelihood** | | | | | | |
| 1. Very low | | | | | | |
| **2. Low** | | | | | **8/25** | |
| 3. Medium | | | | | | |
| 4. High | | | | | | |
| 5. Very high | | | | | | |

## Section 10: Security risk assessors final comments

| |
|---|
| |

Name of Security Auditor.:
Date of Security Risk Assessment:

## Notes

1. If there are any ambiguities, there may be the need for a site visit.
2. Remember the importance of seeking SME advice when calculating likelihood and impact.
3. The risk owner has the final say about how the risk is treated.

# Annexe B

## SECURITY SURVEY TEMPLATE

The Risk Journey

### Introduction

The Security Survey is the second stage in the Risk Journey, and as such the data from the process is critical.

After receiving risk information from the Security Risk Assessment, this is the opportunity for the Security Auditor to carry out an examination of all forms of security on-site, in an effort to understand if the systems deployed meet their Operational Requirements and if they are fit for purpose.

Follow the Security Survey process, but bear in mind, as with the Security Risk Assessment, this is a base document which can of course be adapted to the needs of the client, and his or her circumstances.

## Contents



## Section 1: Survey details

Name and appointment of the client.

| |
|---|
| |

Address (s)

| |
|---|
| |

Point of Contact.

| |
|---|
| |

E mail.

| |
|---|
| |

Telephone.

| |
|---|
| |

Web address.

| |
|---|
| |

Location of Survey.

Name of Surveyor.

Organisation.

Date of Survey.

## Section 2: Initial stages of the survey

General description and business operations.

Reason (s) for the survey.

Assets to be protected

Initial research. This is the phase when as much information as possible about the organisation commissioning the survey should be collated. An important question to ask is: has a Security Risk Assessment been carried out?

Planning and preparation. Think about everything that is required prior to the survey. e.g., Maps and diagrams, authorisation, changes in law and regulations, and point of contact.

Notes:

## Section 3: External

Environment.
Rural/Urban?

Employment rates in the area.

Crime Pattern Analysis

Potential for CPTED

Nearest police station.

Nearest hospital.

Nearest fire and rescue.

Notes:

## Section 4: Perimeter protection

### *Perimeter by type*

**How is the perimeter protected?**

Welded mesh fence, two-metre stone wall, natural bunding etc.

**Example:**

Comments: The site is protected by a two-metre welded mesh steel fence.

Observations: During the Security Survey it was observed that there was a ten-metre gap in the southern fence line.

Recommendations: It is strongly recommended that the fence is repaired as a matter of urgency.

### *PIDS by type*

What, if any, Perimeter Intruder Detection Systems (PIDS) are in place? e.g., Taught wire, underground, and active line of sight. To what standard have they been installed? BS EN, ISO, PAS, etc.

Comments:

Observations:

Recommendations:

### *PIDS activation and response.*

Once activated how are the PIDS responded to? e.g., Manned Guarding response, police response, and keyholder.

| |
|---|
| Comments:<br>Observations:<br>Recommendations: |

### *Topping*

Barbed/razor wire, electrified wire, etc.

| |
|---|
| Comments:<br>Observations:<br>Recommendations: |

### *State of repair*

In what condition, what state of repair, have you found the perimeter protection?

| |
|---|
| Comments:<br>Observations:<br>Recommendations: |

### *Supporting security systems*

If the perimeter is part of an integrated security system, how is it supported? CCTV, PIDS, Lighting, Manned Guarding etc.

| |
|---|
| Comments:<br>Observations:<br>Recommendations: |

### *Supporting security systems specifications*

To the best of your ability, describe the specifications of all supporting systems. You may have to seek the advice of an SME.

| |
|---|
| Comments:<br>Observations:<br>Recommendations: |

### *Supporting systems state of repair*

In what condition are the supporting systems?

| |
|---|
| Comments:<br>Observations:<br>Recommendations: |

### *Entrances*

Number.

| |
|---|
| Comments:<br>Observations:<br>Recommendations: |

### *Entrance types*

Double steel gate, single arm barrier etc.

Comments:

Observations:

Recommendations:

### *Entrance state of repair*

In what condition are the entrances?

Comments:

Observations:

Recommendations:

### *Entrance access control systems*

Keys, swipe cards, bio metrics, or perhaps Manned Guarding.

Comments:

Observations:

Recommendations:

### *Entrance access control systems state of repair*

In what condition are the access control systems?

Comments:

Observations:

Recommendations:

### *Manned guarding*

Y/N. If yes, please describe all services provided

Manned Guarding coverage e.g., Days only and 24/7. Can you access the shift rosters?

| |
|---|
| Comments:<br>Observations:<br>Recommendations: |

### *Security Control Room*

Y/N

| |
|---|
| Comments:<br>Observations:<br>Recommendations: |

### *Security Control Room manning times*

| |
|---|
| Comments:<br>Observations:<br>Recommendations: |

### *Security Control Room duties*

Access control, search, ID issuing etc.

| |
|---|
| Comments:<br>Observations:<br>Recommendations: |

Notes:

## Section 5: Main building (s) external

### *Key personnel*

Who should be interviewed, when, and what information is needed?

Comments:
Observations:
Recommendations:

### *Description of buildings*

Construction, age, number of storeys, state of repair, etc:

Comments:
Observations:
Recommendations:

### *Number of access points*

How are they secured.

Comments:
Observations:
Recommendations:

## *CCTV*

Numbers, type, standard of repair, telemetry, VMD, tripwire etc.

| |
|---|
| Comments:<br>Observations:<br>Recommendations: |

## *Intruder Detection System (IDS)*

Type, hours of operation, standard of repair how received, etc.

| |
|---|
| Comments:<br>Observations:<br>Recommendations: |

## *Lighting*

Type, state of repair, how it is activated, etc.

| |
|---|
| Comments:<br>Observations:<br>Recommendations: |

## *Distance from the perimeter*

| |
|---|
| Comments:<br>Observations:<br>Recommendations: |

### *External utilities*

Gas, electricity, water etc.

| |
|---|
| Comments: |
| Observations: |
| Recommendations: |

### *Areas of concealment*

Walls, bushes etc.

| |
|---|
| Comments: |
| Observations: |
| Recommendations: |

### *Items to help a criminal*

Ladders, drainpipes, tools etc.

| |
|---|
| Comments: |
| Observations: |
| Recommendations: |

### *Restricted areas*

Garages, power plants, utilities, etc.

| |
|---|
| Comments: |
| Observations: |
| Recommendations: |

### *Parking arrangements*

Where and when is the car park accessible to staff and visitors? How is it secured? e.g., CCTV, lighting, and access control Manned Guarding.

| |
|---|
| Comments:<br>Observations:<br>Recommendations: |

Notes:

| |
|---|
| |

## Section 6: Main building (s) internal

### *Access control*

Describe by type and any differences between internal access control systems. e.g., Keys for non-sensitive areas, swipe/smart cards, biometric systems.

| |
|---|
| Comments:<br>Observations:<br>Recommendations: |

### *CCTV*

Describe CCTV by location and type, also the state of repair and any differentiation throughout the building. e.g., Static cameras protecting doors and corridors, 360-degree cameras in cash centres, or pan, tit, and zoom used to observe external areas such as car parks and walkways. Also consider how the CCTV system is managed i.e., locally in a control room, or perhaps via an Alarm Reiving Centre (ARC)

Comments:
Observations:
Recommendations:

### *Intruder Detection Systems (IDS)*

Describe the IDS by type and location, also consider zoning and access privilege e.g., IT and security personnel will have access to server rooms, but admin staff will not.

Comments:
Observations:
Recommendations:

### *Lighting*

Consider the type of lighting and how it is controlled e.g., LED lighting in corridors is activated by movement, whilst tungsten lighting in offices is manually operated.

Comments:
Observations:
Recommendations:

## Section 7: Internal specialist or restricted areas

All locations are likely to have internal specialist buildings or rooms that may contain sensitive equipment or data/information. They should be given special attention, as the safety and security of the organisation and its people may rely on it. In no particular order of priority.

- Server and communication rooms.
- Uninterruptible Power Supply (UPS)/Generator room.

- Stores.
- HR/Payroll.
- VIP accommodation.
- Board rooms.
- Security control rooms.
- Sick bay.
- Armoury.
- Accommodation.
- Car parks.
- Chiller rooms.

For each room, the following information should be supplied.

## Location

It is critical to be precise about the location of any sensitive/ restricted areas. e.g., *Server room. First floor, room number 115 on the right-hand side*

| |
|---|
| Comments:<br>Observations:<br>Recommendations: |

## Function (s)

Server room, communications room, HR, etc.

| |
|---|
| Comments:<br>Observations:<br>Recommendations: |

## Configuration

The layout. e.g., Single room, no windows, one point of access/egress. Solid doors, walls, and ceilings. No underground access.

Comments:
Observations:
Recommendations:

### *Contents*

Once again, it is critical that the full contents of this sensitive/restricted area is made clear. e.g., Communications equipment, CCTV controls, IT network hub, and a/c generator. It is likely that the Security Surveyor will have to take advice on the exact description from a subject matter expert.

Comments:
Observations:
Recommendations:

### *Access control*

What types of access control systems are deployed to secure the room? e.g., Keys, swipe card, proximity card, bio-metric, and PIN.

Comments:
Observations:
Recommendations:

### *Accessed by whom?*

This is particularly important when related to a sensitive/restricted area because of course access will be limited, and an entry/exit log should be maintained.

Comments:
Observations:
Recommendations:

### *Electronic security deployed*

What systems are deployed to protect the location, for example, a server room? Systems such as CCTV, Access Control, Security Lighting, IDS, and Manned Guarding. Is any form of response required, and if so by whom and in what time period?

| |
|---|
| Comments: |
| Observations: |
| Recommendations: |

### *Manned guarding*

How is the location supported by uniformed Security Officers? e.g., Numbers, patrol times, room inspections, etc.

| |
|---|
| Comments: |
| Observations: |
| Recommendations: |

### *Communications systems in place*

How can personnel inside the room communicate with the outside world?

| |
|---|
| Comments: |
| Observations: |
| Recommendations: |

### *Operational hours*

What hours is the room accessible?

| |
|---|
| Comments: |
| Observations: |
| Recommendations: |

### *Back up location*

If the room is operationally critical, is there a backup location with all necessary equipment? e.g., Server Rooms, Power Supply Rooms, and Communications Rooms.

| |
|---|
| Comments: |
| Observations: |
| Recommendations: |

## Section 8: Security Surveyors' Final Comments

| |
|---|
| |

**Name of Security Surveyor:**
**Date of Security Survey:**

# Annexe C

## SECURITY AUDIT TEMPLATE

**Security Audit**

| | | |
|---|---|---|
| Name and location of audit. | InfoTech Data Services.<br>New Forrest Business Park<br>Dirking<br>Hampshire<br>DI217DX | |
| Date of audit. | 22 January 2022 | |
| Audit lead. | Charles Swanson | |

| | |
|---|---|
| **Security Audit Management summary**.[1] | As the result of a Security Survey carried out at InfoTech Data Services, on 12 December 2021, during which a number of vulnerabilities were identified, it was decided by the Senior Manager Team of InfoTech to commission a Security Audit.<br>The majority of vulnerabilities identified during the Security Survey have been rectified, but there are still issues surrounding the credibility of the site Crisis Management Plan (CMP). |

| **Observations from the Security Survey.** |
|---|
| 1. The retractable bollards to the front of the main entrance were deemed not fit for purpose.<br>2. The ICT network was overdue a software upgrade.<br>3. The Crisis Management Plan (CMP) had not been upgraded or tested for three years.<br>4. The Contract Manned Guarding Site Assignment Instructions had not been signed by the client since 2017. |

| **Audit observations** |
|---|
| 1. The retractable bollards to the front of the main entrance have been replaced with a PAS 68 system which is now fit for purpose.<br>2. The ICT network software has been upgraded, and it now meets the requirements of ISO 27001.<br>3. During the Security Audit it was observed that the Crisis Management Plan (CMP) had not been upgraded or tested.<br>4. The Contract Manned Guarding Site Assignment Instructions have now been signed by and agreed with. |

| | |
|---|---|
| **Non-Conformities and actions required.** | 1. The lack of actions taken with respect to the Crisis Management Plan constitutes a non-conformity, which must be resolved before the Security Audit is complete. It is once again recommended that the Crisis Management Plan (CMP) is revisited, and if feasible, tested against BSI 11200. |

| | |
|---|---|
| **Auditors final remarks.** | It is clear that the Management Team at InfoTech have invested heavily in terms of time, effort, and financial support to meet the requirement of the majority of the Security Audit requirements.<br><br>During the course of the audit the Security Auditor was afforded the assistance needed, reflecting a positive security culture at the site audited. |

| *Auditor details* | *Auditor signature* | *Date.* |
|---|---|---|
| Charles Swanson | Online | 29 January 2022 |

## Note

1 This will include an overview of the Security Survey and its overall findings.

# INDEX

Note: **Bold** page numbers refer to tables; *Italic* page numbers refer to figures and page numbers followed by "n" denote endnotes.

For Product Safety Concerns and Information please contact our EU representative GPSR@taylorandfrancis.com
Taylor & Francis Verlag GmbH, Kaufingerstraße 24, 80331 München, Germany

www.ingramcontent.com/pod-product-compliance
Ingram Content Group UK Ltd.
Pitfield, Milton Keynes, MK11 3LW, UK
UKHW022318250926
475702UK00046B/947
* 9 7 8 1 0 3 2 0 3 0 3 4 0 *